Traces in the Way

Traces in the Way
Michi and the Writings of Komparu Zenchiku

Noel J. Pinnington

East Asia Program
Cornell University
Ithaca, New York 14853

The Cornell East Asia Series is published by the Cornell University East Asia Program (distinct from Cornell University Press). We publish affordably priced books on a variety of scholarly topics relating to East Asia as a service to the academic community and the general public. Standing orders, which provide for automatic notification and invoicing of each title in the series upon publication, are accepted.

If after review by internal and external readers a manuscript is accepted for publication, it is published on the basis of camera-ready copy provided by the volume author. Each author is thus responsible for any necessary copy-editing and for manuscript formatting. Address submission inquiries to CEAS Editorial Board, East Asia Program, Cornell University, Ithaca, New York 14853-7601.

Cover illustration by Tomikichiro Tokuriki.
From *Zen Flesh, Zen Bones: A Collection of Zen and Pre-Zen Writings*
compiled by Paul Reps and Nyogen Zenzaki.
Printed with permission of Tuttle Publishing,
www.tuttlepublishing.com.

Cover design Evangeline Ray

Number 132 in the Cornell East Asia Series
Copyright © 2006 by Noel J. Pinnington. All rights reserved
ISSN 1050-2955
ISBN-13: 978-1-933947-02-0 hc / ISBN-10: 1-933947-02-0 hc
ISBN-13: 978-1-933947-32-7 pb / ISBN-10: 1-933947-32-2 pb
Library of Congress Control Number: 2006931865

23 22 21 20 19 18 17 16 15 14 13 12 11 10 09 08 06   9 8 7 6 5 4 3 2 1

This book is dedicated to my beloved daughter

Philippa Aya Pinnington

CONTENTS

LIST OF FIGURES

ACKNOWLEDGEMENTS

First, I must thank my teachers and later colleagues at the University of Cambridge: Richard Bowring, who having put his hand to the plough kept pushing to the end, and others including Peter Kornicki, Carmen Blacker, Mark Morris. My thanks also to Timothy Barrett of London University, who recommended me to Cambridge.

Leiden University accepted me into their community under the auspices of the ERASMUS scheme. I thank the organizers and participants of the *rokurin ichiro* seminar held there, notably Erika de Poorter and Hendrik van de Veere. I am particularly indebted also to Thomas Harper, who, among other things, introduced me to Konishi's analysis of *michi*.

I would like to thank those who read all or part of the book manuscript for me: Susan Blakeley Klein, of the University of California at Irvine, and I. James McMullen, of Oxford University, who were extraordinarily generous with their time, and my good friends and colleagues at the University of Arizona, particularly Anna Shields, Todd Brown and Roel Sterckx, who all made significant helpful suggestions.

I would like to express my gratitude to the International Research Center for Japanese Studies (Nichibunken) for welcoming me as a visiting scholar, 2004–5, enabling me to finish my manuscript in congenial surroundings. Among many stimulating scholars I met there, I should particularly mention Kuriyama Shigehisa, now at Harvard University, for his discussions of academic writing, and Luciana Galliano, of the University of Venice, for her discussions of aesthetics and medieval Japanese music.

Among the many others who in one way or other contributed to this book are Arthur Thornhill III, Tōyama Ichirō, Paul S. Atkins.

One of the most difficult aspects of writing this book was planning its overall structure and scope. In this regard, as in many others, I am indebted to the suggestions of my wife, Michiko Kamitani.

Finally, I would like to thank the editors and staff at the Cornell East Asia Program for their prompt and able help in all aspects of publication, Elaine Baxter for her copyediting and the Kyushu University Asia Research Center for financial and other support.

Noel John Pinnington
Kyushu University Asia Center, 2006

1 Introduction
Traces in the Way

PRACTITIONERS, THE WAY AND SECRET WORKS

My aged heart is so excessively concerned with this way of performance (geidō), the two legacies (niseki) of which I am unable to transmit to future generations, that it is sure to become an obstacle to me at the moment of death.[1]

So wrote the Noh actor and playwright Zeami 世阿弥 (1363–1443)[2] in desperation in old age, after the unexpected death of his successor, Motomasa 元雅. Although these words are interesting in a number of ways—not the least being that they describe the circumstances under which Zeami began to consider his son-in-law Zenchiku 禅竹 (1405–1470?)[3] as an alternative successor—I cite them here for the light they throw on the terms in which one medieval master conceived of his art and his legacy. Zeami calls his art *geidō* 芸道, the two graphs signifying respectively "performance art" and "way." The second of these graphs is read in isolation "*michi*," a term used for the arts in medieval Japan and possessing a complexity of association in its time comparable to that of the word "art" in ours. *Michi* had, and still has, the prosaic meaning of path, or road. From the earliest times, however, the Japanese conceived of life's transitions in spatial terms,[4] and the term *michi* or *dō* was commonly used to refer to

1. Omote Akira and Katō Shūichi, eds., *Zeami Zenchiku* (*Nihon shisō taikei 24*) (Iwanami Shoten, 1974), *Kyakuraika*, 246. (Hereafter I shall refer to this publication as ZZ. I shall as a rule follow it with the name of the work by Zeami that is being cited. All translations are my own unless otherwise noted.)
2. Saburō 三郎 Motokiyo 元清 of (what became known as) the Kanze 観世 line of actors. For simplicity, I will refer to him throughout as Zeami.
3. Zeami's son-in-law, Ujinobu 氏信, of the Enman'i 円満井 / Komparu 金春 lineage. Again, for simplicity (and anachronistically), I will refer throughout to him as Zenchiku, and to the troupe of which he was the leading actor as the Komparu.
4. A point of view argued by Nakanishi Susumu in "The Spatial Structure of Japanese Myth: the Contact Point between Life and Death," in *The Principles of Classical Japanese Literature*, ed. Earl Miner, (Princeton: Princeton University Press, 1985).

ways of living, paths through life. An early example is found in the eighth-century poetry collection *Man'yōshū* 万葉集: *kaku bakari / subenaki monoka / yo no naka no michi,* that is: "are they all such desperate things, lives lived in this world (the *michi* of this world)?"[5] In the Heian period (794–1192) the graph for *michi,* in various combinations, was extended to include paths to spiritual knowledge (as in *butsudō* 仏道, the Buddhist path), to intellectual and artistic vocations (particularly those relating to academic or musical studies deriving from China), as well as to less prestigious areas of expertise (i.e. carpentry).[6] By the Muromachi period (1336–1573) these usages coalesced, so that practices referred to as *michi* would be thought of as sharing qualities belonging to all these types of activity. Thus for Zeami to call his art of performance a "*michi*" was, among other things, to characterize it as a complete way of life, a discipline entered into in early childhood and only left behind when preparing for death, a journey demanding total dedication, and, according to some, a path leading to higher knowledge, a wisdom of universal significance.

If Zeami's art was a single path, why does he talk of two legacies? It is generally agreed that Zeami made a distinction between the traditions of performance he received from his father, Kannami 観阿弥, and the further developments of the art he achieved through his own experiences.[7] Some, however, have found it odd that Zeami should distinguish his art from that of his father. Surely Zeami followed the way taught by his father.[8] In such objections we can see beliefs about medieval *michi* shaping modern readings of their writings. It is generally believed, perhaps on the basis of naive interpretations of medieval writings, that those practicing *michi* did so in an ethos of self-denial and conformity, holding perfect imitation of the teacher to be a primary ideal. The good pupil would not add anything to nor take anything from what he was taught. But there is a contradiction between this belief and the evident fact that both Zeami and his father were considerable innovators. One way to solve this problem is to reconsider the expression Zeami used for the two legacies, that is, *niseki* 二跡, two traces, or remains. In its singular form, *isseki* 一跡, it is relatively common,

---

5. *Manyōshū* 5: 892.
6. Examples of all of these can be found in the *Tale of Genji*. (For a more detailed outline of the development of usages of the term *michi,* see my "Models of the Way in the Theory of Noh," *Japan Review,* 18 (2006), 32–4.)
7. Nose Asaji advances this view in *Zeami jūrokubushū hyōshaku 2* (Iwanami Shoten, 1944), 669. See also the headnotes to ZZ, 246.
8. See, for example, Mark J. Nearman, "Kyakuraika: Zeami's Final Legacy for the Master Actor," *Monumenta Nipponica* 35.2 (summer 1980): 168–9. Kōsai Tsutomu finds the reference to *niseki* problematic for similar, if more complex, reasons, in *Zoku Zeami shinkō* (Wan'ya Shoten. 1970), 396.

signifying an inheritance or legacy (including both land and office). If however we read *niseki* in the context of what it qualifies, *geidō*, the path of performance, another connotation of *seki* 跡 (read as *ato*) comes into prominence. A person's *ato* on a path normally referred to his footprints. The implication of this reading, then, is that what Zeami wished to preserve were the traces left behind by his own and his father's treading of their "way." Thus, while the path may describe a single unchanging realm of activity, the actual "treadings" could be regarded as separate and multiple.

How could footprints on the path be preserved? It is generally thought that the proper way in traditional *michi* was to teach the knowledge of them to a successor directly, while guiding him through an arduous process of training. Each practitioner would then become a bearer of the whole tradition. Zeami, however, for reasons which we will investigate, was particularly aware of the fragility of oral tradition, and tried to transfer much of what he had learned into writing. This approach to the preservation of tradition, as it happens, is closely related to yet another reading of *seki/ato*. What was left behind when a brush moved across a page was also a tracing, something that remained. Thus *ato* could (and did) signify writing. The multivalence of the term allowed Zeami to leave some ambiguity in the passage cited above. Was it the knowledge of himself and his father that he needed to pass on, or was it the two sets of written accounts of that knowledge? Zeami made it clear that one group of his writings recorded his received tradition and another his own ideas.[9] It is quite possible then to read Zeami's remarks as asking: now that Motomasa has died, to whom shall I pass my two sets of writings on Noh?

In this passage then we discover a problematic complex consisting of a way, understood to be in some sense unchanging; its individual practitioners, subject to historical circumstances; and the works they generated and transmitted. This complex is one which scholars of medieval Japanese literary arts repeatedly encounter, and frames the issues that I address in this book.

WRITINGS: TEXTS OR ARTIFACTS?

The immediate subject of this study is the set of works written by Zenchiku, Zeami's eventual "artistic successor." In general, "writings" are both representations of language (broadly conceived) and physical objects, and so the ways in which we can treat them can range from considerations of their textual character (seeing them as codifications of knowledge,

---

9. Most clearly in his colophon to *Kakyō*, ZZ, 109 (where the term *geiseki* 芸跡 (?=*geidō no isseki*) is clearly intended to refer to writings).

statements of positions, tissues of citations and so on), to approaches that highlight their existence as artifacts (noting how they were generated and distributed, what access to them or possession of them was understood to signify). In asking what writings like those of Zeami and Zenchiku were for, we can tend towards the first perspective by referring to their own statements: they were written to preserve knowledge and intended to guide future generations. We can, however, take the other perspective and regard them as artifacts generated by particular groups for symbolic social purposes. It might be thought, for example, that artists created these works out of a desire to provide their art with social distinction, mimicking high court traditions; or again that they used them to confer or withhold authority, controlling succession in their households and manipulating access to patronage (the possession of such works was commonly used to prove claims to artistic authority). These two approaches to so-called "secret" works are interestingly reflected in the categorical terms used by scholars today to refer to them. As *nōgakuron* 能楽論 (discussions of the art of Noh), they are considered to be a kind of *geijutsuron* 芸術論 (discussions of the arts) and are aligned with *karon* 歌論 (on poetry), *rengaron* 連歌論 (on linked verse) and *hairon* 俳論 (on *haikai* verse). The term *ron* 論 is associated with detached philosophical or academic discussions, and seems deliberately chosen to resist social purposes. It is probably behind the common English language misnomer: "treatises."[10] The other categorical term, *hidensho* 秘伝書 (writings of secret transmission), like the closely related *kadensho* 家伝書 (writings transmitted in houses), highlights the material side (*sho* 書, writings on paper) and the social uses of such works (their secrecy and their role in transmission). Any adequate investigation of these works needs to integrate both approaches, taking account of their social roles as well as their intellectual positions.

Those who read these works as disembodied texts—as "treatises"— have tended to resist the legitimating character of their contents as well as their social uses as artifacts. In rhetorical structure, terminology and titles, *nōgakuron* are pastiches of the works produced by court culture or high religious traditions. They present *sarugaku* 猿楽[11] as an illustrious and elevated art, and claim that their authors are its foremost practitioners. They express attitudes to performance that work to the advantage of their authors

---

10. As in "Zeami's treatises." The formal, public and comprehensive connotations are clearly inappropriate since access to *nōgakuron* was strictly limited.
11. *Sarugaku*, also written 申楽, is the performance tradition to which Zeami and Zenchiku belonged. It included various genres, including the plays (*sarugaku no nō*) that are referred to today as Noh.

and to the disadvantage of their competitors. There seems, however, to have been almost a convention among twentieth-century scholars of *nōgakuron* to ignore these aspects, and to present the works as detached disquisitions on aesthetics and metaphysics. This tendency is surely not unconnected to the place occupied by Zeami and Noh in Japan's narrative of its cultural history. To early twentieth-century Japan, discovering Zeami through the publication of his works (from 1907 onwards), he appeared an excellent candidate for a cultural hero. His art was indubitably Japanese, and his life neatly fit the pattern that Ivan Morris would later describe in his analysis of "the nobility of failure."[12] At the same time his interest in the responses of audiences could seem both modern and democratic, so that he could be absorbed into western ideas of the artistic genius and man of the people. Scholars of Zeami focused on issues of grammar and vocabulary, as well as matters of historical fact, and may have worried less about general questions of interpretation. Indeed, there was probably a certain amount that they did not say (concerning, for example, Zeami's pretensions to high *michi* status for his tradition), preferring to couch their readings in a bland tone of reverence. Generally, though, Zeami was (and still is) presented as not just an excellent actor and playwright, but also as a thinker of the highest level, a man possessed of extraordinary virtue, a medieval Japanese ideal.[13] This idealization may or may not be deserved, and it probably has complex causes (including Japanese scholarly style), but it has meant that those closely interested in Zeami have focused the spotlight on those aspects of his works which are likely to be found admirable, and any signs of "lower" motives, or partiality, have been left in the shade.[14]

This idealization of Zeami has been imported into Western scholarship, although it has taken on somewhat different forms. In the main we find a projection of the nineteenth-century "man of genius" complex onto Zeami. For example, in Jacob Raz's well-known study it turns out that Zeami is a "real master," and that "like Molière, Shakespeare and Lope de Vega, he

---

12. That is, the pattern whereby a hero, long on sincerity and purity and short on calculation and practical realism, would at first succeed but in the end fail—described by Ivan Morris in *The Nobility of Failure: Tragic Heroes in the History of Japan* (New York and Toronto: Holt, Rinehart and Winston, 1975). Zeami's early success at the shogun Yoshimitsu's court and his banishment in old age at the hands of the shogun Yoshinori frame his participation in this stereotype.

13. In Japanese studies of Zeami there is a widespread tone of admiration that does not stop at his plays or ideas, but extends to his person. (For example in Kobayashi Shizuo's introduction to *Zeami* (Hinoki Shoten, 1958), 2: "Zeami was not simply a great artist, he was, seen as an individual, a considerable personage. It is this greatness of Zeami that I hope to have my readers . . . understand. . . . I recount his life first and then discuss his art, for I wish to make plain how great a being he was, both as a man and an artist.")

14. The problems arising from the idealization of Zeami are noticed by the essayist Dōmoto Masaki, who criticizes the fictionalization of Zeami's life (in *Zeami* (Geki Shobō, 1986), 134).

was a dramatist, who knew very well that the life of the theatre exists in its 'million' patrons, not in the cultivated few,"[15] to select from a host of universalistic statements. What is going on here? Molière and the rest are listed to construct a hierarchy of prestige within which Zeami can be placed, showing that he had the right attitudes. But what about the words "dramatist" and "theatre"—can we just leave such terms as they are, without qualification, to describe what Zeami was, and what he practiced? And what lies behind the contrast between the millions and the cultivated few?[16] This domestication, or absorption into a European tradition, has its positive aspects, but it has blurred the reading of Zeami's works, for it presupposes a number of value-laden oppositions about which scholars should be more detached. An example is the polarity of ambition (bad) and artistic integrity (good). More than one scholar has found Zeami's equation of fame (*meibō* 名望) and artistic mastery problematic (although I do not recall Japanese scholars having any difficulty with it).[17] Raz translates one of Zeami's passages as follows: "If, however . . . your fame is not so great as you expected, you must realize that, however skillful you are, you are an

15. Jacob Raz, "The Actor and his Audience, Zeami's Views on the Audience of the Noh," *Monumenta Nipponica* 31.3 (1976): 259.

16. Studies relating to Zeami include translations of plays, translations of expository works, detailed investigations of works, and general discussions of his thought. The first two, while sometimes reflecting considerable scholarship (for example, Erika De Poorter, *Zeami's Talks on Sarugaku: An Annotated Translation of the Sarugaku Dangi with an Introduction on Zeami Motokiyo* (Amsterdam: J. C. Gieben, 1986)), generally do not involve appraisal of his thought. Prominent among the third are the studies of Thomas Blenham Hare and Mark J. Nearman. Hare's interest (in *Zeami's Style: the Noh plays of Zeami Motokiyo* (Stanford: Stanford University Press, 1986)) is in the architecture of plays rather than Zeami's thought per se. Nearman is a special case, to which I will return below. Of the last category, there are fewer studies than one might expect, perhaps because of the difficulty of finding a suitable stance. Widely known are Raz (as cited above) and Makoto Ueda ("Imitation, *Yūgen*, and Sublimity, Zeami on the Art of Nō Drama," chapter four of *Literary and Art Theories in Japan* (Ann Arbor: Center for Japanese Studies, University of Michigan, 1967). Ueda adopts a similar stance to Raz. The general presence of this universalistic great man approach is also reflected in the entry for Zeami in the *Princeton Companion to Japanese Literature*, which compares Zeami to Sophocles, Shakespeare, Moliere, Jonson, Corneille and Dryden (263). Nearman (in 1980) makes a valiant attempt to generate a more culturally specific approach to Zeami's "mentality," treating him with spiritual respect, as a kind of Zen master. This has the effect, however, that Zeami's words are assumed to be beyond the appraisal of readers; if a passage is not admirable it is because the reader lacks the spiritual and dramatic experience to appreciate its profundity (Nearman says, for example, that: "Like Zen kōan . . . Zeami's secret-tradition writings are intended to be absorbed, lived with, and contemplated until a link with personal experience catalytically brings about a revelation of significance which transforms his seeming simple observations into profound insights," (Nearman, 1980, 153–97, 160)). A more recent and very welcome study of the fourth kind is Shelley Fenno Quinn's *Developing Zeami: the Noh Actor's Attunement in Practice* (Honolulu: University of Hawaii Press, 2005). I received my copy too late to provide any summary of its stance here, but do briefly discuss some of its arguments in chapter five, below, in relation to Zeami's formulation of stages in training.

17. See also, for example, Nearman's anxieties about Zeami's "social snobbery" (1980, 163, n.59).

actor who still has not mastered the genuine Flower," and then remarks that "the term 'fame' is, in its modern sense, somewhat less than satisfactory, as it sounds like a cheap desire to buy vulgar popularity in the eyes of the masses." But who says that popularity, even among the "masses," is vulgar and cheap? And what is wrong with "buying" it? The point is that Raz has his own ideas of what a "true artist" is and they condition the way he reads Zeami. Perhaps we can say that for similar reasons scholars in general have averted their eyes from the element of self-promotion that informs Zeami's works.[18]

In the next generation, Zenchiku's works can also be seen to be both pretentious and partial, in their own way. These aspects have been even harder for scholars to handle, perhaps because the model of "true artist" is less useful for reading Zenchiku, who was neither tragic nor very popular, and did not care much for the audience either. It is true that he can be (and has been) presented as that ancillary figure, the devoted pupil,[19] but that gives rise to further problems. As I shall demonstrate, Zenchiku's view of the nature of *sarugaku* was quite different from that of Zeami. This needs to be explained, for, as I have said, according to accepted wisdom, an ideal pupil was not supposed to resist the ideas of his teacher. Certain pre-Second World War scholars took this in their stride, declaring Zenchiku simply to be an epigone, not talented enough to match his master.[20] Others have seen his value to be in the access he gives to high intellectual trends of his time, despite the fact that he himself may not have fully understood them. Zenchiku himself, as a thinker and actor, has proved difficult to place, and his works themselves have been difficult to categorize. Their status as discussions of art or aesthetic theory is difficult to maintain, for he does not share Zeami's interest in aesthetic response. The most well-known works are those concerned with the system of diagrams called *rokurin ichiro* 六輪 一露 (six circles, one dewdrop). Here, while much work has been done to elucidate the sources for the commentaries Zenchiku obtained from Ichijō

---

18. There are of course counter-examples, although they are not prominent among those for whom Zeami is a primary focus of study. One meets American and European academics who speak dismissively of secret writings in Noh, which they see as little more than window-dressing. Barbara Ruch ("Medieval Jongleurs and the Making of a National Literature," in *Japan in the Muromachi Age* eds., John W. Hall and Toyoda Takeshi (Berkeley: University of California Press, 1977)) stands out as someone who is particularly unimpressed by Zeami's theorizing about Noh, which she sees as part of a regrettable process by which Noh became an élite art. Donald Keene, in various places in a number of writings including *Some Japanese Portraits* (New York: Kodansha International, 1978), discusses Zeami in a refreshingly detached fashion.
19. See, for example, the account of Takemoto Mikio in "Nōsakusha Retsuden," in *Nō* (*Bessatsu Taiyō No. 25* Winter 1978), 70.
20. Itō Masayoshi refers to such early views in *Komparu Zenchiku no Kenkyū* (Kyoto: Akao Shōbundō, 1970) (hereafter KZK), 72.

Kanera 一条兼良 (1402–1481) and Shigyoku 志玉 (1383–1463), prominent thinkers of his day, the simple question of what the system is about and what it is for has hardly been asked, let alone answered. Arthur Thornhill, in *Six Circles, One Dewdrop*, is primarily concerned to explicate the intellectual worlds in which the *rokurin ichiro hidensho* participate. He considers the "best approach" to the obscurity of the system to be to "excavate deeper to uncover the larger pattern of cultural discourse" that the "facade of discontinuity represents." The goal is "not to interpret, but rather [quoting Foucault] 'to define discourses in their specificity; to show in what way the set of rules that they put into operation is irreducible to any other; to follow them the whole length of their exterior ridges, in order to underline them better.'" Thornhill's stance reflects his wish not to be one of those who "wade" through such writings "to extract a practical meaning, a body of knowledge that can be transferred to another context,"[21] a point that is well taken, but is that the only alternative? Is there no way that we can analyze these difficult works except by "defining their specificity," avoiding all but a general and bland reference to the activities and social circumstances from which they sprung, and averting our eyes from their self-legitimating character?

RADICAL CONTEXTUALIZATION: POSITION-TAKING AND THE FIELD

According to the late Pierre Bourdieu, all artistic stances are deeply embedded in the social structures of the field in which they arise. Bourdieu's general approach has been described by one of his editors as "radical contextualization."[22] As such it appeals to common sense—for it would be odd to refrain from contextualizing texts—and urges us to resist the perception of intellectual history as a matter confined to discourse, what Bourdieu called (criticizing Foucault) a "paradise of ideas."[23] Bourdieu had his own intellectual vision of culture, constructed to bridge the academic disciplines of sociology and the humanities, and, partly in order to avoid the connotations of terms used in either domain, he developed a special terminology which is now used fairly widely: "symbolic capital," the artistic and other "fields," "habitus" and so on. It is not my intention here to base my study on an alignment of Zenchiku's thought with the terms of

21. Arthur H. Thornhill III, *Six Circles, Single Dewdrop: the Religio-Aesthetic World of Komparu Zenchiku* (Princeton: Princeton University Press, 1993), 4.
22. Randall Johnson, "Editor's Introduction" in Pierre Bourdieu, *The Field of Cultural Production: Essays on Art and Literature*, trans. and ed. Randall Johnson (Columbia University Press, 1993), 9.
23. Bourdieu, 1993, 179.

Bourdieu's theories.[24] The organizing ideas for this study are rather the terms of Konishi's analysis of *michi*, as I shall discuss below. Nevertheless, I do find that Bourdieu's general intellectual orientation, in which he is alert to some of the negative consequences of scholastic culture, to be compelling, and indeed of considerable importance. Bourdieu observed that scholars characteristically universalize from particular cases and forget the social conditions that made those cases possible.[25] (That scholars should do so is surely facilitated by their focus on texts, for, especially when printed, texts mask their origins in people and practices, as well as the particularity of those origins.) Thus a scholar confronted by a work discussing art searches for its characteristic ideas and locates them in relation to other works, rather than asking who wrote this, under what circumstances, and to serve what purposes. One cannot avoid feeling a certain ambivalence towards this tendency, for on the one hand it can be seen as the expression of a kind of liberal generosity, to judge by ideas alone, regardless of those bases for prejudice deriving from physical difference that writing hides. On the other, however, it separates academic discussion into a rarified world of ideas, and moreover encourages an amnesia of all those who never learned to write or whose writings never made it into the canon. It has seemed to me that there is a kind of blind-spot among scholars of medieval performance theory that has allowed a "glass barrier" to be erected, detaching works from the practices to which they are related, from the social and economic circumstances in which they arose, and contextualizing them instead in an imaginary world of aesthetic rights and wrongs.

To Bourdieu, artistic manifestos should be understood as adoptions of positions ("position-taking") in a range of competing and mutually defining stances that make up the artistic field. He asserts that the structure mapped out by those positions can then be seen to reflect the distribution of the properties governing success in the art in question. Using his characteristic extension of economic terminology, he states that this structure corresponds to "the external or specific profits (such as literary prestige) which are at stake in the field."[26] This insight points the way towards an important historical context within which we can locate the thought of Zeami and Zenchiku, i.e. the array of social and economic rewards to which their

24. Hearing an application of Bourdieu's theories to a number of Tokugawa period thinkers (at the AAS Annual Meeting, Chicago, 2001), I was struck by the extent to which each thinker ended up sounding the same. Of course this is the aim of scientific theory, to expose commonality, but for me an intellectual history that loses sight of individuality rapidly becomes boring.
25. To paraphrase from the jacket notes of Pierre Bourdieu, *Pascalian Meditations*, trans. and ed. Richard Nice (Stanford University Press, 2000).
26. Bourdieu, 1993, 29–30.

performances could be directed. It might be felt, on first consideration, that the task of recovering the network of discussions of performance within which these actors developed their distinct positions would be prohibitively difficult, for their works represent just two archeological projections from which a surrounding landscape has been swept away. But in fact we can make out a number of different stances in these works. Zeami's writings are, as we have seen, clearly divided between a received tradition and his own views; and while the former is associated with Kannami, it also includes a disinterested[27] report of certain traditional lore which expresses a quite different stance. When we consider what we know of the "external profits" at "stake in the field" of *sarugaku* in the late-fourteenth to mid-fifteenth centuries, we find that there is a relatively straightforward association between them, certain types of performance, and the artistic stances expressed in the writings of Zeami and Zenchiku. Let us without more ado, then, sketch out this association by surveying the patronage opportunities available in their lifetimes and relating them to ideas found in their writings.

The organization within which *sarugaku* performers worked was the *za* 座 or troupe.[28] These *za* were set up by powerful religious institutions to perform at their regular festivals sometime before the period we are considering. In the case of the *Yamato za*, to which Kannami, Zeami and Zenchiku belonged, the establishing institution was the Kōfukuji temple, which was closely associated with the nearby Kasuga shrine. The primary task of the *za* was to offer *okina sarugaku* 翁猿楽, a genre of masked performances involving old men roles, to the Kasuga deities, particularly during the Buddhist ceremony of the Indian New Year (*Shūnigatsu-e*).[29] One set of artistic lore that circulated among the troupes from before Kannami's time addressed this institutional relationship and its duties. It asserted the priority of *okina sarugaku* over other genres, for which it claimed *okina* should be the model, and characterized *sarugaku*'s purposes to be occult, including the pacification of non-Buddhist deities and worshippers, the re-ordering of the world and the attraction of auspicious influences. These beliefs were expressed through accounts of legendary performances closely associated with the cult of Shōtoku Taishi 聖徳太子 and with the Hata 秦 clan, claimed as ancestors of the Yamato troupes,

27. See my discussions of section four of *Fūshikaden* in chapters three and six.
28. The troupes' names changed in the late fourteenth and early fifteenth century. For simplicity, I anachronistically use the later names for troupes—Komparu for that to which Zenchiku belonged (instead of Enman'i *za*), and Kanze for that to which Kannami and Zeami belonged (instead of Yūzaki *za*).
29. For the priority of *okina sarugaku* over other Kōfukuji related duties, see Omote Akira, "Yamato sarugaku no osa no seikaku no hensen (ge)," *Nōgaku kenkyū* 4 (1978): 35.

particularly the Komparu 金春 lineage. This lore then both underwrote the priorities of Kōfukuji patronage and provided them with a spiritual interpretation.

From some time in the middle of the fourteenth century, another performance genre, *sarugaku no nō* 猿楽の能 (i.e. Noh plays), developed and became increasingly popular. Changes in society, such as increasing use of coinage, growing wealth in the middle classes, and a weakening of barriers between classes, led to *sarugaku* and another performance tradition, *dengaku* 田楽, being presented to large paying audiences (such occasions were called *kanjin* 勧進 "subscription" performances). At the same time the establishment of a large warrior class in Kyoto brought a fashion for competition that influenced a number of practices that were to become the characteristic arts of the period, including tea, incense, and Noh. *Sarugaku* players could become widely known—and also earn official titles—by writing new plays and performing them in competitions. Through such activities, Kannami, who had a great impact on the Noh play genre by importing into it other popular traditions, was able to widen his economic base, acting before rural shrines, in mountain temples and in distant provinces. His reputation brought him to the notice of the new metropolitan élite. As is widely known, he won the patronage of Yoshimitsu 義満 (1358–1408), the third Ashikaga 足利 shogun, who himself was intent on constructing a new warrior cultural life.

The artistic positions expressed in those of Zeami's writings thought to reflect Kannami's views relate closely to these circumstances. Therein, he repeatedly urged the mastery of techniques required to win competitions and to please audiences at all levels of society, for example the study of multiple performance styles, and their maintenance in readiness to be able to respond to audience demands. He stressed the importance of composing new plays to bring out the main actor's advantages. He explained the ways in which the actor should focus his attention on the mood of the more powerful members of any audience. These approaches to performance clearly reflect the means by which Kannami gained access to and took advantage of new patronage opportunities.

As Kannami's son Zeami grew up, the patronage of his troupe by the shogun came to be treated as settled and, indeed, hereditary. In general, patronage relations in the arts became less fluid. Competitive performance is hardly heard of in the early fifteenth century; the major known site of such competitions, the Tōnomine temple, for example, was unable to put them on for several decades. Zeami was a personal favorite of Yoshimitsu and his entourage of artistic advisors, and as a result he gained a knowledge of élite tastes and court culture. He adopted a view of performance that corresponded to contemporary high fashion. For example, in line with Confucian inspired anxieties about representations of violence, misery or the horrific, he rejected certain styles of Noh play that were popular among rural audiences, particularly the portrayal of demons and certain speedy movements associated with magical traditions. He fully immersed himself in the metropolitan passion for the earlier Heian court life represented in the *Genji monogatari* 源氏物語 *(Tale of Genji)* and stories of poets and court ladies, as well as in accounts of the aristocratic culture of Heike warriors (described in *Heike monogatari* 平家物語 *(Tale of the Heike)*). Zeami's repeated calls for refinement and restraint in performance, expressed through Tendai and Zen imagery, are appropriate to his established position as the leader of the troupe patronized by an élite warrior society.

When the sixth Ashikaga shogun Yoshinori 義教 (1394–1441) came to power, however, Zeami fell out of favor, and his special relationship with the *bakufu* 幕府 (military government) passed to his nephew, Onnami 音阿弥, rather than to his chosen heir Motomasa. Zeami persisted in a commitment to the values of his maturity, based on his memories of the earlier regime, but he increasingly referred to occult standards that he felt he alone was qualified to certify. The only outsiders whose judgments he felt were worthwhile were certain aristocratic specialists (*mekiki* 目利) with whom he maintained contacts. He appropriated the language of Zen to describe the aesthetic values that he wished to preserve in his lineage, drawing on its capacity to justify a purely private vision.

Circumstances facing Zenchiku growing up and inheriting the Komparu troupe were quite different from those in which his contemporary Kanze 観世 actors found themselves. The Komparu troupe had never shifted its economic base from Kōfukuji to the capital, Kyoto. It had no chance of competing with the Kanze in the warrior arena, or with the Enami 榎並 troupe patronized by the Daigoji Shingon temple, or with other troupes associated with the court of the retired emperor. In his early maturity, Zenchiku associated himself closely with Zeami (marrying his daughter and receiving many of his writings) thus gaining a certain kind of symbolic capital, but not only was the circle of metropolitan patronage extremely difficult to break into, it was also becoming less attractive. Kyoto society was becoming fragmented, and the risks for the individual were becoming higher, as was evident in such events as the beating to death of the leading Enami performers and Zeami's banishment. The Komparu in any case had significant symbolic capital at the Kōfukuji in Nara, for the earlier lore declared them to be the premier group of actors through their descent from participants in the legendary beginnings of *okina sarugaku*. Zenchiku cultivated his priority in Kōfukuji in a number of ways. In each case he located *sarugaku*'s role squarely in spiritual processes and showed no interest in audience response. Kōfukuji was not just a temple; it had the rights of the *shugo* 守護 (constable) of Yamato province, as well as being the clan temple of the Fujiwara. Zenchiku persuaded among others the leading aristocrat of his day, the clan head Ichijō Kanera, to underwrite his attempts to establish *sarugaku* as a manifestation of spiritual processes as well as his claims to be its foremost hereditary exponent. Kanera was the father of Jinson 尋尊 (1430–1508), the superintendent of Kōfukuji. Zenchiku also studied poetry under Shōtetsu 正徹 (1381–1459), the leading Reizei 冷泉 poet, out of favor with the shogun but patronized by Kanera, and sought to identify Reizei poetic traditions with his own particular style of *sarugaku* plays. Poetry was, of course, the most prestigious practice in the field of *michi*. Finally, when Kyoto was collapsing in civil war, and Kōfukuji emerged as an island of aristocratic culture amidst chaos, Zenchiku resuscitated the legendary lore concerning *okina sarugaku* and rewrote it as a legitimation of his own troupe and a "return" to spiritual motives in performance. As a result he won a reputation as the primary actor in Nara, comparable to that of Zeami's successor, Onnami, in Kyoto.

In the above survey we can see that the attitudes to performance expressed in early *nōgakuron* are profoundly intertwined with the particular performance occasions, patronage opportunities and types of cultural capital available to their authors. Unlike the language of genius and universal aesthetic values which forces us to take sides, or agonize over apparent contradictions with our preconceptions, the relationship with historical circumstances is a context within which we can investigate both the intellectual worlds and the legitimating rhetoric of *nōgakuron*. Such an approach should not be understood to imply that Zeami or Zenchiku's works were in any way the mechanical products of social forces. Both men applied considerable ingenuity to reconcile contemporary intellectual fashion, their inherited traditions, and their experience of performance, to create visions of their art that could be admired by the world.

ENTERTAINMENT OR RITUAL?

Bourdieu alerts us to the connections between social demands and the stances artists adopt in relation to them. But are there any inherent stances available for performance artists to choose from? The cyclic character of the artistic positions outlined above, which might be thought of as progressing from ritual to entertainment and back to ritual, fits neatly into a model of performance ideology developed by the ethnographer, Richard

Schechner.[30] Schechner notes that the common teleological model in which primitive ritual performances are seen to be the forerunners of fully-fledged theatrical arts does not reflect ethnographic observation. Rather it seems that performance traditions inherently possess the capacity to be presented more or less as ritual practices or entertaining practices depending on circumstances. Where the aims of performance traditions are stated, they are found to oscillate between ritual and theatre rather than merely to develop in one direction. In general, the discussion of the relation between ritual and drama has been bedeviled by arguments over turf among anthropologists who regard ritual as their domain and strain at its definition. Schechner puts himself beyond the reach of such arguments by making no essentialist claims about the performances themselves. He rather interests himself in the motives for performance expressed by practitioners. Performances which have efficacy as their aim he determines through a list of qualities: looking for results, linking to an absent Other, abolishing time, making the Other present, believing the performer to be possessed or in trance, having the audience participate and believe in something, forbidding criticism, and creating collectively. These performances approximate to those we might consider ritual, whereas those that have entertainment as their aim—looking for fun, focusing on the human audience, emphasizing the present moment, having the performer act deliberately, encouraging the audience to watch, appreciate and criticize, and prizing individual creation—are those we might consider to be theatre.

Of course, these axes do not exhaust the ways in which performance of *sarugaku* in particular has been represented; nevertheless, the terms of Schechner's analysis are useful for clarifying Zenchiku's stance and contrasting it with that of other performers. In particular we find that Zenchiku is not only uninterested in audience appreciation and uncomfortable with criticism, he repeatedly finds ways to locate performance's value in the manifestation of a number of formulations of the "Other." He is also always more interested in the mental field of the performer, which he again represents variously but always in terms more or less understandable as trance, marked by a lack of deliberation, or possession by transforming forces. While Zenchiku does not directly refer to the priority of the collective over the individual, he is consistently unhappy with what might be thought of as individual creativity, that is with the presence in performance of elements arising from the personal.

30. Schechner, Richard, "From Ritual to Theatre and Back," in *Ritual, Play and Performance: Readings in the Social Sciences/Theatre*, eds. Mady Schuman and Richard Schechner (New York: Seabury Press, 1976), particularly 207–211.

Zenchiku often justifies his views by claiming that they are *watakushinaki* 私無き, not derived from the individual self. He also finds change problematic and struggles to reconcile differences between the old and the new. Anxiety over change is of course a characteristic of the Noh tradition up to the present day, and it is interesting to see in Noh's inception the presence of multiple views attributing to it contrary aims. The sense in which there is a mystical or spiritual tradition at the heart of Noh performance owes a considerable amount to ideas that can be traced back to Zenchiku, especially concerning *Okina* 翁, but also in the performance of Noh plays.[31]

THE FIELD OF *MICHI*

As I have mentioned above, there is another context that has been used to locate the attitudes of early performers of Noh, and that is the ideology of *michi*. In European culture, the concept of art has until recently acted as an umbrella for a clearly defined hierarchy of practices: painting, sculpture, literature, drama and music and so on, all thought to bear some fundamental identity of values. In medieval Japan, there was no meta-field equivalent to "art." From medieval discussions of such practices (for example, in *Tsurezuregusa* 徒然草 (*Essays in Idleness*, by the poet-priest Yoshida Kenkō 吉田兼好 (1283?–1352?)) it seems that the closest category was *michi*, the field of more or less prestigious traditions of expertise. When, then, we distinguish among *michi* those that are religious, artistic or technical, we must remember that we are importing distinctions from outside. Like the European field of art (of which the most prestigious were perhaps music and sculpture), *michi* was believed to possess an intrinsic hierarchy—Buddhism and *waka* 和歌 (courtly poetry) standing at the top. All *michi*, however, were felt to be fundamentally similar and to share important characteristics. I shall put forward in this book my views about just what the perceived commonality was. In his comprehensive analysis of *michi*, Konishi Jin'ichi presents these shared qualities in platonic terms, as reflected in the title of his famous monograph: *Michi: Chūsei no rinen* (The

---

31. For an illustration of the former, see the account of *Okina* given in Richard Emmert, "Okina—the ritual piece of ritual theatre," *In the Noh* (Electronic Newsletter of *Theatre Nohgaku*, found at www.theatreNohgaku.org), 1.2 (March 2004): 2. This account clearly shows its roots in the Yoshida Shinto secret interpretation of *Okina* that was used in initiations throughout the Tokugawa period, which was itself derived from Zenchiku's interpretations, as I demonstrate in Noel J. Pinnington, "Invented origins: Muromachi interpretations of *okina sarugaku*," *Bulletin of the School of Oriental and African Studies* 61.3 (1998). Note that I italicize the word *Okina* when it refers to the play or the role, but not when it is the name of a deity (i.e. Okina). Zenchiku, of course, did not make such distinctions in his orthography.

path: a medieval ideal).[32] He writes as if *michi* were an unchanging essence
to which practices within Japanese institutions or traditions at one time or
other more or less approximated. He explores the statements of medieval
writers to abstract the qualities of this ideal, and derives five elements: a
michi is a *specialization*, demanding that its practitioners refrain from other
arts; it needs to be *transmitted* unchanged over several generations; its
practitioners must suppress their individuality, following a *conformist ethic*
in training; it is expected to lead to a wisdom of *universal* value; and, being
possessed of these qualities, it is accorded *authority* by society. This
analysis is well observed, giving a convincing and explicit overall shape to
something immediately recognizable by most readers familiar with
Japanese traditions. It suffers from some limitations, however, in my view.
Primarily, it seems clear that *michi* meant different things in the mouths of
different authors, or, rather, that a number of different models of *michi* have
been available for people to claim for their activities. That there should
have been at any time one particular ideal of *michi* seems to me doubtful.
This is important because idealizing *michi* turns one's attention away from
the extent to which it was actually underpinned by the structures of
institutions.[33] Shadowing discussions of *michi*, particularly its demands for
conformity, its transmission of knowledge, and its social authority, are the
structures in which it was practiced, structures such as performing
households, which controlled transfers of office, access to social rights, and
insisted on control over their members. The materials that Konishi reads are
in fact ideological and as such mask structures of control and power that
they naturalize; it is not surprising, then, that they succeeded in diverting
his attention from these aspects.

Despite my differences of approach, I consider Konishi's elements to
constitute an important model within which to discuss medieval artistic
writings and have therefore given them a major role in the structure of this
book. I have in fact used each of Konishi's elements (italicized above) as a
springboard from which to discuss particular aspects of Zenchiku's life and
thought. This enables me to make this book into a radical critique of the
michi ideal, at least as it is applied to medieval *sarugaku*, and also to

32. Konishi Jin'ichi, *"Michi" Chūsei no Rinen* (Kōdansha, 1975). Konishi also expounds his
theory in English in "Michi and Medieval Writing," in *Principles of Classical Japanese
Literature.* ed. Earl Miner (Princeton: Princeton University Press, 1985), chapter six, as well as
in *Nihon Bungei Shi III* (Kōdansha, 1986), 145–164, an English language version of which can
be found in his *A History of Japanese Literature Volume Three: the High Middle Ages,* trans.
Aileen Gatten and Mark Harbison, Ed. Earl Miner (Princeton: Princeton University Press,
1991), 139–165.
33. In this study I use the term "institution" to signify any systematic organization of people (a
common usage in sociological studies). It thus includes the family or household.

highlight important characteristics of Zenchiku's works. However, it is clear that some of these elements, especially the matter of Zenchiku's conformity to Zeami's teachings, and the way in which Zenchiku tried to authorize or legitimate his own tradition, have a relevance to all of his works, not just the groups of works discussed in individual chapters.

ZENCHIKU MISREADING ZEAMI

An important characteristic of Zenchiku's writings is their problematic use of terms and ideas from other texts. A major set of these allusions is to Zeami's works. Indeed, Thornhill states that "perhaps 90 percent [of Zenchiku's] 'content'—that is teaching on the art of performance—is based upon principles expounded by Zeami."[34] Zenchiku's presentations of these teachings, however, are fundamentally different in tone and implication from Zeami's. A number of questions arise from this, including one about which Thornhill's words are perhaps intentionally neutral: the extent to which Zeami, in turn, is the originator of the ideas he expounds. In general, Japanese scholars write as if all the ideas in Zeami's post-*Fūshikaden* 風姿 花伝 writings were his personal invention. This perhaps springs from the common fallacy that only those who have left written records can have thought about anything. Actually there are reasons, both general and specific, for taking a different view. The matter is important because it impacts on the way we interpret Zenchiku's deviation from (or "misreading" of) Zeami. If Zenchiku met these ideas and associated vocabulary through Zeami alone, then we have to treat his presentations of them as distortions of his teacher's ideas. Whereas, if they were part of the general teachings of *sarugaku* masters, then we might see them as merely his adoption of a particular position within a number of contemporary interpretations.

Even given this possibility, however, it is clear that Zenchiku did pore over Zeami's writings and use them in the creation of his own systems. This activity was in fact part of a larger pattern of "mixing and matching" of ideas (and citations) from a wide variety of written sources, in poetics, religion and elsewhere. The innocent reader might wonder why Zenchiku did not simply express his views in his own terms. One way to approach this matter is to see Zenchiku's writings as exemplifying a special type of intertextuality. While texts can be understood as tissues of citations from a range of language uses, in Zenchiku's writings citations and allusions describe a deliberate hierarchy of authority. Zenchiku mainly drew his

34. Thornhill, 1993, 4–5.

material from written sources, and he particularly favored those of restricted circulation and associated with élite or spiritual traditions. Towards these texts he displayed a certain deference. He did not, for example, contradict or criticize them; rather he changed their emphasis, recontextualized or recombined them. Thus we might say that he used them to appropriate their authority and he re-read them because he needed to express or find new meanings. This is an issue to which I will return in later chapters. Here, however, I would like to suggest that this strategy is one that we might expect given the conflicting requirements in *sarugaku* traditions of conformity and change.

MICHI OR ORAL CULTURE: WRITTEN TRADITION AND THE PROBLEM OF CHANGE

While Konishi sees the *michi* ideal as something specifically Japanese, it is notable that his model has much in common with descriptions made elsewhere of oral traditions. Konishi's discussion of transmission, the conformist ethos and authority in *michi* traditions, is not far from a specific instance of Ong's observation that "oral societies" have a "highly traditionalist or conservative set of mind that with good reason inhibits intellectual experimentation. Knowledge is hard come by and precious, and society regards highly those wise old men and women who specialize in conserving it."[35] If *michi* then belong to a general set of conservative oral traditions, it is interesting to observe how such traditions deal with changing conditions. Anthropologists have frequently observed in oral traditions the operation of "structural amnesia," whereby that which "has no utility in terms of current social institutions . . . is forgotten in a process of natural selection."[36] Those who practice this structural amnesia invariably fail to notice its existence.[37]

With Zeami's writings, a tradition that was formerly oral began to have written aspects. Did it thereby become less oral, less conservative? Probably not. In general, *michi* arts up to the present day continue to stress

35. Walter J. Ong, *Orality and Literacy* (London: Routledge, 1982), 41.
36. Matthew Innes, "Memory, Orality and Literacy in an Early Medieval Society," *Past and Present* 158 (1998): 31.
37. It may be objected that these observations are irrelevant to *michi*, which was pursued in a literate society, but what I am considering here is the impact of writing in traditions which considered themselves to be primarily oral, or at least can be described as possessing considerable "residual orality." (Anthropologists, having first characterized two types of tradition—oral and literal—noticed that some traditions in literate societies possess characteristics that properly ought to belong to oral societies. To deal with this, Goody developed his concept of "residual orality," a quantity that can be calculated from the amount of memorization involved in education. Jack Goody, *Literacy in Traditional Societies* (Cambridge, UK: Cambridge University Press, 1968), 13–14.)

the importance of orally transmitted elements. Japanese performance arts are still passed down from generation to generation within the ethos of oral traditions. Nevertheless, despite the ideal of preservation, expressed in such images as the passing of a given liquid from bowl to bowl, there has been, as can be readily observed in specific traditions, a persistent need to adjust to historical conditions. Even in *gagaku* 雅楽 (the musical traditions of the Nara and Heian court), the raison d'etre of which was the preservation of an ancient form, we have evidence in fact of a good deal of change.[38] There was even more need for change in an art like *sarugaku* that depended on evolving bodies of patronage. Its history, at least in the fourteenth and fifteenth centuries, clearly demonstrates its continuous adjustment to fashion. Nevertheless, it should be noted that *nōgakuron* never discuss artistic development in terms of the alteration or adjustment of tradition. Thus *Fūshikaden* addresses the need for flexibility in performance by recommending the maintenance of a wide range of techniques, all apparently drawn from fixed traditions. This pattern of generating the new by patching together elements of the old, while more or less preserving each element's integrity, can be seen both in the libretti of Noh plays themselves, as well as in works theorizing about Noh. Thus, while *nōgakuron* would appear at first to be an obstacle to structural amnesia, they can be seen to exemplify another technique that manages to remain faithful to older forms (appropriating their authority if you will) while enabling change and development.

Such change can be finessed by recombining textual elements, by recontextualizing them through association with other equally or more prestigious writings, and by misreading or over-interpreting cited passages and phrases. It is my argument that this is precisely what is happening in Zenchiku's writings. Far from presenting Zeami's ideas in a systematic form (as most scholars assume), they use Zeami's writings to say something quite different. Actually, we can observe something similar in Zeami's own writings. He more than once radically reinterpreted his own written account of his received tradition—i.e. Kannami's teachings. A good example is the matter of "doing nothing." In an early part of *Fūshikaden*, Zeami described how, after fifty, there was nothing left for an actor but to "do nothing." Context makes it quite clear that this signifies just what it says; the older actor, devoid of charm, should not perform on the stage. In later writings, however, Zeami converts this "doing nothing" to a profound technique

---

38. As is evident from any historical study of *gagaku*. See for example chapter three, volume 1 (1981) and chapter five, section three, volume 2 (1982) of Geinōshi Kenkyūkai eds. *Nihon geinōshi* (7 vols.) (Hōsei Daigaku Shuppan Kyoku, 1981–1990).

(associated with Zen/Taoist ideas of *wu-wei* 無為) whereby an actor is able to fascinate the audience even when "doing nothing." This is a re-reading of the phrase with completely different intention, and marks an advance of ideas on Kannami's view of acting.[39]

RE-READING AND LEGITIMATION

This way of dealing with the grip that the past exercises over the present is closely related to the matter of legitimation. Students of East Asia and, of course, other "old worlds," repeatedly come across cases where the new has been justified through a re-reading of the old. This should not lead them, however, to the reductionist position whereby such re-reading is seen as a deliberate ploy, the expression of the conscious insincerity of the authors. There is another way of looking at the phenomenon, which entails a shift to the writer's worldview. Here I am particularly interested in the case of Zenchiku, the generalization of which is naturally open to doubt. There is no sign that Zenchiku, at least, was not deeply serious in his readings of the array of prestigious citations that he amassed. It seems that he was convinced of their power to answer the questions that faced him. At the same time he had certain expectations about the nature of the knowledge that they should yield. This is a matter embedded in his metaphysics or cosmology, which was characteristic of a certain stream of medieval thought. Zenchiku understood the phenomenal world, whether natural or the product of human culture, to be both a mask over and also a manifestation of spiritual forces. Among phenomena certain things were expected to be especially representative of deeper reality. These included writings associated with ancient personages and events, shrines, striking natural phenomena, and also the Chinese characters use to signify such things. Zenchiku's intellectual procedure was to treat such phenomena as hidden guides to the action of invisible forces. For him, the authority of prestigious texts lay in their possession of this quality (being amenable to creative and multiple interpretation). Thus his special readings of such texts spring from his attempt to look beyond them or behind them to the truths at which they hint. This could explain why Zenchiku treats Zeami's works in ways that often seem to us inappropriate; for him, their immediate meanings were superficial and did not exhaust their ultimate significance. We can thus see Zenchiku as both a searcher for barely glimpsed truths and as a man with an

---

39. Another example is his development of the structure of *jo* 序, *ha* 破, *kyū* 急 from a theory about the overall structure of a performance session into a minute analysis of each moment of performance.

agenda, bending his materials to support his own arguments. It is in the nature of human psychology that these two cannot be entirely distinguished. What then was Zenchiku's agenda? At its heart was the establishment of the priority of his group of actors over others, primarily in its sphere of activity, the Nara temples. Zenchiku's method was to apply a rhetoric of legitimation that had been developed by the imperial family and the court as well as Shinto apologists.[40] Necessary for this argument was his position that *michi* were sacred—if we use Mircea Eliade's framework—*michi* were cultural spaces where forces from the spiritual world interacted with, or entered into, the human world. The prime example of this in the courtly arts was *kadō* 歌道, the way of poetry. Insofar as Fujiwara Teika 藤原定家 (1162–1241) had been consecrated as a deity (as famously expressed in Shōtetsu's writings), anything deriving from Teika, which effectively meant the whole tradition of court poetry in Zenchiku's time, could be regarded as sacred tradition. Thus Zenchiku's early writings start from an attempt to discover in traditional poetic texts, as well as in Zeami's writings, evidence for an identity between *sarugaku* and poetry (expressed in a series of taxonomic works starting with the work entitled *Go on no shidai* 五音之次第). This led to certain practical approaches to performance which, interestingly enough, can be observed informing the discussions of *sarugaku* lore of early Edo Komparu masters two centuries later. At the heart of this approach was the idea that it was the field of awareness of the actor that was the source of his performance, and also the significant stage on which the important processes of performance were played out. True performance could be verified as such if the conscious impulses that it expressed were the same "movements of the mind" that emerged in the words of the poetic tradition. If *sarugaku* was an entry of the spiritual into the phenomenal world, then one route to understanding *sarugaku* was to be found in the statements in religious and cosmological theories concerning the relation between the absolute and its manifestation. Zenchiku investigated these relations in his series of works on the *rokurin ichiro* (six circles, one dewdrop) diagrams. In these works he traced the process by which the invisible became visible and then reverted to the invisible. He expected this process to be observable in the processes of performance art and also Buddhist and Chinese delineations of the manifestation of the phenomenal world. Thus while the poetic model focused attention on the mind of the actor, the *rokurin ichiro* system moved from the actor to

40. I use the term "Shinto" here and elsewhere in this book to refer to the traditions developed in shrines in relation to the native deities worshipped there. In particular I am thinking of Watarai and Miwa Shinto traditions.

universal processes. This, however, stretched to its limits Zeami's images of the *sarugaku* path, and we see that Zenchiku was forced to invert and manipulate Zeami's structures in order to integrate them into his system. Another way in which Zenchiku tried to develop the idea that *sarugaku* was a locus through which invisible powers emerged into the human world was through the ritual performance pieces grouped together as the *Shikisanban* 式三番, core performances of the *okina sarugaku* genre. As I have said, *okina sarugaku* before the Kasuga shrines was the most important of the regular *sarugaku* performances in Nara. Zenchiku expanded and systematized *okina sarugaku* lore, integrating traditions related to other deities, to posit the existence of a new deity called "Okina," which he claimed took physical form in the *Shikisanban* performance itself. This lore, happily, included a rudimentary set of stories about the origin of *sarugaku* that he could claim as his family's legendary history. This is the reason for Zenchiku's construction of family trees and histories, armed with which he successfully had his troupe accepted as the most ancient and hence leading troupe at the Kōfukuji-Kasuga institution. The delineation of Okina, through its manifestations in history and in human culture, and the construction of a religious basis for performance art, equipped with a ritual calendar and a theory of spiritual transformation through performance practice, were never completed. A draft of work in progress (*Meishukushū* 明宿集) is extant, however, and, as well as showing us an important dimension of Zenchiku'[41]s thought and intellectual procedures, it preserves a number of folk interpretations of *sarugaku* that otherwise are little known.

Before we move on to an outline of the structure of this study, let us look at a characteristic statement by Zenchiku to get some flavor of his approach to the relation between the actor, the path and the embodiment of its knowledge in secret works of Noh theory. These are the opening words of his most well-known work, *Rokurin ichiro no ki* 六輪一露の記 (*Record of the Six Circles, One Dewdrop*):

> Now, the way of the household task of *sarugaku* is to exhaust beauty with the body and to "create pattern with the voice." Hereby "unwittingly the hands gesture and the feet tread." Consequently, this must surely be the mysterious operation (*myōyū* 妙用) of what is fundamentally without master (*mushu* 無主) and without phenomena (*mubutsu* 無物). That is why I have provisionally acquired the forms of the six circles and the dewdrop; the first is called the circle of life (*jurin*

41. In medieval artistic works, the graph 用 when contrasted with *tai* 体 is often pronounced *yū* (see entry in *Kōjien*).

寿輪), the second is called the circle of the vertical (*shurin* 竪輪), the third is called the circle of abiding (*jūrin* 住輪), the fourth is called the circle of images (*zōrin* 像輪), the fifth is called the circle of breaking (*harin* 破輪), the sixth the circle of emptiness (*kūrin* 空輪), the dewdrop (*ichiro* 一露) is the highest, most important stage.[42]

We see immediately that Zenchiku refers to his "way" as a household task or karmic duty (*kagyō* 家業). As we shall see in the discussion of specialization in chapter two, this was a term associated with those groups of people of common social status who gained privileges (like tax exemptions) by a kind of contract between their families and powerful institutions. Their part of the bargain was to offer the practice of their inherited expertise at certain times under agreed conditions. These are the groups referred to as *shokunin* 職人 by the late Amino Yoshihiko. Such groups were often related to their patrons through guild organizations (*za*, that we have translated "troupes," as is usual in relation to groups of actors). For Zenchiku, unlike Zeami, this relationship, between his family, the Enman'i 円満井 troupe that it traditionally dominated, and the Kōfukuji-Kasuga complex, was central to the legitimation of his performance style and his claims of priority over other traditional actors. These claims were not based on the successes of actors in living memory. The next important assertion made by this passage is almost invisible in translation, but any contemporary of Zenchiku's familiar with the élite *michi* of poetry would have seen it. The passage itself not only quotes from the *Great Preface* (to the Chinese *Classic of Poetry*[43]) (in quotation marks), it also mimics certain of its phrasings (the opening phrase and the final sentence), thus making it look like a similar piece of writing. Now some phrases from the same *Great Preface* were cited and re-read in the prefaces to the first imperial collection of Japanese poetry (*waka*), the *Kokinwakashū* 古今和歌集, and interpretation of these usages had long formed a part of discussions of the deeper significance of that art's "way" (*kadō*). It is generally recognized today that that attempt to apply the terms of Chinese poetry to *waka* was not particularly successful intellectually, but that it served another purpose: the assertion by Ki no Tsurayuki 紀貫之 and his co-editors that Japanese poetry could be as valid a vehicle for public and formal expression as

---

42. Itō Masayoshi and Omote Akira, eds., *Komparu kodensho shūsei* (Wan'ya Shoten, 1969) (hereafter KKS), 197.
43. The *Shi jing* 詩経 also known as the *Book of Songs* or the *Book of Odes*. This collection was handed down in four schools, each with its own interpretations. Only one traditional text remains, the so-called Mao text. The passage prefacing the first poem in that version is known as the *Great Preface* (as I shall term it in the rest of this book) to distinguish it from introductory remarks to subsequent poems.

Chinese poetry. We can similarly interpret its appearance in Zenchiku's introduction, albeit formal and visual, as a parallel assertion that *sarugaku* (as practiced in his family) could range itself alongside *waka* as a similarly prestigious human path. This proposition, which is only made implicitly in this passage, is fundamental to Zenchiku's works of aesthetic classification.

The phrases Zenchiku quotes directly from the *Great Preface* happen to be ones that were not employed by Ki no Tsurayuki and Ki no Yoshimochi 紀淑望. In the *Great Preface* there are two brief accounts of processes by which poetry (or song) are produced. In one the process is seen as a social phenomenon. Emotion emerges in voice, voices make patterns, and the resultant melodies reflect the quality of government. It is from here that Zenchiku picks out the phrase: "to create pattern with the voice." The other account maps the natural expression of profound emotion onto the cultural forms of speech, dance and song:

> Residing in the heart the emotions become active, emerging in words they make poetry. When emotions move within and take the form of words, if the words are inadequate, then there is heaving and sighing, and if the heaving and sighing is inadequate, then there is chanting and singing, and if chanting and singing are inadequate, then, unawares, the arms gesticulate and the feet tread.[44]

The force of this account lies in its blurring of the lines between learned and instinctive reactions. Heaving and sighing are perhaps not learned, but chanting and singing surely are. In the case of movements of the limbs, the immediate image we receive is the familiar one of someone pacing up and down beside himself with emotion. We can, however, read this as a statement about dance, arguing for its basis in natural reactions. The pretence that acquired culture is actually innate is common in aristocratic societies, because it contributes to myths that naturalize upper-class privileges. (We see a similar general conceit in the writings of Ki no Tsurayuki, where uncultured peasants on occasion happen to speak in the rhythms of *waka*.) Zenchiku, however, found this celebrated conflation to be useful in two quite different ways. Elsewhere in his writings we see that he understood it to confirm a fundamental identity between poetry, song and dance—all were expressions of the same mental states. And here it gave him a basis for arguing that performance manifested something that went beyond the conscious mind. Gesticulating and treading are described

---

44. My translation from the version cited in Siu-kit Wong, ed., *Early Chinese Literary Criticism* (Hong Kong: Joint Publishing Company, 1983), 167.

as unwilled action, occurring "unawares." For Zenchiku, this "unawares" does not point to the "natural" basis of dance, but rather to its transcendence of the personal mind. He argues that anything that happens unwittingly must be an expression of that part of the mind that is beyond self. It is a "mysterious function"—i.e., the functioning (*yū* 用) of the absolute (*myō* 妙)—of what is "originally masterless and without phenomena"—i.e. not consciously controllable (*mushu*) and having no basis in form (*mubutsu*). In other words it is an expression of absolute and sacred forces.[45]

This introduction to the *rokurin ichiro* diagrams shows the terms in which Zenchiku thought of his profession. It was an inherited tradition, a path through which the sacred was made manifest in the human world, a means by which what was beyond man could enter the phenomenal world through man. For Zenchiku, his art was a technique given to his ancestors to be used in service of religious institutions, equivalent in its essential functioning to the classical poetry of Japan and China, an art that could only be expressed in cryptic and mysterious terms evoking the ancient formulations used in those traditions.

ORGANIZATION OF THIS STUDY

As I have mentioned above, I have organized this study of Zenchiku's works around the elements of *michi* identified by Konishi. In each of the following chapters I shall discuss one of those elements as a starting point from which to approach certain sets of writings and certain themes. The first of Konishi's elements is specialization, and I start my second chapter by distinguishing two aspects—exclusive practice and whole-hearted dedication—and tracing their relations to the social groups that were forerunners of *michi*. I then consider what such an ideal could have meant for *sarugaku* actors, who participated in the radical borrowing and adaptation of their time, resulting in a complete reconfiguration of such arts, the loss of many old traditions, and the emergence of new arts. I then survey a number of historical contexts necessary for our study, including the organization of actors into troupes and their arrangements with patrons, and aspects of the cultural world of those patrons: warrior leaders, the court, the capital and the religious institutions in Nara. I complete this survey of contexts with an account of the Komparu troupe and of Zenchiku's forebears, and a biographical sketch of Zenchiku himself.

---

45. For further discussion of the term *mushu* see the section titled "*Rokurin ichiro* diagrams as stages in the way of performance" in chapter five.

The second of Konishi's elements is transmission, referring to the ideal that a medieval art should be passed down unchanged from master to pupil across several generations. In my third chapter I look closely at Zeami's transmission to Zenchiku. I first consider how idealized images of transmission (a harmonious process undertaken in dedication to the art and leading to the mutual benefit of master and pupil) deflect one's attention from the fact that the process of artistic transmission accompanied the transfer of relations to patronage networks. In general, the management of succession has been markedly problematic in Japanese history. In the early Muromachi period succession disputes were endemic in office-bearing families of many types, from the imperial family, to military officers, to poetic specialists. The case of Zeami's transmission to the next generation, taking place within an unstable patronage environment, is exemplary of the tensions inherent in artistic successions. House writings occupy an important place in the transmission of *michi*, for while internally they embody the knowledge being transmitted, externally they acted as symbols of their possessor's authority. The play of such aspects is even seen in their formal organization, with legitimating aspects clustering in the introductions and colophons, and technical aspects found nearer to the center. In Zeami's case, the demands of office and of art proved irreconcilable. He therefore finally sought to transmit his knowledge independently of the transfer of power in his house, of which he had lost control. This placed the recipient, Zenchiku, in an invidious position, for his access to patronage derived from his own family, whereas his "secret" knowledge came from Zeami. Contrary to commonly asserted views, Zenchiku maintained his commitment to his own house and its traditions rather than to Zeami's house, with which there were significant matters of contention. An understanding of these conflicts is all-important in understanding Zenchiku's problematic reading of Zeami's works.

From the fourth to sixth chapters I embark on a closer study of Zenchiku's works themselves. These works are notoriously difficult—they are far from discursive (rather exploiting specifically written characteristics), use obscure vocabulary (exploiting its particularity and resisting translation) and operate through extensive citation and allusion. I would like then briefly to foreshadow how these difficulties impact on these three chapters. The fourth chapter deals with musical and aesthetic works, which have their terminological challenges, but the introductions to the works make the task of interpretation less difficult than it might be. The arrangements of material in these works are important to our discussions and will be represented through tables. The fifth chapter handles the works related to the "six circles, one dewdrop" diagrams. These textually complex works have been closely studied by a number of scholars for many decades, and their interpretation is controversial. I adopt a specific stance from which to investigate anew fundamental questions, and therefore must present complex arguments and analyze difficult material. The result, however, is I believe worth it, for I arrive at a new understanding of what kind of works these are, and what they were designed to do. The difficulty in the sixth chapter lies primarily in the incomplete and fragmentary nature of the primary text under consideration, the quasi-religious *Meishukushū*. Fortunately an analytical approach reveals that its aims, methods and assertions are relatively straightforward.

Associated with the element of transmission in *michi* is the ethos of conformity. My fourth chapter considers the nature of this conformity when transmission becomes textual. Konishi claims that resistance to change dominated the transfer of knowledge from one generation to the next, and that this conservatism was achieved through the willing suppression of the pupil's individuality. It is surely true that training in *michi* required submission to a regime of practicing standard patterns. On the other hand we have seen that artists were forced to respond to changing circumstances. It is my view that Zenchiku managed to adopt a fundamentally different attitude to performance, its purposes and processes, by misreading Zeami's texts (as well as many others, including the *Great Preface*). In this chapter I focus on a set of works that Zenchiku developed from a restatement of Zeami's system of five voices. This family of works has been treated as merely concerned with aesthetic typology, but in fact in Zeami's hands it is clear that they answer one distinct set of aims, whereas Zenchiku applied them to quite others. Zeami developed the five voices as a training method to enable actors to have a direct impact on the emotions of an audience through different styles of singing. Zenchiku used the same theory to explore identities between the states of mind expressed in poetics and in singing. This shift was enabled through textual methods. I shall investigate Zenchiku's development of these aesthetic identities, and show the lessons he drew from them about the acting process, which he began to see in terms of the manifestation in the physical actions of the actor of deep universal impulses acting through his mind.

The next of Konishi's elements is universality. He describes an expectation that the practitioner of a true *michi*, artistic, religious or otherwise, should arrive at a wisdom common to all. He sees the roots of this expectation in certain beliefs characteristic of medieval Buddhism. I would rather interpret such ideas, however, in terms of the participation by medieval writers about *michi* in a number of universalistic discourses and associated textual techniques. These include discussions identifying poetry and Buddhism, the extension of investigations of commonalities among *michi* traditions beyond class boundaries, developing uses of the rhetoric of the "unity of the three creeds," and textual methods used in Shinto works to reinterpret ancient Japanese history. The last two of these I find particularly useful for an understanding of Zenchiku's works concerned with the *rokurin ichiro* set of diagrams. A prominent aspect of medieval hermeneutics is the exploitation of the spatial possibilities of writing. By attending to this aspect of the *rokurin ichiro* works as well as the process by which they were produced, I argue that they were not constructed to represent the ideas Zenchiku inherited from Zeami, as generally believed, but rather derived from Shinto traditions, which Zenchiku had come to believe would usefully organize patterns in *sarugaku* traditions. In fact they proved to be singularly unsuccessful in the representation of the theory that Zenchiku most identified with Zeami, the theory of nine levels. This failure is no accident; it results from fundamental differences in the images of "the way" that were developed within Buddhism and Shinto.

In my sixth chapter I take up the issues of authority and the legitimacy that the master of a culturally sanctioned *michi* possessed. Artistic authority was not something that men of *michi* could expect automatically to accrue to them, for we can see in the theorizing of medieval artists and religious thinkers the careful development of legitimating ideologies. In the cases of Zeami and Zenchiku, the logic of legitimacy that they produced reflects different theories of political legitimacy current in their time, in each case associated with the rhetoric of their prime or target patrons. Whereas Zeami's view of his art moved from an ideology of demonstrable technical superiority to the independence from external judgment of one who has achieved Zen enlightenment, reflecting his service of the warrior government and later disassociation from it, Zenchiku developed an ideology of descent from a divine being in the ancient past. Expressed in the possession of three treasures, this lineage gave him authority over a performance ritual with which it had always been associated, the *okina sarugaku* plays called *Shikisanban* performed before the Kasuga shrine. This adoption of Shinto—and imperial—rhetoric made perfect sense in Zenchiku's situation, for late in his life it seemed that the Komparu ties with the Kōfukuji-Kasuga spiritual complex and the networks of aristocratic and imperial institutions were the most secure patrons to which to entrust his troupe's future. From certain traditions in which an argument for the special nature of the Komparu lineage was embedded, Zenchiku created a new ritual understanding of performance art, one which reversed much of Kannami's and Zeami's achievements, reducing the effects from entertainment to spiritual blessing, reinstituting ritual performance's priority over Noh plays and finally making the transformation of the actor's consciousness rather than the audience's awareness of beauty the goal of the actor's art. In this vision of *sarugaku*, Zenchiku drew on a stratum of *sarugaku* lore that has been overshadowed by Zeami's revolutionary theories, but has left its impress on Noh traditions up to the present day.

In conclusion, I reflect back on the issues raised in this introduction and consider this study's significance for our image of *michi* in medieval Japan. *Michi*, far from being a static end-point of a number of intellectual tendencies, was rather a focus of struggles between competing ideas. By negotiating these ideas, practitioners could reinterpret their practices and define their social relations. Secret writings themselves were tools in this self-definition. In the case of Zeami's works, their distribution described his attempts to control and transmit the social authority of his household, while their citations mapped his tradition's self-location in the cultural field. Zenchiku's access to those works became possible when they had lost some of their immediate authorizing power in the Kanze troupe, but he managed to combine them with a number of élite texts to shore up the position he adopted as the representative of an ancient ritual tradition. At the same time, specifically textual methods, spatial arrangement and visual interpretation, developed on the model of other contemporary intellectual practices, enabled him to generate a mysterious knowledge, the kind of knowledge that the person he claimed to be might have been expected to possess.

2 Specialization
Sarugaku, Patrons, Komparu Lineage

In this chapter we shall survey a number of historical contexts important for our analysis of Zenchiku's writings. As noted previously, this study is organized around the five elements of Konishi's analysis of medieval *michi*, which we shall use to discuss aspects of Zenchiku's writings. We begin here with the first of these elements, the principle of exclusive specialization. This principle has hardly any explicit function in Zenchiku's thought, and has only a very slight presence in Zeami's, but it does perhaps have a close relationship with something which both authors take for granted: an ethos of total dedication and the identification of practitioner, household and profession. This expectation, certainly present in many medieval *michi*, has a number of roots in both intellectual and social history which we will briefly survey, but it does not necessarily entail the further element of exclusivity, which is central to Konishi's vision of *michi*. The discussion of specialization will lead us to aspects of the changing social position of *sarugaku* actors—an important context for the appearance of *sarugaku* writings. Having identified the social group to which practitioners of the *michi* of *sarugaku* belonged, we shall advance to an outline of other historical, geographical and biographical contexts for Zenchiku, which include the culture of the new military ruling class in the capital, Kyoto; the ideological constructions of the imperial court; and life in the capital and in the ruling and religious institutions of Nara. Finally we shall summarize and interpret what can be known of Zenchiku's own life and family background.

SPECIALIZATION AND THE PEOPLE OF *MICHI*

In his account of the medieval ideal of *michi*, Konishi uses the term "specialization" (*senmonsei* 専門性) for the expectation that a practitioner devote himself whole-heartedly to one path and refrain from the practice of any other. [46] According to Konishi's interpretation, this exclusivity lay behind the belief that *michi* could lead to universal knowledge, and that in turn earned for *michi* its authority in human affairs. In general, specialization, insofar as it signifies the dedicated concentration of all one's powers on the mastery of a particular branch of endeavor, is something that is celebrated throughout Japanese culture (a modern example is the film *Tampopo*). From the late Heian period in particular we find a number of writings which extol its virtues. Naturally there are some pretexts, for example there is the compelling illustration of total dedication in the *Zhuangzi* 荘子, where the master cook (or butcher) Ding describes his training:

> When I first began to cut up oxen I saw nothing but oxen. After three years of practicing, I no longer saw the ox as a whole. I now work with my spirit, not with my eyes. [47]

But it is in *setsuwashū* 説話集 (story collections) like *Konjaku monogatari* 今昔物語 that one finds such dedication develop into a topos. In a number of late Heian and early medieval collections there appears a new category of stories concerning specialists or devotees of particular arts. A regular theme of these stories is intense dedication. In the story about Minamoto no Hiromasa 源博雅 and his receipt of lute pieces from Semimaru 蝉丸, for example, the narrator tells how Hiromasa secretly traveled every night for three years to Semimaru's hut vainly hoping to hear him play, and then he remarks, "Now think: this is the sort of devotion that should be shown towards each of the many Ways." [48] Another case of single-minded devotion is seen in the story of the painter of Buddhist pictures, who seeing his house on fire, and faced with the loss of his wife, children and possessions to the fire, comments to shocked onlookers: "What a stroke of luck! . . . Now that I've seen this, I've learned what a fire really looks like. . . . If you want to make a living at this branch of art, you can have any number of houses you like, provided you're good at painting. . . .

---

46. See Japanese version in Konishi, 1986, 154–155, and English translation in Konishi, 1991, 146–47.
47. Using the version in Gia-Fu Feng and Jane English, trans., *Chuang Tsu Inner Chapters: A New Translation by Gia-Fu Feng and Jane English* (London: Wildwood House, 1974), 55.
48. Using Marian Ury's translation in *Tales of Times Now Past: Sixty-Two Stories from a Medieval Japanese Collection* (Berkeley: University of California Press, 1979), 145. (I do not know whether this "three years" has any connection with the three years in the *Zhuangzi* story.)

It's only because you have no talent for art that you set such store by material things."[49]

We notice in these stories (and in other writings) that the dedicated expert is thought to have a special quality unobtainable by the occasional amateur. This is a reversal of the attitude typical of mid-Heian courtiers that belittles experts, seen for example in the *Tale of Genji*, where the polymathic but essentially dilettante Genji and his friends are portrayed as superior to the dusty "professors" and expert painters. The new valuation of intense dedication is particularly apparent in discussions of poetics and music, expressed in the new usage of the term *suki* 数寄 to signify a "single-minded devotion to an artistic pursuit."[50] It continues to be expressed into the thirteenth and fourteenth centuries. A particular later locus for the expression of this ideal is Yoshida Kenkō's *Tsurezuregusa*. A well-known passage tells the story of the poet-priest Tōren who is so impatient to learn anything related to the poetic tradition that, hearing the remark that a certain holy man knew a secret tradition about the pronunciation of the name of a particular plant, would not wait for the rain to stop before rushing out to try to find him.[51] In general, in writings from the late Heian period onwards, we find a strong interest in specialists of every sort of art, and an admiration of single-minded and intense devotion to arts, as opposed to the effortless and natural felicity in many that was the ideal of earlier courtiers.

Most of the illustrations of this new interest in *setsuwa* 説話 and elsewhere describe well-educated individuals who take a particular interest in a single "*michi*" but are quite aware of, and probably participate in, the practice of others. When Konishi talks of specialization as an element of the medieval ideal of *michi*, however, he goes beyond mere dedication to stress the quality of exclusiveness; the practitioner of one *michi* should not practice any other. This principle is essential to Konishi's formulation of *michi*, but we find little sign of it in discussions of courtly experts. Konishi cites a statement of it in the writings of the thirteenth-century founder of the Japanese Sōtō Zen sect, Dōgen 道元 :

> If a person is born into a household and enters its occupation (*michi*), he should above all study and understand the work (業 *gyō* or *waza*) of

49. This version from Douglas E. Mills, trans., *Collection of Tales from Uji: a study and translation of Uji Shūi Monogatari* (Cambridge, UK: Cambridge University Press, 1970), 197.
50. Following the definition in Rajyashree Pandey, *Writing and Renunciation in Medieval Japan: the Works of the Poet-Priest Kamo no Chōmei* (Ann Arbor: Center for Japanese Studies, University of Michigan, 1998), 92.
51. Section 188 of *Tsurezuregusa*. See Donald Keene's translation: *Essays in Idleness: The Tsurezuregusa of Kenkō* (New York: Columbia University Press, 1967), 161–2.

that house. It is therefore wrong for him to study and know about matters that are not part of his occupation (*wagamichi* 我が道), not part of his lot (*onogabun* 自が分).[52]

The kind of person Dōgen has in mind here seems quite different from say, Hiromasa, or Tōren, whom we have seen above. He is not an educated courtier who has chosen to dedicate himself to a particular art for its intrinsic value to himself, but rather someone born into a house who has a duty imposed on him by social expectation, as it were.

We will come back to the question of what kind of person this was, but let us now survey statements of this restrictive principle that appear in later writings about *michi*. The prominent example, which Konishi cites, is from Zeami, who in his preface to *Fūshikaden* writes:

> Anyone who intends to master this *michi* should not practice the arts of other *michi*.[53]

While Zeami refers to this restriction, we should note that he does so only to immediately invoke the exception to the rule:

> Still, the way of poetry is an elegant and life-extending decoration, and so it alone can be made use of.[54]

How serious could the restriction be in Zeami's mind? As we know very well, some of the admiration he inspired in his youth derived from his skill in courtly pursuits, including linked verse and kick-football. If we take Dōgen's reference to the importance of ignorance of other fields seriously, then certainly it could not apply to Zeami, whose writing depended on an extraordinary knowledge of other paths, artistic, military and religious. The same could be said about Zenchiku, and we see no direct reference to a restrictive rule in his writings. The writings of Zenchiku's grandson, Zenpō 禅鳳 (1454–1530), too, make clear his close familiarity with the gentle arts of his day. Indeed polymathic knowledge and participation in a range of arts are characteristic of men of *michi* in the fifteenth and sixteenth centuries, whether aristocratic polymaths like Sanjōnishi Sanetaka 三条西実隆, or tea-masters like Takeno Jōō 武野紹鴎, Murata Shukō 村田珠光 or Sen no Rikyū 千利休. Even the expert in the way of the sword, Miyamoto Musashi

---

52. *Shōbōgenzō zuimonki* 正法眼蔵随聞記, from sn. 2, chap. 2. Yamazaki Masakazu, ed., *Shōbōgenzō zuimonki* (Kōdansha, 1972), 60–61.
53. *Fūshikaden*, ZZ, 14. This injunction is not as clearly expressed as its translation might indicate. Zeami uses the term *hidō* 非道 for "not of this *michi*," a term that might be interpreted differently: "against this *michi*." The main reason the term is interpreted the first way is because of the subsequent qualifying sentence.
54. *Fūshikaden*, ZZ, 14.

宮本武蔵, found time between fights to master calligraphy and ink painting.[55] Nevertheless, we do find some, albeit very rare, mentions of the principle of exclusive practice. For example, Zenchiku's contemporary, the linked verse master Shinkei 心敬 (1406–1475), writes (in "question and answer" *mondō* 問答 style):

> Q: Surely one who enters the way of poetry and combines with it the practice of various other arts is not acting in error, is he?
>
> A: I have referred to former masters. In the "various *michi*" it is said that one who truly excels cannot have ability in other arts. Still in the various *michi* there are those mutually helpful and those mutually opposed, and there are definitely some which can be studied without harm. For the way of poetry, Buddhist training, study of Chinese and calligraphy are mutually helpful, and are surely useful. Go, *shōgi*, backgammon, gambling—such things are all one path, and are mutually helpful. Again, playing musical instruments, dancing, Noh chanting and such like are of the same type, and can be practiced together without harm. Again kick-football, sumo, and martial arts are the same path. For one wishing to master a *michi*, it is vital to pay attention to this matter of helpful and opposed types. Indeed, it is said that of the people of old, even in the great countries, people who walked a single path, alone, were the ones who achieved fame in the realm.[56]

It seems that for Shinkei exclusive practice was an ideal that one did hear of from former times, but he saw that it required sensible modification.

When we ponder Dōgen's prescription of specialization, we find that it is associated with certain other questions that are very important for an understanding of the predicament that faced early *sarugaku* performers like Kannami and Komparu Gonnokami. That predicament concerned the social position in which they and other performance traditions found themselves in what was a watershed period of Japanese history.[57] As we have said, it is clear that Dōgen's words do not refer to aristocratic lovers of the arts

55. In fact, Musashi recommends a wide knowledge of other *michi*: "if you know the various *michi* widely, you can handle anything," Kamiko Tadashi, ed., *Gorin no sho* (Tokuma shoten, 1963), 57.
56. Ijichi Tetsuo, Omote Akira and Kuriyama Riichi, eds., *Rengaronshū, nōgakuronshū, haironshū (Nihon koten bungaku zenshū 51)* Shōgakkan, 1973, 151–2.
57. This seems to have become a widely accepted characterization. For a survey of the historiography of the fourteenth century see Ōyama Kyōhei, "The Fourteenth Century in Twentieth Century Perspective," in Jeffrey P. Mass, ed., *The Origins of Japan's Medieval World: Courtiers, Clerics, Warriors, and Peasants in the Fourteenth Century* (Stanford: Stanford University Press, 1997), 345–365.

(*sukibito* 数寄人). It is surely more reasonable to think of them as denoting members of families dedicated to specialist professions, more or less coincident with the class of people that the late Amino Yoshihiko and others identified as deriving from a special kind of late Heian period commoner that they name *shokunin*.

Who were these *shokunin*? In Amino's usage they were not simply "artisans" but rather a particular class affiliated with powerful clans, especially the imperial family or high aristocrats, or else religious institutions. As such, they received exemptions from taxes on the food they cultivated on lands provided for them, and from such public service as army duties. They had a certain freedom to travel from area to area and were allowed unusual access to the upper classes. In return they had to provide specific services for the *kenmon* 権門 (powerful clans or institutions) who protected them. These rights and duties were generally transmitted through households (but not always) and mediated through higher-level organizations, by which they identified themselves. Amino was particularly interested in the ambiguous social position of these groups, who were often despised and were forerunners of outcastes in later times. Such groups were both privileged and dependent. It is amid the transformations of the fourteenth century that a number of such traditional groups began to disappear. It seems very likely to me that Dōgen in fact had these kinds of people in mind, considering his identification of person, household, work and the household's social obligations.[58]

If so, then we should note that it is to just this class that the *sarugaku* troupes of the fourteenth century belonged. In that period the *shokunin* were known as *michimichi no tomogara* 道々之輩, people of the various paths, and they included, in addition to magicians, traders, artisans, hunters and fisherman, a series of performance traditions, including *sarugaku*, *dengaku*, *shirabyōshi* 白拍子, puppet masters (*kugutsu* 傀儡), and so on.[59] Yamaji Kōzō surveys a whole range of such performing traditions that still existed in the fourteenth century, and confirms their similarity with the groups described by Amino.[60] He understands them in the main to have been organized by provincial government to perform at important festivals.

These local organs confirmed their special tax-free status. Performers identified themselves in relation to their particular provinces and became closely involved with individual shrines and temples where they performed at events organized by the calendar and received traditional rewards. (We can immediately see the relevance of this analysis to *sarugaku*.)

A striking aspect of Yamaji's account is the sudden disappearance in the early Muromachi period of so many of these traditional artistic lineages and the appropriation of their arts by competing non-hereditary performers. Indeed in the fourteenth and fifteenth centuries, it seems that a whole traditional culture disappeared. The reasons for this destruction are clear enough: the patronizing institutions on which their status depended became poorer and weaker, new patrons appeared with different tastes and different styles of patronage (for example, local warriors, as well as the new aristocratic warriors associated with the Ashikaga shogunate and also new religious institutions), and finally, a general loosening of class barriers meant that there were new groups willing and able to jump in and establish themselves with new arts.

The traditional arts, which Yamaji refers to as *michi* arts (following such usages as Zeami's "*michi no kusemai*"[61]), struggled to maintain their position in a number of ways. Naturally they declared the importance of traditional roots and fought to preserve their rights and precedence both over new groups of performers (*te* 手 performers, usually mistakenly translated as "amateur" groups) and over competing *michi* performers. Under pressure, they reinvented their arts or appropriated others likely to be more popular with contemporary patrons; and they sought to establish hereditary ties with those new patrons.

Of the many *michi* performance groups—*kusemai* 曲舞, *jushi* 呪師, *dengaku*, *kugutsu*, *shishimai* 獅子舞, *shirabyōshi*, etc.—only Yamato *sarugaku* and *heike biwa hōshi* 平家琵琶法師 survived the fifteenth century, that is to say, only in these two arts did traditional lineages and their associated *za* or traditional organizations survive. Many of the other arts, however, persisted in some form or other in the repertoires of other groups (a well-known example is the survival of *kusemai* in Noh).

In the case of Yamato *sarugaku*, whose lineages dominate Noh today, we can see that they successfully applied all the strategies enumerated above. In the first place we see in the writings of Zeami and Zenchiku repeated expressions of their self-consciousness as practitioners of *michi* arts developed in various directions. This is particularly visible in

Fūshikaden and is characteristic of most of Zenchiku's works, which open with such phrases as *"Somo somo sarugaku kagyō no michi wa . . ."* ("Now the *michi* of the household task of *sarugaku . . ."*). Several events recorded in the fifteenth century reflect the struggle over traditional rights.[62] Furthermore, while determined to preserve *sarugaku* prerogatives, performers such as Kannami did not hesitate to study and adopt the arts of other groups—particularly *dengaku*, which was the prime performance favored by the high warrior class, and *kusemai*, a popular syncopated style of singing and dancing. His generation of *sarugaku* and *dengaku* performers developed what became the Noh play, almost certainly drawing also on the monastic entertainment known as *ennen* 延年.[63] This new and fashionable form of entertainment was inserted into the traditional calendar of performances at the Kōfukuji, Kasuga and Tōnomine temple rituals, although it did not supplant the centrality of *okina sarugaku* there.[64]

Finally, Kannami's troupe led the field in targeting new sources of patronage. They modified the Yamato style of *sarugaku* by adopting Ōmi characteristics popular among the warrior aristocrats in Kyoto.[65] Once Kannami's troupe became the favored *sarugaku* troupe of the shogun and his society, Zeami had to accept the typical personal patronage that had been common in relations between warrior leaders and *dengaku*, with its pedophilic and homoerotic overtones. The relationship forged by the Kanze troupe with the *bakufu* became hereditary if not formally defined, but it was a new kind of hereditary relationship, involving a restructuring (and perhaps rethinking) of the *za* from what it was under the religious institutions from which it derived. Moreover, it constituted a more personal and less contractual set of duties and rewards.[66]

---

62. For example the attack on *dengaku* performers in Nara by *sarugaku*, who claimed that the *dengaku*'s use of a mask was a usurpation of *sarugaku* prerogative, discussed in further detail below.
63. For connections between *ennen* and *sarugaku nō*, see Omote Akira and Amano Fumio, eds., *Nōgaku no rekishi (Iwanami kōza nō kyōgen 1)* (Iwanami Shoten, 1987), 11–19.
64. Other traditional *sarugaku* arts, for example, *hōgatame* 方固 (exorcisms of land to be built on), were meanwhile fading out (see Nose Asaji, *Nōgaku genryū kō* (Iwanami Shoten, 1938) (hereafter NGK), 884–5 for discussion).
65. Playing down the vigorous traditions of *monomane* (vigorous mimicry) and adopting the *yūgen* (subtlety and elegance) aesthetic, ZZ, *Fūshikaden*, 42–3. For convenience I use the name Kyōto for the capital formerly known as Heiankyō and usually referred to in contemporary records as Kyō or Miyako.
66. The new *za*, seen in Zeami's *Shūdōsho* 習道書 is fundamentally different from the traditional *za* structure as seen in the troupe rules of the Kanze in *Sarugaku dangi* and of the Komparu, seen in *Enman'iza kabegaki* 円満井壁書. The old patronage involved a fixed calendar of performances, and fixed rewards, whereas military patrons wanted to have performances on invitation, and rewards reflecting their enjoyment. I note that the Kanze also pursued older-style patronage, notably at the Daigoji temple in Kyōto.

This then is an all-important context for the writings of Zeami and Zenchiku: the great struggle by the old *michi* traditions to find a firm place in a new world. Zenchiku himself identified strongly with the ideology of ancient lineage that his forebears at some point had invented. This cannot be unrelated to the fact that in his lifetime the new forms of patronage turned out to be more problematic and less reliable than they had appeared in Kannami's time. To see why that might have been so, we have to consider the changing nature of the shogunate from the time of Zenchiku's birth, just before Yoshimitsu died, to the time of his death, in the early years of the disastrous Ōnin War.

THE SHOGUNATE AND CULTURAL TRENDS

Political power, centered on Kyoto, shifted wildly in the fourteenth and fifteenth centuries. For a few years after the collapse of the Kamakura military government in 1333, all political authority was concentrated in the hands of the emperor Go-Daigo 後醍醐. It became clear shortly that imperial power could only be exercised with the support of the warrior class. The Ashikaga shoguns manipulated conflicts between two imperial lines while gathering power to themselves. The third shogun Yoshimitsu (1358–1408), like Go-Daigo, worked to acquire both symbolic and real power. He succeeded in usurping a number of imperial and aristocratic rights and seems to have been about to establish his family as a new imperial dynasty when he died.[67] The hard-won system of authority he had constructed began to fragment after his death. This time it was primarily conflict among warrior officials, capital and regional, that undid the Ashikaga shoguns. The sixth shogun Yoshinori tried to control these conflicts by directly intervening in succession and other disputes as well as by reassigning offices at will. This was not appreciated and led to his assassination in 1441. The eighth shogun Yoshimasa 義政 (r. 1449–1473) was passive politically, concentrating instead on his extravagant artistic lifestyle. Uncontrolled disputes among the warrior clans and disaffected members of the lower classes eventually became ranged on two sides of Kyoto under the banners of competitors for the post of shogunal deputy. The resulting Ōnin civil war (1467–77) laid waste to a great part of the capital city, destroying the remains of Heian culture, as well as *bakufu* and *gozan* 五山 edifices and

---

67. See Imatani Akira and Yamamura Kōzō, "Not for Lack of Will or Wile: Yoshimitsu's Failure to Supplant the Imperial Lineage," *Journal of Japanese Studies* 18.1 (winter, 1992): 45–78.

aristocratic libraries.[68] The consequent social and geographic fragmentation of the country was to last for a century.

Thus in Zenchiku's lifetime the governance of Japan, radiating from the capital in Kyoto, traced a relentless path into chaos. There were changing cultural styles, too, and these are often imagined through two architectural sites that remain in Kyoto today.[69] Yoshimitsu's Kitayama residence, now chiefly known for the structure that became the Rokuonji reliquary, more commonly known as Kinkakuji, the Temple of the Golden Pavilion, is considered representative of the tastes of Yoshimitsu's era and court. Yoshimitsu was a cultural as well as political leader, inheriting and refining the lifestyle that nouveaux-riches warriors in the capital had developed, centered on aesthetic and sensual discrimination. We see him composing *waka, renga* 連歌 and Chinese poetry, watching *sarugaku* and *dengaku*, collecting and displaying imported Ming objets d'art and ink paintings, tasting tea, playing court football and carousing in boats. This culture, marked by discrimination and fashion, combined aristocratic and warrior traditions and was enriched by Yoshimitsu's erudition in Confucian arts of rule and his involvement in Zen meditation and Amidist practices.[70]

Yoshimasa's Higashiyama residence, the Kannon Hall of which exists still as Ginkakuji, the Temple of the Silver Pavilion, is similarly taken to represent the cultural tastes of the second half of the century. It is thought to be the culmination of certain trends away from the lavish and aristocratic tastes to which Yoshimitsu aspired. From the time of the fourth shogun Yoshimochi 義持 (r. 1394–1423), expertise in Chinese paintings and plastic arts developed and spread among Kyoto merchants, who sought to satisfy an increasing interest in the stark and unadorned tastes characteristic of the Sung period in China. This new style was accompanied by a withdrawal from the flashy to the quiet and intimate, and from the overwrought to the natural. A new form of architecture, later to be called the *shoin* 書院 (study room) style, developed, reflecting a new vision of the aesthetic possibilities of daily life. The new style served in the display of works of art, the study of books, writing and painting; and it facilitated gatherings for *renga*, Noh and banquets that were more informal than the ceremonial requirements of former aristocratic styles. Among aristocratic intellectuals, there was a rise

68. The *gozan* (five mountains) were leading Zen temples.
69. See Hayashiya Tatsusaburō (with George Elison), "Kyoto in the Muromachi Age," in *Japan in the Muromachi Age*, eds., John W. Hall and Toyoda Takeshi (Berkeley: University of California Press, 1977), 15–36.
70. For details of Yoshimitsu's life see Usui Nobuyoshi, *Ashikaga Yoshimitsu (Jinbutsu sōsho 38)* (Yoshikawa Kōbunkan, 1960).

in interest in Taoist works, reclusion and inwardness.[71] If the Kitayama palace was an external display of political supremacy and wealth, the Higashiyama villa was a place of withdrawal from an unpredictable world of violence into a life of the arts.

Zenchiku's life started in the last years of Kitayama culture and ended in the early Higashiyama culture.[72] It is possible to see the shift from Zeami's youthful confidence in the tastes of Yoshimitsu's court to Zenchiku's restless search in the next generation for the sources of authority and significance in the arts—a search for something justified by inner experience rather than external success—to be simply a reflection of Zenchiku's participation in the cultural trends of his day.[73] But the above summary is based on Kyoto, so first we must enquire about the significance of Kyoto culture for Yamato performers in this period.

Zenchiku was considered one of the great performers of his age, but we only hear of his appearing on the stage in the capital area once, in his early youth. Although later the Komparu possessed a certain prestige, Noh performance in Kyoto in Zenchiku's maturity was dominated by Zeami's nephew, Onnami. Each fifteenth-century shogun surrounded himself with a constellation of cultural dependents—a Zen priest, an aristocratic intellectual advisor, *sarugaku* and *dengaku* performers and so on. For his performers, Yoshimitsu favored Kannami (Yamato *sarugaku*), Inuō 犬王 (Ōmi *sarugaku*), and Kiami 亀阿弥 (*Shinza dengaku*). Yoshimochi patronized their heirs in each case: Zeami, Iwatō and Zōami, and although Yoshinori had Onnami, Zeami's heir, as his primary performer, he liked to have a representative of Ōmi *sarugaku* and Shinza *dengaku* in attendance as well. This settling of patronage into a hereditary pattern corresponds to general policies Yoshimochi adopted after Yoshimitsu's death as he tried to codify and place a limit on *bakufu* structures. Yoshinori subsequently increased this formalization. The *bakufu* calendar of artistic activities became fixed, with monthly *waka*, *renga* and *sarugaku* meetings, and the *dōbōshū* 同朋衆 system of cultural aides was established.[74]

In Yoshimitsu's era, shogunal patronage had been far more fluid, and struggles among *sarugaku* performers were expressed through a creative effort to win audience acclaim. From Yoshimochi's time, however, artistic

---

71. For a study of this culture, see Haga Kōshirō, *Higashiyama bunka* (Hanawa Shobō, 1962).
72. In fact, Yoshimasa did not move to the Higashiyama mountain residence until 1483, but the artistic style that it came to symbolize is thought of as beginning earlier.
73. This is more or less how Haga Kōjirō does see it, in *Higashiyama bunka no kenkyū* (Kyoto: Shibunkaku Shuppan, 1981), 627–635.
74. See Murai Yasuhiko, *Kyōyōjin no nihonshi (2) (Gendai kyōyō bunko 582)* (Shakai Shisō Sha, 1966), 256–257.

changes reflected the formalization of patronage connections: plays started to have fixed titles, reflecting the fact that older ones were more frequently performed, and appreciation was extended to older performers whose reputations were already established. The form of the Noh play became relatively fixed, although there were still to be moves towards more dramatic and less "operatic" plays. There was perhaps a greater connoisseurship in appreciation—the rise of professional experts in taste reflected this—a general artistic trend of the capital at the time. On the other hand the increasing number of plays presented at performances shows a desire for quantity rather than quality. Behind the settlement of patronage networks we see the struggles of traditions that did not make it into the big league. In the second half of the fifteenth century, traditional troupes other than the Kanze and Komparu (such as Hōshō 宝生 and Kongō 金剛) had no role at all in the capital region, although they were visible here and there in the provinces. On the other hand, non-established performers, forerunners of "*te-sarugaku*," did appear in the capital. The *shomoji* 唱門師 Koinu, for example, performed before aristocrats and warriors, but when he attempted a *kanjin* (public performance before a paying audience) in 1450, the *bakufu* closed it down because of Kanze and Komparu objections. There are also records of female *sarugaku kanjin* in 1432 and 1436, though on the second occasion Yoshinori forbade priests to watch. In 1466 Yoshimasa also attended female *sarugaku*.[75]

The two most prestigious performers of lineage in the mid-century were Kanze Onnami and Komparu Zenchiku.[76] Except for the one performance noted above, we have very little evidence that Zenchiku ever appeared in the capital. Not only did the Kanze hold the *gakutō* 楽頭 position (master of entertainments) at Daigoji and the hereditary right to performances in the *bakufu* calendar, it seems that Yoshinori's patronage of Onnami gave the latter complete priority in Kyoto. It should not be imagined that Onnami had an easy time, however. Yoshinori was a capricious patron and was regarded with a good deal of fear. It is generally assumed that Onnami was performing at the famous occasion when Yoshinori was assassinated in 1441. For ten years or so subsequently, his troupe appears to have been in hardship, putting on very cheap *kanjin* in the effort to survive.[77] This was a period of general social misery. The *bakufu* had made cash rather than land the basis of its economy, and the new

75. For more details of this history, see Omote and Amano, early chapters.
76. As famously remarked by Shinkei 心敬, but such opinions are also reflected elsewhere. See the citation of colophon of *Hitorigoto* in Omote and Amano, 59.
77. For details of Onnami's career see Omote and Amano, 59–61 and 63–65.

financial structures brought abuses, price fixing and hoarding. As peasants banded together to attack Kyoto institutions, the capital suffered from repeated depredations, with widespread looting and arson. There was a horrifying famine in 1460–61. In 1462, fires lit by peasant rebellions destroyed thirty *machi*. Finally in 1467, as we have described, the Ōnin War broke out leading to widespread destruction.[78] So although Onnami and later his son, Matasaburō 又三郎, had the continuous support of the shoguns Yoshinori and Yoshimasa, there are a number of signs of Kanze poverty in the decade leading up to the Ōnin War, when it seems that having duties in Kyoto was not necessarily advantageous.[79]

Thus, whatever the polarity of Yoshimitsu and Yoshimasa signified to Zenchiku, whether a move towards a Sung aesthetic, or a move towards increasing insecurity, probably a more significant polarity was that between patronage in the capital and patronage elsewhere. The primary alternative for Zenchiku was the Kōfukuji-Kasuga institution in Nara. This was a center of a more or less distinct cultural world, connected to imperial institutions, to native deities and to the Fujiwara family, and also to a more coherent form of social organization.

KŌFUKUJI, KASUGA AND NARA

Muromachi Kyoto, with its court, *bakufu*, *shugo daimyō* 守護大名 (provincial lords), warriors, merchants and financiers, within a province of independent and warlike landholders, was increasingly unstable. Twenty-five miles to the south, in the old capital of Nara, a quite different organization of society had developed, which integrated its people more successfully, allowing its city to ride out the terrors of the time a little longer and with fewer scars.[80] The "sacred province" (*shinkoku* 神国)[81] of Yamato bound together its people through a structure of religious institutions that acted as a partial alternative to the weakening bonds of class, clan, and family that obtained elsewhere. Into these ecclesiastical

78. See, for example, the account of Hayashiya, 1977, 27–30.
79. Omote and Amano, 65.
80. The sources for this section are works by Nagashima Fukutarō, especially "Kōfukuji no rekishi," *Bukkyō geijutsu* 40 (1959): 1–22; *Nara bungaku no denryū*, (Chuōkōronsha, 1944); "Kasuga taisha no rekishi," in *Kasuga Myōjin: ujigami no tenkai*, ed. Ueda Masaaki (Chikuma Shobō, 1987). Other scholars referred to are Hiraoka Jōkai, *Tōdaiji* (Kyōikusha, 1977) and Tagawa Shun'ei, *Nara Kōfukuji: ayumi, oshie, hotoke* (Shōgakkan, 1990), these authors being abbots of Tōdaiji and Kōfukuji, and the other articles in Ueda Masaaki, 1987, referred to above, on the Kasuga deity. Good treatments in English are Royall Tyler, *The Miracles of the Kasuga Deity* (New York, Columbia University Press, 1990), concentrating on a former period and Allan G. Grapard, *Protocol of the Gods: a Study of the Kasuga Cult in Japanese History* (Berkeley: University of California Press, 1992).
81. Referred to as such in *Gukanshō* 愚管抄 (early 13th century), according to Nagashima, 1987, 59.

bodies were brought the small independent landowners, the commercial groups and other professions, warlike families and nobility, within a particular theory of land operating under the singular assertion that Yamato province was the spiritual and worldly domain of the Kasuga shrine. A marked contrast with Kyoto is that there was little place within this structure for the military élite and their religion, Zen.[82]

When Nara was built, the Fujiwara took the most scenic spot in the area and established therein Kōfukuji as their clan temple, to mark and guard the supremacy of the family within the court. In the eighth century, on the eastern side of this area, an ancient sacred spot on the flanks of Mount Mikasa was developed as the Fujiwara clan shrine, Kasuga Taisha, gathering four deities, three male and one female, that the family appears to have taken as tutelary gods.[83] It would be a mistake to assume that the interests of Kōfukuji and the Fujiwara coincided in subsequent ages. The Heian period saw a struggle between temple and courtiers for control of the Kasuga shrine, specifically the rights of access to its sacred space bestowed by involvement in its rituals. It was understood to be the key to possession of the province.[84] Kōfukuji eventually won the battle. From the late eleventh century, Kōfukuji promoted and disseminated a cult in which the composite deity was protector of the Hossō (Yogācāra) sect, and the temple was the shrine's provider. Parts of Fujiwara manors dedicated to Kasuga came under Kōfukuji administration. Gradually, by means fair and foul, Kōfukuji expanded its lands to fill the province and beyond. Within Yamato its monastic and Shinto armies became the predominant power.

The way in which the Kōfukuji system had come to operate in the Muromachi period is perhaps best understood in terms of its relations with other social groups. Minamoto Yoritomo 源頼朝 had informally accepted Kōfukuji as the *shugo* of Yamato, meaning that it was the one province in which a military representative of the *bakufu* was not placed.[85] The Genji felt gratitude and sympathy for Nara's suffering at the hands of the Heike and were conscious of the dangers of challenging the military power of Kōfukuji. These *shugo* rights were confirmed by the Muromachi *bakufu,*

82. "Yamato is the fief province of Kasuga shrine, Kōfukuji grasps the administration of the province, with Tōdaiji in attendance. The new Buddhist sects like Zen are expelled . . . " complained a Muromachi Zen priest, Ishō Tokugan (Nagashima, 1987, 63).
83. See Tyler's discussion, 52–4.
84. Nagashima interprets the establishment by Kōfukuji of the Wakamiya shrine and its festival in 1135–6 as a ploy to get the rights to Kasuga rituals. Nagashima, 1959a, 9–10.
85. Yoshimoto was to describe this as Yoritomo offering Yamato to the Kasuga deity. Tyler, 153.

and this was no doubt the reason for the lack of influence in Yamato of the military élite.[86]

The key to Kōfukuji's power was its relation to other religious institutions in Yamato and Nara. As its wealth and influence had grown, it had forced all other major temples (except Tōdaiji and Tōnomine) to become its subtemples. They were quite free to practice religion as they wished, but their financial and political activities were subordinate to Kōfukuji.[87] Tōdaiji preserved its independence at a loss of economic power and some subtemples such as Hasedera, which were taken by Kōfukuji. Tōnomine, a temple dedicated to the Fujiwara ancestor Kamatari 鎌足 and belonging to the great Ōmi institution of Mt. Hiei and the Sannō shrine, was the object of frequent armed attacks.

Kōfukuji maintained its relations with the court nobility through its many private subtemples and retreats. Theoretically there were procedures within the Kōfukuji hierarchy that provided for promotion from lower to higher positions in line with Buddhist traditions. In the Muromachi period, however, it was routine for the sons of court families to be appointed to head Kōfukuji institutions (*inge* 院家) whose mutual hierarchy mapped their importance at court.[88] The two leading *inge,* Ichijōin and Daijōin, were exceptional in various ways. Known as *monzeki* 門跡, their abbots were always appointed from the *gosekke* 五摂家 (the five noble families from which chancellors and regents could derive) by the Fujiwara clan head. The two alternately held the position of *bettō* 別当, superintendent, the nominal head of Kōfukuji and ultimate possessor of the rights of *shugo* and provincial governor. Moreover, their temples and lands were independent of Kōfukuji management.

The main focus of faith of the mid-fifteenth-century superintendent, Jinson, was the deity Kasuga Daimyōjin 春日大明神. The cult of Kasuga was a universalization of a history of legendary assertions of Fujiwara hegemony into a religion of personal devotion. As *ujigami* 氏神 (clan deity), the Daimyōjin was a central symbol of the clan's solidarity. It was also a spiritual power that numbered in its manifestations those deities that had served Amaterasu in the pacification of rebels, and the deity Amanokoyane

---

86. The Ashikaga shōguns seem to have wanted to get back control of Yamato—this is how Nagashima interprets Yoshimitsu usurpation of the Fujiwara progresses to the Southern capital and payments for the regular reconstructions of Kōfukuji buildings (see 1987, 63–4).
87. Most temples had developed multiple denominations.
88. Originally worthy monastic edifices degenerated into private shelters to protect noble sons from the rigors of monastic life. Nagashima, 1959a, 14–5. Tyler, 76–7.

to whose descendants Amaterasu entrusted the affairs of government.[89] Each of the four sanctuaries and the added Wakamiya shrine had developed Buddhist identities (*honji* 本地). In the medieval period Kasuga Daimyōjin became a personal deity not just for Fujiwara, but also for any who felt connected to the shrine—by being a member of Kōfukuji or of Yamato province, or simply by the wish for personal salvation.[90]

Yamato province was understood to belong to the Kasuga deity. Kōfukuji had used this as a rationale for placing shrines throughout Yamato under its control. It had thus been able to influence local families that administered the shrine rituals—closely linked to agricultural life—and it gave them the status of priests associated with the Kasuga, using the designation *kokumin* 国民, people of the province. Similarly temples in the province were taken under Kōfukuji command, and monks sent to them accepted that abbotship belonged to local powerful families and landholders to whom was granted the title *shuto* 衆徒, monks of the Kōfukuji. In this way rural communities, which elsewhere were developing greater self-consciousness and solidarity—setting up self-governing and defense organizations and resisting traditional external authority under the militarized land-holders known as *jisamurai* 地侍 or *kokujin* 国人—in Yamato were integrated into the provincial administration. These *shuto-kokumin* made up the body of armed forces of Kōfukuji capable of mobilizing local forces whenever required. Twenty members of the monastic group were chosen as representatives to reside within Kōfukuji for three-year periods.[91]

This system of a sacred province run by monks balancing the needs of local powers and the nobility had inherent weaknesses that led to its collapse towards the end of the fifteenth century. The *shuto-kokumin* were

---

89. The question of the identity of the Kasuga Daimyōjin, and how it could be at the same time one and many is discussed interestingly in Tyler, 111–26. It is related to questions of the ultimate nature of reality, in which enlightenment and illusion are not different, and the *Lotus Sutra* conception of the Buddha whose appearances and teachings correspond to the capacities of the taught. Amaterasu is the ancestral deity of the imperial family worshipped at the Ise shrine.

90. See Tyler, 90–110, for the development of the Kasuga cult.

91. The organization of the various groups within Kōfukuji is not absolutely clear, and changed over the years. Higher class members of the monastic body at large made up a group called the *gakuryo* 学侶 (scholars) and at their command were youths selected from subtemples known as *roppōshū* 六方衆 (the six regions). These acted as officers to the *shuto* under arms. These armed men however had their own representatives mentioned above, the *shūchū* 衆中, and an executive body in the temple complex, the *satashū* 沙汰衆. The day-to-day running of the temple, its finances and festivals came under the *goshi* 五師 (five masters) and the *sangō* 三綱 (temple council) and the officers below them who came from the *gakuryo*. The superintendent of Kōfukuji had to utilise these organs to balance the powers of the region. Tyler, 83 has 2000 *shuto* resident in Kōfukuji for the period, but Nagashima refers to 20 in 1959a, 17.

an unruly horde with their own agenda. It is not clear that they were ever fully under the control of the superintendent. Armed monks were originally subject to the East and West Kondō (two of the seven temple halls) which came under the control of the two *monzeki*. Their competition spread to the *shuto*, who fought on different sides in the dispute between the northern and southern courts in the fourteenth century. This rivalry surfaced again in the Ōnin War, when the armies divided and fought on opposing sides. The temple itself held aloof at this time, providing an island of comfort for high courtiers such as Ichijō Kanera, who took refuge with his son Jinson, *monzeki* and superintendent. But the wars divided the local armies, and these turned more and more to aggression for private benefit, making alliances with powers outside Yamato. Already in the fourteenth century they administered through the *shūchū* 衆中 the central festival of Kōfukuji, the Takigi, and this was the start of their taking control of the city. In the end the temple authorities became powerless. The *satashū* 沙汰衆 made an alliance with the Tsutsui clan, who eventually became the dominant power in the province.

In the time leading up to the Ōnin War, however, while the nobility in Kyoto were suffering from shrinking incomes and being absorbed into new cultural forms, the *monzeki* and *inge* of Nara managed to maintain a more traditional aristocratic lifestyle. Their private residences were constructed in *shindenzukuri* 寝殿造り style and possessed of plentiful manors and income.[92] It seemed that their estate did not hold them back from the entertainments of the poetry and court music of their worldly brothers.[93]

As we discussed above, Yamaji Kōzō understands traditional groups of performers to be a subset of the *shokunin*, as envisaged by Amino. The origins of the *sarugaku* troupes associated with Nara are particularly unclear, but the name for the groups into which they were organized by Kōfukuji, *za*, was also the name used for the guilds of artisans, builders and craftsmen that lived in particular areas belonging to the temple, known as *gō* 郷. These apparently can be traced to the great Kamakura-era rebuilding of Nara after its destruction in 1180 at the hands of Taira Shigehira 平重衡. Perhaps the great development of festival and ritual at the same time led to the organizations of troupes of *dengaku*, *sarugaku* and other performers. The *sarugaku za* begin to appear in fourteenth-century records when they numbered four, known in the Muromachi period as the "four troupes of

92. The Ōnin war itself appears to have had quite a severe effect on the incomes of Kōfukuji, however, as is seen in the inability to fund the Takigi performances in 1474. KKS, 63.
93. Nagashima Fukutarō, *Ichijō Kanera*, (Yoshikawa Kōbunkan, 1959) (hereafter Nagashima, 1959b), 47–8.

Yamato" (*yamato yoza* 大和四座). These are the origin of the official troupes of the Tokugawa period and still exist today. They belonged in the sense mentioned above to Kōfukuji, and owed the temple a calendar of ritual performances as well as readiness to appear as needed on special occasions. For each performance they received payment in various media—sake, rice, cloth and so on.[94] The number of troupes probably derived from the four sanctuaries of the Kasuga shrine before which they performed simultaneously the sacred *okina sarugaku* at the start of each year's performance calendar. The offering of scriptural readings to the Kasuga deity by the monks that started in the Heian period is taken to be part of Kōfukuji's project to get control of the shrine—either to be understood as gaining the blessing of the deity or the right of access to its sacred space. One might interpret the dispatch of the four *sarugaku* each year in the same light. Kōfukuji also coveted Tōnomine, the Mt. Hiei subtemple mentioned above, and it is noted that the same four troupes were sent to perform there as a regular part of their duties.

By the fifteenth century, the origins of the four Yamato *sarugaku* troupes had become shrouded in mythical stories that generally dignified and justified their activities, giving them ancient origins and magical political significance. There were also old troupe rules, essentially contracts, which summed up troupe duties, the rights and rewards of internal troupe offices, and matters of precedence. It was possible for the dominating families within these troupes to feel themselves to be an important part of an old world under threat, allies of Shinto shrine families, aristocrats and the old imperial order, and at the same time similar to high poetic traditions. In particular the Komparu troupe was taken to be the "original" troupe, and we find that Zenchiku took these pseudo-traditions very seriously. The island of Nara and its older culture, more able with its armies and privileges to resist the radically new world of the Muromachi warriors, could seem representative of a lasting and profound culture and polity to which *sarugaku* belonged.

KOMPARU ZENCHIKU—BIOGRAPHICAL DETAILS [95]

Zenchiku was awarded the title of *tayū* 太夫 [96] in the Enman'i [97] troupe sometime before his twenty-third year.[98] The significance of such titles is a

---

94. To what degree such payments were actually paid in equivalent cash is unclear to me.
95. Documentary information concerning the life of Komparu Zenchiku is summarised in KKS, 56–63. An analysis of data relating to his friends, acquaintances and relatives can be found in KZK, 11–45, summarizing previous research. A number of contemporary documentary references to the Komparu house are reproduced in NGK.

matter that has not been completely settled and in any case was changing in the fourteenth and fifteenth centuries. Young actors who performed Noh plays particularly well were awarded the title of *tayū* by the monastic bodies in Kōfukuji and Tōnomine. Similarly a successful and mature *tayū* would be awarded the rank of *gonnokami* 権守. These titles, however, were not equivalent to positions in the *za*, the troupe itself, which had its own ranking system.[99] In the case of the Kanze *za*, however, the two people who evidently controlled the troupe, at least outside Nara, were *tayū*, Kannami and Zeami. It is generally accepted that Zenchiku was, from the time he became *tayū*, if not the leader of his troupe, its primary actor at least.[100]

The relationship between the titles *tayū* and *gonnokami*, and the *za* are not clear, and similarly the relationship between the *za* and *sarugaku* lineages or households is unclear. In Zenchiku's case, he understood himself to be the recipient of a household that traced itself back to a contemporary of Prince Shōtoku, Hada no Kōkatsu 秦河勝,[101] through his third son.[102] A line of thirty generations was traced back to a tenth-century man in that line, Hada no Ujiyasu 氏安.[103] He nowhere stated that his line was equivalent to membership of, or headship of any given troupe, but he notes that the twenty-sixth incumbent was "Bishaō Gonnokami 昆沙王権守 of Takeda, in the Enman'i troupe."[104] We do not know the status of household heads from Bishaō to Zenchiku within the troupe, but we can see that the headship of the house did not correspond to attainment of titles: thus Bishaō had three sons, the youngest of whom, Komparu, became Gonnokami. The headship, however, went through the eldest Mitsutarō, also a well-known actor. The house was next passed to Mitsutarō's son, Bishaōjirō, but then moved sideways to Komparu Gonnokami's son,

96. *Tayū* was a title bestowed on a leading performer in a troupe. See ZZ, supplementary note 175, 502–3.
97. Hirose Mizuhiro suggests that the name Enman'i derives from Enman'in, or Enmanji, an ancient Nara temple, an explanation rejected by other scholars. See Hirose Mizuhiro, *Nō to Komparu* (Shoon Shobō, 1969), 140–1, and ZZ, 434.
98. The date is discussed below.
99. Apparent in the Kanze and Komparu troupe rules: see discussions in the works listed in the next footnote.
100. See Amano Fumio, *Okina sarugaku kenkyū* (Osaka: Izumi Shoin, 1995), 303–336, and Omote Akira, "Yamato sarugaku no osa no seikaku no hensen" parts 1, 2, and 3 (*jō, chū and ge*)," *Nōgaku kenkyū* 2, 3, 4 (1976, 1977, 1978).
101. Also read as "Hata no Kawakatsu." Both Zeami and Zenchiku read "Hata" as "Hada."
102. These legends are recounted in the fourth section of Zeami's *Fushikaden* by Zeami and in Zenchiku's *Meishukushū*. The role of this lore in Zenchiku's thought is discussed further in chapter six.
103. Not now believed to correspond to a historical figure. See chapter six.
104. KKS, *Sarugaku engi*, 311. Omote and Amano, basing their observations mainly on the Kanze troupe, conclude that hereditary leadership of the troupe was a fifteenth-century development (Omote and Amano, 58).

Yasaburō 弥三郎 Tayū. From there it was passed to Zenchiku, whose title, like that of most actors in his generation, did not advance beyond *tayū*.[105]

We know very little of these former heads of Zenchiku's house. The Yamato actors were noted for their performances of the role of the *oni* 鬼, or demon,[106] and it seems that Mitsutarō, among them, was considered particularly fine, so that Zeami compared his own style of *oni* to Mitsutarō's.[107] Komparu Gonnokami appears as the representative of his lineage's acting style in both Zeami and Zenchiku's writings, receiving better treatment at Zenchiku's hands than the heavy criticism he is subjected to by Zeami.[108] His representative function is also indicated by the fact that the troupe was subsequently named after him, even though he did not succeed to its leadership. He was also known as a playwright. Both Zeami and Zenchiku name him as the author of *Ōshōkun* 王昭君, an old name for the current play *Shōkun* 昭君, which, as might be expected, is a demon play.[109] It seems that Komparu Gonnokami either retired or died before Zenchiku was more than a few years old.

Zenchiku inherited the Komparu lineage from his father, Komparu Yasaburō. One would expect Zenchiku to acclaim Yasaburō as a master performer and express great regret at his death, for it is a cliché of traditional writings in *michi* houses that they establish their credentials by the magnitude of the inheritance received.[110] Furthermore, it is fundamental to the ideology of *michi* that the appropriate attitude of a successor must begin with the desire to reproduce the techniques of the previous master.[111] Given the personal tone that appears in some of Zenchiku's writings,[112] one might even expect some mention as a result of natural affection alone. It is therefore extraordinary that the Komparu Yasaburō cited in a minimal way in both family trees does not figure anywhere else in Zenchiku's writings. Neither is he described in Zeami's writings. As both *Sarugaku dangi* 申楽談儀[113] and *Kabuzuinōki* 歌舞髄脳記[114] survey the performances of

---

105. It seems that from this time, *tayū* began to take precedence over *gonnokami*.
106. ZZ, *Fūshikaden*, 25.
107. In ZZ, *Sarugaku dangi*, 266–7, notes that he had never seen Mitsutarō's *oni* (demon), but that when he himself performed as a youth, the audience acclaimed him as the image of Mitsutarō.
108. See chapter three.
109. ZZ, *Go on*, 210. KKS, *Kabuzuinōki*, 134.
110. See for example such court performance writings such as *Kyōkunshō* 教訓抄, or the later *Taigenshō* 体源抄, or else, of course, Zeami's references to Kannami.
111. At least in Konishi's account. See Konishi, 1985, 183.
112. Mention of his wife, their poetic exchanges and her dreams, as in *Inariyama sanrōki*, is perhaps unusual (KKS, 317–22)).
113. A record of Zeami's words written by his son Motoyoshi, the full title of which is *Zeshi rokujū igo sarugaku dangi* 世子六十以後申楽談儀.

contemporary and former masters, the absence of Yasaburō demands investigation.

A certain Komparu Tayū appears in a Kasuga record for 1385.[115] In the next year, 1386, someone called the *ko-otoko* 小男 (small man) of Komparu is made *tayū*.[116] This last is likely to be the successor Yasaburō, receiving the headship from Bishaōjirō. The only explanation of the term Komparu Tayū in 1385 that can be suggested by scholars is that Komparu Gonnokami was the de facto leader, and the head priest of Kasuga called him *tayū* in error.[117] If this is accepted, then Yasaburō is called *ko-otoko* here, and subsequently, in 1392, *Komparu otoko*,[118] and then again in 1400 is the person referred to by Zeami as just Komparu.[119] Nose Asaji proposes a thirty-year period for generations, which results in Yasaburō being eleven years old when he receives the position of *tayū*. If Komparu Gonnokami was forty-one at the time, the succession seems singularly inexplicable. Itō Masayoshi regards *ko-otoko* as an unlikely term to be used for a youth. Another possibility is that Yasaburō was adult but a dwarf or physically deformed.[120] There is a problem with using this physical characteristic to explain Zenchiku's lack of reference to him, however. We are then left to ask how he could have performed at Shinto festivals, where taboos concerning physical oddity would be likely to obtain, particularly in an art form that considered physical beauty of great importance.[121]

This particular question may be difficult to resolve, but in any case, it seems reasonable to accept that Yasaburō died when Zenchiku was quite young. Not only does this explain Zenchiku's lack of memory or feeling towards him, it also explains the early age at which Zenchiku took up the leadership of the Komparu troupe, and the apparent backing he received before that time from Ōkura Tayū.[122] The lack of a father might be seen as a

114. A work by Zenchiku combining aesthetic classifications, written in 1456 (KKS, 121–42). See discussion in chapter four.
115. In *Shitoku ninenki*, of the priest Moromori of Kasuga, quoted in KZK, 16.
116. In *Shitoku sannenki*, again quoted in KZK, 16.
117. See KZK, 17. Itō suggests in a note that *gonnokami* may have been a position of control over all four troupes, which would explain the term Yamato Gonnokami used by Zenchiku in *Kabuzuinōki* to refer to Komparu Gonnokami. See KZK, 44, note 3.
118. In *Kōjin Nichinikki Nukigaki*, cited in KZK, 17.
119. ZZ, *Fūshikaden*, 40.
120. KZK, 16.
121. ZZ, *Fūshikaden*, 18. The application of taboo to shrine *sarugaku* is apparent in the heavy punishments meted out to performers urinating near the stage under cover of rain. NGK, 268–9.
122. The Ōkura group was a collateral branch of the Komparu family. There are reports of a *kanjin sarugaku* in Kyōto in 1424, in which it was uncertain whether the leading performer was Ōkura Tayū or Komparu Tayū. From these we might imagine that Ōkura Tayū had taken on the leadership in Zenchiku's minority. See KZK, 18. This Ōkura branch of the family seems to have had its origins in Ōmi, at the Hie shrine. It may be that Zenchiku's father was also

psychological matter, but within a traditional *michi* it was much more than that. Zenchiku believed himself to have inherited an ancient tradition, but he surely would have expected it to be accompanied by some ancient teachings. He had an exaggerated respect for what he believed was passed down from the past. When we look at his over-reading of Zeami's works, he appears to be searching for hints of a secret knowledge, which we, as readers, do not feel is there. His researches into hidden Shinto and poetic teachings also show his belief in some profound unifying knowledge below the surface.

There is, in fact, a tone of searching in his writings, which contrasts strongly with Zeami, who always seems to know what it is he wants to say, but searches for vocabulary from other fields to express it. Zenchiku, however, uses the other kinds of knowledge to which he gained access as a path to knowledge itself. This lends to his writings an odd lack of confidence. The knowledge that he gains is never enough, and we find him returning repeatedly to new combinations of the same material in the hope that they might yield new insights. A lack of direct tuition from a former successor would have created serious doubts concerning his legitimacy within the social ideology of *michi*, which may have influenced Zenchiku to turn away from conceptions of *sarugaku* as mere performance art, towards the examples of poetics or Shinto ritual. His undoubted capacity as a performer implies that he possessed the training in techniques, which other professionals in the troupe could have passed on to him in his childhood. It is in the secret knowledge believed to pass privately from former to succeeding master that he would have felt poorly qualified, and this may be considered one personal element that drove him to the persistent metaphysical questioning and search for inner validating factors expressed in his writings. For Zeami, on the other hand, this may well have been a factor behind his odd belief that Zenchiku could have been a potential successor in his lineage, as we shall discuss in chapter three.

Let us now turn to what can be known about Zenchiku himself. He was born in 1405, three years before Yoshimitsu's death.[123] A major event in his

---

closely connected with the Ōmi *sarugaku*. Speculations concerning this material can be found in NGK, 304–22.
123. The post-script of *Rokurin ichiro hichū (bunshōbon)* 六輪一露秘注文正本 (hereafter *Bunshōbon*) has the age "62 years" written alongside the signature, and is dated the spring of *Bunshō* 1 (1466) (KKS, 262). Another work, *Sarugaku engi*, is dated Ōnin 2.3.20 (1468) and is accompanied by the remark "64 years" (KKS, 57). These ages are of course according to the traditional system of calculation whereby age at birth is one year, subsequently increasing every new year. This system is followed in this study, for it allows an age to be calculated without knowing the day and month of birth. The modern style of age can be calculated by subtracting either one or two. Thus in Ōnin 2.3.20 Zenchiku was sixty-two or sixty-three years old by our reckoning. Dates will be given as here in the order year, month and day. These do

life must have been his assumption of the position of *tayū*. The first definite identification of Zenchiku as Komparu Tayū is in Zeami's hand, written in 1428,[124] but because we know so little about his father, we cannot be sure to whom earlier references to Komparu Tayū might refer. The report of a Komparu Tayū appearing in a *kanjin sarugaku* in the capital in 1424 might indicate that Zenchiku was made *tayū* by his nineteenth year.[125]

In these early years the Komparu troupe can be expected to have continued to fulfill its duties in Nara, performing at Kōfukuji, before the Kasuga shrine, at the *monzeki*, Daijōin and Ichijōin, at the Nandaimon, at the Chūin for the *roppōshū* 六方衆, and at the Wakamiya festival, as well as at the eightfold reading of the *Vimalakirti Sutra* at Tōnomine. The Kanze and other troupes would also have been present, and so it is to be expected that Zenchiku became familiar with Zeami's sons Motomasa (?1401–1432) and Motoyoshi, and nephew, Motoshige 元重 (Onnami) (1398–1467), all perhaps somewhat older than he. The nature of the relationship between Zenchiku and the Kanze troupe will be looked at in detail in chapter three. Suffice it to say here that as well as becoming *tayū*, Zenchiku married a daughter of Zeami and received from Zeami a number of playscripts and two secret writings on *sarugaku*: *Rikugi* 六義 and *Shūgyokutokka* 拾玉得花, by the end of Ōei 35 (1428).

At this time Yoshimochi was shogun (1408–1428). Kōfukuji leaders must have felt a reprieve from Yoshimitsu's ambitions concerning the court and Yamato province. It was a period when the Kanze fully established the priority that they had in Kyoto, when Zeami (or Motomasa) received the position of *gakutō* at the *Seiryūgū* 清滝宮, a shrine that was part of the *Daigoji* temple complex (1424). This had formerly been a post passed down in the Enami troupe, and gave the bearer the power to decide which troupes to bring to perform in the capital. The Kanze had often performed there, and the appointment was marked by gifts from the nobility as well as the monastic body, who recalled Zeami's performances there as a child.[126] 1428 is the same year as the Komparu *kanjin sarugaku* referred to above, but it is

not correspond to Western months. Intercalary months will be preceded by the letters "int." A Japanese year does not coincide precisely with a Western one, either, so that an equivalent of 1468 given for Ōnin 2 is no more than an approximation based on standard tables, correct for months in the middle of the year, possibly in error at year-ends.
124. *ZZ, Rikugi*, 182.
125. A record of the temple *Tōji*, preserved in *Nochi Kagami*, and cited in NGK, 470. Nose takes this to be Yasaburō, Zenchiku's father, but more recent scholars consider it to be Zenchiku, cf. KZK, 18.
126. NGK, 718–22. The story of the nasty fate that met the Enami brothers and the significance of the *gakutō* post is discussed in Hayashiya Tatsusaburō, *Chūsei geinōshi no kenkyū* (Iwanami Shoten, 1960), 477–8.

notable that the Komparu troupe in Zenchiku's lifetime never otherwise figures in Kyoto performances or performances before the shogun and his circle except simply as one of the four Yamato troupes performing together, usually on the occasion of the shogunal progress to the southern capital.[127]

It was perhaps some time before this that Zenchiku began his association with Shōtetsu, leading poet of the Reizei tradition. There is a copy of the poetic work *Saigyō shōnin danshō* 西行上人談抄 which includes a postscript by Shōtetsu dated Ōei 31 (1424) and a note to the effect that it was shown to "Lord Komparu."[128] *Saigyō shōnin danshō* is in fact quoted in Zenchiku's *Kabuzuinōki*, so there is no reason to doubt the note's veracity. Furthermore, a draft collection of poems by Shōtetsu tells of an occasion, probably much later, when Zenchiku obtained from him an inscription for a sacred image of Okina.[129] It seems that Shōtetsu mediated Ōuchi patronage of Zenchiku.[130] It is generally accepted that Shōtetsu was Zenchiku's poetry teacher. Shōtetsu placed Fujiwara Teika and the aesthetic of *yūgen* 幽玄 at the centre of his poetics, which he regarded as a kind of spiritual task. Shōtetsu felt that a return to Teika's conception of poetry was required to re-establish its proper significance. A well-quoted remark of his states: "In the path of poetry, any who criticize Teika must surely forfeit even divine favor."[131] His account of *yūgen* takes place within a whole context of contemporary discussions.

In the Muromachi period *yūgen* is characterized in different ways, on the one hand in terms of elegant court ladies in scenes of natural beauty and on the other as something richly beautiful, veiled by mist or cloud. Both are part of a general idealization of the Heian court that gripped the fifteenth-century imagination. The former characterization was clearly apparent in both the works of Nijō Yoshimoto 二条良基 (1320–1388), principal supporter of the Nijō faction,[132] and of Zeami; but Shōtetsu leaned more towards the latter.[133] This is in line with the definitions that were thought to

127. A collection of records of Komparu performances in this time can be found in NGK, 469–79. These are the source of unnoted references to Komparu troupe activity below.
128. Quoted in KZK, 28.
129. See chapter six.
130. See the section of chapter four entitled: *Go on jittei.*
131. 歌道に於いて定家を難ぜん輩は冥加もあるべからず in *Shōtetsu monogatari* 正徹物語 in Hisamatsu Sen-ichi and Nishiō Minoru, eds., *Karonshū nōgakuronshū (Nihon koten bungaku taikei 65)* (Iwanami Shoten, 1961), 166.
132. Konishi, 1991, 392.
133. "*Yūgen* may be comprehended by the mind but it cannot be expressed in words. Its quality may be suggested by the sight of a thin cloud veiling the moon or by autumn mist swathing scarlet leaves on a mountainside" (from *Shōtetsu monogatari*, as translated and quoted in Tsunoda Ryūsaku, Wm Theodore de Bary and Donald Keene, eds., *Sources of Japanese Tradition I* (New York: Columbia University Press, 1958), 285). The author is well aware that assertions of influence and of shared aesthetic views are complex matters and has no wish to

be Teika's. The Reizei ideal of poetic composition rising from the depths of "deep, silent contemplation"[134] can be seen to correspond closely to Zenchiku's derivation of excellence in performance from the achievement of a state of mind-transcending mental activity.[135] That Zenchiku was familiar with and had a great regard for the poems and theories attributed to Teika is apparent from the fact that of eighty poems illustrating aesthetic qualities in Noh in his work, *Kabuzuinōki*, forty-three are found in *Sangoki* 三五記 and thirteen in *Shūigusō* 拾遺愚草, both works attributed to Teika.[136] Zenchiku quotes from the former work frequently. The only two Noh plays that quote from Teika's poetry are *Teika* 定家 and *Oshio* 小塩, both attributed to Zenchiku.[137] Thus one can see some convergence of views between Zenchiku and Shōtetsu.

Zenchiku understood poetics to be a basis for *sarugaku* aesthetics. A series of searches for direct parallels between terms arising in the two arts is seen in his works of classification.[138] The first sign of this kind of approach appears in the work *Rikugi* that Zeami wrote at Zenchiku's request in 1428. This relates the nine levels of *sarugaku* performance as described in Zeami's *Kyūi* 九位 to the six types of poetic form found in the *Great Preface*. The result is not at all successful, but the attempt is interesting. The reading of the six poetic forms derives from the introductions to the *Kokinwakashū*.[139] Ki no Tsurayuki attempted therein to relate the six forms to styles of *waka*. There is, of course, no reason why a set of three types of poetic device and three conventions of poetic format in the Chinese

go into them here. The relationship between Nijō Yoshimoto's concepts of *yūgen* (the style of court ladies of the *Genji Monogatari*) and more particularly *hana* and the related *kakari* are discussed usefully in Janet Goff, *Noh Drama and the Tale of Genji: the Art of Allusion in Fifteen Classical Plays* (Princeton: Princeton University Press, 1991), 37–8.

134. Konishi Jin'ichi, 1991, 390. Konishi's account of Shōtetsu's aesthetics in the surrounding pages seems to over-emphasize the elegant and aristocratic aspect of *yūgen*, while the poems given in example clearly illustrate the phantasmagoric, covered, and spare quality that it can also be thought to denote. The move towards such Higashiyama aesthetics as *hie* (chill) in his pupil, Zenchiku's contemporary, Shinkei (1406–75), and the use of synaesthesia are also mentioned (392).

135. As described in chapters three, four, and five, below.

136. Falsely so, in the case of *Sangoki*.

137. The evidence for Zenchiku's interest in Teika given here derives from KZK, 50–1. The fact that both plays given do not use any material from *Sangoki* may require some explanation. The attribution of *Oshio* is pretty strong, as Zenchiku performed it at a Tōnomine-style *sarugaku*, when it was common to present newly written plays. Kawase Kazuma (according to KZK, 49) held that *Teika* was by Zeami, and modified subsequently by Zenchiku. This would explain the extraordinary structure of the play which appears to be the combination of two halves of different plays, a standard *mugen* play by Zeami, and plant play in which a creeper fails to find release by listening to the *Lotus Sutra*, by Zenchiku. This intriguing play deserves to be better known.

138. As discussed in chapter four.

139. The opening words of *Rikugi* make this plain. ZZ, 180.

tradition should correspond with subsets of the single poetic form of *waka*. The purpose of Tsurayuki's combination is generally thought to be ideological. Tsurayuki wished to bring to literature in Japanese something of the regard that was reserved for composition in Chinese. In the same way, the aesthetic analyses of the prefaces to the *Kokinwakashū* had themselves become a source of authority from which Zenchiku attempted to dignify *sarugaku*.[140]

In 1428, the shogun Yoshimochi died and Yoshinori was chosen by lot to replace him. The emperor Shōkō 称光 abdicated and Go-Hanazono 後花園 acceded to the throne. The first great uprising of peasants demanding from the *bakufu* a remission of debts occurred in Ōmi province. This period of Yoshinori's rule was to prove disastrous for Zeami. Yoshinori had formerly supported the Enami, and also favored Zeami's nephew, Onnami. The Kanze troupe appears to have split about this time, 1429, with one group led by Motomasa, supported by Zeami, and the other by Onnami.[141] A performance of Zeami and Motomasa at the Sentōin (the retired emperor's residence) was forbidden, by Yoshinori it seems.[142] In the next year, 1430, the shogun had Onnami take over the role of *gakutō* at Seiryūgū at Daigoji.[143] Zeami's son Motoyoshi retired from *sarugaku* and took holy orders after making a record of Zeami's teachings, *Sarugaku dangi*.[144] In 1432, Zeami's chosen heir, Motomasa, died while traveling in Ise province—probably not a natural death.[145] From this time Zeami showed interest in the possibility of his son-in-law, Zenchiku, continuing his artistic lineage. In 1434, Zeami was banished to Sado Island, and his subsequent activities are not clearly known, although he replied to letters from Zenchiku and in 1435 composed the work *Kintōsho* 金島書. It is thought that Zeami returned from Sado after Yoshinori was assassinated in 1441, and died in 1443.[146]

---

140. The pseudo-Chinese of *Rikugi* accords with these intentions. Zeami himself does not seem to have been particularly enamored with the project. In itself it lacks the clarity of Zeami's other works, and the postscript rather deliberately records Zenchiku's request that it be written. (ZZ, 162.) The next work passed to Zenchiku a few months later, *Shūgyokutokka*, is a return to topics about which Zeami himself wished to write.
141. A *tachiai* (competition) performance in 1429 figured two Kanze troupes, along with the Hōshō and the Jūni troupe, according to the entry for Eikyo 1.5.3 in *Manzai Jugō Nikki*, quoted in NGK, 724.
142. *Manzai Jugō Nikki*, Eikyō 1.5.13, who gives no reason, but expresses regrets. NGK, 723.
143. At least the entry in *Manzai Jugō Nikki*, Eikyō 2.4.17, is generally interpreted in that fashion (see NGK, 725–6).
144. As described in the postscript of that work, ZZ, *Sarugaku dangi*, 310.
145. The circumstances are unknown, but he was in his thirties and there is no indication of illness. Zeami's despair at this apparent end to his lineage is recorded in *Museki isshi* 夢跡一紙 written in the same year. ZZ, 242–3.
146. For this period see Kobayashi Shizuo, 65–71.

The only glimpses available of Zenchiku at this time show him continuing his duties in Nara. A son, Shichirō Motouji Sōin 七郎元氏宗筠 (1432–1480), is born, who eventually inherits the troupe. Zenchiku manages to get his hands on a number of Zeami's family writings and playscripts, and appears to be studying them carefully, perhaps developing his own understanding of *sarugaku*.[147] He takes on responsibility for the upkeep of his mother-in-law, Zeami's wife, Juchin 寿椿. A letter to the banished Zeami sends money and enquires about the demon Noh, the specialty of the Komparu house.[148]

It is after Zeami's death that Zenchiku embarks on his own writing career. The idea of using the *rokurin ichiro* set of diagrams came to him while in retreat at the Hasedera in Yamato.[149] In 1444, the eminent Tōdaiji spiritual leader, Shigyoku, wrote an erudite commentary on the diagrams, with references to Buddhist scripture. This is clearly the product of serious attention and is an impressive display in its own right. Shigyoku's biography can be found in *Honchō kōsōden* 本朝高僧伝. He descended from an aristocratic family and entered the Kaidan'in of Tōdaiji while young. In his early youth he showed great intelligence and mastered Kegon theory. In Ōei 24 (1417) he went to Ming China for five years where he lectured the emperor on the Avatamsaka Sutra and received the title Fuichi Kokushi 普一国師. Returning to Japan loaded with scriptures, he lived in Tōdaiji. His eloquence in lecturing on the Kegon sutras persuaded Emperor Shōkō to award him the *kokushi* 国師 title ("national teacher") a second time. Shigyoku thereafter studied in different schools, the vinaya from Fukai, and Zen from Zuikei Shūhō of Shōkokuji, the major *gozan* temple. He even preached the Buddhist law to a Shinto deity that attempted to frighten him, and received a *waka* in return.[150] Tōdaiji records tell how in 1429 Shigyoku, as master of the Kaidan'in, ordained the shogun Yoshinori, an indication of his worldly eminence.[151]

---

147. This appropriation of texts including several of Zeami's playscripts, *Fūshikaden*, *Shikadō* and copying of important works, *Kakyō* in 1437, and *Besshi kuden* in 1441, will be discussed in chapter three.
148. See Zeami's reply, ZZ, 318–9.
149. Kōfukuji had taken control of Hasedera by this time. The temple figures prominently in *sarugaku* traditions. See chapter five, below for a discussion of the passage, which is found in *Rokurin ichiro no kichū*, KKS, 220.
150. This summarises the account in section 18 of *Honchō kōsōden*, an eighteenth century collection of hagiographies of great Japanese Buddhist monks (Bussho Kankōkai, ed., *Honchō kōsōden I* (Bussho Kankōkai, 1913), 264).
151. Hiraoka Jōkai (abbot of Tōdaiji) discusses this and other aspects of Shigyoku's career in 1977, 166. The Kaidan'in was the first ordination platform properly established in Japan. It was burnt down in 1446, two years after Shigyoku completed the commentary on *rokurin ichiro* diagrams.

Considering Shigyoku's stature and the seriousness of his commentary on Zenchiku's system, we find the tone of the eminent monk's closing remarks to be extraordinary: "This Komparu Tayū Ujinobu is a famed master in his art inherited from a long lineage, excellent to a degree not to be equaled in times ancient or modern, a master artist rarely found in these latter days, the most skillful in the world. Above all, intelligent and awakened to Buddhist and non-Buddhist knowledge, superior and excellent, the inner significance of this work is extremely profound. Thus, overwhelmed with admiration, writing with some restraint, the details are as recorded above."[152]

How Zenchiku achieved an intellectual association with Shigyoku is unknown, but it is one sign of his increasing prestige in Nara from this time on. Temple records mention Zenchiku socializing with the Daijōin *monzeki* and Kōfukuji superintendent Jinson, and taking part in *renga* sessions with Jinson and the former incumbent Kyōgaku 経覚 (1395–1473) at his retreat, the An'iji.[153] In 1451 Zenchiku's troupe is *gakutō* of the Kasuga shrine. Zenchiku and Onnami are the leading actors of their day. In 1454, his grandson, Hachirō Motoyasu 八郎元安 Zenpō, is born. By 1455, Zenchiku has managed to gain a further commentary to add to that of Shigyoku from Jinson's father, Ichijō Kanera, also grandson of Nijō Yoshimoto.

Kanera had risen quickly through the court ranks and held the positions of chancellor, regent and prime minister, and clan head. He was a prolific author whose scholarly sobriety marks him out from his predecessors.[154] He was favored by Yoshinori, receiving land-rights from him, and was called upon to write the introductions to leading poetry collections. He was an expert in court culture, writing commentaries on the *Tale of Genji* and *Ise monogatari* 伊勢物語, and works on *waka* and *renga*, and is renowned for his contributions to the studies of the *Nihonshoki* 日本書紀. He was an influence on Yoshida Kanetomo's Shinto, perhaps a conduit to him of Watarai ideas.[155] Zenchiku called upon his expertise in Chinese non-Buddhist thought for a "Confucian" commentary to his *rokurin ichiro* system. Kanera's contribution begins with an invocation of the unity of the three creeds,[156] and some choice quotations from Confucius and Mencius

---

152. KKS, 206–7.
153. KZK, 25.
154. See the discussion by Richard Bowring, "The Ise Monogatari: a Short Cultural History," *Harvard Journal of Asiatic Studies* 52.2 (December 1992): 450–4.
155. A chronology of Kanera's life can be found in Nagashima, 1959b, 194–7. For Kanera's connection to Kanetomo, see Mark Teeuwen, *Watarai Shintō: An Intellectual History of the Outer Shrine at Ise* (Leiden: Research School CNWS, 1996), 183.
156. That Taoism, Buddhism, and Confucianism express the same truth—a fashionable doctrine in the fifteenth century—discussed in chapter five.

on the role of music in society. He then adds an outline of the way in which *sarugaku*—both the art and its name—is derived from the events in the section of the *Nihonshoki* concerning the "age of the gods."[157] The rest of his contribution relates each of the theory's diagrams to elements of Neo-Confucian thought.[158] Zenchiku was to take the Shinto elements and incorporate them into his own assertion of the preeminence of his troupe's lineage in the later work *Sarugaku engi* 猿楽縁起. There are references to a Noh playscript written by Kanera for Zenchiku, and to his continued patronage of the Komparu troupe after Zenchiku's death.[159] This patronage included a work by Kanera that asserted in the clearest terms the supremacy of the Komparu tradition over the other three Yamato troupes, and the superiority of the late Zenchiku and his line.[160]

Although Kanera was Jinson's father, his relationship with Zenchiku may have been supported by another connection. The poet Shōtetsu was out of favor with the shogun Yoshinori, supporter of the Nijō school, who caused his work to be omitted from the Imperial collection *Shinshokukokinwakashū* 新続古今和歌.[161] The poet and the Reizei school did have the support, however, of Kanera, who took him up after Yoshinori's death, and wrote a preface to his personal collection, *Sōkonshū* 草根集.[162]

The building of such relations bore fruit in 1457. During the Takigi performances,[163] on the day when Komparu and Kongō performed before Jinson at the Daijōin, the Komparu claimed the right to perform the first (*waki* 脇) Noh. Lots were drawn, and Kongō was chosen, but the superintendent shortly issued a decision that former precedents clearly gave the Komparu priority. The former precedents invoked appear to have been faked, and it is clear that the Kongō found the decision extremely difficult to accept. The next year the elderly Kanze *osa* 長 attempted to intervene, suggesting a compromise, which Jinson flatly rejected. The Kongō then refused to show up, for which they were strongly censured and ended up having to write an abject apology.[164] The situation can only be explained in

---

157. That is *kamiyo* (or *jindai*) 神代, history prior to the emperor Jinmu. Subsequent history is known in contrast as the age of human kings (*ninnō* 人皇).
158. See KKS, *Rokurin ichiro no ki*, 208–12.
159. See KZK, 24–5.
160. KKS, *Sarugaku kōshōki*, 568.
161. The last of the twenty-one imperial *waka* collections. The final three collections were ordered by the Ashikaga shōguns and represented their tastes.
162. After Shōtetsu's death, it seems. Nagashima, 1959b, 196.
163. The series of performances put on at the Kōfukuji-Kasuga complex in the second month, the first of the Yamato *sarugaku* troupes' annual calendar of duties in Nara.
164. The records describing the event and an evaluation of the material can be found in NGK, 472–4.

terms of Jinson's strong support for the Komparu. Komparu precedence was apparent in Kōfukuji thereafter, except when the shogun was present and the Kanze went first.[165]

A much fiercer conflict occurred at the Wakamiya festival of 1458. A *dengaku* player performed with a mask. The *sarugaku* claimed that the use of a mask was their prerogative and stormed the *dengaku* lodgings, stole the mask and smashed it. A go-between trying to intervene in the violent struggle of the two sides was shot with an arrow and died. The *sarugaku* troupes were banned from the province forthwith on pain of death, so that there was no Takigi Noh the next year. The ban appears to have been soon rescinded however, and the Komparu were to be seen giving thanks and performing at the two shrines of Hachiman and Kasuga in the fifth month.[166]

Tours of the provinces are assumed to be a part of the life of these troupes. Zeami's letter from Kiya congratulates Zenchiku on his visits to the North and refers to performances in Ōmi.[167] In 1456, Zenchiku journeyed down to the West of Japan where in the ninth month he hastily committed *Go on jittei* 五音十体 to paper at the request of the prominent enthusiast of the arts, Ōuchi Norihiro 大内教弘 (1419–1465). The work is presumably a record of ideas that Zenchiku had expressed in conversation.[168] This visit seems likely to be connected to the invitation that Norihiro had issued to the aging Shōtetsu in the same year to come to Suō province to combine poetry and sightseeing, rejected on the grounds of failing health.[169]

Japanese regard their sixtieth year as the completion of a cycle, representing as it does a return to the element-zodiac combination of the year of birth. The sixty-first year (*kanreki* 還暦) is then a new birth, and can be taken as an occasion for renaming in the Buddhist path. It is at about this age that Zenchiku stops using the name Ujinobu in his postscripts. In 1466 he signs himself Zenchiku-ō—the first use of the name Zenchiku.[170] It is taken to be a Buddhist name (*hōmyō* 法名). In 1468 this has been absorbed into a Zen-style name, Ken'ō Zenchiku 賢翁禅竹, in which Ken'ō could be a *dōgō* 道号, that is, a name conferred at the achievement of awakening.[171]

165. As mentioned in *Inryōken Nichiroku* for Kanshō 6.9.25, with the reason for Kanze priority given. See NGK, 478.
166. See NGK, 475–7.
167. ZZ, 316.
168. See Komparu Zenpō's appended postscript, KKS, 148.
169. KZK, 29–30.
170. KKS, *Bunshōbon*, 262. The name Zenchiku also appears in the Yasaemon copy of *Kabuzuinōki*, but as it is not in the other copy, it is taken to be a copyist's addition.
171. In KKS, *Sarugaku engi*, 311.

It is reminiscent of Zeami's name, Shiō Zenpō 至翁善芳, but unlikely to be directly connected. Zeami's relationship with the family temple Fuganji and its Sōtō sect masters is well known,[172] but there is no sign that Zenchiku had equivalent Zen connections.[173] In fact, the various changes of name are more likely to be related to the roles within the troupe. In 1464, Zenchiku used the name Chikuō Koji 竹翁居士.[174] In his work *Meishukushū* referring to the role of *Okina* in the performance he notes that *"osa* is the status of *koji.*"[175] *Koji* is a translation of the second of the four stages of man in the Hindu conception: celibate student, householder, forest-dweller and renunciate.[176] By its use in the story of Vimalakirti,[177] it came to mean one who physically lives in the world but in spirit is a renunciate—a popular reconciliation of spirituality and worldliness. In Japan it became a suffix for older men who had entered religion. *Osa* is the name for the traditional elder of the *za*. It may be then that Zenchiku's use of the suffix *koji* refers to his attainment of the position of *osa*. Among various duties, the performing role of the *osa* was that of *Okina*, which Zenchiku understood to be a divine essence pervading the universe. It is perhaps for this reason that he adopts the character as part of all his subsequent self-namings.

The aged Zenchiku, along with Onnami, is commanded to perform a Noh play, before the shogun Yoshimasa in 1465.[178] He is referred to as Takeda 竹田 Tayū, presumably to distinguish him from his son, going now by the name of Komparu Tayū. In 1466, however, a set of Zenchiku's poems refers to life in his hermitage. The colophon of *Sarugaku engi*, completed in 1468, tells of his "living in the mountains of Takigi in Yamashiro, at the Tafuku hermitage." This is probably the place to which he retired in his sixty-first year. Ikkyū Sōjun 一休宗純 moved here a year

---

172. See "Zeami no shukke to kie," in Kōsai Tsutomu, *Zeami shinkō* (Wan'ya Shoten, 1962) and summarized in additional note 149, ZZ, 493.
173. The unlikelihood of Zenchiku's formal Zen affiliation or close connection with either Fuganji or Ikkyū Sōjun is argued in KZK, 31–40. The interpretation of Zenchiku's religious names is found in KKS, 61–2. Zenchiku points to the presence of the character ō (翁) in the Buddhist name of Zeami and another leader of a troupe and takes it to be a sign of the mysterious power of Okina (in KKS, *Meishukushū*, 295.) This implies that there was not a more obvious connection.
174. In *Rokurin ichiro hichū (kanshōbon)* 六輪一露秘注文寛正本, (referred to hereafter as *Kanshōbon*) KKS, 246.
175. 長者居士身, KKS, *Meishukushū*, 279, n.5. This collection of characters, however, affords different interpretations, for example to identify the term *chōja* and the state *koji* (see chapter six).
176. Sanskrit: *grhapati*.
177. Known to Japanese as *Yuima Koji* (維摩居士).
178. When the shōgun visited Nara, as recorded in *Inryōken nichiroku* for Kansho 6.2.25 (1465). Quoted in NGK, 478.

later fleeing from the Ōnin war, and there are records of Ikkyū writing Zenchiku a religious tract in the autumn of 1468.[179]

In Zenchiku's works there are mentions of his going on spiritual retreats to Hasedera[180] and the Sumiyoshi shrine.[181] In the sixth month of 1467, Zenchiku and his wife entered a retreat at the Inariyama shrine near Kyoto, and Zenchiku appears to take a priest of the institution, Zengan 善岩, as preceptor. An account of the retreat is preserved as *Inariyama sanrōki* 稲荷山参籠記.[182] After 1468 the next mention of Zenchiku is in 1471, when Ichijō Kanera refers to him as "the late Komparu *tayū*, Zenchiku."[183] In 1473, a Tendai priest called Senkai 仙海 copied out passages of a commentary on the *Lotus Sutra* that discussed the hidden significance of the *okina sarugaku* piece *Shikisanban*. In his explanatory colophon Senkai referred to the "dying wish of the hermit Zenchiku."[184] The circumstances of Zenchiku's death are unknown.

From the above account, one can see that Zenchiku's life, although perhaps cut short by the civil war, was an extremely successful one. At his birth the supreme attainment for a *sarugaku* troupe—the backing of the *bakufu* (led by Yoshimitsu) and of the court elite (led by Nijō Yoshimoto)—had been achieved by Kanze leaders Kannami and Zeami. Taking the *gakutō* position of Seiryūgū at Daigoji in 1424 sealed this preeminence in Kyoto. The Komparu troupe on the other hand had probably the lowest rating for performance,[185] and Zenchiku himself lacked an accomplished predecessor from whom he could inherit the house. Zenchiku married into Zeami's family and managed to receive most of the secret works of Zeami, at least some of which he subsequently refused to hand back.[186] From the time of Zeami's death, he himself began to produce his own secret writings and to build a network of supporters among the great authorities of Nara—the Tōdaiji leader Shigyoku, and Kōfukuji superintendents Jinson and Kyōgaku. Through Shōtetsu he was connected to leading Reizei poets and perhaps to the provincial cultural leaders, the Ōuchi, who requested from him a work on aesthetic classification. His connection with Ichijō Kanera, chancellor and intellectual authority, led to

179. See KKS, 74.
180. In *Rokurin ichiro kichū*, KKS, 220.
181. In *Meishukushū*, KKS, 282, and 299–301.
182. KKS, 317–22.
183. KKS, *Sarugaku kōshōki*, 568.
184. KKS, *Hokegobukukanshojo*, 564.
185. See chapter three.
186. See the account of Kanze Motoyoshi, in *Shiki shūgen* 四季祝言, quoted in KZK, 21–2. The fact that one of the works referred to, *Sandō* 三道, is not found in Komparu possession subsequently and that the extant versions seem to have derived from the Ochi Kanze line implies that it, at least, was returned. ZZ, 559–60.

his troupe being validated as the *honza* 本座 of all troupes. In his lifetime and after, he was ranked alongside the Kanze leader, Onnami, as one of the two leading performers of his day. While in Kyoto the Kanze continued to have the backing of the shogun, in Nara and in intellectual and literary circles the Komparu achieved the greatest possible prestige.

3 Transmission
Zeami to Zenchiku

Zenchiku alludes to Zeami's theories and terminology throughout his works.[187] How we interpret these allusions is crucial to our reading of Zenchiku. In general, scholars have assumed Zenchiku's attitude to Zeami's tradition to be one of respect and loyalty, as appropriate in a pupil of a medieval *michi*. They have accordingly interpreted Zenchiku's writings as attempts to systematize Zeami's work, or to provide it with metaphysical foundations.[188] Zeami and Zenchiku are, indeed, sometimes thought of as exemplars of the medieval master-pupil relationship. Such a relationship is thought to have entailed the pupil's denial of his own ideas in favor of a wholehearted identification with his master's teachings; for the teachings in a *michi* should transmit something more significant than what a mere individual could discover on his own. A master of a *michi*, for his part, would not accept a pupil who lacked such dedication. Zeami, as the exemplary master, certainly could not have done so.

Such assumptions, however, are misleading, and have distorted readings of Zenchiku's work. Zeami's major concerns—his analysis of the impact of performance on audiences and his delineation of the structures in the artist's path—hardly appear at all in Zenchiku's theoretical systems. Zenchiku scarcely discusses, for example, the concept of *hana* 花, a concept so dominant in Zeami that its graph appears in the title of all of his major works. Again, fundamental intellectual structures that Zeami repeatedly applied to his formulations of the way have no presence in Zenchiku. Consider, for example, the pattern that traces development from *waza* 態 (technique), through *kokoro* 心 (understanding) to *mu* 無 (unconscious skills), or the distinction between elements that are *tai* 体

---

187. Much of the material in this chapter appeared in my "Crossed Paths: Zeami's transmission to Zenchiku," *Monumenta Nipponica*, 52:2 (Summer 1997), 201–234.
188. See Nose Asaji, *Kodai geki bungaku (Nihon bungaku taikei 21)* (Kawade Shobō, 1939), 165–6.

(primary) and those that are *yū* 用 (secondary), or that dominant image of Zeami's later work, the return (*kōkokyakurai* 向去却来) of the master from the heights of purity.[189] While it is true that Zenchiku sometimes draws on the vocabulary associated with these ideas, the structures on which they were built have no formative presence in his work. We must put aside the assumption that Zenchiku was either intent on supporting or systematizing Zeami's teachings.

TRANSMISSION IN *MICHI* INSTITUTIONS

The conventional view of Zeami and Zenchiku's relationship appears to be based on general images of the transfer of knowledge from one generation to the next in the medieval arts. Such transmission (*keishōsei* 継承性) is central to Konishi's model of *michi*, for he writes that "*michi* is found in the act of transmission."[190] Konishi holds that one reason various *michi* accrued general authority was because people believed them to be transmitted unchanged over several generations. It was on this basis that they were felt to have the authority to order individual lives, to take precedence over individual impulses. By submitting himself to the process of training and suppressing his "small ideas," the pupil could hope eventually to break through to a superior and universal knowledge that was beyond the powers of an ordinary individual. It was only by submitting to the standards applied by the master that the pupil could hope to reach this final stage. This achievement of mastery brought with it a "higher freedom."[191] While the artist sought these personal benefits he was also committed to the preservation of the path itself; it was his duty to find appropriate pupils to pass it on to. Konishi inferred the character of these ideals from the writings of medieval masters and certain accounts of experts in various paths. Particularly prominent among these were the writings of Zeami himself. How could it be then that Zeami espoused certain ideals that in practice are so little illustrated by the behavior of his artistic successor?

Michi is described as an ideal. But what were the social circumstances within which the ideal was pursued? The fundamental institution was the

189. The term *kōkokyakurai* is made up of two contrasting terms, *kōko* 向去 (otherwise read *kōkyo*), meaning abandoning the world and making for the mountain tops to achieve the heights of purity, and *kyakurai* 却来 (otherwise read *kyarai*), meaning coming down in old age with a head of white hair to the market place (see entries for the two terms in Koga Hidehiko, ed., *Zengo jiten* (Kyoto: Shibunkaku Shuppan, 1991). Thus For further discussion in relation to Noh, see chapters four and five below, Noel J. Pinnington, "Models of the Way in the Theory of Noh," *Japan Review* 18 (2006): 42–3 and Konishi Jin'ichi, *Nōgakuron kenkyū* (Hanawa Shobō, 1961): 231–7.
190. Konishi, 1986, 155, translated thus in Konishi, 1991, 147.
191. Konishi, 1986, 155.

household, which we can understand to have been related to society in something of the manner that we have seen generally described for *shokunin* organizations.[192] When we compare the transfer of power in such households with the transmission of knowledge in *michi*, we immediately observe a relationship. This is because the idea of *michi* is an ideology naturalizing the power structure of the institution of the household, which mediated the relations between its members and society at large, distributing work and rewards. For simplicity at this point, let us discuss this in the general terms of the "traditional Japanese household," i.e. the *ie* 家, as described by social scientists.[193] (We shall refine this below in relation to conditions in fourteenth-century households). Within such a household, authority belonged to a single head (*iemoto* 家元). Subject to him was the next generation, consisting of his children and adopted children. From these he had to train and nominate a successor. The *iemoto*'s ultimate responsibility was the continuity of the house and its fulfillment of the professional task with which it was identified. If we consider the career of a potential successor, he had to both master the technical business of the house and satisfy the present head. This clearly corresponds to the *michi* ideal of self-denial and conformity in training. A junior member of the house who gained the headship, however, suddenly found himself in the position of considerable autonomy, free to practice as he wished and endowed with authority, both within the household and with regard to external society, concerning the practices and rights of the household. This stage corresponds to the "breakthrough" to artistic freedom and the general artistic authority in society claimed for masters of *michi*. These correspondences are hardly surprising, for *michi* was indeed a name for the business of households. We can see then that the transfer of knowledge in *michi* was simply one face of a larger process, the transfer of power, resources and autonomy in traditional households.

The ideal of *michi* thus emerges as an ideology, masking and justifying a structure of power. The relationship between the transfer of knowledge and skill and the transfer of power in the house was of course obvious to everyone. This is apparent from the apophthegm invoked by Zeami himself, among others: *ie ie ni arazu, tsugu o motte ie to su; hito hito ni arazu, shiru o motte hito to su*—a household is only a household insofar as it is transferred across the generations, a man is only a man insofar as he has

---

192. As Konishi points out (1986, 154–5), although there were exceptions among the kind of performing *michi* we are concerned with, for example, blind musicians (who would seek blind pupils, unlikely to be among their own progeny).
193. As described, for example, in Joy Hendry, *Understanding Japanese Society* (London: Croom Helm, 1987), 21–37.

acquired knowledge.[194] This connection between the transfer of knowledge and the transfer of power lies behind the odd fact that, although the relations of masters and pupils in *michi* are regularly described in their works, and in the writings of those who idealize the Japanese arts as mutually beneficial and harmonious, the actual history of the transmission of knowledge in the medieval arts is marked by conflicts and lawsuits.

"Secret" writings (*hidensho*) play an important role both in the ideology of artistic lineages and in their conflict-ridden histories. Much in the manner of *kuden* 口伝, the written records of oral transmission in Tendai esoteric Buddhist initiations, they had a dual character—internally concerned with abstruse unworldly matters, and externally used as evidence of the possessor's authority. Thus we see that *hidensho* were used (and forged) in poetic lineages throughout the Kamakura period both to validate the poetic beliefs of lineages and to support claims to succession to the Mikohidari tradition. The use of *hidensho* to validate claims to authority was of course widespread in all court traditions. In Zeami's case, it is clear that his works had different extrinsic or social roles at different periods in his life. We shall find that his transmission of them had three distinct phases: the first period in his thirties and forties when he wrote down his received tradition adopting the conventions of writings in the courtly arts; the second when his children and pupils were in their twenties and he attempted to control the family succession and the inheritance of his acting troupe; and the third when, having lost control of the succession in his lineage, he looked to Zenchiku to carry his artistic ideals to future generations. This last transmission of knowledge carried no authority in the Kanze households, nor any patronage relations associated with them. In some ways this was ideal for Zenchiku, however, in that there is no sign that he inherited any kind of inner transmission from his father Yasaburō. He did however succeed to the Komparu lineage, which had its own place in the *sarugaku* world. We shall explore therefore the significance of Zenchiku's commitment to that lineage and investigate the differences that this entailed between his and Zeami's views of performance. Finally we shall consider how Zenchiku might have viewed the works he received from Zeami and the uses he found for them.

CREATING A WRITTEN *SARUGAKU* TRADITION

Zeami's first version of *Fūshikaden* consists of three sections, which, combined with an introduction and colophon, make up a single short work.

---

194. ZZ, *Fūshikaden*, 64–5.

As the first record of the *sarugaku* tradition, it marks a momentous shift from oral to written transmission. Scholars do not agree on Zeami's motives. As I have demonstrated elsewhere, Zeami borrowed for the work both structural and ideological elements from secret writings in the court performance arts.[195] There was a taboo in those arts against writing their traditions down, though court *hidensho* routinely excused the breaking of this taboo by referring to imminent danger facing the tradition. Usually the author was an elderly man who, lacking a talented pupil, saw his knowledge dying with him. Now Zeami was not an old man, and he was to have a number of pupils, but he still makes statements that echo these excuses. He says, for example:

> For the preservation of the house, out of respect for the art, I stored away in my heart the things my late father told me. I have recorded their essential meaning, regardless of people's criticism, because I am concerned that this art (*michi*) will be lost. It is definitely not in order to contribute to the knowledge of outsiders.[196]

In essence, the situation seems to be this: a tradition received orally from a great master is in jeopardy, and thus needs to be put into writing. Are we to take this avowal at face value? Actually, this situation is one found not only in the hereditary writings of court performance families, where it is used to excuse the dangerous precedent of putting what should be oral into writing, but also in popular court stories of musical lineages.[197] When we consider a number of other elements of the early volumes of *Fūshikaden*—opening with a (mythical) account of the art's ancient and illustrious origins, Zeami's signing himself with an ancient surname and court rank both of which are dubious, and the prominent use of terms like *michi, kuden, keiko* 稽古, *ichidaiji* 一大事, and others found in works on *gagaku* and *bugaku* 舞楽 (imported court dance and associated musical traditions)—we cannot help feeling that there is an air of pretension or pastiche about the whole work. Taken one by one, scholars have explained away such characteristics, but we should not forget the scorn with which some aristocrats of the time looked down on *sarugaku* actors—as beggars who should not be receiving

---

195. Noel J. Pinnington, "Crossed Paths: Zeami's Transmission to Zenchiku," *Monumenta Nipponica* 52.2 (summer 1997): 204–207.
196. ZZ, *Fūshikaden*, 37.
197. For the musical treatises, see Pinnington, 1997, 205–6. A case of such a situation presented in a *setsuwa*, accompanied by a discussion on the effect that, while carelessly allowing secret knowledge to be broadcast was regrettable, keeping it too secret was a profound sin, originating in *Kokon chomonjū* 古今著聞集, volume 15, is discussed in Ishiguro Kichijirō, *Chūsei geidōron no shisō: Kenkō, Zeami, Shinkei* (Kokusho Kankōkai, 1993): 38–39.

the favor of the young shogun.[198] The sense of pretension probably accounts for the reductionist view of many Western scholars who feel that Zeami wrote his works simply because he wanted his family to be able to pose as transmitters of an élite art.[199] If the works are fraudulent, then we can dismiss Zeami's excuses as window-dressing. Japanese scholars, however, have in the main taken these works at face value and interpreted such passages as expressions of anxiety over superficial artistic trends in his time and of respect for his father's legacy.[200]

How are we to choose between these two positions? The evident seriousness of Zeami's writings makes it unlikely that they were mere accessories for posing. The fundamental problem in the reductionist argument, though, is that there is no evidence at all that anyone even knew of the existence of Zeami's writings outside of his extended family. Before whom, then, was Zeami posing? There is another way to interpret what appears to be pastiche, however, and that is to see it as an almost inevitable result of the transition from orality to literacy. The difficulty of the task facing Zeami, of putting a tradition that he had received orally into writing for the first time, was considerable. It is generally held that actors in previous generations were not even literate. Zeami was bound to have looked for prior models for the organization of his writing, and the writings passed down in the court performance arts, as well as similar works written in poetics and in *renga* were the nearest genre to his purpose. Zeami seems to have been familiar with Nijō Yoshimoto's works on *renga*, with which his own writings share both ideas and stylistic characteristics.[201] We may not find it so surprising then that his borrowing of style and organization entailed some adoption of authorial stance.

It is important to note, however, the sophistication of Zeami's borrowing. If we look at how he uses the conventional courtly terms related to secrecy: *kuden*, *ichidaiji*, and so on, we see that he brilliantly reinterprets them to his own purposes. The secrets of court performance were largely related to particular pieces with imperial or divine connections that were forbidden to those without sanctioned transmission.[202] But in *Fūshikaden*

---

198. I am referring to the well-known entry concerning the young Zeami in Sanjō Kintada's diary, *Gogumaiki* 後愚昧記, cited and discussed, for example, in Kitagawa Tadahiko, *Zeami* (Chuōkōronsha, 1972): 31.

199. Such views are more often expressed informally than in print.

200. See the discussion in ZZ, 433–4, and also my discussion in 1997, 206, esp. fn. 14.

201. See Goff, 35–41, for Yoshimoto's intellectual influence on Zeami, as well as Pinnington, 2006, particularly 34, 37–8. Zeami's close relationship with Yoshimoto in his youth would explain his familiarity with his works on *renga*, and also suggest the means by which Zeami found access to court works normally well outside a *sarugaku* actor's reach.

202. Ueki Yukinori, "Gakusho no seikō to geiron," *Geinōshi kenkyū* 45 (1974.4): 33.

we find that the secrets to which Zeami applies the terms *ichidaiji* or *kuden*, are in fact strategies for winning performance competitions. Such issues did not apply in *gagaku* or *bugaku* but were of course to be jealously guarded in the Kanze house, for they were the means by which Kannami had won the shogun's notice and eventual patronage. Thus an apparent borrowing becomes in Zeami's hands a way of talking about certain new practical issues. Such re-reading and re-application of clusters of ideas drawn from different contexts are indeed characteristic of Zeami's thought.

Thus we return to his avowals of his motives for writing and see them as simultaneously echoes of convention and also coded expressions of his actual predicament. When Zeami started writing *Fūshikaden*, he was thirty-seven years old and his eldest son was either an infant or not yet born. Calculating his own lifespan on the basis of his father's age at death, fifty-one, he may well have thought the remaining fourteen years insufficient to pass on the strategies on which the house's priority depended. This reading also explains his frequent references to the well being of his house and his descendents. Thus he was not simply committed to his *michi*; rather he was concerned about his family's position from which it was indistinguishable, the preeminent position which his father and he had worked so hard to achieve. Thus the avowals of *Fūshikaden* can be seen as indeed borrowings, which we should not read at face value; but they are not empty pretensions. They are rather the expression of genuine concerns through conventional formulae—an appropriate strategy, perhaps, for a Noh actor.

SUCCESSION, INHERITANCE AND TRADITION

The centrality to the *Fūshikaden* series of strategies for winning audience acclaim is made plain in its seventh and final volume. This work, foreshadowed more that once in earlier sections, is marked and placed on a different level from the rest by its oxymoronic title *Besshi kuden* 別紙口伝 (Oral Transmission on Separate Papers). Actually the title is only apparently a self-contradiction. It is true that *kuden* literally signified oral tradition. It derived from Buddhist training, where oral transmission was considered particularly important. Even in Buddhist traditions, however, *kuden* had come to refer to a class of written materials, notes intended to serve as reminders, that accompanied oral teachings, and were copied, collected and preserved. The possession of these *kuden* (or *kuketsu* 口訣) in the *taimitsu* 台密 tradition was treated as a proof of authority.[203] Among

---

203. For a discussion of such writings, see Kuroda Toshio, "Historical Consciousness and Honjaku Philosophy in the Medieval Period on Mount Hiei," in *The Lotus Sutra in Japanese*

works on poetic theory we find that a number contain the term *kuden* in their titles. Thus *kuden,* as well as meaning oral teaching, signified a class of document expounding particularly profound issues, the transmission of which conferred authority. The subject matter of Zeami's *Besshi kuden* is the strategies for winning performance competitions. *Hana* (the flower), an image repeatedly referred to in *Fūshikaden,* is finally explained explicitly. *Besshi kuden* was clearly something that the Kanze would have been unwise to let out of its possession. Zeami proclaims its special character in a colophon:

> This oral tradition on separate pages [contains] the great essential (*daiji* 大事) of the house, a tradition for one man in each generation. If there is a successor without talent, it should not be passed on to him. It is said, "A house is not a house but through transmission; a man is not a man but through knowledge." This [teaching] can lead a person to a full grasp of the complete and mysterious flower.[204]

This particular passage comes from a copy Zeami wrote in 1418, when he was in his mid-fifties. His attention has turned from the need to record his tradition for unspecified descendants to the choice of a particular recipient, his qualifications, and the relationship between the receipt of family secrets and succession. From this colophon we can conclude that anyone receiving this work could thereby claim to be the most talented performer of his generation, and probably the household head's choice for the succession. Before we investigate Zeami's distribution of this and other works, we should consider what it would mean to succeed to the Kanze household.

As we have seen, since its establishment by Kannami, the Kanze house had developed three spheres of performance activity. Firstly, as one of the four troupes attached to the Kōfukuji-Kasuga religious complex, it was required to carry out a calendar of festival performances at religious sites in the Nara area. For these performances, the control of the troupe and of its economic rewards was at least nominally in the hands of an elderly performer, the *osa* (or chief elder), who performed the most important role on such occasions, that of the old man *Okina.* A second sphere of activity was as the leading performer of a traveling band of actors. Performance troupes had a number of opportunities to travel the country giving performances. These could be *kanjin* performances, where a patron would fund a performance as a means to raise money, or private performances at

Culture, ed. George J. Tanabe Jr. and Willa J. Tanabe (Honolulu: University of Hawaii Press, 1989), 143–158.
204. ZZ, *Fūshikaden,* 64–5.

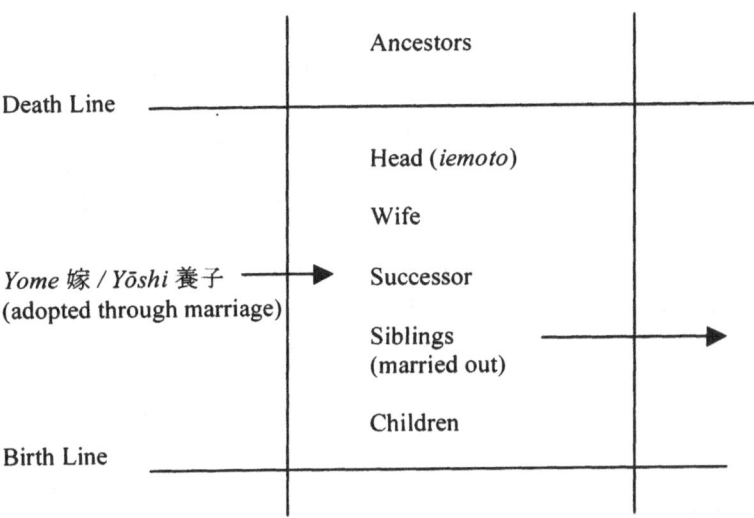

large residences. The rewards were high, especially in Kyoto, where wealth, power and discrimination were concentrated. If we look at performance records when Zeami was an adult, we find that his is the only Yamato troupe with frequent shows in Kyoto, whether in *kanjin* or at the *bakufu*.[205] It seems that this Kanze privilege was the result of the shogun Yoshimitsu's patronage, which first went to Kannami, and then after his death to Zeami. The third area of activity was as the *gakutō* of Daigoji. This position was formerly held as a hereditary office by the Enami troupe, but it was given to the Kanze *tayū* in 1424.[206] Under Enami control, the performers had for half a century or more included Yamato *sarugaku*; and in recent years, both Kanze and Hōshō had also performed there. Now, as the holders of the post, the Kanze could employ themselves.

This last was only relevant to Zeami's succession after the event, for we see Zeami referred to as "Kanze Nyūdō 観世入道" (the "lay priest" i.e. retired Kanze) in 1422. Even so it is clear that the Kanze had accrued substantial official and semi-official positions to pass to Zeami's successor. How was succession in such a case likely to be handled? To some degree we can analyze it in terms of the "traditional household" model, and then

205. See NGK,715–720.
206. For the documentary evidence related to the appointment at Daigoji, see NGK, 722–733.

we can get a clearer picture by considering conventions applying to other office-bearing households linked to the shogunate at the time. Let us start with a review of the *ie* model, referring to the diagram on page 71.

The household head is the *iemoto*; below him are members of the next generation. One of them has been nominated as successor. The siblings of the successor are expected to marry out of the family, and if they attempt to set up a new household, they will receive some support from the main house (*honke* 本家), of which they will now be regarded a junior line (*bunke* 分家). The household itself possesses property and social rights; members, including the household head, only have access to them through their membership. Within the household, the head has total authority; outside the household, he takes responsibility for its actions.

Now let us consider the social expectations and conventions that were likely to apply to succession and inheritance by looking at disputes occurring in other households under medieval *bakufu* law. Jeffrey Mass has collected many cases of official judgments in his study of the *sōryō* 惣領 system of extended families bearing political and military offices. In a typical case, a dying household head chose his younger son as heir-designate (*chakushi* 嫡子) and left just one quarter of the land to the elder son to set up his own household. The elder son claimed that he was the rightful heir, as he was generally known to be such and was acting as his father's deputy. The younger son produced the father's testament in his favor and hereditary documents proving land rights. The Dazaifu judgment was in favor of the younger son on the basis that the former head's discretion was paramount. Thus, the elder son took priority over the younger until the father's death, at which point he suddenly had to accept being second.[207] In general, from Mass's accounts we see that houses transmitted both indivisible office, which had to go to one successor, and property—including land—which could be divided among siblings, albeit with the major share going to the successor. It was widely accepted that fathers had an absolute right to choose an heir and also to revoke that choice at any time. The most common basis cited for passing over older sons was lack of ability.[208]

As we have seen, the Kanze family held what amounted to a hereditary post under the Muromachi *bakufu*. We can expect then to see parallels

---

207. Jeffrey Mass, *Lordship and inheritance in early medieval Japan: a study of the Kamakura sōryō system* (Stanford University Press, 1989), 64, 149–52.
208. Mass, 1989, 73–5. A case of "lack of ability" cited is that of the post of shrine head, 177–9.

between the succession in the Kanze house and in vassal households.[209] Precedence of talent over birth was likely to be the rule in the arts as in other spheres and for the same reason: the *raison d'etre* of the house was the preservation of its monopoly over the family task. Loss of patronage would have been disastrous. Another parallel is likely to be seen in the right, often mentioned in contemporaneous documents, of household heads to alter their choice of successor at any time. Zeami in his writings certainly assumes that right, and it seems that he resisted external pressure to change his mind. The performance rights of the Kanze house were indivisible and hence could go to only one son, but the option for siblings to set up junior houses can be seen in earlier records of *sarugaku* families. Kannami himself was a younger brother who set up his own acting household, and it seems that Zeami's second son, Motoyoshi, did something similar, creating the so-called Ochi Kanze line. If performance rights were equivalent to office, then the traditions and training preserved within the family can be seen as a kind of divisible property that could be shared among siblings in each generation. Of course, intellectual property does not need to be divided; knowledge can be shared without being diminished. Still, when we look at Zeami's distribution of his writings, we see that they, at any rate, were treated as a divisible intellectual property. The bulk of more valuable (i.e. secret) writings went to the chosen successor, and the rest were distributed among the other members of the house or accompanied his daughter marrying into another house. We can read the distribution of Zeami's writings as a story of his choices for the succession and his appraisal of the next generation.

Besshi kuden is clearly an important element in the story. There is however a complicating factor apparent in the passage from the 1418 colophon that I have cited above. Zeami writes that *Besshi kuden* is "a tradition for one man in each generation. If there is a successor without talent, it should not be passed on to him." This raises the possibility that someone without talent might be made the head of the household. Is Zeami visualizing the possibility that there may one day be a talented son who fails to get the succession, while a mediocre son is made the next household head? Or is he simply thinking that there might be a generation where all the sons are untalented? If the first, then Zeami had begun already to foresee the possibility that artistic inheritance and inheritance of the household could be separate matters, as they indeed turned out to be. If the second case, then he must have imagined that *Besshi kuden* would in such a

---

209. Note, however, the changing trends mentioned in footnote 211 below.

case have been kept unopened in the family awaiting the talent of future generations. We should then understand the transfer of *Besshi kuden* to represent a kind of higher qualification, one even more stringent than the transfer of the household. The oddity of this passage is compounded as the colophon continues:

> Although it is true that in a previous year I passed on these separately written details to my younger brother Shirō, Mototsugu is an extremely capable performer, and so again I pass them on to him. Secret tradition, secret tradition![210]

If the work was intended for one person in each generation, why did he give it to his younger brother Shirō 四郎 who, obviously, was of his own generation? Surely Shirō would have been justified in considering it to be an indication that the troupe was to pass on through him. It is probably on this basis that Dōmoto Masaki concludes that Shirō's son was Zeami's "adopted eldest son"[211] although it is clear from the evidence that I provide here that if so, Zeami must have changed his mind, as conventionally he had every right to do.[212] Zeami, by giving out two copies of the work, was bound to exacerbate any conflicts associated with succession. These speculations are far from idle, for in fact a conflict within the *za* over the succession did ensue. In time Shirō's son was accepted by the *bakufu* and by society at large as the next leader of the Kanze troupe, while Zeami's own choice, his son Motomasa, and Zeami himself, fell into disfavor. Zeami's awareness of a split between an artistic and social inheritance was to open a door for Zenchiku to become his artistic successor. The following diagram may help our discussion at this point.

210. *ZZ, Fūshikaden*, 65.
211. Arthur H. Thornhill reports Dōmoto Masaki's assertion in "*Yūgen* after Zeami," in *Nō and Kyōgen in the Contemporary World*, ed., James R. Brandon (Honolulu: Hawaii University Press, 1997), 61, n.25, but it is not clear what "adopted" is intended to signify. Onnami's father, Shirō performed as one of the Kanze players at the Daigoji in 1415. What would the adoption of his son by his brother amount to?
212. Actually, it is generally thought that the absolute right of a household head to determine the succession was weakened in the Muromachi period in two ways. Among *bakufu* officers, it seems that it became increasingly common for the *bakufu* itself to intervene in succession in the fifteenth century (see Ienaga Saburō et alia, eds., *Iwanami kōza: Nihon rekishi (7 Chūsei 3)* (Iwanami Shoten, 1967), 28–30). This kind of assumption is obviously relevant to Yoshinori's support of Onnami in the present discussion. It also seems that there was a increasing tendency from the fifteenth-century onwards in family-based institutions to give weight to senior advisors in determining succession (as brought out in Imatani Akira's discussion of the case of Ashikaga Yoshimochi, in *Kujibiki shōgun Ashikaga Yoshinori* (Kōdansha, 2003), 25–41). The relevance here to Zeami's succession is less striking, for we know nothing of his discussions with advisors within the troupe.

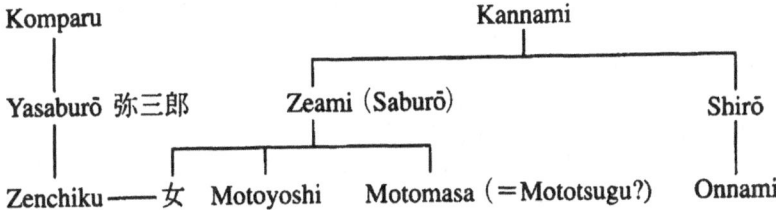

The unidentified Mototsugu 元次, second recipient of *Besshi kuden*, shares the first element of his name, *moto*, with other family members of his generation. *Tsugu* may derive from Kannami's name Kiyotsugu 清次 or it may imply succession, although it would normally be associated with a second son. We can read the passing of the 1418 copy to Mototsugu as a reflection of Zeami's choice of a successor, and it is indeed on this basis that Mototsugu is taken to be Motomasa, who Zeami declares in later writings was his choice.

DISTRIBUTION OF ZEAMI'S WORKS

In *Fūshikaden*, Zeami recorded the teaching that he had received from Kannami, probably completing the full seven sections by about 1403. From then until the end of the 1420s, he wrote several new works that owed less to his father and more to his own developing ideas. The question of who was to receive them must have become critical as the following generation began to grow up. All of Zeami's potential successors mentioned above received writings in this period, and who received what has been seen as a reflection of his assessment of their different levels of ability and areas of interest.

The evidence for the distribution of Zeami's works among his disciples is complex. There are internal and contemporaneous references that are relevant; some works, for example, are marked with the names of their intended recipients. Another kind of evidence lies in the distribution of works among the various overlapping collections that came to light in the twentieth century. Texts found in the main Kanze family alone and clearly not copied from other collections were probably passed by Zeami to his brother Shirō or to his nephew Onnami, from whom the main Kanze line derives. The so-called Yoshida collection, destroyed in the Kanto earthquake of 1923 but fortunately previously transcribed in *Zeami jūrokubu shū*,[213] is believed to have been handed down in the Ochi Kanze

---

213. Yoshida Tōgō, ed., *Zeami jūrokubu shū* (Nōgaku Kai, 1909).

troupe and to consist of writings passed to Zeami's sons, Motomasa and Motoyoshi. Works available only in the Komparu family collections were probably intended for Zenchiku.[214]

On this evidence Onnami appears to have received some sections of *Fūshikaden*, *Kashūnai nukigaki* 花習内抜書 and *Ongyoku kowadashi kuden* 音曲声出口伝, a summary record of Kannami's teachings on chanting—all relatively early works. It seems likely from this transmission, and from the second colophon to *Besshi kuden* discussed above, that Zeami early on considered his nephew as a probable successor. But something changed his mind, leading him to want to pass the house to his own son, Motomasa. We need to distinguish those in the Yoshida collection intended for Motoyoshi from those for Motomasa. Motoyoshi himself in *Shiki shūgen* 四季祝言 stated that Motomasa received *Kakyō* 花鏡, while he himself received *Sandō* 三道.[215] Motoyoshi's own record of Zeami's teachings, *Sarugaku dangi*, both mentions and appears to quote from *Fūkyoku shū* 風曲集, another work in the Yoshida collection. *Sandō* discusses the process of writing plays, and *Fūkyoku shū* is concerned with chanting, skills which Zeami regarded as part of a single art (*ongyoku*音曲). Motomasa, whom Zeami eventually chose as successor, is believed to have received the rest of the works: *Shikadō* 至花道, *Nikyoku santai ningyō zu* 二曲三体人形図, *Yūgaku shūdō fūken* 遊楽習道風見, *Kyūi*, and others in addition to *Kakyō*. Most of these are major texts, concerned with higher aspects of performance, and it is striking that none of them has the recipient indicated in the colophon. Perhaps Zeami was reserving his right to alter his choice, directing the possessor to pass them to the new favorite. All these works were completed before 1424, by which time Zeami had taken Buddhist vows and the position of leading actor of the troupe had passed to the next generation.

THE MARRIAGE PORTION

Zenchiku was *tayū* of the Komparu troupe in 1425 and fathered a son in 1432. It seems likely, then, that his marriage to Zeami's daughter took place between these dates. As it happens, Zeami gave two works and several playscripts to Zenchiku in this period. The two works, *Rikugi* and *Shūgyokutokka*, the only ones explicitly addressed to Zenchiku, have colophons dated 1428, when Zenchiku would have been twenty-three years old. Zeami had retired from active performance by 1422. He was to describe the transfer of his writings to the next generation in terms

---

214. The history of these collections is sketched in ZZ, 549–551.
215. Quoted in KZK, 21–2.

suggesting the settlement of a legacy and the renunciation of attachment to prepare himself for the next world.[216] We can understand the writings that went to Zenchiku to represent a dowry of intellectual property accompanying Zeami's daughter to her husband's house.[217] We would expect the choice of *Rikugi* and *Shūgyokutokka* to say something about Zeami's assessment of Zenchiku's interests and talents at this time. In light of the parallel between the distribution of such works as intellectual property and the distribution of wealth in land-owning families, we might expect that the texts should provide the basic grounding in the family tradition required for the prosperity of the family into which Zeami's daughter was entering. We would not, however, expect to find anything passed that might threaten the preeminence of the Kanze. As it happens, one of the works is an outline of fundamental issues that are taken up in Zeami's thought, while the other deals with topics typically of interest to Zenchiku. The playscripts are of particular interest in that they contain virtually no overlap with lists of plays that Zeami recommended as exemplary to his son Motoyoshi in the same period.

Rikugi and *Shūgyokutokka* are concerned with quite different topics. *Rikugi* proposes equivalences that link a subset of the nine levels of performance described in Zeami's *Kyūi* to the six poetic categories deriving from Chinese poetics that were elaborated in the *kana* 仮名 preface of *Kokinwakashū*. Several of Zenchiku's own writings generated equivalences between categories in different intellectual realms, for example, between the five modes of chanting (*go on* 五音) and the ten poetic styles (*jittei* 十体) in *Go on jittei*. On this basis alone it might be conjectured that Zenchiku had something to do with Zeami's decision to write *Rikugi*. It is a sufficiently unsuccessful work for some to have doubted Zeami's authorship. The tone is somewhat half-hearted, and we can read the final colophon as something of a disclaimer, including as it does the following words: "This volume has been handed on at the request of Komparu Tayū."[218]

There is something odd about the production of this work, the holograph of which is still extant. The handwriting of the colophon has been identified as Zeami's, but the rest of the work is in another hand (not Zenchiku's).[219] The paper, thick and decorated, is exceptional for Zeami's writings. Even if we accept that *Rikugi* was composed by Zeami for

216. ZZ, *Kyakuraika*, 246.
217. For contemporary dowry practices see Mass, 1989, 149–52.
218. *"Kono ikkan, Komparu dayū shomō ni yori sōden seshimuru nari,"* ZZ, *Rikugi*, 182.
219. See discussion ZZ, 564.

Zenchiku, it is likely, all things considered, that the contents were a response to Zenchiku's own interests.[220]

The other text transmitted to Zenchiku in this period, *Shūgyokutokka*, is more typical of Zeami, both in terms of topic and style. It takes the form of a series of questions and answers, the format known as *mondō* and commonly found in Zen works. The first question asks why well-prepared performances sometime fail—a topic of abiding interest to Zeami. Subsequent questions introduce discussions of key terms in his thought— *hana, omoshiroki* 面白き, *yasuki kurai* 安き位, *jōju* 成就, and *gaibun* 我意 分, terms that Zenchiku uses in his own works, but in peripheral contexts. Zeami justified his transmission of *Shūgyokutokka* to Zenchiku in terms of his performing ability:

> This work is a secret teaching in the training of this art. As Komparu Tayū's performance is evidence of his attainment (*kenjo* 見所), I hereupon transfer it to him.[221]

An oddity of this transmission is that *Shūgyokutokka* refers to other works by Zeami: *Fūshikaden, Shikadō,* and *Kakyō*, but it is unlikely that Zeami intended Zenchiku to have access to these other texts at this time.[222] It may be that *Shūgyokutokka* was not initially written with Zenchiku in mind.

Thirty-five playscripts were copied out in the Kanze house and passed to Zenchiku, and a list of their titles, in a hand believed to be Zenchiku's, is extant. Of the actual playscripts, only a few survive; of these, those that are dated were written out between 1423 and 1429. As *Rikugi* and *Shūgyokutokka* were transmitted in 1428, it is probable that Zeami regarded the playscripts as part of a single act of transmission together with these two works. Two aspects of this set of plays have struck scholars as peculiar, and both conform to our model of a distribution of intellectual property as a wedding portion. The first is that not all the plays were composed by Zeami; on the contrary, some are by Kannami, some by Zeami, and some

220. The only similar work in Zeami's output is *Goi*, and this is only found transmitted in the Komparu house collection, implying that it too was perhaps written for Zenchiku.
221. ZZ, 196. ZZ glosses the term *kenjo* as superb points (*sugureta ten* すぐれた点). Zeami uses this term variously. See for example ZZ, *Kakyō*, 104, or 109, (where it might be read as *miru tokoro*). My translation follows other usages in which the context is similar to the present case, in *Kyūi* and particularly in a letter to Zenchiku where Zeami refers to visible evidence (of the receipt of the Dharma—*tokuhō no miru tokoro* とく法の見所). The Buddhist context indicates that the term is equivalent to *kenshō* 見証. ZZ, 176, and 316.
222. All three works were passed down in the Komparu line (see *Komparu ke shomotsu no nikki*, dated Genna 7 (1621).10.8, reproduced in KKS, 20–21), but they were later copies. If Zeami had intended Zenchiku to see these works in 1428, his remarks made five years later (ZZ, *Kyakuraika*, 246) that Motomasa had let Zenchiku see just one of them makes little sense.

by Motomasa; others are conjectured to be by Motoyoshi. Some of the plays are not even by the Kanze; *Kashiwazaki* 柏崎 was in a version that derived from Saemon Gorō 左衛門五郎 of the Enami troupe. The plays represent, in fact, a broad range of basic types. Zeami may well have considered them as a suitable basis for a young *tayū* of another troupe starting out to build his own reputation. The plays do not overlap with the exemplary list given by Zeami to Motoyoshi in 1423 in *Sandō*, nor with the list that appears in *Sarugaku dangi* in 1429, except possibly in the case of the first play given to Zenchiku (*Yumiyawata* 弓八幡). Zeami famously (and correctly) predicted that many of the plays in these lists would continue to be popular in future generations, so he may have wanted to keep them within the Kanze house.[223]

We may conclude from this transmission that Zeami felt Zenchiku to be of sufficient talent to merit teachings on the elements of successful performance. He attempted to provide him with the basic plays and theoretical considerations necessary for success. There is no sign, however, that he wished to bring Zenchiku into the Kanze line, nor to give him his best works. Zenchiku, for his part, appears to have already shown signs of his interest in theoretical questions relating *sarugaku* to the typologies found in other arts.

THE SPLITTING OF THE KANZE TROUPE

Considering Zeami's dispositions to his family in the context of the model of the *sōryō* system, it is less surprising than has perhaps been believed to discover that rivals for succession in the following generation founded their own separate lines, with Motomasa, as far as Zeami was concerned at least,

---

223. The plays are listed as: *Yumiyawata, Tamamizu, Taema, Fuseya* (= *Tokusa?*), *Hanjo, Tsunemori, Tōgan koji, Sumidagawa, Yamamba, Senju,* **Kashiwazaki, Tomonaga, Koremori, Shirotori, Hōjōgawa, Yoshino saigyō, Matakashiwazaki, Mimosusogawa, Izutsu,* **Unrin'in,* **Morihisa, Tatsutahime, Utaura, Ishikawa no jorō, Sumiyoshi no monogurui, Ushihiki no nō, Matsu no o, Hikaru Genji* (=*Suma Genji?*), **Tadotsu Saemon,* **Eguchi, Nokiba no ume, Tamura,* **Tomoakira,* **Yoroboshi,* and *Sao no uta no nō* (=*Murogimi?*). Those preceded by asterisks are extant. Nishino Haruo in his study of these, takes the line that Zeami must have given his best plays to Zenchiku, and so the lack of coincidence in this list with those in *Sandō* and *Sarugaku dangi* reflects Zeami's changing tastes. He himself rejects Kawase Kazuma's suggestion that the transmission of the plays could have taken place at a later period (despite the dates of extant copies). It is not at all clear, therefore, when Zeami's tastes could have found time to change so radically. Even if they had, it seems unlikely that almost all of his former recommendations would have been omitted. Nevertheless Nishino's analysis of the unconventional handling of the material in these plays is of great interest, and this list demands further study. Cf. Nishino Haruo, "Zeami bannen no nō: Nōhon sanjūgoban mokuroku o megutte," *Bungaku* 39.5 (1971). For other lists of plays and Zeami's prediction see: ZZ, *Sandō*, 142–4, and ZZ, *Sarugaku dangi*, 291. Zeami's criticism of Enami's *Kashiwazaki* is found in the same section of *Sarugaku dangi*, where he says that he has himself written an improved version. This may be *Matakashiwazaki* in the list.

the main line, and Onnami and his father, Shirō, establishing a branch troupe. It will be recalled that Zeami passed an early version of *Besshi kuden* to his younger brother, Shirō, when he was in some anxiety about the loss of traditional strategies. This work was passed down in Onnami's line to the present day, although its colophon is unfortunately missing.[224] Zeami's later version, which went to Mototsugu, survives only in copies, but the original is believed to have been part of Motomasa's collection. Armed with their own copy, Shirō and Onnami began to perform separately from the main Kanze troupe.

The Kanze family was appointed to the post of *gakutō* for the Seiryūgū festival at Daigoji in 1424, two years after Zeami's retirement.[225] The Kanze, along with several other troupes: the Hōshō, Hiyoshi 日吉, Umewaka 梅若 and Jūni 十二, had in previous years taken turns performing for the Enami at the Seiryūgū festival.[226] In 1415, it was Kanze Shirō, Zeami's brother who performed, and again in 1417, a Kanze actor, it is not known which. In 1422, a record states that a Kanze Gorō 五郎 and Onnami performed there backed by the retired Zeami. Finally in 1424, the post of *gakutō* passed from the Enami to the Kanze. In Kōfukuji, in 1427, Motomasa, Zeami's choice for successor, and Onnami performed separately on a single occasion. In the same year, Onnami put on an independent subscription (*kanjin*) performance in the Fushimi area. He was supported in this by the cleric Gien 義円, who became shogun in the following year, taking the name Yoshinori. From then on there were two Kanze groups of actors, Onnami supported by Shirō, and Motomasa backed by Zeami. Important in this story is the tastes of the shogun Yoshinori. He had been a keen supporter of the Enami. After the Enami demise, his enthusiasm shifted to Shirō's son, Onnami. He not only backed his *kanjin* performance, he thereafter frequently had him perform at the Muromachi palace. Both Kanze troupes performed in 1429 on the riding grounds of the Muromachi estate. In 1430, Motomasa's younger brother, Motoyoshi, decided to retire to monastic orders. This need not necessarily have been the result of the shogun's oppression of the main house. As a sibling who failed to be made successor and yet did not feel able to strike out on his own, he may have concluded that he had little future left in the Kanze line.

---

224. That the colophon has been destroyed cannot be insignificant, for as we have seen, the transmission of *Besshi kuden* was intimately bound up with the succession. If the colophon had favored Onnami's line, one would expect it to have been carefully preserved.
225. The evidence for the following discussion consists of entries in *Manzai jugo nikki* and other diaries, as cited in NGK 718–733, and elsewhere as noted below.
226. See discussion in NGK, 1028–1029.

Zeami never referred to Onnami in his writings. He made it plain after Motomasa's unexpected death in 1432 that he regarded no actor in the Kanze line other than Motomasa qualified to receive the full transmission. If the appointment of Onnami as successor would have pleased the shogun, consideration of the welfare of the Kanze house might have persuaded Zeami to be flexible. The Kanze troupe had gathered to itself more public positions than it had possessed in Zeami's youth. For the troupe to disregard the tastes of the ultimate public authority was surely foolish. Zeami seems to have placed a higher priority on the absolute significance of the artistic knowledge that he had to transmit. We have seen signs that Zeami was aware of a potential conflict between the inner and outer faces of the *sarugaku* line, between the requirements of public office and the conditions for the transmission of *michi*, in the 1418 colophon to *Besshi kuden*, in which he distinguished a mere successor from one qualified by talent to receive that work. *Besshi kuden* itself, however, set forth as its prime objective winning the favor of people with power. That Zeami could have considered that he had something to transmit of supreme value, quite separate from the destiny of the troupe, is probably not unconnected with the fact that he increasingly thought of the *michi* of *sarugaku* in terms of the Zen path to spiritual liberation.

SATORI IN *SARUGAKU*: ABSOLUTE AESTHETIC STANDARDS

After the completion of *Fūshikaden*, Zeami's terminology increasingly reflected the influence of Zen. [227] The Zen characterization of the relationship between practice and enlightenment provided him with a useful vocabulary of ideas for a discussion of training and mastery in *sarugaku*. But the concept of legitimacy found in Zen placed absolute authority in a line of enlightened masters and spurned external opinion. This was a fundamental theme of the Zen tradition, one that conditioned the way in which Zen attempted to establish legitimacy, internally and externally. The problems involved are clearly apparent in the legendary story of the succession to the fifth patriarch in the *Platform Sutra of the Sixth Patriarch* (*Liuzu tanjing* 六祖壇経). Although the leading Chinese monk, the highly educated and popular Shenxiu 神秀 (605?–706) publicly received the headship of the temple, he was not to be regarded as the legitimate sixth patriarch. The true line had passed through the illiterate barbarian Huineng 慧能 (638–713) who was such an unpopular choice that he was advised to flee under the cover of night. The symbol of the transmission was

---

227. For details of Zen language and thought in Zeami's work, and his connection with the Sōtō sect, see Kōsai Tsutomu, 1962, 1–68.

Huineng's reception of a cloak and a bowl. But how were the unenlightened to judge the legitimacy of his claim? A cloak and bowl were no more reliable signs than temple headship. By the time Dōgen (1200–1253) went to China, it had become customary for Zen masters to keep documents of succession (*shisho* 嗣書) to confirm their enlightenment. Dōgen himself stressed the necessity of such documents, without which it was impossible to tell who had genuinely received the transmission:

> The buddhas always transmit the Dharma to the buddhas, the patriarchs always transmit the Dharma to the patriarchs; this is called the bond of evidence, this is called the single transmission. . . . No one but a buddha can bestow the seal of approval upon a buddha, and no one is a buddha without receiving the seal of approval. . . . Without determining to whom the Way of the Buddha is to be transmitted, how could it have reached this day? For this reason, in order to become a buddha, there must be a document of succession that is to be granted from a buddha to a buddha and to be received by a buddha from a buddha.[228]

Dōgen managed to get a look at five *shisho*, in which the line of masters back to the historical Buddha were enumerated. When he pointed out discrepancies between different documents, he was told:

> Even if there are differences, the buddhas of the Yun-men School must be accepted as indicated in the document. Why do people venerate Shakamuni? It is because he realized the Way. Why do we venerate the Great Master Yun-men? It is because he realized the Way.[229]

Dōgen was apparently deeply moved by this explanation, yet it exposes a central problem. The document's purpose was to authenticate the master's enlightenment, but ultimately the document was verified by that enlightenment. Whereas other institutions or lineages embody and preserve skills mediating their relations with society, the training in Zen serves in the first instance the interests of the acolyte alone, at least in its own terms. Enlightenment justifies itself and scorns society's evaluation.[230]

Zeami did not go so far as to believe that the actor performed simply for himself. Nevertheless, he steadily shifted from an early justification of

---

228. Taken from the translation of *Shōbōgenzō* 正法眼蔵, section 39, (*Shisho* 嗣書) in Takashi James Kodera, *Dogen's Formative Years in China: An Historical Study and Annotated Translation of the Hōkyō-ki* (London: Routledge and Kegan Paul, 1980), 45–6.
229. Quoted in Kodera, 43.
230. Of course Zen achieved its own accommodation with social realities. Zen monks in Japan were prized for their knowledge of Neo-Confucian texts on government, and for their literary ability. Both depended on their expertise in Chinese, the medium of the Zen transmission to Japan.

performance in terms of audience reaction toward a self-justifying aesthetic. In *Fūshikaden*, the acclaim of audiences, both culturally sophisticated and untutored, was seen to be the basis for the troupe's survival. In Zeami's later writings there is a tension between this ideal of pleasing all types, associated with Kannami, and that of exquisite moments of perfection, only appreciable by those of refined tastes. This second ideal predominated in works such as *Shikadō* and *Kakyō*, where Zeami developed theories of grades of artistic ability and levels of audience response. He associated these standards more and more with the remembered tastes of the great cultural polymaths of his childhood, the associates of the shogun, Ashikaga Yoshimitsu. As he grew older, Zeami changed from a performer who pandered to the tastes of a rarified society to one who remembered a great age that had passed. In *Sarugaku dangi* it is the past period of Yoshimitsu that is constantly referred to as the standard by which performance should be judged. Zeami had finally arrived at a point where his aesthetics were independent of any contemporaneous assessment.

ZENCHIKU: ZEAMI'S LAST HOPE

After Motomasa's death, Zeami began to view Zenchiku as a possible successor to bear his artistic legacy to future generations. In *Kyakuraika* 却来華, 1433, he discusses him thus:

> Now Komparu *Tayū* is correct in the fundamental elements of performance and is a man who will preserve the Way, but he does not yet appear to be one who can found a lineage that will lead others to enlightenment. If he increases his success in artistic power and achieves a ripe age, definitely he will become one who is "an exception among exceptions." But it is unlikely that I will live that long. It is unfortunate, but who might there be in this path who could test him and prove his attainment with the seal of enlightenment? Nevertheless, Motomasa appears to have believed that there was no one apart from Komparu who could bequeath to future generations the family name (*iena* 家名) of this *michi*, for he allowed Komparu to look at an important volume of secret tradition.[231]

This passage is expressed in terms derived from Zen. In Zen, the seal of enlightenment (*inka no shōken* 印可の証見) is given when a master is convinced that his pupil's enlightenment is genuine. Zeami used the term to refer to the certification of an actor's ability. Because the Japanese language can leave number unmarked, we do not know whether Zeami here

231. ZZ, *Kyakuraika*, 246.

envisaged for Zenchiku a single, once in a lifetime seal, or an ongoing process of training and certifying. Scholars disagree, although there is some indication in a letter by Zeami that there were different types of certification (see below).[232] In any case, Zeami seems to believe that Zenchiku would require the seal(s). As we have seen, Zenchiku lacked a Komparu forebear from whom he could receive the tradition. Although he had been the Komparu *tayū* from four or more years before and had the backing of the Ōkura performers from Ōmi, he may have felt a need for further certifications of ability, especially from a famous master in the Yamato tradition. Zeami refers to the "family name of this *michi*." Did he mean to absorb Zenchiku into the Kanze family? Actors certainly moved between troupes in the fifteenth century, but Zenchiku was profoundly committed to his own Komparu lineage, which he regarded as the senior line of the Yamato troupes. Zeami was no longer in a position to bequeath the Kanze line to anyone. We can only conclude that he had come to believe in a higher understanding of *sarugaku* that could be passed from generation to generation, that would be independent of family and troupe affiliation, something more profound and universal than the concerns of a single *ie*.

ZEAMI'S LETTERS TO ZENCHIKU

The only substantial material we have bearing on the personal relationship between Zeami and Zenchiku during the period in which Zeami tried to pass on his legacy is the two letters written by Zeami. To get much information from them, we need to penetrate the Zen terminology in which they are couched. It is particularly unfortunate that Zenchiku's side of the correspondence is missing. Zeami wrote the first of his letters to Zenchiku two months after *Kyakuraika* and one year before he was banished to Sado Island. Zeami must already have informed Zenchiku of the role he intended for him. The letter appears to have been a reply to a message from Zenchiku expressing doubts about his ability, or about the level of his attainments. Zeami starts by reassuring him with a poem:[233]

> *oroka naru / kokoro yo to miru / kokoro yori / hoka ni wa nani no /*
> *tama o mimashi ya*

232. See discussion in P. G. O'Neill, "The Letters of Zeami: One Received from Jūni Gonnokami and Two Sent to Zenchiku," *Nōgaku kenkyū* 5 (1979): 134–150.
233. In my analysis of this letter, I pursue certain issues in order, rather than cite the letter as a whole. This results in a fragmentation that enables me to come to my conclusions. For a full sequential translation see O'Neill.

What inner jewel remains to be seen other than the mind which sees that the mind is deluded?[234]

That is, awareness of imperfection is itself a sign of enlightenment. Similar encouragement is found throughout Zeami's letter:

> As I told you the other day, I have certified you to lead a group of actors. . . . I had already certified that you have attained the Dharma with regard to being secure in performance. . . . Your performance is visible evidence that you have attained the Dharma. . . . From the beginning you had attained the Dharma, and so, after weighing everything up, I felt that you were accomplished.

It seems that at least two certifications (*inka*) are referred to here. The earlier is that of having "attained the Dharma." Zeami mentions this *tokuhō* 得法 elsewhere in his writings; it signified the "settled mastery" (*an'i* 安位) of certain fundamental skills: the two arts (singing and dancing) and three forms (old man, warrior, woman), and the main roles of all types of plays.[235] The qualification he describes in the letter as "being secure in performance" (*ando no bun* 安堵の分) is probably equivalent to this "settled mastery." Perhaps Zeami gave this certification on a much earlier occasion, for example when Zenchiku married his daughter. "Accomplishment" (*jōju*) was a higher stage, the ability to give a complete shape to one's performance, one which stirred the audience's emotions.[236] It is not clear whether this required certification. Zeami says that he gave the certification to "lead a group of actors" "the other day," implying that Zeami had started elevating Zenchiku shortly after his decisions of *Kyakuraika.*

It is a bit odd to find Zeami justifying his earlier assessments ("after weighing everything up, I felt . . . "). As we have seen, he felt that time was short. Perhaps he was in more of a hurry than Zenchiku to get on to the transmission of more profound matters. Zenchiku, however, seems to have been anxious about technical questions. Zeami writes:

> I received your questions concerning performance. . . . Beyond this point you should follow your own feelings. . . . Even in the Buddhist Dharma, according to the second head of Fuganji, there is 'the study of a master' which means the study after attaining the Dharma. . . . As to the matter of the arms (*te no koto* 手のこと), you must simply gain a

234. This and other citations from this letter are taken from ZZ, 316–7.
235. ZZ, *Kyūi*, 176.
236. Discussed in *Shūgyokutokka* in terms of *jo, ha* and *kyū*, ZZ 190–191.

full understanding of the appearance and sound of the two arts and the three forms.[237]

Even though Zenchiku had been certified for his mastery of the basic elements, he would still need to go on practicing them. This reflects Zeami's well-known view that an actor should keep practicing the techniques learned as a beginner, summed up in the famous phrase: *shoshin wasurubekarazu* 初心忘るべからず ("do not forget your early training").[238]

In his reassurances to Zenchiku, Zeami refers repeatedly to the assessments of others:

> Lord Mimura saw your performance at Omi. He said that you had developed great ability. He is a man of discernment and his judgment can be trusted, so it is not a matter for concern.

Further on he writes:

> I heard that you yourself felt that your ability had increased since your performance at Tamba. Also Lord Mimura observed you. Again another not inconsiderable person in the audience at the subscription performance in Kawachi praised your acting.

But he concedes that it is necessary that he see Zenchiku's performance himself:

> Still, a thousand reports cannot match a single viewing, so once I have seen your performance I will be able to decide for myself.

Zeami writes this more than once in his letter. How well did Zeami know Zenchiku's performance? He refers to great improvement, but his evidence for this is all second-hand. We do not know whether Zeami witnessed the "performance at Tamba," but since then he heard reports of Zenchiku's improvement from Zenchiku himself, and from Mimura who saw him in Ōmi, and from someone else who saw him in Kawachi. Now that Zenchiku was traveling the northern provinces, he had developed doubts and written about it to Zeami. Japanese scholars generally assume that Zeami must have had a close knowledge of Zenchiku's acting, and therefore take it that Zenchiku must have been asking about a particular issue which Zeami had not yet been able to observe. This may well be true, but it is striking the number of performances Zeami had missed. Of course Zeami was old, and

---

237. ZZ, 316–7. *"Te no koto"* is perhaps to be read: "the matter of (a certain) technique."
238. ZZ, *Fūshikaden*, 60 (and elsewhere).

shattered by the loss of his favorite Motomasa and of the control of the Kanze troupe. He probably did not want to traipse around the countryside watching the Komparu perform. The general question still arises how close Zeami and Zenchiku's association was. Even in *Kyakuraika*, Zeami had relied on Motomasa's inferred attitude to Zenchiku for his assessment of his suitability.

The next letter, written by Zeami from exile, probably in 1435, increases the impression of a lack of mutual familiarity. Zenchiku certainly was taking his duties towards Zeami seriously. Zeami thanks Zenchiku for caring for his elderly wife, and for sending 10,000 *mon* 文, by which he is able to maintain a reasonable standard of living. He promises in the unlikely event that he returns to the capital to visit and express his gratitude in person. But the letter seems again to have at its center a reply to a question from Zenchiku. Zeami writes:

> I read what you said in your letter about the performance of the demon. In this lineage (*konata no ryū* こなたの流) it is not known. In general, apart from the three forms, we only go as far as the *saidō* 砕動 style. Things like the *rikidō* 力道 style belong to other lineages. My father sometimes performed the demon, but he would only express the demonic vigor in his vocalization, as a result we too learned it. I only performed it after I took vows on my retirement. You also should take care that you only try to perform the demon when you have retired, after many years of experience.[239]

The phrase "this lineage" shows that Zeami was conscious of a distinction between Kanze and Komparu traditions. The demon was a specialty of the Yamato style, closely associated with the Komparu (and also with the Enami). Where Zeami says, "it is not known," he means the true demon, the "demon from hell." Zeami had made it plain in the second book of *Fūshikaden* that there were other roles in which ghosts or possessed people appeared in demonic guise, which refined the violent actions of the true demon, and therefore were acceptable. The style of these roles was called *saidōfū* 砕動風, the style of subtle movements, but the classic demon style was *rikidōfū* 力動風, the style of violent movements. Kōsai Tsutomu, discussing Zeami's attitudes to the violent demon, concludes that it was popular at this time among young actors and ordinary audiences.[240] Zeami always disapproved of it. It seems that Zenchiku, however, even at this stage in their relationship, was unaware of Zeami's feelings towards it.

239. Citations from this letter taken from ZZ, 318–9.
240. Kōsai, 1962, 131–7.

Perhaps Zeami kept his feelings about it private among members of his own troupe. It may be then that before now Zenchiku had been excluded from such discussions. As we shall see below, it also seems that Zeami kept from Zenchiku his true feelings about other aspects of Komparu tradition.

In this second letter, there still seems to be a gap between Zenchiku's expectations and Zeami's responses. However much Zeami may have intended to transmit his enlightenment by a close union of minds, he closes with a promise to send a written account. Zen itself boasts a tradition independent of verbal and written representation, but the teaching that Zeami passed to Zenchiku concluded by relying on the written word. This perhaps helps to explain the intense over-reading that Zenchiku himself applied to Zeami's works, many of which he was able to copy later under circumstances that are unclear. There just does not seem to have been sufficient time for the development of the close intellectual intimacy of teacher and pupil that would have made the works into reminders of insights already received, rather than a set of clues to a knowledge otherwise out of reach. Zeami may also have underestimated the extent to which his tradition was designed for someone committed to the Kanze line. Even if the two men had spent more time together, it is questionable how well they would have understood one another, for there are signs of fundamental differences in attitude.

ZEAMI'S ATTITUDE TOWARD KOMPARU TRADITIONS

There were in fact contentious issues concerning *sarugaku* likely to divide the two men. The difference between the image of the Komparu tradition that appears in *Sarugaku dangi* and that found in Zenchiku's works indicates a general rift among the Yamato troupes. Related to this were different interpretations of *sarugaku* history and associated conceptions of artistic authority.

Behind the apparently detached aesthetic judgments of *Sarugaku dangi* lies a network of alliances and oppositions. Performers who contributed to the hegemony of Zeami and Kannami are approved and those who compete with it are criticized. The attitudes adopted therein toward the Komparu and Kongō troupes cannot be read simply in light of artistic differences. The Komparu considered themselves descended from an extremely ancient line—a view generally accepted by their contemporaries. The Kongō also traced itself back through several generations, having a long prior association with Horyūji, a fact not mentioned in the *Sarugaku dangi* account of its origins.[241] Zeami's family, on the other hand, neither wished to nor could claim a comparable depth of lineage. In a discussion of "the style of the countryside," Zeami (through the brush of Motoyoshi) singled out the performers of the two older troupes in particular for devastating criticism:

> Komparu Gonnokami and Kongō Gonnokami in the end failed to advance themselves. Even at *kanjin* performances in the capital those of the shogun's line did not attend. After two days performing a *kanjin* in the capital, Komparu went back to the countryside. Even in a competition in Nara, Kongō was made to stop and leave after two pieces. In that period, when the Way was at its height, to be famed for one's skill was a considerable feat.[242]

Here, Zeami takes popularity among the shogun's entourage in the capital, and during Yoshimitsu's hegemony, to be the standard of correct taste, and it is against this that he finds the Komparu and Kongō wanting. He reserved for Komparu Gonnokami, Zenchiku's grandfather, the harshest treatment, asserting that not only the spectators but even the Kongō considered his oddities of performance too much.[243] Komparu Gonnokami perhaps employed techniques of performance that were popular before rural audiences but considered too vulgar for the city. Zeami seems to have regarded him as the representative of those techniques and tastes. There probably were two general styles among the Yamato troupes, one more traditional and the other more refined, and each may have been supported by its own ideology. Kannami's approach to performance, preserved in *Fūshikaden*, was intimately related to the Kanze troupe's success in the capital. How Komparu Gonnokami understood his art is unfortunately lost, but indications of his self-justification are apparent in Zenchiku's fixation on his family history.

Commentators on Zeami's works have accepted the artistic judgments on the Komparu and Kongō in *Sarugaku dangi*. Still, the use of the word "countryside" (*inaka* 田舎) is itself tendentious. A contrast seems intended with Kyoto, but the site of Komparu and Kongō supremacy was, in fact, the religious institutions of Nara, especially the Kōfukuji-Kasuga complex,

---

241. Zeami derives the Kongō troupe from "two people called Matsu and Take coming up to the capital from Kamakura. They had no surname." (ZZ, *Sarugaku dangi*, 302.) The Kongō family records trace themselves back to the sixth century. Nose Asaji manages to confirm their association with the Hōryūji back to the early 1300s, and shows that they were probably active there as far back as the early twelfth century, in NGK, 286–98.
242. ZZ, *Sarugaku dangi*, 298.
243. "*Kongō ga kata yori amari no koto tote nan zeshi nari.*" ZZ, *Sarugaku dangi*, 298

which ill deserves the perjorative epithet *inaka*. It was, after all, the ruling
élite of this vast organization dominating the province of Yamato that was
able to both maintain continuity with Heian courtly culture and resist
warrior influence at this time. It is hardly surprising that the two troupes
with greatest prestige in Nara should seek legitimacy via claims to ancient
lineage, for this was the traditional strategy of those who governed
Yamato—the Fujiwara aristocrats. On the other hand, that Zeami and
Kannami should stress repetitive training leading to performance judged by
its effectiveness in competition is compatible with their hegemony in a
warrior-dominated Kyoto.

ZENCHIKU'S ATTITUDE TOWARD KOMPARU TRADITIONS

We would expect Zenchiku's attitude to his own tradition to be apparent in
his references to his predecessor in the Komparu troupe, but as we have
seen, he never mentions his father, Yasaburō, apart from listing his name in
family trees. It is from Zenchiku's descriptions of his grandfather, Komparu
Gonnokami, therefore, that we must gauge his attitude to his family style.
Even here his remarks are somewhat obscure. In *Kabuzuinōki*, Zenchiku
describes four types of leading role: old man, warrior, woman, and
"various." He lists plays under each heading and adds to them indications of
their aesthetic qualities. The section ends as follows:

> Broadly speaking, all the above roles, from the three higher forms to
> the "various," are in the original style, possessing the Way (*michi*), and
> are appearances that eschew vulgarity (*zoku* 俗). People ignorant of the
> Way consider plays expressing the pathos of parents and children, or
> the duty and fate of warriors, to be best, but I fear such plays are
> merely worldly roles. Yet even when vulgar, disordered styles are
> performed by one who has attained the discrimination of a superior
> man, they can be of unexpected interest. It is my humble view,
> however, that such a performer does not suit such techniques. The role
> of the shore-dweller who gathers seaweed appears to be worldly, yet it
> has superb points. My grandfather had sublime moments of the "bone"
> style, but now it is like gazing down a deep ravine and trying to grasp
> the jewels at the bottom. If anyone managed to attain this feeling, the
> performance of the role would then be appropriate for *yūgen*.[244]

Zenchiku attempts to distinguish plays or roles that accord with the Way.
Ama 海士 is an example of a play on the borderline; it is not included in

Zenchiku's preceding list. He tells us, however, that Komparu Gonnokami's performance in it had sublime moments out of reach of contemporaneous players. But it was precisely Komparu Gonnokami's performance of *Ama* that Zeami singled out for scorn in *Sarugaku dangi*.[245] One of the plays listed by Zenchiku in the mixed category is *Ōshōkun*—the modern *Shōkun*—written by Komparu Gonnokami. Zenchiku characterizes this play by quoting two poems that he considers to express equivalent aesthetic moods.[246] He then adds:

> The element of appearance here particularly bequeaths the single stream of my grandfather's aesthetic style. It has sublime moments of one appearance, one sound, and one step.[247]

These two references to Komparu Gonnokami involve no quotative structure; Zenchiku writes from his own experience. There is no sign that he believed that his grandfather's style lacked taste. In a later passage of *Kabuzuinōki*, Zenchiku recalls Zeami's judgments of four famous performers of the past. Among them is the following:

> Grandfather [Gonnokami] was like the frost upon a mossy bough of a twisted pine tree, he said. . . . Again, if we were to compare him to a flower, he said that it would be like seeing red plum double-blossoms in full bloom.[248]

In *Shūgyokutokka*, Zeami used the metaphor of flowers when discussing differences between audiences; some flowers are admired by ordinary people and rustics, while others are savored only by those of real breeding.[249] Plum blossom represented the middle grade of performance. What Zeami meant to say about Gonnokami in the present case is open to interpretation. It is believed that he hid his real feelings about him from Zenchiku out of kindness. Be that as it may, Zenchiku must have known that his grandfather failed in the capital, and that the Komparu and Kongō troupes used techniques eschewed by the Kanze and their supporters. He himself never disavowed Komparu traditions, however, and made it clear elsewhere that he considered his lineage preeminent.[250] Whatever Zenchiku

245. ZZ, *Sarugaku dangi*, 298.
246. The demonic barbarian in *Shōkun* seems to have no conceivable link to Zeami's style of tranquil flowering (*kankafū*) nor to *uruwashiki tei*, the mood of someone driven mad by love (in Zenchiku's definition: KKS, *Go on sangyoku shū*, 164), nor do the poems quoted seem appropriate.
247. KKS, *Kabuzuinōki*, 134.
248. KKS, 136.
249. ZZ, 186–7.
250. As we discuss in chapter six.

was to inherit from Zeami, the idea that the ultimate style of performance was the one admired by Yoshimitsu and his contemporaries conflicted with his allegiance to his family. The fact that the Komparu and Kanze styles were quite different lies behind remarks that Zenchiku makes in his introduction to *Bunshōbon*:[251]

> The Way of *sarugaku kagura* arose in the age of the gods. It had the stages of the sixty-six performances that were condensed into *Okina shikisanban* and, following Shinto and Buddhist rituals, this was not performed for private benefit. Still, becoming a medium for flowers, birds, wind, and moon, it developed into an entertainment for the whole realm. Let us suppose that there is a house in service to a shrine with a reputation not justified in practice. Even so, by performing the functional forms of *kagura* and preserving the Way, the house must qualify for the gaze of the hidden gods. Evil activities not in accordance with the Way must surely receive punishment, but each house severally founding various Ways and determining different varieties can in no way be an obstacle. This is why my grandfather's Way and Zeami's transmission are a single stream.[252]

The asserted conclusion can have been worth making only in view of evident differences. Zenchiku characterizes the task of *sarugaku* here in terms of ritual performance that wins divine, rather than human, favor.[253] Within such parameters, the refinement and aesthetic analysis pursued by Zeami and the "rural" style of Komparu Gonnokami need not be in conflict.

TRADITION AND INNOVATION

Zeami held a progressive view of history in which Kannami's enrichment and refinement of *sarugaku* under the influence of Yoshimitsu's entourage brought the art to its highest expression. Zenchiku, on the other hand, felt that *sarugaku*'s cultural claims depended on its ancient origins, and as a result he seems to have had some difficulty in accepting alterations to tradition.

> The ancients simply treated the old style of *kagura* as the Way, but ever since the functional forms of sixty-six pieces were refined it became a poetic entertainment, and eventually attained artistic elegance; it was decorated with flowers and polished jewels....[254]

---

251. That is, *Rokurin ichiro hichū (bunshōbon)*.
252. KKS, 249.
253. Kagura 神楽 is the name of traditional musical performances offered before shrines.
254. The passage breaks off here and starts on a new line.

It flourished especially since the time of Yoshimitsu, who comprehensively judged the performers of Yamato and Omi provinces, rejecting the vigorous and vulgar, and demanding *yūgen*.[255] He clearly informed the famous masters of the various houses of his evaluation of their good and bad points. When the levels and varieties of the structure of the Way had later been distinguished, the old investigated and the new understood, choices made and fixed, then the Way of performing skill was surely not a matter of personal opinion. Still, it is said, "The superior man hears of the Way and works to attain it; the middling man hears of the Way and it is as if he has suffered a loss or is destroyed; and the inferior man hears of the Way and claps his hands and laughs out aloud. If it is not laughed at, then it cannot be the Way." Even if a man achieves the laughter of inferior people, then truly will he qualify for the gaze of the deities if his mind is full of the Way and without thought of self—and why should this not extend to the eyes of the nobility and the higher levels? There must not be any intention to do as one pleases.[256]

Here Zenchiku justifies Yoshimitsu's refinements by noting that they did not arise out of "personal opinion," for it is the lack of "thought of self" that validates performance. In another passage, Zenchiku considers an occasion in the *Tale of Genji* where the emperor judges Genji's dancing to be superior to that of traditional experts:

As told in the *Genji* as well, the highest level is not so much that of the traditional style of specialists of court dance. Rather, it is that of members of the imperial court who, carried away by the mood, perform pieces such as *Waves of the Blue Sea*, dancing forth from the shade of the autumn leaves. At this level both brilliance and emotional quality must have been profound. It is out of our reach, but if a person is steeped in that feeling, it can serve as a reminder of the Way. How

255. The conception of *yūgen* that contrasts it with *tsuyoki* appears in *Fūshikaden* (ZZ, 50) and is thought to derive from *renga*, perhaps via Nijō Yoshimoto (cf. Goff, 1991, 37.) Ideally they have equal positive status, with the danger that they might degenerate on the one hand to weakness and on the other to roughness. Ōmi *sarugaku* tended towards pieces exemplifying *yūgen*, whereas Yamato *sarugaku* was fiercer, concentrating on warrior roles, expressing nobility and anger, but Kannami was particularly known for his *yūgen* roles (ZZ, *Fūshikaden*, 42–3).
256. KKS, *Kabuzuinōki*, 140. The phrase: "investigation of the old and understanding of the new" in this passage is a reference to Confucius's definition of the quality required of a teacher: he goes over his old knowledge to develop new. This passage has acquired a variety of interpretations. See James Legge, tr. and ed., *Confucian Analects, The Great Learning, and The Doctrine of the Mean*, (Volume 1 of *The Chinese Classics*, 2nd edition) (Oxford: Oxford University Press, 1893), 149.

valuable the awareness and understanding of this feeling is! Reaching the level of style that integrates the traditional manner with new feeling should be the initiation into the Way.[257]

Zenchiku manages here to reconcile traditional or ritual *sarugaku* with subsequent developments. In *Meishukushū*, however, probably written late in life, his account of *sarugaku* history (and of his family line, with which it was identified) shows his deep conservatism:

> Long ago in Prince Shōtoku's age, they performed the *sarugaku* dance in the Tachibana court. The prince intended the performance to settle the country and establish peace in the realm, and he asked Hada no Kōkatsu to dance *Okina* in the *Shishinden* 紫宸殿. . . . Later, after many generations and in the time of Murakami, the emperor saw what Shōtoku had written and he believed that the performance of the *sarugaku* dance could settle the country and establish peace in the realm. So he commanded Hada no Kōkatsu's descendants to perform in the *Shishinden*. But after that, as generations passed, the art became superficial and merely the diversion of entertainers. What regrettable development could possibly match this?[258]

The phrases in this passage, and several like them appearing throughout Zenchiku's writings,[259] are similar to those of the opening section of *Fūshikaden*. The implications are, however, quite different, for Zeami says:

> That [*sarugaku ennen*] has become in recent times everybody's entertainment. But in Empress Suiko's reign, Prince Shotoku commanded Hada no Kōkatsu to perform it, on the one hand for the safety of the realm, and on the other, for everyone's enjoyment. The sixty-six-piece carnival was put on, and called *sarugaku*. Since that

---

257. KKS, *Kabuzuinōki*, 140–1. Almost certainly Zenchiku is referring to the imperial remark translated as: "There is something about the smallest gesture that tells of breeding. The professionals are very good in their way—one would certainly not wish to suggest otherwise—but they somehow lack freshness and spontaneity" in Edward G. Seidensticker trans., *The Tale of Genji (Volume 1)* (London: Secker and Warburg, 1976), 133. The compounds rendered "the traditional manner and new feeling" in Zenchiku's words differ in various copies of *Kabuzuinōki* (KKS, 141; ZZ, 352). The term "initiation" (*kanjō*) is noticeable in that it acts as an external confirmation of the reception of spiritual knowledge in esoteric Buddhism, and may play in Zenchiku's thought something of the part that the Zen seal (*inka*) came to have for Zeami.
258. KKS, 283–4.
259. I.e. *Kabuzuinōki, Kanshōbon, Bunshōbon* and *Meishukushū* (as here), in KKS, 140, 231, 249 and 283–4.

time, generation by generation, men have borrowed the scenes of wind and moon[260] and made them the medium for this diversion.[261]

Zeami's terminology (*ennen, moteasobu tokoro* もてあそぶ所, *kairaku no tame* 快楽のため, *yūen* 遊宴 ["carnival"]) contrasts strongly with Zenchiku's. In the latter's account, Shōtoku's and Murakami's motives for having *sarugaku* performed did not include entertainment. In fact, Zenchiku never mentions entertainment as a proper goal of *sarugaku*. For him, its ultimate significance lay in its being a magical ritual bringing order to the world. In *Meishukushū*, Zenchiku proposed *Okina shikisanban*, the least entertaining and most ritual of pieces, as the major task of *sarugaku* players. The delight of audiences, the kernel of Zeami's thought, has no role at all in Zenchiku's writings.

ZENCHIKU'S ATTITUDE TOWARD ZEAMI

Our outline of the way in which Zeami took Zenchiku on as his final pupil has largely depended on Zeami's words. The one-sidedness of the evidence even extends to the letters; indeed, it may be significant that Zenchiku's half of the correspondence has not been preserved. But what of Zenchiku's references to Zeami? He mentions him by name only a few times and what he has to say tells us little. Zenchiku actually describes Zeami only once, in an account of famous actors of the past:

The above assessments [of former actors] were made by the lay priest Zeami. His knowledge, compositions, and acting were all of the highest level. He was like the moon remaining in the blossoms at dawn.[262]

The purpose of this description appears to be to validate the quoted judgments. Apart from this passage, there are only passing references to Zeami by name: he "repaired" the nine levels of performance (i.e. *kyūi*);[263] he declared that a certain dance should start from the right;[264] and his Buddhist name contained the character for *okina*.[265] This is not the praise of his character and account of his lineage that might be expected from the major recipient of his tradition. Zenchiku twice gives detailed accounts of his own lineage back to the time of Prince Shōtoku, without mentioning

260. The descriptions of the natural world found in poetry.
261. ZZ, *Fūshikaden*, 14.
262. KKS, *Kabuzuinōki*, 137. The simile is typical of contemporaneous definitions of *yūgen* in poetry.
263. KKS, *Yūgen sanrin*, 264–5. Zenchiku uses the term *iyasu*—implying that Zeami is not the originator of the nine levels.
264. KKS, *Meishukushū*, 286.
265. KKS, *Meishukushū*, 295.

either Zeami or Kannami. It is clear that he had no wish to claim Zeami as his artistic master.

The ambivalence of Zenchiku's attitude is also apparent in the colophons that he added to his copies of Zeami's major works. As mentioned above, *Rikugi* and *Shūgyokutokka*, as well as several playscripts, had colophons written by Zeami authorizing their transmission. Some time after Zeami's banishment to Sado, Zenchiku copied other works, including *Fūshikaden*, *Kakyō*, and *Shikadō*, which were central to Kanze tradition. These copies are not accompanied by authorizing statements.[266] On the contrary, Zenchiku behaves as if he is aware that his copying is not strictly legitimate. He adds to *Kakyō* the following remarks:

> Zeami passed this volume to his grandson's house and it should not go to any outsider. But the mind that reveres the Way penetrates to divine will and so I have acquired this work. As it is the essence of that lineage, I have copied it myself for the sake of the Way and for the sake of our house. By no means should it be shown to outsiders.[267]

The grandson's house is the Kanze troupe in Ochi that centered on Motomasa's son. The "divine will" that has arranged for Zenchiku's temporary possession of the work is used as an excuse.[268] In 1441, having copied *Besshi kuden*, Zenchiku appended another colophon, now partially destroyed, including the following: "This single section has been obtained by divine will."[269] This has similar implications.

Zenchiku does not attempt to justify these appropriations by referring to his relationship with Zeami. He does, however, mention a teacher on occasion. That this teacher was Zeami is apparent from the colophon appended to his holograph of *Shūgyokutokka* in 1453: "This single collection was passed to me by my teacher when I was young."[270] Zeami's own colophon makes it clear that he was the source of the work. We have suggested that Zeami may have been unable to establish the intellectual intimacy that was expected of a medieval teacher and his major pupil. We have surmised that the eventual transmission became almost wholly dependent on Zeami's writings. Such a conclusion is supported by

---

266. The transmission of these works to another troupe was sufficiently unusual for later generations to conclude that it was Zeami's favoring of the leader of another troupe over his own heir that caused his banishment. Given that the heir was Motomasa, the theory does not fit the evidence–see Kobayashi Shizuo, 66–7.
267. ZZ, *Kakyō*, 109.
268. When Motoyoshi retired into Buddhist orders, in 1430, he entrusted both *Kakyō* and *Sandō* into Zenchiku's keeping, as he wrote in *Shiki shūgen* (KZK, 21).
269. See ZZ, 553.
270. ZZ, *Shūgyokutokka*, 196.

Zenchiku's references to his teacher, which act as authorizations of Zenchiku's ideas. For example, in *Kabuzuinōki*, Zenchiku states:

By and large, this volume has resulted from the extremely hard work that I have done upon receiving my teacher's explanations; I have repeatedly thought over them and dwelt upon them.[271]

This was characteristic of Zenchiku's uses of Zeami's writings; they seem to have been for him sanctioned works encoding profound knowledge, just as were "secret" works of Shinto and poetics. His approach to them was to look beyond or behind them for hidden patterns of ideas. In his own writings Zenchiku cited passages from them out of context to draw conclusions for which they were never intended. We shall consider such "creative misreading" or "over-reading" directly in the next chapter.

TRANSMISSION OF WHAT?

Konishi says that *michi* is found in the act of transmission. What was being transmitted, however, was not just an unchanging knowledge, poured each generation from an old vessel to a new vessel. It was also authority, and a place in society, bearing rights and responsibilities. In the abstract it has been assumed that these two coincide, but in accounts of poetic, artistic and religious history, the tension between them is met with on every side. It was present in Zeami's mind when he distinguished the qualifications for inheriting *Besshi kuden* from mere succession. Insofar as the Kanze house was an institution with relations to various organizations and patrons, one might naively expect the ideal of talented and skilful performance and the requirements of paymasters to have been identical.

To practitioners of *michi*, however, as Konishi observes, conservation of tradition is fundamental. In Zeami's case, there were a number of things he wished to conserve. What he saw as his received tradition, however, was in reality no ancient tradition; it was rather the product of, and rationale for, extensive innovation. Kannami created his plays by bringing into Yamato *sarugaku* popular elements of other traditions—*dengaku*, Ōmi *sarugaku*, *kusemai* and others. It was by ideological innovation, moreover, that he gained access to power and high culture. The metaphor of *hana*, the apparent novelty of old techniques resulting from their use "in season," was inspired by the developing poetics of *renga*, and was one of a number of ideas that drove Kanze to success in performance competitions. When Onnami became Yoshinori's favorite, he was surely fulfilling the family

271. KKS, *Kabuzuinōki*, 140.

task as Kannami saw it. But it came up against Zeami's wish to conserve his tradition.

How was it that Zeami became so attached to an artistic ideal, the tastes of connoisseurs exemplified by Yoshimitsu and his entourage of literary and artistic experts? We can speculate about the idealization of the past common among those who have been successful. No doubt Zeami was attached to the great achievements of his youth, as well as feeling loyalty to his father. I would like to highlight, however, unexpected effects that may have arisen from his creation of his writings. The very act of translating his knowledge into the idiom of written conventions may have influenced the way he read his own past. In *Fūshikaden*, as we have seen, he cleverly reinterpreted the language of court artistic traditions, especially of secrecy and tradition, to represent his father's insights. In later works he generated a reading of Zen terminology to contain his aesthetic and performative insights. Both of these rhetorical moves separated *sarugaku* from its dependence on audiences. In *Sarugaku dangi* he recounted *sarugaku* history in terms of Yoshimitsu's court, pitching one group, those who had succeeded in that environment—Kannami and his friends, Zeami himself, Yoshimitsu's advisers, Jūni Gorō, and so on, against other more traditional actors who had not—Komparu, Kongō and others. For Zeami, good acting was something that had happened in the past. Zeami appears to have been convinced by his own stories to put himself on the side of what proved in his later years to be society's losers.

There is another way in which Zeami's writings may have intensified the split between traditional and popular performance. Leaving aside the transfer of social position and considering the passing of tradition itself, we have to admit that the image of human beings as temporary vessels containing an unchanging fluid of knowledge is unrealistic. Oral traditions commonly have a conservative ethic, but notoriously change from generation to generation. When the aging master passes knowledge to the pupil, he effectively loses control of it; the pupil's tendency, as the master fades away, is to put his memories to the service of present concerns. When the tradition is written, however, it becomes frozen. This may seem to strengthen the hand of conservatism. The master not only gains control of the content of the future tradition, but with the quasi-commodification of the tradition, he at least for a while controls its distribution. But even these works, manifestations of a longing to conserve as well as instruments of control, are vulnerable to the inevitable tactics of future writers with their own agendas, misreadings and distortions. In the next chapter we shall consider a test case in Zenchiku's misreading of Zeami.

4 Conformity
Misreading Zeami

Where Zenchiku refers to an idea originating in Zeami's writings, it frequently appears to us to be distorted in some way—either it is used for purposes with which it is unconnected in Zeami, or else some fundamental structural aspect or context is altered. A particular group of these "misreadings," is the focus of this chapter.[272] There are many uses of, or references to, Zeami's ideas throughout Zenchiku's writings, but some are more difficult to evaluate than others. Not knowing the whole of either man's thought on any issue, we often have to guess at the nature of the gaps between what they both wrote. Here, rather than attempt to cover or summarize all Zenchiku's readings or misreadings, I will scrutinize a particularly exemplary subset of works that are based on theories we find in Zeami. The works we shall consider here are among those generally understood as aesthetic typologies, that is *Go on no shidai*, *Go on jittei*, *Go on sangyoku shū* 五音三曲集 and *Kabuzuinōki*. Those with the words *go on*, the five voices,[273] in their titles have the advantage for us that they constitute a series. The first of these is little more than Zeami's own *go on* theory, especially as he presented it in the second of the two works he wrote on the subject, *Go on* and *Go ongyoku jōjō*. We are thus able to trace very clearly how Zeami established the theory of the five voices and how Zenchiku took it up and developed it.[274] There is a fundamental difference

272. I will demonstrate just what I mean by "misreading" in this chapter, but I do not mean to indicate by this term that I believe Zenchiku's use of Zeami's theories to be anything that might have been felt at the time illicit or inappropriate.
273. I use the term "voices" for *on* 音 in the compound *go on* 五音 as a neutral expression of what I consider the theory to describe, that is types of vocal production used in singing passages appropriate to types of aesthetic or other content. The compound *go on* has to be distinguished from the contemporary *go in*, with the same orthography, signifying the five vowels (Zeami uses it with this meaning, in, for example, ZZ, *Fushizuke shidai*, 73). The inspiration for using the graph *on* 音 with the meaning of voice or vocal style probably derives from its similar use in the *Great Preface*, cited by Zeami in ZZ, *Go ongyoku jōjō*, 202.
274. The system of five voices was to be influential in future generations, particularly in puppet theatre, where Uji Kaganojō 宇治加賀掾 (1635–1711) made it the basis of *ningyō*

99

between Zeami's use of this theory and Zenchiku's adoption of it; for this reason we shall be careful to analyze its precise nature in the first two works. Zenchiku's *Kabuzuinōki,* the last work in the list above, has much in common with the others, but here it is Zeami's theory of the nine levels, *kyūi,* that takes on the role played by *go on.* We shall see that the clinamen (or "swerve") that Zenchiku applies to these two important analyses, of vocal qualities and of styles of performance, is similar, and that he puts them in service of a theory of acting radically different in kind from Zeami's.[275]

CONFORMING TO MICHI: ORAL AND WRITTEN STYLES

Before we explore these particular works, let us consider some general questions. The first is the relation of Zenchiku's misreading to the *michi* ideal. A fundamental element of Konishi's analysis is the "conformist ethic" (*kihansei* 軌範性) that he describes governing the transmission of knowledge across the generations. This idea of conformity to the past has two distinct functions in Konishi's vision of *michi.* The first relates generally to practical training, where the pupil was enjoined to reproduce precisely the example set by his master. Konishi discusses this in terms of a strict restraint on the expression of the pupil's own ideas and creativity, a denial of the lower self that made possible the breakthrough into the higher artistic freedom typical of true mastery.[276] Thus the conformist ethic in training acted as a narrow restriction leading to transcendence, a kind of "strait gate." In *sarugaku* in Zeami's times, some ethos of this kind was probably operative, as we see in his repeated prescriptions for the training path and his insistence on the order of skills to be controlled before the master could perform freely.[277] Zeami says nothing about the pupil exploring his own interpretations of roles, emphasizing rather the need for

jōruri 人形浄瑠璃 vocal styles. Within Noh, Zenchiku's reading was taken up and developed further, being transmitted from generation to generation. Note that *Zenpō zōdan 's* reading of the five voices as "*kokoromochi nari*" bears the mark of Zenchiku's "swerve," away from technique to "state of mind" (KKS, 448).

275. My use of the word *clinamen* derives from Harold Bloom's *The Anxiety of Influence: A Theory of Poetry* (New York: Oxford University Press, 1973). However, Bloom's theory is based on argumentative disagreements found in the romantic period, which Bloom himself considers different in kind from the more subtle shifts of emphasis of earlier more conservative European tradition and terms "heresy." I find little in common between Japanese medieval masters and nineteenth- and twentieth-century European poets (despite the apparent coincidences between Tsurayuki and Wordsworth noted by Ueda Makoto in 1967, 1–24). We would be unlikely to find any recipient of a Japanese *michi* claiming that his master's way was, at a particular point, mistaken, as Bloom's poets claim concerning their forerunners. I also see little generalized application for Freudian theory to Japanese relations in the arts.

276. Konishi, 1986, 155 (1991, 148).

277. Such ideas deeply inform, for example, ZZ, *Shikadō,* 111–118, which we shall consider in chapter five.

him to control precise technical skills. Another aspect of the conformist ethic in Konishi's model is the idea that it guaranteed the preservation of a *michi*'s practices and essential spirit (*ōgi* 奥義), and thereby brought to the art a kind of authority that could not be possessed by something merely resulting from a single human being's discoveries. It was something that transcended the individual and remained unchanged from age to age.[278]

If this second aspect, unchanging practice, was essential to *michi*, then we might think that Zeami knew his claims for the status of his art as *michi* to be false. It was obvious that the practice had changed since the time of his father and even more since prior generations. The Noh play was a recent development and was still in flux, partly as a result of Zeami's own innovations, innovations that went beyond mere practice; for Zeami was also developing a number of new ways to think about and transmit the arts of performance. Still, *sarugaku* was not a free-for-all. Though Noh had not become the relatively rigid tradition that it was to become in the Tokugawa period, it is true, we do see in Zeami's writings several signs of his belief in the authority of traditions handed down from the distant past. He clearly felt that the profound attitudes to art that he had inherited from his father had a universal validity and had to be preserved for future generations.

How did he, and Kannami, too, for that matter, balance such respect for tradition against the need for change to which they both responded? I do not intend to go very deeply into this question here, where our focus is more on Zenchiku, but I will note three ways in which this problem was finessed, ways that are perhaps typical of Japanese medieval cultural practices. One of the major innovations that Kannami made was to introduce the form of song called *kusemai* into Noh plays. When Zeami describes this process he is careful to state that it was *michi no kusemai*, and also that Kannami had received it by a proper transmission.[279] It is clear from his remarks that he understood *michi no kusemai* to refer to authorized lineages. If Yamaji Kōzō's suggestions that we saw in chapter two are right, this authorization essentially derived from the special status of those *kusemai* lineages, based on their traditional relations with élite institutions. Thus, in this case at least, the change in *sarugaku* practices could be thought of not as alteration, but as the addition to its own practices of another, equally sanctioned, tradition. In early writings Zeami talks about *sarugaku* as if it was comprised of a number of discrete traditions, and indeed when we consider the modular character of Noh plays, we can see that he could have understood them to

---

278. Konishi, 1986, 155, 158 (1991, 147, 151).
279. ZZ, *Go on*, 223.

be an arrangement of forms rather than a development of something new.[280]
Another way in which change was managed is exemplified by the
curtailment of the *Okina* performances, the removal of one section of which
was made by the Kanze troupe in Kannami's time. This change was
justified by the attendance of the shogun. Zeami subsequently saw this as a
precedent to be followed by the Kanze troupe in Kyoto.[281] As we shall see
in chapter six, this is one of a number of invocations of originating or
founding occasions, usually dignified by the presence of powerful or semi-
divine figures, that were routinely used to justify change.[282] Finally,
concerning traditional teachings about *sarugaku*, we see that Zeami often
applied a kind of over-reading to phrases deriving from his received
tradition.[283] Within oral tradition, this kind of development of theory would
be unlikely to attract notice, for it was the mnemonic formulae that were
transmitted, and such formulae were expected to produce different
interpretations according to context.[284] We can observe how by such means
Zeami regularly re-interpreted formulae from his art (and, of course, from
other "legitimate" traditions) to effect a gradual change in the deeper aims
of his arts as he had received them. To sum up, it seems that the addition of
practices taken from other equally authorized traditions, the setting of new
precedents on the basis of founding occasions before powerful leaders, and
shifts in meaning deriving from stretched interpretations of formulaic
phrases passed down in the tradition were all somehow felt to be legitimate,
not really "change."

As we discussed in chapter one, it is common for oral traditions to be
deeply conservative. To the methods of managing the conformist ethic that
we have surveyed above, then, we can probably add the "structural
amnesia" that we discussed at that time. When we come to Zenchiku,
however, another factor becomes important which was not relevant in the
case of Zeami, and that is the fact that Zenchiku's received tradition was to

---

280. There are many outlines of the modular character of Noh plays, but an example is Konishi,
1986, 167. For Zeami's conception of Noh as a series of separate techniques, see, for example,
section five of *Fūshikaden*, especially ZZ, 43–44.
281. See Pinnington, 1998, 494–5.
282. We see similar processes in *gagaku*, both the collection of disparate traditions, and the
justification and sacralization of new modes deriving from performances before the emperor.
See Ueki, 31–43.
283. For example, when he changed the interpretation of the words: "doing nothing" from a
plain instruction that old people should stop performing to a profound mental technique based
on Zen traditions (ZZ, *Kakyō*, 100–1), or when he developed a progressively universal
application of the formula: *jo, ha, kyū* (ZZ, *Shūgyokutokka*, 190–2), or again when he turned
the tradition of *kagura* origins of *sarugaku* into an analysis of audience response (ZZ,
Shūgyokutokka, 188–9).
284. Ong, 33–57, particularly 41–42.

a substantial degree embodied in written works. Zenchiku's management of change and difference is conditioned greatly by this fact, and his misreading of Zeami is in large part achieved through specifically textual practices. If we understand Zenchiku's own production of works in this light it saves us from being caught between two unsavory positions, either seeing Zenchiku's misreadings as deliberate distortions, meaning that we must take him to be dishonest and disloyal; or seeing them as misunderstandings, in which case we must think him to have failed to grasp Zeami's real intent. Actually, the textual techniques Zenchiku employs were characteristic not only of his uses of a wide variety of other sanctified written materials, but also of intellectual life in his day. Ultimately they were entwined with a sense of the nature of reality and its expression in phenomena. Just as holy sites and other sacred objects of all kinds were considered to hint at profound truths, to require creative interpretation, and to have nothing about them that was contingent, it is clear that Zenchiku expected certain texts to be productive of endless new and significant readings. How such interpretations were controlled is a matter we shall see more clearly in chapters five and six. For the moment, what we should note is that the kind of interpretative reading that we might expect to see today, that is, guided essentially by the desire to recover the intentions of a human author, by situating a text in its original context, was not a prominent part of medieval approaches to texts.

This surely lies behind our sense of the discontinuity between Zeami and Zenchiku. Zeami himself, at least in his early writings, seems to have used writing "innocently," as it were, that is to record what could be expressed orally. Zenchiku, however, does not read those writings in that way, that is, to try to recover the oral traditions that Zeami wanted to preserve. This is clear from the cut-and-paste quality of Zenchiku's citations; by concatenating textual elements set free from their contexts he generates new patterns. It is not only Zenchiku who operates in this mode; as we shall see in the next chapter it was a common textual practice of his time.

This matter of the difference between how orally transmitted and written tradition is treated is an important aspect of a general process that we notice in Zeami and Zenchiku's writings, that is, the way in which their writings reflect an increasing exploitation of the particular possibilities of writing itself. Scholars of orality and literacy have argued over the past forty years or so about the new intellectual modes that writing enables or stimulates. Theories about these modes generally focus on four issues— writing's persistence in concrete form, resulting in new patterns of communication which of course are central to the politics of access, copying and possession, so important in élite *michi*; its spatial and visual character (about which more below); its tendency to stimulate metalinguistic activity (in other words, texts themselves become objects of thought and discourse); and the new intellectual modes that arise from learning to read and write.[285] The first three issues result from the media used in written communication, and are clearly interrelated. The bringing together of passages of texts in new arrangements to generate new readings, which is so characteristic of Zenchiku, clearly depends on all of them. When we consider the second issue, the spatial and visual character of writing, however, we see a progressive development in usage from Zeami to Zenchiku. Zeami's early writings hardly utilize visual possibilities at all. In many cases they rather declare their allegiance to oral modes, as when he uses the *mondō* format (which operates through an imaginary dialogue between master and pupil) and when he uses the mnemonic formulae typical of oral tradition, following them with expanded interpretations, and then restatements of the original formulae.[286] He does employ one of the simplest visual possibilities of texts in *Nikyoku santai ningyō zu*, where he adds diagrams of the postures appropriate to stereotypical roles, but here of course he is finding a substitute in writing to compensate for what is lost from face-to-face teaching, that is, physical demonstration. One of the well-known discussions of the differences between oral and literate modes relates to the use of lists—in oral culture lists tend to be additive, narrative, repetitive and redundant (like the lists of "begats," originally oral, and now preserved in the Old Testament). In writings, however, new possibilities of lists in the form of tables and charts emerge. A whole series of ways of looking at listed material becomes available—for example multiple routes can be taken through them, and complex relationships can be observed (note the visual word) by considering spatial relationships and qualities. Ong notes the sophisticated use of charts commonplace in our own culture reflecting our "deep interiorization of print."[287] Zeami's later writings—particularly those connected to Zenchiku, as it happens—are often organized in tables—for example *Kyūi*, *Rikugi*, and *Go on*. *Rikugi* is interesting in that it does not quite work as a systematic presentation because Zeami attempts to match the elements of two systems that are numerically different. *Kyūi*, though, is striking for its proposition of an

---

285. This summary is derived from David R. Olson, "Literacy as metalinguistic activity" in *Literacy and Orality*, edited by David R. Olson and Nancy Torrance (Cambridge, UK: Cambridge University Press, 1991), 251–270, esp. 254–260.

286. Those of us who lecture (i.e. teach orally) are familiar with these modes, discussed in Ong, 33.

287. Ong, 99–101.

alternative route to be taken through the nine levels—the basic one being the order of degree of quality of performance, and the alternate one being the order of training.

Thus Zeami begins in later works to exploit the spatial possibilities of writing, but it is Zenchiku who really embraces the possibilities of such non-oral characteristics. The classificatory works we analyze in this chapter make their arguments visually, by arranging material of disparate origins into a number of repeated patterns. They also use different colored inks. The oral aspects of those arguments are notably absent. The *rokurin ichiro* works, which I discuss in the next chapter, are all based on the interpretation of diagrams. The family trees that are central to the legitimating theories that I discuss in chapter six express not only relationships but also the relative importance of people by the location and size of the characters by which they are represented. As we have said, Zenchiku's works often consist of rearrangements of textual elements from elsewhere. The visual has a great importance in Zenchiku's (and his co-authors') interpretative modes, as we shall demonstrate in our discussion of Kanera and Shigoku in the next chapter. We see use of the visual as well in Zenchiku's participation in the characteristic "readings" of phenomena and of writing that Susan Blakeley Klein has called in poetic *hidensho* "etymological allegoresis."[288] Of course Zenchiku did not somehow on his own suddenly "deeply interiorize [brush] writing." These modes came to him through his familiarity with secret works in poetic, Shinto and other traditions. We might observe that the striking characteristic of the genre of *kuden*, so-called "oral transmissions" that constitute the secret writings of the period, is precisely its exploitation of the non-oral possibilities of texts.

ZEAMI'S THEORY OF FIVE VOICES

As we noted above, the first of Zenchiku's completed works, *Go on no shidai*, appears to be a simple restatement of elements of Zeami's theory of *go on*, five voices. Nevertheless, it is a selective restatement. Much that we find in *Go ongyoku jōjō* has been left out. Zeami and Zenchiku typically organized their works with an introduction, a central discussion and a conclusion. Zenchiku's *Go on no shidai* is exceptional in that it has none of the usual "wrapping" of introduction and conclusion. Zeami's fragmentary *Go on*, essentially a list of representative passages of chanting and accompanying musical notation organized in terms of five styles of vocal

288. Throughout Klein, Susan Blakeley, *Allegories of Desire: Esoteric Literary Commentaries of Medieval Japan* (Cambridge (Massachusetts): Harvard University Press, 2002).

production, does have an explanatory introduction. *Go ongyoku jōjō*, on the other hand, which gives a full description of the five voices themselves, has no introduction, but it has a number of discursive closing passages in place of a conclusion. By considering these sections of both of Zeami's *go on* works, we can get a clear idea of the concerns that led to his development of the theory of five voices, and also information that helps us to interpret certain problematic aspects of the theory itself. I shall start then by exploring the main characteristics of Zeami's theory before proceeding to Zenchiku's restatement. Scholars in general have failed to notice how fundamentally different the theory is in the writings of the two men, mainly, I suspect, because in Zeami's hands it is seen as an obscure part of his musical treatises, and has not received the attention it deserves. The main interest of scholars concerning these works has been focused on the exemplary passages of singing included in them, which have been treated as useful evidence in tracing the history of plays. In any case, in order to bring out the particular quality of Zeami's construction of the theory, I shall subject it to a fairly detailed analysis.

Go on opens as follows:

> The vocal art of this *michi* must derive from one of the following three traditions: Yamato, Ōmi, and *dengaku* vocal music. Now in Yamato there are many performers of *sarugaku*, but in this lineage we make my late father Kannami's vocal music our basic training. In Ōmi they use Inuō's music. *Dengaku* vocal music comes from Kiami, and that too is a single lineage. These great masters were in the old *michi*, and their old styles of vocalization have been passed down through the generations to the present. Recently, however, people of real ability have died out, and there are no qualified masters of those lineages. No one writes plays now in the Ōmi or *dengaku* traditions. In form at least, in this lineage, we have received my late father's tradition, and we preserve and transmit it in the form of the "three ways" (seed, construction, composition). We train in this art of performance and preserve this *michi*, so that this vocal music has spread of its own accord. Since the turn of the century it has become the musical performance of this era.[289]

Zeami asserts the legitimacy of his tradition as one of three, the other two of which are moribund. (*Ongyoku* or "vocal art" embraced the composition of the words of plays, the addition to them of musical notation,

---

289. ZZ, *Go on*, 206.

and singing in performance; that is why traditions in which plays were no longer written were considered to have died out.)[290] He does not claim however that his is the only legitimate Yamato tradition; merely that it derives from his father and has become widely popular. It is unclear whether "spread" means that performers in other traditions (or of no legitimate tradition) adopted his style. Zeami continues:

> Nevertheless, everyone now just enjoys this vocal art, and no one understands even the basic difference between *tadautai* 只謡 and *kusemai*. The distinctions between the vocal styles of celebration (*shūgen* 祝言) and sorrow (*bōoku* 亡臆) are even less understood. Therefore I shall provisionally divide the way of music into celebration (*shūgen*), veiled artistry (*yūkyoku* 幽曲), amorous longing (*renbo* 恋慕), grief (*aishō* 哀傷) and mature artistry (*rangyoku* 闌曲), calling these the five voices. These five voices should be taken as benchmarks in the path of training in singing, and one should practice them having deeply pondered their aesthetic flavors (*kyokumi* 曲味).[291]

We know from Zeami's report (discussed above) that it was Kannami who had imported a modified version of *kusemai,* a rhythmic style of singing used in *shirabyōshi* traditions, into Noh plays, where it was added to the older *tadautai*, plain singing. We might take it, then, that what Zeami meant when he said before that his father's style had spread, was that other well-known *sarugaku* performers had copied the *kusemai* form from his lineage's performances. This would explain why he says that "no one" understands the basic difference between *kusemai* and *tadautai*, for the new form would have been copied rather than learned by the proper method—transmission in training. This reading, however, is problematic for we have to wonder for whom Zeami was writing. Surely those outsiders who did not properly understand Kannami's tradition would not have access to Zeami's writings. This is an unanswered problem.

In any case, it becomes clear as we read on, that the system of five voices is actually not specifically aimed at the difference of *kusemai* and *tadautai*. Rather it is meant to develop the other distinction that Zeami refers to, between the vocal styles of celebration (*shūgen*) and sorrow

---

290. "Learning *ongyoku* has two aspects: the beautiful stringing together of syllables by the one who writes the libretto and understands the different song types, and the distinguishing of the syllables by adding musical notation by the one who sings." ZZ, *Ongyoku kowadashi kuden,* 74. In the following translations, my interpretations of musical terms differ somewhat from those of other scholars. This does not affect my primary argument, however, which is that Zeami is attempting with these terms to specify methods of vocalization.
291. ZZ, *Go on,* 206.

(*bōoku*). This polarity is a fundamental opposition that Zeami had written about in earlier musical works, describing it in terms of a number of contrasts. (The celebratory derived from the *ryo* 呂 mode, stressed vital energy rather than syllabic pronunciation, was strong and emerged from the outgoing breath, while the sorrowful had arisen from the *ritsu* 律 mode, was based on pronunciation rather than vital energy, was soft and weak, and was like the ingoing breath.)[292] In the *go on* system he extends these two styles of vocal production to five styles, with the celebratory constituting the first, and grief (renamed from the mysterious *bōoku* to the poetically sanctioned *aishō*)[293] the fourth. An important aspect of the five voices is that they are each a modification of the one before, proceeding from simple to complex, making them particularly well designed for a system of training.[294] They were in fact styles of vocal emission—we must note that they did not correspond in any way to such notated musical qualities as pitch.[295] To describe such vocal emission, Zeami struggles with the vocabulary available to him. The result is not unproblematic, but is more or less successful.

As Zeami describes the five styles of vocal production in *Go ongyoku jōjō*, he also attempts to characterize the corresponding passages of singing to which they should be applied. This results in a typology of sung passages, distinguished by what Zeami called *kyokumi*, a word that was to become of great importance in Zenchiku's reading. I have translated this above as "aesthetic flavor," but this is not always appropriate, for the *kyokumi* of a piece of chanting was not restricted to its aesthetic quality, and sometimes referred to its intellectual stance or its topic. A form of thematic unity applied in Noh singing, much like the *hon'i* 本意 that bound such aspects

292. ZZ, *Ongyoku kowadashi kuden*, 76.
293. The meaning of *booku* is not absolutely clear (probably sorrowful, but perhaps mournful, or cowardly—see Kōsai, 1962, 228–32). It has been thought to be a mispronunciation of the term *bōkoku* 亡国, which derives from a celebrated passage from the *Great Preface*, where it refers to the fallen nation, whose songs are sorrowful. Zeami knew the passage in question, for he cites it in *Go ongyoku jōjō*, (ZZ, 202). Perhaps his own doubts about the provenance of the term led him to adopt the more established *aishō* (grief), which was not only a hoary Chinese poetic category but was used as a topic in *Kokinwakashū* (book 16) and subsequent collections.
294. The main source of technical musical vocabulary in Zeami's earlier musical works is the Chinese twelve-note system employed in *gagaku*, but it seems that the actual singing of *sarugaku* was based on the characteristic tetrachords of Buddhist music composed in Japanese. See Akira Tamba's demonstration of this in *La Structure Musicale du Nô: Théâtre Traditionnel Japonais*, translated by Patricia Matoré as *The Musical Structure of Nō* (Tokyo: Tōkai University Press, 1981), 49–53.
295. This is clear from the notations in the passages given, and is also mentioned by Zenchiku's grandson in *Zenpō Zōdan*: "*Utai no fushi ooku wa nashi. Jū bakari nari. Koutai no hitotsu no uchi ni kotogotoku nari. ... mata shūgen o hajimete, go on kotogotoku, fushi wa onajiku shite kawaru koto nashi. kokoromochi kawaru nari.*" KKS, 447–8. The last phrase reflects Zenchiku's misreading of the system, as we shall see.

together in poetry.[296] Even if we consider the simple polarity in examples of the celebratory and sorrowful, we can see how *kyokumi* unites such aspects. Celebratory passages describe a world in which things are in their proper order; they refer to lineage and the sacred, and express wishes for long life. Passages sung in the mode of sorrow, on the other hand, are imbued with the idea of impermanence, of the struggle for detachment and enlightenment as well as the mood of sadness. Zeami used various striking means to identify the five *kyokumi*, including lists of poems, botanical metaphors and exemplary passages. Thus Zeami's theory amounts to a matching of descriptions of vocal style—essentially a musical and technical matter—and an analysis of the *kyokumi*—the import of the words—to which they were to be applied.

Go ongyoku jōjō opens with definitions of the five voices and brief indications of the types of songs to which they should be applied. The first is celebration:

Celebration (*shūgen*) is the sound of the enjoyment of simplicity. It is vocalized plainly, proceeding simply, the style of a world in its proper order, a regular flowing voice.[297] It is very important to understand the significance of this simply flowing style, and it should be deeply pondered.[298]

Here, the term *shūgen* refers to the content rather than the style of singing. The style of singing is explained through an allusion to the *Great Preface*, a canonical statement of the Confucian theory of music associating the mood of popular song and the quality of government: "The songs of an orderly world express enjoyment in simplicity, and its governance is harmonious." The vocal style is described as plain, simple and flowing.

The second voice arises from a modification of the first:

Next is Veiled Music (*yūkyoku*). This adds a stylish flow to the previous voice of celebration. The words are sung in a continuous flow of sound and the "notes" (*fushi* 曲) are covered over, what is above is made attractive, but there is still a correct musical flow. It is like viewing the blossom and moon of dawn and dusk at the same time. In

---

296. *Hon'i* refers to the idea that a proper treatment of a poetic topic must draw on the traditional imagery associated with it. For a discussion see Robert H. Brower and Earl Miner, *Japanese Court Poetry* (Stanford: Stanford University Press, 1961), 253–7, and for a practical examination see chapter one of Kōji Kawamoto, *The Poetics of Japanese Verse: Imagery, Structure, Meter* (University of Tokyo Press, 2000), 1–44.

297. There is a visual pun here: *chisei* in *chisei naru kakari nari* is written: 治声 "an ordered voice," but the allusion to the *Great Preface* clearly brings to mind the word 治世, "the ordered world." I therefore translate the phrase twice, once with each reading.

298. ZZ, *Go ongyoku jōjō*, 198.

terms of what is primary and secondary, the secondary is made central, and the primary is covered over.[299]

There are two problems that arise in the interpretation of this passage, and I will propose a single solution to them both. The first problem lies in the name of the vocal style, *yūkyoku*. This is generally take to be a synonym of the aesthetic classification *yūgen*, to which it is certainly related for, as we shall see, it was *yūgen* pieces that were to be sung with the *yūkyoku* voice. Why then does Zeami call the vocal style *yūkyoku* and not *yūgen*?

The second problem is how we read the character 曲 that I have in the citation here translated with the word "notes." Zeami actually used this character to represent two words, *fushi* and *kyoku*, which have quite different meanings. Which reading is correct? [300]

Let us consider this second matter first. In Zeami's musical contexts, *kyoku* signified an unnotatable element in singing, the product of the singer's higher musicality or artistry, something that drew an emotional response from the audience. Zeami contrasted *kyoku* with *fushi*, which signified the notated elements of singing, the framework of notes and melismata applied to a written passage to clarify and distinguish its syllables. [301] He famously described the relationship between *kyoku* and *fushi* in the formula: "*kyoku* is the flower above *fushi*." [302] We might say that this means: "What makes us emotionally affected by singing is an attractiveness that is beyond the mere musical notes." If we read 曲 in the definition of *yūkyoku* cited above as *kyoku*, musicality, the passage does not make sense. Why would the continuous flow of the voice lead to a covering over of "musicality"? Surely it is the correctness of the notes that is generally regarded as primary and the resultant musicality that is secondary. If, however, we read the character 曲 as *fushi,* the notes—as I have above—the passage makes much more sense: *yūkyoku* is then a vocal style that takes the plain unadorned singing of *shūgen* and partially covers over the notated elements with a "stylish flow" (*kakari*) The primary element, the "notes," is made secondary, and the overall flow is given precedence.

This reading now leads to the solution to our first problem, the significance of the term *yūkyoku*. It is now clear that *yūkyoku* is derived from a key phrase in the explanatory statement of the vocal style, which we

299. ZZ, *Go ongyoku jōjō*, 198.
300. This double use of a character strikes us as being irresponsible, of course, but is less so when we consider the nature of *hidensho*—ideally a record of knowledge that has already been communicated orally.
301. ZZ, *Ongyoku kowadashi kuden*, 74.
302. ZZ, *Fūshikaden*, 57.

read as *fushi o uzumite*, "covering over the 'notes.'" This is an example of a typical rhetorical mode found in medieval interpretation, for *fushi o uzumite* is a *kun* reading (or Japanese translation) of the pseudo-Chinese compound *yūkyoku* 幽曲, because of the semantic connection between *yū* 幽, meaning veiled, partially obscured, or indistinct and *uzumu,* meaning to veil or cover something,[303] and because *fushi* is a *kun* reading of *kyoku*. The explanation, then, of the term *yūkyoku* is that it describes (in fact is a *kanbun* version of) the style of vocal production in question, whereas *yūgen* describes the *kyokumi* of the passages to which it should be applied.[304] Zeami's use of the character 曲 for *fushi*, when he could have used the less ambiguous 節, was because he wished to display visually the relationship between the *on* form of the name of the voice, *yūkyoku*, and its relation to its *kun* expansion, *fushi o uzumite*.[305]

Yūkyoku, the second voice, then, takes the plain vocalization of the notes found in *shūgen* and adds to it a stylish flow which, without making the singing musically incorrect, nevertheless covers it over, giving it a veiled quality.

The next of the five voices is *renbo*, or amorous longing:

> Amorous longing is also soft and harmonious, but added within it is *aware*—deep emotion. An indefinable emotion reverberates in the sound, affecting the listener. It is a singing that expresses emotion by adding color so that the words are somewhat distorted, as well as the *fushi* being covered over. This handling of the voice so that the syllables are distorted must be well understood. . . . The difference between good and bad distortion must be clearly grasped. Good distortion gives singing charm. It is not heard as distortion.[306]

Renbo adds to *yūkyoku* the element of deep emotion (*aware* アハレ). While in *yūkyoku* a "stylish flow" softened the musical distinctions, in *renbo* intense emotion was expressed by a distortion, or mispronunciation, of the syllables of the text.

The next voice is *aishō*, grief. As we have stated, it derived from a poetic classification that Zeami adopted in place of a former term: *bōoku*, sorrowful, in contrast to *shūgen*, celebratory.

---

303. Morohashi gives *uzumeru* as a "*kun*" reading for *yū* (*Dai kanwa jiten* entry for 幽).
304. The editors of ZZ attempt to explain the term *yūkyoku* as Zeami's adjustment of the word *yūgen* to fit the pattern of the fifth voice *rangyoku* (ZZ, additional note 122, 482).
305. My argument here is supported by the fact that in *Go on,* Zeami says concerning *yūkyoku: fushi o uzumu yoshi narubeshi.* In this case the other graph 節 is used, the reading of which is not ambiguous (ZZ, 208).
306. ZZ, *Go ongyoku jōjō,* 198.

Aishō has *aware*, too, but its fundamental feeling is one giving rise to tears of emotion. It should be a voice with a sound that communicates the impermanent character of life.[307]

Zeami's description of *aishō* is very brief. Its vocal style adds to *renbo* the feeling of weeping and is used to sing passages expressing the awareness of impermanence. Zeami goes on to explain that this voice was not to be overused, because "nowadays in any field, *shūgen* is taken to be the main style, and one must avoid *aishō*." We note that there seems to have been a widely held belief that such verses could bring ill luck, just as *shūgen* could bring blessings.[308]

The last of the five voices is *rangyoku*, mature artistry:

Rangyoku is the highest vocal quality. It is that stage arrived at when one has completely mastered the study of singing, arrived at the highest level, mixed the orthodox and unorthodox in a single voice, and produced that sound which is "similar and not the same." In poetics, there is among the ten styles the one called catching and overpowering a demon (*rakkitei* 拉鬼体), which must be this level. This is that level of singing where one, having reached the heights, turns back (*kōkokyakurai*), yet more mature.[309]

Like *yūkyoku*, the term *rangyoku* describes the singing technique rather than the content, but the nature of that technique is made clearer in a passage in *Go on*:

307. ZZ, *Go ongyoku jōjō*, 199.
308. This idea is seen in other arts, too. For example, the imperial *renga* collection, *Tsukubashū* 菟玖波集, followed imperial *waka* collections in its classification of poems, except that it lacked a volume on *aishō* poems. The root of this taboo was probably the Confucian theory of music mentioned above. It was part of Confucian theories of government that we know were taught to educated warriors like Yoshimitsu and that are evident in warrior writings of earlier periods. In Confucian theory, songs of loss, *bōkoku*, presaged the downfall of the state. Zeami's shift to the new term *aishō*, may in fact have been to avoid the earlier term's dangerous connotations. The seriousness with which such ideas were taken is evident in the use of a related term *bōshitsu* 亡室 presaging the fall of a lineage or house. It was believed that *bōshitsu* elements (mourning the death of a spouse) were apparent in the poems of Fujiwara Ietaka, and that they were fulfilled when his line died out (as related in *Shōtetsu monogatari*—see Steven D. Carter, ed., *Conversations with Shōtetsu: (Shōtetsu Monogatari)* translated by Robert H. Brower (Ann Arbor: Center for Japanese Studies, University of Michigan, 1992), 63). We notice however that in the next generation, Zenchiku's contemporary, the *renga* poet and theorist Shinkei opposed such conventional attitudes: "People in the country admire *shūgen* in every verse and frown at even slightly unlucky verses . . . but impermanence and regret are central to the ideas and language of this *michi*. . . ." Even Shinkei, however, recommends they be avoided at New Year poetry meetings or before nobility or strangers (in *Sasamegoto*, see Kidō Saizō and Imoto Nōichi, eds., *Rengaronshū haironshū (Nihon koten bungaku taikei 66)* (Iwanami Shoten, 1961), 139).
309. ZZ, *Go ongyoku jōjō*, 199.

Rangyoku is a special sound. It is the essential level where, having mastered the other voices, one sings as one wishes. In general if one sings according to the notation, then one can sing in unison with others. But this is in truth solo singing. Hence it is the level where one sings freely as the mood takes one.[310]

It seems here that the singer can ignore the notated elements and sing the passage simply as he wishes, regardless of whether it accords with the rules (which covered the distribution of notated elements over given song styles). This is an example of the freedom earned by the actor who has submitted himself to rigorous training, a stage which Zeami generally in the arts of performance referred to as *ran'i* or *taketaru kurai* 闌位, what we might call the level of mastery. In *Shikadō* he described it in the following terms:

> Now the technique of *taketaru kurai* is as follows. When one has trodden this artistic path and thoroughly mastered each of the steps in training from youth to maturity, gathering the good and rooting out the bad, and when one has gone beyond these stages, there develops an inner power of performance that is always accomplished. Then at this stage one mixes in with the good style slight elements of bad styles that one has throughout one's training rejected and rooted out.[311]

Similarly *rangyoku* (= *taketaru fushi*) is conceived of as a vocal technique that allows the use of heterodox elements for effect. *Rakkitei* (the demon-quelling style) was a style in *waka* that was forbidden to students until they had mastered all other, milder styles.[312] Again *kōkokyakurai*, the Buddhist term, represented the freedom of those who had attained enlightenment to return to the lower realms without being sullied. In both cases the rules restricting those traveling on the path were relaxed once mastery was attained.

This completes Zeami's technical descriptions of the five vocal styles. *Shūgen* is plain and ordered vocalization; *yūkyoku* adds a stylistic elegance that made a continuous vocal flow and caused notated elements to be obscured; *renbo* adds deep emotion, resulting in a distortion of the pronunciation of syllables, *aishō* adds to this the sound of immanent tears;

310. ZZ, *Go on*, 212.
311. ZZ, *Shikadō*, 114.
312. This common idea in the poetic systems of schools tracing themselves back to Fujiwara Teika probably had its roots in the remarks in *Maigetsushō* characterizing *rakkitei*, the demon quelling style, as one not to be attempted until the other nine styles had been mastered (Hisamatsu and Nishio, 127).

and *rangyoku* mixes in heterodox elements for effect, overruling the musical notation.

Corresponding to these five styles, Zeami characterized five types of passages to which they should be applied. He did this by setting up a number of arboreal similes, citing poems from the Heian court tradition, and giving passages from current Noh plays as examples. *Shūgen* was represented by the pine tree, which Zeami illustrated with the poem:

> *Yorozuyo o / matsu ni zo kimi o / iwaitsuru / chitose no kage ni / sumanto omoeba*

> As the crane longs to dwell in the shade of a thousand years, I celebrate my lord, that he should, like the pine tree, wait for ten thousand ages.[313]

The pine tree is associated with waiting (from the polysemy of its name, *matsu*) and with long life (its being evergreen, and also long-lived). A further association is with the tradition that *kami* 神 (gods) appear beneath them in the form of old men. This poem was classified in the *Kokinwakashū* as an *iwai uta*—a celebratory poem. In the *kana* preface to the *Kokinwakashū*, such poems were described as "praising the world, reporting to the gods." The term for "world" in this phrase can also be understood as "realm," i.e. the political *status quo*. In the given poem, the poet praises the world and expresses his sense of safety in dependency and his wish that the state of affairs should persist. Zeami also provides an exemplary passage of Noh singing, from an old form of the play *Fushimi*, which expresses similar ideas, describing the divine descent of the emperor, the tranquility he confers on the realm, and the luster he gives to the world. *Iwai uta* 祝ひ歌 generally include requests for blessings on the emperor and his court. In the preface to the *Kokinwakashū*, one finds the belief that such poems could influence spiritual powers and elicit rewards. The significance that Zeami saw in the plain and correct singing of celebratory songs is related to this belief. In *Ongyoku kowadashi kuden*, he stated that such spiritual influence was dependent on "correct feeling." He explained this as follows, referring to the traditional Noh style of *tadautai* (plain singing):

> *Tadautai* is not rhythmically decorated, rather it is chanted just as it is, and so there is no confusion in the pronunciation of the syllables. Thus the essence of the passage is manifest from the declamation and

---

313. ZZ, *Go ongyoku jōjō*, 200. The poem is *Kokinwakashū*, 356.

recitative, each phrase, each song clarifies the ear, calms the mind. Both singer and listener are of a single mind responding to the emotion of a single passage. This is "correct feeling."[314]

The ideas are similar to those in the *shūgen* vocal style, which were to be sung in a plain and simple fashion.

Yūkyoku was represented by the flowering cherry, which Zeami says is another "spiritual" tree, the emblem of spring. Its poem is:

Mata ya mimu / katano no mino no / sakuragari / hana no yuki chiru / haru no akebono

Shall we ever see its like again! Searching for cherry blossoms, on the imperial meadows of Katano, on a dawn in spring, with the blossoms scattering like snowflakes.[315]

Zeami also gives an exemplary passage of *utai* 謡 celebrating the beauty of cherry blossoms. The common elements here are blossoms and whiteness. As it happens fifteenth-century references to *yūgen* in poetry highlight such elements (in contrast to the somber profundity of Heian usages).[316] So it seems that Zeami is identifying such *yūgen* poetic themes as appropriate for his vocal style of *yūkyoku*. This connection is in fact made explicit in one section of *Go ongyoku jōjō*, where Zeami replaces the word *yūkyoku* with *yūgen* in his summary of the five voices.[317]

Renbo is represented by autumn colors and the poem:

Shita momiji / katsu chiru yama no / yū shigure / nurete ya hitori / shika no nakuran

Is a lone deer crying out, wet from the evening shower on the mountain where the lower autumn leaves are all falling?[318]

The autumn colors of the maple tree "display the feeling of the close of autumn, dyed with color (passion), arrayed with dew, expressing the emotion of amorous longing." The accompanying passage of *utai* is one in which a lover tells of a secret passion that shows itself in her embarrassed blushes.

---

314. ZZ, 78.
315. ZZ, *Go ongyoku jōjō*, 200. The poem is *Shinkokinwakashū* 新古今和歌集, 114.
316. See Hisamatsu Sen'ichi, *The Vocabulary of Japanese Literary Aesthetics* (Tokyo: Tōyō Bunko, 1963), 33–44.
317. "*Shūgen* must be the essential character. The aesthetic form that softens this essence and adds to it elegant style is called *yūgen*. Again the stage that deepens *yūgen* and adds emotional decoration is called *renbo*," ZZ, *Go ongyoku jōjō*, 202–3.
318. ZZ, *Go ongyoku jōjō*, 200. The poem is *Shinkokinwakashū*, 437.

The bare trees of winter represent *aishō*, exemplified in the following poem:

Ashikareto / omowanu yama no / mine ni dani / ounaru mono o / hito no nageki wa

I do not think you bad, but complaints do arise, just as, on the mountain peak, while there are no reeds to cut, it seems that trees grow.[319]

This complex poem juxtaposes growing trees and rising bitterness. Zeami has chosen an exceptionally gentle complaint, perhaps reflecting his concern over mournful songs. *Aishō* poems in *Kokinwakashū* are mainly poems mourning the deaths of important or greatly loved personages or written facing one's own death. The passage of *utai* that Zeami offers is: "A lifetime is like a cloud before the wind, easily scattered as in a dream, the three realms disappear like froth on the waters before the shining sun," and so on, which seems to capture the "impermanent character of life" mentioned in his definition, rather than the lover's complaints in the poem.

The tree for *rangyoku* is the cedar and the poem also refers to cedars:

Itsushika to / kamisabi ni keru / kagu yama no / musugi ga moto ni / koke no musu made ni

When did the spear cedars on Mount Kagu become so venerably aged that moss grew at their base?[320]

Zeami explains his choice as follows: "The cedar's foliage looms higher, the sacred trees surrounding the old shrine look from a distance like other trees but are not the same. Thus the cedar symbolizes *rangyoku*, which sounds unlike other songs, possessing a unique resonance." This does not seem to indicate what types of passage should be sung in this way, rather it describes the qualities of the singer who has attained this level of singing. Of the exemplary passages of Noh singing, the first is a section from an early version of the play *Jinen Koji* 自然居士. In this play the preacher Jinen explains how he had practiced eremitism in order to achieve spiritual knowledge, but having awakened, left the mountains and returned to associate with the ordinary world as a madman. This, in other words, is a passage recounting an example of *kōkokyakurai*, returning to the world after enlightenment. As such it parallels the artist's disregard of the rules of good and bad vocalizations after the achievement of mastery, rather than expressing any particular aesthetic mood. The relationship between the

---

319. ZZ, *Go ongyoku jōjō*, 200. The poem is *Shikawakashū* 詞華和歌集, 333.
320. ZZ, *Go ongyoku jōjō*, 200. This poem is a medieval version of *Man'yōshū*, 259.

vocal style and *kyokumi* in *rangyoku* is thus fundamentally different from that given in the other four styles.

This in short is Zeami's system. At a superficial glance, it might be taken simply to be an aesthetic typology of sung passages based on categories adopted from poetics, and indeed that is how scholars do generally seem to have understood it.[321] Such a view, however, masks its relation to Zeami's own particular interests, for it is much more than a typology. Zeami develops a series of progressively more complex vocal styles, for which he presents a corresponding series of types of passages. The styles themselves are structurally coherent, each one adding some specific vocal quality to the prior simpler one, rendering them suitable as stages in training. The typology of passages, too, is at least superficially well organized, through the metaphors of five types of trees. There is also an element of the Buddhist sentimental education in the system: plain reality (*shūgen*) is perceived as beautiful (*yūgen*), whereupon attachment arises (*renbo*); this leads inevitably to loss (*aishō*); realization of the impermanence of the world brings about detachment resulting in a freedom from good and bad (*rangyoku*). The idea that a progressive series of techniques should be effective in expressing a series of contents (or aesthetic moods) is a striking one, reflecting the inherent integrity of Zeami's worldview.[322]

ZENCHIKU'S THEORY OF FIVE VOICES: *GO ON NO SHIDAI*

We now turn to Zenchiku's works incorporating the theory of the five voices. The first is *Go on no shidai (Details Concerning the Five Voices)*. The extant version is a copy, and there is evidence that certain elements

---

321. See for example the explanatory headnote to *Go on no shidai*, KKS, 107: "*Go on*, the five voices, are a typology of aesthetic qualities (*kyokumi*) of sung passages, developed previously by Zeami."

322. Zeami was deeply interested in the question of what it was in singing that enabled it to affect the emotions of audiences, something that he felt must be more than simply the notated elements, but at the same time he found it difficult to locate outside its musical qualities. He closes *Go ongyoku jōjō* with profound questions about musical performance: "Musicality is a principle that cannot be learned. Thus what is called musicality is in truth something that does not exist. If there is such a thing then it must just be in the notes. Thus there is no system whereby it can be taught. It is a charm that arises of its own accord when a singer has studied fully [all technical aspects of] singing and achieved certain mastery. . . . Thus music exists as phenomenon but musicality is *mu* (i.e. unmanifest reality). . . . And so, where is this non-existent musicality to be found? Is it just the music of the voice? They say that there are places where one uses the voice, and places where one is used by the voice. The first is melody; the second is vocal color or timbre. *Kyoku* lies in the second but how does it communicate to the ears of the audience? The audience is not necessarily trained how to listen. What affects the feelings of children and women, this is probably *kyoku*, although it could be the vocal color. These are all emotional qualities heard arising from the five sounds and the four tones, unawares, without being understood. It is incomprehensible, incomprehensible!" (ZZ, 204)

were added after the date of Zenchiku's colophon (an auspicious day in early autumn, 1455), although when and by whom is not known. The original material, however, is a brief and systematic presentation of matter found in Zeami's *Go on* and *Go ongyoku jōjō*. The work is reorganized into five clusters of material, each with the same structure: the name of the voice (i.e. *shūgen, yūkyoku, renbo, aishō, rangyoku*) written with large characters in black, a brief summary of Zeami's explanation followed by the arboreal image written below in red ink, and Zeami's exemplary passage of singing written to the left. In *Go ongyoku jōjō* the exemplary passages were indicated by their opening phrase, but in *Go on no shidai*, they are written out in full, with their musical notation added in red. The poems that Zeami provided to exemplify the arboreal associations are omitted. There is no explanatory introduction.[323]

This is a slight work, and contains very little that cannot be directly traced to Zeami's two works. We do see, however, some interesting tendencies. First of all is the simple fact that this work is a selection from and reorganization of Zeami's writings. Although we know nothing of what oral communication there might have been between Zeami and Zenchiku concerning the five voices, certain patterns make it seem likely that Zenchiku's primary reference was to Zeami's written versions. This is apparent from a close reading of Zenchiku's elements. An example is the summaries of Zeami's descriptions of the five voices. In each case Zenchiku takes a brief phrase from either *Go on* or *Go ongyoku jōjō*, and expands it with one or two words (so that, where Zeami states that *yūkyoku* is "*shūgen ni kakari o soetari*" (the addition of a stylish flow), Zenchiku has "*shūgen ni uraranaru kakari o soetari*" (addition of a bright stylish flow).[324] This process has a physical and mechanical feel to it, as if Zenchiku is applying a routine to written material he had before him, rather than, say, recalling something that he had been taught. The primary point that I want to make here, then, is that Zenchiku is from the beginning treating Zeami's writings in a way that is characteristic of the use of written texts. Zeami's record of his thought has converted it into texts, open to specifically textual treatment. While Zeami's works operate through a series of lists, Zenchiku gathers together their elements into a more synthetic set of clusters, creating a kind of visual summary that encourages multiple routes through them, a system of organization that is grasped visually and would be difficult to present orally.

---

323. See discussion KKS, 69–70.
324. KKS, 109.

A second point is that Zenchiku does add (perhaps at a later date) a very few notes that do not derive from Zeami's theory. For example he adds the remark to *rangyoku* that "at this level there is also *kan*; that is, the elegant, still form (*miyabi shizuka katachi*)."[325] This shows that the material is not something that Zenchiku regards as transparent in the form Zeami gave it, but something that needs his own shaping to bring to completion. (As it is addition rather than alteration, it is perhaps felt to be legitimate.)

The third point is the nature of the selection that Zenchiku applies to Zeami's theory. The most striking aspect of this is that Zenchiku either omits or veils all Zeami's attempts to create technical descriptions of the vocal styles in his system. As we saw, Zeami tried to describe these using the vocabulary of *fushi*, *kakari* and *kyoku* and the idea of various distortions, of *fushi* and of syllables. These vocal styles were in fact the primary elements of his theory, which was concerned to teach singers the techniques by which singing could communicate emotion; the aesthetic typology was secondary, arising from the need to distinguish exemplary passages suited to each voice. The vocal styles were, moreover, the basis of the five voices as a method of training. The training depended on the progressive modifications of the vocal styles, one after the other. In Zenchiku's system then the technical and pedagogical aspects of the theory are ignored. It is only with this shift of emphasis that it becomes possible to think that "*miyabi shizuka*," the elegant and still, could be inserted alongside *rangyoku*, for it describes a "*katachi*," that is, a poetic mood, not a way of singing. Once Zeami's system has been reduced to a typology of aesthetic categories, *rangyoku*—which essentially was a kind of free singing and lacked a clearly defined corresponding *kyokumi*—becomes problematic, and so we see Zenchiku looking for a more useful aesthetic quality to put in its place.

GO ON JITTEI

Zenchiku's next work on the five voices takes spatial logic a step further. It is also exceptional in that it is the first Noh treatise written for someone outside the profession. A colophon dated 1490 added to *Go on jittei (Five Voices and Ten Styles)* by Zenchiku's grandson, Zenpō, describes the circumstances of its composition:

---

325. KKS, 116.

When the late Zenchiku was visiting the western provinces, Lord Ōuchi asked him and he immediately wrote this document for him. It should on no account be shown to outsiders.[326]

The work is dated 1456.9.2. Lord Ōuchi is almost certainly Norihiro (1419–1465),[327] a powerful *tozama* 外様 leader in possession of several provinces in West Honshū. Norihiro was an avid poet, sufficiently highly rated to have been asked by the Shogun Yoshinori to act as his teacher. He also contributed to the *renga* collection *Shintsukubashū* 新菟玖波集. It is sometimes suggested that Norihiro might have been an early case of an amateur practitioner of Noh, and thus he wanted *Go on jittei* to help him with his singing. If so, then the work seems singularly ill chosen for the task, as will become apparent. More likely Norihiro was fascinated by Zenchiku's theories concerning the essential unity of *sarugaku* and poetics. Norihiro had in the same year invited the poetic theorist Shōtetsu to visit him too, and the latter had declined. As Zenchiku had close relations with Shōtetsu from at least his twenties, it could well be that there was a connection between the two invitations. In any case, let us start by looking at the central material of *Go on jittei* before we conclude what there was in the work that might have interested Norihiro. The reader is recommended at this point to refer to table 1 in which the material of *Go on jittei* is summarized to clarify its spatial organization. It will again be seen that Zenchiku generates a complex table made up of repeated clusters of material, allowing a number of parallels and contrasts to be observed.

The central matter of *Go on jittei* falls into two halves: the first a representation of Zeami's system of five voices, the second a system of ten poetic types (usually translated "styles"). Each of the five voices is numbered, accompanied with an explanation (building on Zeami's descriptions but taking them in new directions) and illustrated with a poem. The ten poetic types are also numbered, and each is accompanied, in contrast, by the title of a Noh play as well as a poem. As the reader will see, this simple arrangement amounts to a powerful visual argument, which is that the five voices of Noh can be used as a typology of poems and the ten poetic types as a typology of plays. This implies that Noh plays and court poetry are essentially the same kind of thing. This point is driven

---

326. KKS, 148.
327. See KZK, 28–30, also, for Ōuchi patronage, see Stephen Carter, *Literary Patronage in Late Medieval Japan* (Michigan Papers in Japanese Studies, 1993), 8–9 (Carter seems to confuse the fifteen-year-old Masahiro with Norihiro).

Table 1
Arrangement of *Go on jittei*

1 Introduction		
2 Five Voices:		
Voice	*Descriptions elaborating Zeami*	*Exemplary poems*
Shūgenkyoku		
Yūgenkyoku		
Renbokyoku		
Aishōkyoku		
Rankyoku		
3 Ten Poetic Styles:		
Poetic style or equivalent	*Exemplary noh play(s)*	*Exemplary poems*
Shūgen (=*take takaki tei* (sonorous style))	*Aioi no Matsu*	
Yūgen (like a spring dawn)	*Yuya*	
Renbo (like an autumn eve)	*Matsukaze Murasame*	
Aishō (=*mono aware naru tei* (style of impermanence))	*Ono Komachi*	
Ran or *Kan* (mature or quiet) (=*rakki tei* (demon-quelling style))	*Aridōshi*	
Uruwashiki tei (splendid style)	*Ohara Gokō*	
Enpaku tei (far white style)	*Shio Kama (=Tōru)*	
Komayaka tei (rich detailed style)	*Hyakuman*	
Ushin tei (educated feeling style)	*Ashikari*	
Kotoshikarubeki tei ("how things should be" style)	*Eguchi*	
4 Closing remarks		
5 Colophon		

home by certain specific changes that have been made to conventional aspects of the two systems: The names of Zeami's five voices have been altered to read: *shūgenkyoku* 祝言曲, *yūgenkyoku* 幽玄曲, *renbokyoku* 恋慕曲, *aishōkyoku* 哀傷曲, and *rangyoku* 闌曲. This intensifies the sense that they are a mere classification of equals, simply types of *ongyoku*, sung pieces.[328] In the process it also erases the technical origins of *yūkyoku*—

---

328. This representation of the five voices illustrates the characteristic flattening out of categorical types that is noted by scholars when lists are put into writing. Goody describes how writing extends the possibilities of classificatory systems, but lessens the toleration of ambiguous categories. The manipulation of written signs weakens the awareness of contingent significations, and leads to a flattening of categorical types, giving them apparently equal valences. (Jack Goody, *The Interface Between the Written and the Oral* (Cambridge, UK: Cambridge University Press, 1987), 274–277.

fushi o uzumu—replacing it with the purely aesthetic *yūgen*. [329] The structure of the ten poetic types, which derives from early Kamakura poetic systems as expressed in *Sangoki* [330] or other similar works, has been reorganized as follows, in such a way as to make the first five match the five voices (omitting the suffix *kyoku*): *shūgen* (which a note tells us is equivalent to *taketakaki* 長高 *tei*, the lofty style, the second of the ten types in *Sangoki*); *yūgen* (the first type in *Sangoki*); *renbo* (explained in a note to be a subsection of *yūgen*); *aishō* (noted to be equivalent to *monoawarenaru* 物哀なる *tei*, the style of the sadness of things, a subtype of the third *ushin* 有心 *tei*); and a composite type, *ran* 闌 (transcendent) or *kan* 閑 (quiet) (explained as "probably" equivalent to *rakkitei*, the demon-subduing style). The remaining five styles (*urawashiki* 麗 *tei*, *enpaku* 遠白 *tei*, *komayaka* 濃 *tei*, *ushin tei*, and *kotoshikarubeki* 事可然 *tei*) are taken from others listed in *Sangoki*.

Thus, with a certain amount of fiddling, and with some places where he himself expresses uncertainty, Zenchiku has created a new version of the ten poetic styles in which the first five coincide with the five voices. Without it being explicitly stated, the spatial symmetry of the system leads us to the conclusion that the typologies of poetry and Noh, whether plays, roles, or sung passages, are equivalent. Not only can a classification of poetic types be applied to Noh performance and vice versa, but also culturally sanctioned typologies (i.e. one supposedly derived from Fujiwara Teika and the other actually derived from Zeami), which must reflect profound essential truths, are seen to coincide.

Why might that be important to Zenchiku or to Ōuchi Norihiro? On its own, it is probably only of mild interest. Zenchiku's prefatory remarks, however, explain a theory that he was developing, one in which this coincidence becomes much more significant:

> That which should be known concerning the way of "the single mind of song and dance" (*kabu isshin* 歌舞一心) in *sarugaku* is stated as follows: "What is in the mind is called intent and what emerges in words is poetry. Without stopping at that poetry, it is transferred to chanting and singing, and unawares the hands gesture and the feet tread." The arising of intent we base on *yūgen*, and as it appears as profound emotion and lingering feeling, the words are subtle and the

---

329. An explanation of this misreading could be that Zenchiku was unaware of this connection, which he might have been if his knowledge of the system was based on reading alone, without the support of the oral transmission that should have accompanied it.
330. See chapter two for an overview of Zenchiku's use of this and other treatises attributed to Fujiwara Teika.

form elegant. Thus all actions that contain that principle are songs/poems. They are also dance. That is why I have recorded what I find difficult to keep quiet about, simply considering the vital importance of aesthetic types (*kyokumi*). It is just dedication to this way, that what is said should be what is meant; the inner feeling (*isshin*) should be the same as the appearance (*ikken* 一見).[331]

This typically gnomic introduction is a first statement of a theory that was to be of fundamental importance to Zenchiku. It refers to a Chinese theory of the origins of poetry, found in the *Great Preface*. Zenchiku (mis-) quoted it from memory (perhaps as he was writing it on the spot). It was the same passage that Ki no Tsurayuki and his associates used to assert the "expressive" function of poetry, that is, that poetry was simply the expression of the poet's mental and emotional activity. What arose in the mind demanded expression, first in words, but then if the feelings were too strong to be adequately expressed in words only, in chanting and finally in unconscious gesticulation and striding about. This is an account of the instinctive reaction to mental turmoil, but in its uses in poetic theory in China and Japan it was projected onto cultured activity, particularly the composition of poetry. Zenchiku, however, was to endow this projection with a number of meanings that became an important pillar of his artistic theory. In this introduction, his main point is that it is the same mental energy that emerges as poetry and song (i.e., *utai*) and gestures and treading (i.e., dance). If the same impulses, deriving from the same mind, lie behind these activities, then we would expect classifications of them to coincide. Now in poetry the knowledge of and the ability to distinguish the classifications of poetry, the *jittei*, had become a central matter in the secret transmissions from Fujiwara Teika. Thus for Zenchiku, the *kyokumi*, the aesthetic types, which he extended both to songs (*ongyoku*) and dance (as we shall see), were of "vital importance." It was also important that what was within the mind in performance should conform to what was expressed outwardly.

We can read this construction of equivalence between poetry and performance in a number of ways. Firstly, poetry was the supreme form of court culture, possessed of essential artistic and spiritual significance, and so *sarugaku*, which was still historically near its plebeian origins, could legitimate itself by the association. In the second place, since Teika's time poets had repeatedly tried to formulate the practice of poetry as a *michi*, a path, and had developed various conceptions of training, of techniques to

331. KKS, 143.

advance along that path. Once Zenchiku could establish *sarugaku* as a form of *waka*, he could apply those techniques, as he knew them through his relations with Shōtetsu, to the practice of Noh. We shall see reference to these aspects in other works.

Some of the significance of other parts of the above introduction only becomes apparent when we look further at Zenchiku's writings. I would just like to foreshadow certain aspects that we will meet with later. The first is the idea of the origin of poetic qualities in performance. Zenchiku states that "the arising of intent we base on *yūgen*, and as it appears as profound emotion and lingering feeling, the words are subtle and the form elegant." This sentence reflects the tri-partite structure of the quotation it follows: mind, poetry, performance. Profound emotion and lingering feeling are of course poetic terms. That words should be subtle (*kasuka*, another Japanese reading of *yū* 幽) and form elegant are the standards that Zeami demanded for *sarugaku* performance, to distinguish it from vulgar rural styles. For Zenchiku, however, these external elements proceed from the state of mind of the performer; the "arising of intent" should be "based on *yūgen*." This clearly demonstrates a shift of the meaning of *yūgen* from an aesthetic quality to a state of mind—a shift that is seen in contemporary poetic theorists such as Shinkei. For Zenchiku, indeed, *yūgen* was much more than a mere mental impulse; it was, in fact, the inner presence of absolute reality. It was this higher and yet unconscious inner source of activity that was *yūgen*, and once the actor harmonized his mind with it, then automatically his performance would have the appropriate qualities. This idea occurs repeatedly in Zenchiku's writings. Another aspect of this passage is that it shares a structure with Zenchiku's metaphysics, his view of the structure of reality, that is particularly apparent in the arguments of *Meishukushū*. In the human being, what is in the mind, being associated with ultimate reality, shows itself in human appearance, imbuing actions with an ineffable aesthetic quality. So, in the world outside the mind, the expression of that ultimate or divine reality in the phenomenal world can be recognized by the presence of certain structural qualities. Thus there are certain cultural expressions, as well as natural formations that closely express a hidden structure of spiritual relations that have their root in the absolute. The path to higher knowledge lies in the recognition and interpretation of these traces in the world.

In his closing words to *Go on jittei*, we see something of Zenchiku's view of *sarugaku* history (we have cited this passage in chapter three). He tells how two generations previously, the Shogun Yoshimitsu had viewed the performances of Kannami's generation, including Kannami, Inuō and Komparu Gonnokami, and rejected what was vulgar, and established levels and grades of quality. He made lingering feeling and subtle beauty the basis of *sarugaku*. The present generations, however, were in the process of abandoning the path that these performers had left behind. Zenchiku, ignoring the "laughter of inferior men" aimed to have his performance polished by the "clear sight of superior men." Out of these words we can imaginatively reconstruct the discussion between Zenchiku and Norihiro that might have given rise to the composition of *Go on jittei*. Norihiro, interested in contemporary poetic theories, especially as taught by Shōtetsu, heard from Zenchiku that Noh was actually an equivalent art, a kind of acting out of the mentalities expressed in poetry. Zenchiku flattered his host by explaining that while vulgar performers sought the acclaim of inferior audiences, he aimed only to have the refined appreciation of the cultured and poetically knowledgeable. His host then asked for a demonstration of the equivalences between poetry, which was well known to have ten fundamental styles, and the types of performance. *Go on jittei* was a diagrammatic demonstration of those relations.

Before we move on to the next of Zenchiku's *go on* works, it is worthwhile just noting the way in which he extends the definitions of the five voices. These passages set a pattern for statements of the theory in future generations, which generally followed Zenchiku's lead. The main addition is of imaginative images intended to express the aesthetic flavors of the five voices, for example under *yūgenkyoku* we find:

> It is like a white thread dyed with the five colors. The root feeling is like the bursting open of the color and scent of blossom in a gap in spring mists, or the scent of wild plants in the dew in autumn, that is deep and elegant, profound and yet containing an element of transience....[332]

This is a further move away from the technical and practical in Zeami's theory towards the impressionistic.

GO ON SANGYOKU SHŪ

The next work drawing on the theory of five voices, *Go on sangyoku shū (Collection of Five Voices and Three Qualities),* describes a considerably more complex system of classification than *Go on jittei.* It again combines poetic categories, deriving from *Sangoki*, with the five voices, this time to classify passages of *utai*, that is, vocal passages found in Noh plays. A further typological device is also applied, that is, the triad of skin, flesh and bone (*hi* 皮, *niku* 肉, and *kotsu* 骨, called here *sangyoku* 三曲, which I shall

332. KKS, 144.

translate as the "three qualities"). This triad has its immediate origins in Zeami's work, in particular in *Shikadō*. Zeami's use of this triad derives from poetic *hidensho* which in turn referred to its role in calligraphy where it described three qualities in brushwork that were all present only in the hand of Kūkai.[333] Zeami mapped the three qualities onto elements of performance skill—bone corresponded to innate talent, flesh to acquired skills, and skin to an easy elegance on stage—and asserted that they could only very rarely be combined in one actor. Thus the triad contained a kind of structural idea of different types of ability and also an idea of the rarity of the all-rounded actor. In Zenchiku's explanation of the three qualities we have an ideal example of misreading. It is clearly an elaboration of Zeami's ideas but it also draws on Shinto theorizing, and is put to the service of Zenchiku's own obsessions (we will return to it below).

The work that is represented in *Konparu kodensho shūsei* (KKS) as *Go on sangyoku shū* appears to concatenate one integrated work with a number of passages on music tacked onto the end. The reader may wish to consult table 2 to trace our discussions of the organization of the work. Here I am not concerned with the appended passages on music.[334] The rest of the work is again an attempt to combine the aesthetic analysis of the five voices that we have seen above with another set of distinctions based on the three qualities, and to further connect those to the ten poetic styles, including a number of sub-styles, as presented in *Sangoki*, and believed to have originated with Fujiwara Teika. Now, it is not my aim to go any further here into the definition of these aesthetic styles, nor to explain how they are exemplified in the passages of *utai* Zenchiku cites. While the connection between the five voices and Zeami's exemplary passages are relatively straightforward, Zenchiku's complex schema, like the aesthetic systems of such poetic works as *Sangoki*, are more difficult. I have heard it said that medieval aesthetic distinctions are swamps into which scholars enter at their peril and therefore will keep them at a respectful distance. My purpose here will be merely to clarify the intellectual processes informing Zenchiku's writings. Keeping that particular end in mind, then, let us survey the classification system as Zenchiku applies it in this work.

Referring to table 2, then, we find, as in *Go on jittei*, that Zenchiku constructs a series of repeated groups, each one this time containing the

333. For a discussion of the origins of Zeami and Zenchiku's uses, see Minemura Fumito "Nōgakuron to chūseikaron," in Nihon Bungaku Kenkyū Shiryō Kankōkai, eds, 94–100, *Yōkyoku kyōgen*, (Yūseidō, 1981).
334. KKS, 171–184.

Table 2
Arrangement of *Go on sangyoku shū*

1 Introduction
2 Five Voices (*shūgen, yūgen* etc., each divided into several subsections):
shūgen

Types of shūgen	poems	quality	chanted passages	further material
Celebration		bone	from *Kinsatsu*	
Settling the realm, caring for the people		flesh	from *Hōjōgawa*	poems, explanation from *Sangoki*
Pine style		bone	from *Awaji*	explanation from *Sangoki*
Bamboo style		skin	from *Saoyama*	explanation from *Sangoki*
Lofty style		bone	from *Hōjōgawa*	explanation from *Sangoki*

yūgen

Types of yūgen
Etc.

Similar sections for *renbo, aishō,*

rankyoku

Types of rankyoku	poems	quality	chanted passages	further material
Rakkitei (grasping the demon style)		bone	from *Utaura*	explanation from *Sangoki*
Etc.				

3 Closing discussion of three qualities (*sangyoku*)
4 Unconnected discussions of vocal arts
5 Colophon

following elements: one of the five voices, a definition of a particular type of content (aesthetic or thematic), an expanded explanation, one or more exemplary "old poems," one of the three qualities (skin, flesh, bone), and finally a passage of *utai*. Under each of the five voices there are several subdivisions, for example *shūgen* is treated five times, first with the *kyokumi* of "the sound of an ordered world enjoying ease," second with a *kyokumi* of "settling the realm, caring for the people," third with the "pine style," fourth with the "bamboo style," and fifth with the *kyokumi* of *taketakaki tei*, the sonorous or lofty style. The *utai* passage of the first of these is *kotsu mi* 味, the feeling or mood of bone; the second is *niku mi*, the feeling of flesh; the third, bone; the fourth, skin; and the fifth, bone. Most of the poetic categories used to create subsections of the five voices, such as "settling the realm, caring for the people," derive from the poetic categories of *Sangoki* and most of the exemplary poems come from the same work (although, occasionally, from different categories).

It is even clearer in this work that Zenchiku has turned his attention away from Zeami's interest in vocal production. It is now only the classification of the content of passages that interests him, particularly as they can be represented in terms deriving from poetics. This makes sense in terms of the theoretical position Zenchiku put forward in *Go on jittei*, and is further clarified in the preamble to *Go on sangyoku shū*:

> The element of vocal art of the performance tradition of *sarugaku* takes its source in *waka* (Japanese poetry). *Waka* is a cultural tradition of *wakoku* 和国 (Japan), and so even the bright deities (i.e. kami) accept it and respond to it. That is why, if one sings with the aesthetic mood of those old poems composed with such care held within one, then one's singing should be called *ongyoku*, vocal art.[335]

Zenchiku is generating another set of ideas to support his contention that holding a particular inner mood adds something special to performance. Whereas before it was an inner impulse based on *yūgen* which endowed performance with ineffable aesthetic qualities, now the holding within of the moods found in "old poems"—*kouta* 古歌, a term Zenchiku used for poetry from the court period—renders the performance acceptable to *kami*, native deities, who will respond to it. This is an early sign of Zenchiku's attempt to reinstate what he understood to be the original ritual function to performance. It should be noted that the idea that *sarugaku* performance could be used as an offering to the gods (when it was called *hōraku* 法楽), and that it could draw blessings from them, was widely held in medieval times, as many records attest.[336] One source of these beliefs was the *Great Preface*, or rather, the version of it found in the *kana* preface to the *Kokinwakashū* that we have mentioned before. Zenchiku invokes these passages again:

> Even in Chinese poetry "what is in the mind is called intent, what emerges in words is called poetry." And the Chinese preface to the *Kokinwakashū* also says, "*waka* makes its roots in the mind-ground, and its blossoms open in the forest of words." These are all aesthetic moods arising from the mind-ground and so singing containing these

335. KKS, *Go on sangyoku shū*, 149.
336. In *Sarugaku dangi* there is an account of a spirit requesting Zeami to offer ten plays at the Inari shrine to cure a man on the verge of death (ZZ, 305). There are other cases of such performance offerings, for example to the Hachimangū by the Komparu in 1459 (NGK, 476).

mental states should be understood to be *ongyoku*. Singing without mind is just sound (*on* 音) and there is no artistic effect (*kyoku*). Thus, there are in this school of training the levels of five voices. They are *shūgen, yūgen, renbo, aishō, rangyoku*. In addition there are added the three qualities of skin, flesh and bones. These need to be explained through oral transmission.[337]

It is clear here that Zenchiku understood old poetry to reflect certain privileged inner impulses, these impulses gave singing its vitality (in Zenchiku's use here, the *on-kyoku* polarity seems to draw on the Indian one of *shabda-mantra*, mere sound and spiritual utterance), and these impulses were classified in Zenchiku's received tradition.

Zeami's interpretations of *hi, niku* and *kotsu* (skin, flesh and bone), seem to have no connection at all with their appearance here in *Go on sangyoku shū*. It is not known why Zenchiku felt justified in converting them into aesthetic classifiers, nor why he called them the three "*kyoku*." Although he disappointingly relegates his discussion of them to oral transmission in this introduction, he relents in the final passage of the work:

Now, as I stated in the introduction, the three elements are to be orally transmitted and consequently are difficult to express in writing, but under pressure I will record their general import. The three devices are skin, flesh, and bone. Skin arises from flesh, flesh from bone, and bone from the five organs. The impurity of the five organs arises from the single water, and the single water's place of emergence is from the single thought of the Sanskrit graph 'A.' From what does this character arise? What indeed? This is inexplicable, simply inexplicable. We must hold within us that flavorless wisdom-water of this inexplicability and then sing. Then, directly, will the voice become the superb sound of bodhi that creates Buddhist ritual. Unless we understand this seed of impurity, the bone and the flesh will not be made just like skin, however much we may think so. Knowing the seed and bone, we hide it with the flesh; knowing the flesh, we hide it with the skin; and so it appears as truly attractive skin.[338]

This does not help us to understand why a certain passage of chanting is to be understood as having a "bone mood" and another a "skin mood," but it does advance the idea of the ritual purpose of *sarugaku*

337. KKS, *Go on sangyoku shū*, 149.
338. KKS, *Go on sangyoku shū*, 170–1.

performance.[339] A certain indefinable consciousness (flavorless wisdom-water) emerges via the organs through the voice in the sound of bodhi, transforming the performance in Buddhist ritual. It is striking that the same kind of structure of progressive manifestation (that might in Hindu discourse be described as proceeding from subtle to gross) is expressed in *Go on jittei* in terms of the poetic tradition alone, and then in the introduction to *Go on sangyoku shū* set within a discourse of *kami* and the sacred land (*wakoku*) (also derived from poetics). In this postscript, via the skin, flesh and bone theory, this same structure of the relations between mind and manifestation is presented in Buddhist terms: the primordial consciousness, the primary manifestation of the unborn, the mantra "A" (that is, the first graph of the Sanskrit syllabury), is progressively covered and expressed by the organs, then bone, then flesh and then skin. Viewed as an inner procedure that transforms performance into Buddhist ritual, consciousness of the seed and bone is covered over with flesh, this consciousness is hidden within the skin, and the result of all these awarenesses is an appearance that is truly charming or attractive.

As Thornhill has convincingly demonstrated, this last reading of the relations between the absolute and levels of manifestation mapped onto the mental events of an actor has its roots in medieval Shinto writings. This is particularly evident in the terminology of one of the appended sections of *Go on sangyoku shū* in which the concept of "flavorless wisdom-water" (*mumi chisui* 無味智水) is elaborated.[340] Thornhill explores this passage in some detail,[341] so I will only pick out points relevant to my argument here. Zenchiku starts by drawing a parallel from the widely known theory of five flavors (*gomi* 五味). People have individual preferences, so if a given flavor is too strong, some will like it and some not. Water, however, has no flavor, so it can be flavored to suit individual preferences. In performance, too, one should act lightly, without emphasizing a particular flavor, preserving the qualities of water: fresh moisture (*uruoi* 潤ひ—hence charm and vitality), and an easy free flow from element to element. Thornhill traces a network of relations between this passage and Buddhist and Chinese cosmological systems, and their syncretic appropriations by Shinto specialists. It is also interesting, however, to look at the immediate connections within Noh writings. The discussion of how to handle different tastes clearly links to

---

339. Zeami did make a connection between the five organs and singing, drawing on Buddhist musical theory, in *Kakyō*, but he made no mention in that context of bone, flesh and skin, going rather directly from the five organs to the breath, ZZ, 87.
340. KKS, *Go on sangyoku shū*, 181–3.
341. Thornhill, 1993, 156–164.

Zeami's treatment of the same problem in *Besshi kuden*. Zeami, needless to say, couches his answer in terms of *hana*—the flower, and associated botanical images. For Zeami the answer is to maintain a rich repertoire of styles:

> Moreover, the people have different preferences, and singing, dancing and mimicry are different from place to place, so one should not leave out any particular style. Thus it is like having the seeds for all the flowers throughout the year, from the plum blossom in early spring to the final flowering of the chrysanthemum in the fall. Every flower can then be produced in response to the wishes of people or the occasion. . . . The flower is the experience of novelty in the mind of the audience; that is why I wrote formerly in *Fūshikaden* that one can only know the flower that does not fade when one has achieved mastery of all roles and practiced them thoroughly.[342]

Zeami stresses mastery of all styles and continuous practice. The flower is in the mind of the audience. Zenchiku, however, places the solution firmly in the mind of the performer, in the achievement of a fundamental state of consciousness that can be perceived in an ineffable ease that pervades his performance.

Before we leave the topic of the flavorless wisdom water, we must note for the moment that Zenchiku for the first time in these works relates their ideas to the other theory about which he was writing at this time, i.e., the *rokurin ichiro* diagrams. When discussing the wisdom water (*chisui* 智水), Zenchiku describes the moistness of water as the virtue of the primal water (*issui no toku* 一水の徳) and asserts that this primal water is the basis for all things.[343] He then mentions the "volume on training in the art called *Rokurin ichiro*" and states that the *ichiro*, the single dewdrop, is the inception of the primal water (*issui no hajime* 一水の初).[344] Thornhill's suggestion that this should not be taken to be the "missing key" to the *rokurin ichiro* system is surely entirely appropriate; it was probably a connection that occurred to Zenchiku after the system was established. As will become progressively apparent, though, no such serendipitous connection would have seemed insignificant within Zenchiku's worldview.

We have seen Zenchiku focus on the theory of five voices as an expression of a typology of *kyokumi*—aesthetic and thematic content. We

342. ZZ, *Fūshikaden*, 56.
343. Evidently Zenchiku's *issui no toku* is closely connected to *suitoku* 水徳, translated by Mark Teeuwen as "the working of water," the name given in Watarai Shinto to their primary deity, the origin of life. (Teeuwen, 43–4).
344. Using Thornhill's translations of these terms in 1993, 156.

have seen also that the technical and pedagogical elements that were central to Zeami's own intentions for the theory were set aside so that the system could be put to the service of Zenchiku's own vision of *sarugaku* as ritual. A similar tendency can be observed in Zenchiku's appropriation of Zeami's theory of nine levels—*kyūi*—in *Kabuzuinōki*, the remaining typological work that we shall consider. The role of *kyūi* in this work is not so central, but we do see a swerve away from Zeami's original intentions. Again the material surrounding the typological clusters will be seen to fill out Zenchiku's own particular interests.

KABUZUINŌKI

Let us start by briefly considering Zeami's work: *Kyūi*. This is a widely admired work, but it is not generally noted that there is evidence that Zeami did not develop the system *ab initio*. Zenchiku says that, "in piling up the classes of grades, Zea[mi] cured (*iyashi okaretari*) the ninefold essential levels," which implies that a similar system of grading performances was already a part of *sarugaku* traditions, and that Zeami recast it to make it more effective.[345] Moreover, Zeami himself complained that "nowadays, there are actors in this way who start their study with the lowest three grades. That is not the correct order." It seems reasonable to assume that the concept of nine stages was a common element of *sarugaku* tradition.[346] This would explain the bipartite structure of *Kyūi*: the first section describes in descending order a series of nine qualitative levels of performance, supplying for each a name accompanied with a brief phrase derived from Zen traditions, followed by a few lines of explanation. (For the organization of the nine levels, see table 3.) The second section of Zeami's work tracks a new path through these levels, starting at the lower of the middle three (i.e. the sixth from the top), and progressing upwards step by step to the highest. This is Zeami's recommended training route. He notes that among actors who have achieved this highest level of mastery, some have then chosen on occasion to amuse themselves with the styles of the lowest three levels, but he condemns those who start with the lowest levels and attempt to rise from there to the top. Zeami's order of training is summed up in his formula: first the middle, then the upper, and last the lower.[347]

---

345. KKS, 265.
346. ZZ, 177.
347. ZZ, *Kyūi*, 174–7.

Table 3
Zeami's system of nine levels

Groups	Levels		*Translation*
上三花			Upper Three Flowers:
	妙花風	*myōkafū*	Absolute Flower
	寵深花風	*chōshinkafū*	Charming Profound Flower
	閑花風	*kankafū*	Still Flower
中三位			Middle Three Levels
	正花風	*shōkafū*	Correct Flower
	広精風	*kōshōfū*	Broad and Pure
	浅文風	*senmonfū*	Shallow and Patterned
下三位			Lower Three Levels
	強細風	*kōsaifū*	Strong and Detailed
	強麁風	*gōsofū*	Strong and Crude
	麁鉛風	*soenfū*	Crude and Leaden

Let us just consider what it is that the nine levels categorize. Insofar as they represent stages that actors pass through in training, they can be thought of as levels of performance ability or skill. The descent of the master actor to the lower ranges (which Zeami calls *kyakurai*—return from the heights), on the other hand, does not refer to a loss of ability, but rather an adoption of a lower style of performance. This probably does not seem a very important distinction, but when we look at the way Zeami describes the system, we find he slides from the one to the other. Actually this is one of a number of problems inherent in the term *kurai* as Zeami uses it generally; it is usually translated "level" (i.e. stage), but sometimes is more appropriately interpreted as "quality."[348] The problem is inherent in the concept of *michi qua* "the path." On a physical path, each place is passed through and left behind. In training, however, the skills that are acquired remain in the adept's repertoire. Thus, describing the middle levels, Zeami writes:

> If one starts training at the beginning and practices the two arts of song and dance, that is the style of "shallow decoration" (*senmonfū* 浅文風). If one keeps practicing this repeatedly, adding decoration to the shallow style going step by step along the path, one finds one has already arrived at the broad and fine style.[349]

348. See Nose Asaji's essay: "Zeami no geijutsuron ni okeru 'kurai,'" in *Nose Asaji chosakushū 5* (Kyoto: Shibunkaku Shuppan, 1983).
349. ZZ, *Kyūi*, 176.

The master of the broad and fine style would presumably never again perform in the style of shallow decoration—the grades at this point seem to clearly represent stages in the development of skills. When we look at the first section of *Kyūi*, however, the levels are clearly intended to represent styles of performance. The ambiguity in the system becomes apparent when we find Zeami distinguishing the lower levels as performed by inferior actors and as performed by experts "amusing themselves" below. Those who failed to achieve the broad and fine style, "sink to the lower three levels and ultimately fail to win acceptance in the world." Great masters, however, "even while performing at the lower three levels, create a spectacle of the highest order." The question of whether we are to regard the levels as marking the quality of performance or levels of skill remains. Such problematic aspects probably result from the attempt to combine a pre-existing theory of nine grades of performance with the system of orderly training that Zeami frequently refers to. Like the *go on* system, we can see in *Kyūi* that the same set of issues concerns Zeami—how to train actors so that they can give effective performances. Underlying the system that Zeami comes up with is his usual pattern delineating first a period of restricted practice leading to controlled mastery, followed by a period of freedom to perform at will. Zenchiku's use of the nine levels typically takes it into a new and unexpected dimension.

Like the other works we have considered, *Kabuzuinōki (Record of the Essence of Song and Dance)* has at its center a typological arrangement, a number of clusters of material arranged according to an overall plan (the reader may wish to refer to table 4).[350] Each group again brings together materials from Noh and an analysis from Zeami, treated as an aesthetic category, with a poetic category developed from works ascribed to Teika, and one or more *waka* and Chinese poems. This time the material from Noh consists of both the title of a Noh play and a corresponding aesthetic category taken from the *kyūi* (nine levels). These groups are organized into larger groups, depending upon whether the main roles are old men, warriors, women or "various" (almost all corresponding to "group 4" plays). It would seem that what is being arranged here are the major roles of plays, and that they are both being analyzed in terms of Zeami's performance levels and

---

350. In table 4, I use the unusual translations: "old body," "woman's body" for *rōtai* 老体, *nyotai* 女体 etc. to highlight the shift of meaning deriving from the polysemy of the graph 体, *tei* or *tai*. Zeami's use emphasizes the physical aspect (according to Steven T. Brown's reading in *Theatricalities of Power: The Cultural Politics of Noh* (Stanford: Stanford University Press, 2001), 23–9) whereas Zenchiku's reflects the taxonomic.

Table 4
Arrangement of *Kabuzuinōki*

1 Introduction

2 Clusters of material arranged in turn under each of four "bodies" (*tai* 体)

The Old Body (*rōtai*)

Play	level	description of sugata (combines material from Zeami and poetic works)	poem(s) (exemplary of sugata)
Oimatsu	myōkafū	Based on Zeami's Kakyō	"Ume no hana", from the play.
Aioimatsu	shōkafū	Pine (Sangoki) Distant white	Waka for each sugata plus a Chinese poem
Saigyō-zakura	kankafū		Poem from Teika's Shuigusō
etc.			

The Warrior Body (*guntai*)

Yorimasa	chōshinkafū	Outstanding style (batsugun from Sangoki) Indistinct (honokanaru)	Waka and Chinese poem from batsuguntai in Sangoki Waka from Sangoki (yūgen) Waka from the play
Michimori	shōkafū	Direct style (sonchoku)	Waka from sonchoku in Sangoki

etc.

The Female Body (*nyotai*) (similar groups of material following)

The Various Body (*zattai*) (similar groups of material following)

3 Discussion of plays which are *michi*, plays which are *zoku* (vulgar).

4 Assessment of famous actors (partly ascribed to report from Zeami and illustrated by arborial imagery and exemplary poems).

5 Analysis of two qualitative differences between plays: *yūgen* words and import but having *kyokumi*, and clever words and import, vulgar but stirring. Illustrated through poems.

6 Discussion of *kan* (still) and *ran* (mature) as highest performance levels.

7 Concluding remarks

8 Colophon

also into poetic categories. What then is the purpose of this elaborate typology? For the answer we have to consider the introduction to *Kabuzuinōki*.

Zenchiku opens with a preamble that distinguishes *sarugaku* from worldly entertainments, appropriating for it the same origins as were claimed for *kagura* 神楽, in the events in the age of the gods.[351] He describes the moment of the emergence of Amaterasu, the sun goddess

351. See chapter six, below.

from the cave of heaven, when brilliant light burst forth on a world of eternal darkness, and all the gods were overwhelmed with exhilaration. As well as being a standard myth of the rebirth of the sun, this could be viewed as a Shinto model of spiritual experience, describing the state of mind, moving from an endless night of darkness to a fullness of inner light, achieved by Shinto ritualists entering into union with the gods. Zenchiku relates this state of mind to performance:

> Therefore, if one dyes his mind in this spiritual state, and makes manifest the aesthetic flavor of profound emotion in song and dance, according to the formula "in the midst of mind, images, in the midst of images, mind," if one offers the performance to the gods and Buddha, then truly there can be no doubt that "wild words and fancy phrases, too, will become a cause for the worship of the Buddha and turning of the wheel of Dharma" and the "purpose behind the spiritual connection made through the softening of the light and mingling with the dust and the eight phases of the Buddha's life was to bless mankind."[352]

In other words, if one attains the state of mind of the moment of Amaterasu's emergence from the cave, then performance will be transformed into a spiritual act. This familiar message—the use of performance as an offering to the gods, and the role of the mental state of the performer in that use—is elaborated here in new terms. The phrase "in the midst of mind," etc., that is, *ichū no kei, keichū no i* 意中景、々中之意 (sic) derives from the Sung collection of poetic texts *Shirenyuxie* 詩人玉屑 (*Poets' Jeweled Scraps*), where it referred to a rich rhetorical style in which descriptions of external appearances and inner emotions were combined.[353] Zeami cited the phrase in various works, but he most clearly explained what it meant to him in *Goi*, "The Five Levels." This work outlines five types of artistic effect (or "styles" *fū*). One of these is *ifū* 意風, the effect from the mind:

> "Mind" means that the "artistic effect from the mind" is made within, appears without, and creates extremely subtle emotional impact. It highlights what is shallow and deep and is the root effect (*fūkon* 風根) of the many types of roles. This is the seed that causes the fascinating flower to appear. The work of poetic criticism *Yuxie* says: "In the mind are images, in images is mind."[354]

---

352. KKS, *Kabuzuinōki*, 121–2.
353. See headnote ZZ, 171.
354. ZZ, 170–1.

I 意, which I translate here as "mind," is often translated as intent, but it can signify a wider range of mental contents—thoughts, feelings, moods. Could it be that Zeami is actually talking about the same kind of thing that Zenchiku is interested in, a kind of ineffable quality in performance arising from an actor's maintenance of a special state of mind? Zeami certainly did believe that a sort of inner concentration held by the actor could radiate an attractive quality even when he was "doing nothing."[355] We should, however, consider the overall character of the work *Goi* to get a clearer idea of what he meant by the "effect from the mind." As in *Kyūi*, Zeami enumerates a series of elements from the highest, the extremely subtle, to the most elementary. The fifth level is the effect proceeding from the voice: "Even if the appearance is crude, the voice's emotion penetrates to the ears of the audience . . . giving rise to emotion." The successively finer levels include visual appearance, mind, spontaneous emotion and finally the highest, the presence of non-dual reality, *myō*. This is an analysis then of the sources of artistic emotion experienced by the audience: the sound of the actor's singing, the appearance of his dance and gesture, his ideas/mental state, his emotions, his spiritual transcendence of opposites. In this context it seems reasonable to understand the effect arising from the mind to be something close to Zenchiku's conception. Still, the phrase that the "the effect from the mind is made within," has led scholars to conclude that Zeami is describing an actor visualizing or imagining a particular effect and then presenting it to the audience.[356] Thus in singing and dancing the actor is merely following the rules laid out in his training, but in *ifū* he actually visualizes his performance in a way that emphasizes what is significant ("highlights what is shallow and deep"). This is probably achieved by identifying with the role, which, after all, is the fundamental source of acting ("the root effect"). This reading accords with Zeami's other citations of the "images in the mind" formula.[357]

Zenchiku's uses of the "images in the mind" formula, however, are always associated with the relation between absolute reality experienced within (in Buddhist terms, the Buddha Nature) and the aesthetic quality perceived from without. For example, in *Bunshōbon*, he uses the phrase to symbolize the playful emergence of performance from the void, likening it

355. See ZZ, *Kakyō*, 100–101.
356. See the headnotes to the passage in ZZ, 170–1.
357. ZZ, 113, 165. Paul Atkins discusses these and other passages citing *"ichū no kei, keichū no i"* in his Ph D dissertation, *The Noh Plays of Komparu Zenchiku* (Stanford University, 1999), 52–60, where he relates it to Zenchiku's use of imagery in his plays (see also his *Revealed Identity: The Noh Plays of Komparu Zenchiku* (Ann Arbor: Center for Japanese Studies, University of Michigan, 2006), 46-52.

to the moon floating on the water, or the flower sending out its fragrance.[358] These are both images of the external manifestation of spiritual reality. For Zenchiku, it seems, the phrase meant: when inwardly the actor experiences the absolute, then it is experienced externally in the form of aesthetic quality.

Returning to the passage cited above from Zenchiku's preamble to *Kabuzuinōki*, we see that he cites two other gnomic phrases. The first is that "wild words and fancy phrases too will become a cause for the worship of the Buddha and turning of the wheel of Dharma." This is of course an allusion to the famous statement of Bai Juyi 白居易, which had been converted by Heian poets into a justification for poetic activity. To the Japanese the statement was read as a declaration that poetry could, with the appropriate seriousness of intent, be transformed into spiritual activity. Zenchiku as we have seen saw acting as an extension of poetry. Thus the appropriate intent could transform acting too.[359] The third quotation, "[the] purpose behind the spiritual connection made through the softening of the light and mingling with the dust and the eight phases of the Buddha's life was to bless mankind," is a slightly garbled version of a passage from the *Moho zhiguan* 摩訶止観: "The softening of the light and mingling in the dust [of the Buddha] was the beginning of his establishment of a spiritual connection with living beings, and his showing the eight appearances and achieving buddhahood was the end of his blessing of living beings." This again is a reference to the relationship between the absolute and its manifestation. The Buddha never actually needed to be born and gain enlightenment, but he simply pretended to do so to bless living beings (i.e. he was "acting"). Zenchiku's version of the passage emphasizes the purpose of the Buddha's appearance, to bless living beings. The implication is that performance too blesses the world when the actor is rooted in the highest spiritual awareness. That the aim of performance was to bring spiritual blessings to the audience was an idea associated with the *Okina* ritual pieces, which Zenchiku developed further in *Meishukushū*.

There is just one final aspect of Zenchiku's vision of the role of the actor's state of mind in performance that I wish to draw out from his preamble to the typology of *Kabuzuinōki*. What is the purpose of the typology itself? Zenchiku proceeds by giving a number of arguments why the same aesthetic moods must inform poetry, dance, and song. We have seen his reading of the *Great Preface* by which he argued that the same

---

358. KKS, *Bunshōbon*, 258.
359. We shall consider the use of Bai Juyi's formula more closely in chapter five.

impulse gives rise to poetry, singing, gesticulating and treading. He also refers to the idea that poetry was formless dance, and dance formless poetry. He continues:

> Considering the matter deeply, the same aesthetic flavor (*kyokumi*) is present in both poetry and dance. Awakened to the significance of this, one who wishes to understand and distinguish its levels must honor the way of poetry. Not that he should attempt to compose poetry beyond his abilities, rather that he should dye his mind in old poems (*kouta*). Then if he chants passages, dances and sings, surely the ultimate profound emotion will be present.[360]

It seems then that the purpose of the clusters of material associated with the different plays (or main roles) in the body of the work is no longer simply to demonstrate the coincidence of poetic and *sarugaku* aesthetics, but rather to provide a practical key of poems corresponding to major plays in the repertoire. The performer of any of these roles could then "dye his mind" (*kokoro o somu*) in the mood of the poems before performing. With one's mind in the right state, one's performance would be transformed and fulfill its higher purpose.

To anyone familiar with Teika's writings on poetics, and especially the re-reading of Teika's tradition in the Muromachi period, Zenchiku's theory here sounds familiar. The statement that one should dye his mind in old poems so that when one performs the ultimate emotion is sure to be present, recalls the dictum of Teika as invoked by Shōtetsu: "Dyeing his mind in the old poetic styles and learning his diction from the great poets of the past, what person could fail to compose poetry?"[361] Did Shōtetsu take Teika's remarks to mean that one should constantly dwell on poetry from Heian imperial collections? It is possible, for in his pupil Shinkei's remarks on the relationship between *waka* and *renga*, we find that a "former master" said "above all one should hold outstanding poems in one's breast, and strive to contain their image in every verse one composes."[362] We do not know the details of Zenchiku's relationship with Shōtetsu, but if, as generally thought, he was his poetic pupil, then we have here two of Shōtetsu's students applying a certain idea of *waka* practice to their own literary arts. Actually, it will be seen from table 4 that Zenchiku lists Chinese verses as well as *waka* as expressions of moods in which to dye the mind for particular performances. This again reverberates with the sentence Shinkei adds to the

360. KKS, *Kabuzuinōki*, 122.
361. In *Eiga taigai*, Hisamatsu and Nishio, 115.
362. In *Sasamegoto*, Kidō and Imoto, 132.

one above: "And it should not only be *waka*; all day you should inwardly recite good Chinese poems." There are a number of similarities between Shinkei's thought and Zenchiku's, but it is striking here that if Zenchiku developed his idea that inner states, manifest in old poems, should be used to transform performance, from Shōtetsu's poetics, then this points back to another chain of creative misreading. Teika himself, as is well known, was actually concerned that poets should derive their diction (*kotoba*) from old poetry, and stressed that they should find new conceptions (*kokoro*) for their own poems.

The nine levels in the clusters of material centered on plays seem to fulfill the role of aesthetic flavors, as did the five voices in other works; still their function is obscure. They do not correspond in any way to the poetic categories, for if we line up a group of plays belonging to the same level they do not have the same poetic category. In Zeami's theory we noticed an ambiguity over whether the levels should be applied to particular performances (the quality of their style) or to the people who perform them (the degree of their skill). Zenchiku's application of them to the plays themselves takes them into a new area. If we consider how Zenchiku actually produced this work, we can see the concrete quality of his methods. It seems clear that he sat down with the work *Sangoki*, with its poetic types, explanations, and lists of exemplary Japanese and Chinese poems, and with a copy of the nine levels, and with a list of plays, and then juggled them around to create his own combinations. It will readily be seen that this process was a kind of exploration, a way to discover and establish new connections. At the same time it flattened out contingencies in the systems he was dealing with. Thus it mattered less that the nine levels were not really intended to categorize plays. Indeed, one striking problem of Zenchiku's idea of *kyokumi*, once it becomes extended to whole plays, is that poetic categories, insofar as they represented single mental flavors, could not have embraced the varying of moods that occurs through individual Noh plays, which of course unfold over relatively extended periods of time. It is clearly the shifting emotions in such plays as *Sumidagawa* 隅田川 (which takes us through bullying and mockery, through playful allusion to the *Azuma kudari* 東下り section of *Ise monogatari*, to the sadness of the death of a loved one/child, and finally to a mystic meeting and spiritual acceptance) that constitute their compelling interest. To regard plays as having single aesthetic moods is to ignore their dramatic force.

CONCLUSION

In the theories of the five voices and the nine levels that Zeami developed we can see his continuous concern with the training of actors to give performances that impact on the emotions of audiences. His various discussions of training generally outline a number of stages of progressively more complex skills leading to a skill level from which the actor could freely act as he wished, putting aside the rules to which he had earlier to conform. Zeami's aim was always to generate responses in audiences, but he certainly placed these in a hierarchy, corresponding to the sophistication and knowledge of the audiences on the one hand, and the refinement and depth of the aesthetic communicated on the other. In Zenchiku's typologies, however, the surrounding material makes it clear that his interest in the audience is slight. He sees performance as a kind of impersonal expression of deep mental forces that find their way into the forms of song and dance, imbuing them with spiritual powers, bringing blessings to the world and pleasing the gods. Ultimately Zenchiku's focus is the mental state of the actor himself.

Zenchiku, invoking Zeami's analyses, detaches them from their contexts, and puts them to quite different tasks. We can see this in two different ways. Was it that Zenchiku believed Zeami's works to be, like traditional poetic secret works, essentially mysterious objects demanding and available for radical interpretation, obscure signs through which he could rediscover an inner and higher science of performance? Or was it that Zenchiku, needing to establish his position in a progressively chaotic age, generated a theory of performance that could convince a class of patrons with a smattering of poetic and spiritual knowledge that he was a bearer of a spiritual art form, a possessor of spiritual secrets? Probably both are true.

Two characteristics of the works we have looked at here lead us into the other set of works on which he was working at this time, which we will investigate in the next chapter. One is Zenchiku's repeated reference to the question of manifestation, which Zenchiku saw in terms of deep, impersonal forces, acting through the universe and man to emerge in form, in human behavior, or in other external phenomena. This image lies at the root of the *rokurin ichiro* system, which attempts to identify the processes of cosmic manifestation and the structures of performance traditions. The second is Zenchiku's habit of saying the same thing through formulations deriving from quite different traditions: Shinto, Buddhist, poetic, and *sarugaku*. This mode of concatenating traditions and reading them as equally reflecting universal truths was of course characteristic of

Zenchiku's time and will be explored in the next chapter as a primary context for his development of the *rokurin ichiro* works.

5 Universality
The Theory of Six Circles, One Dewdrop

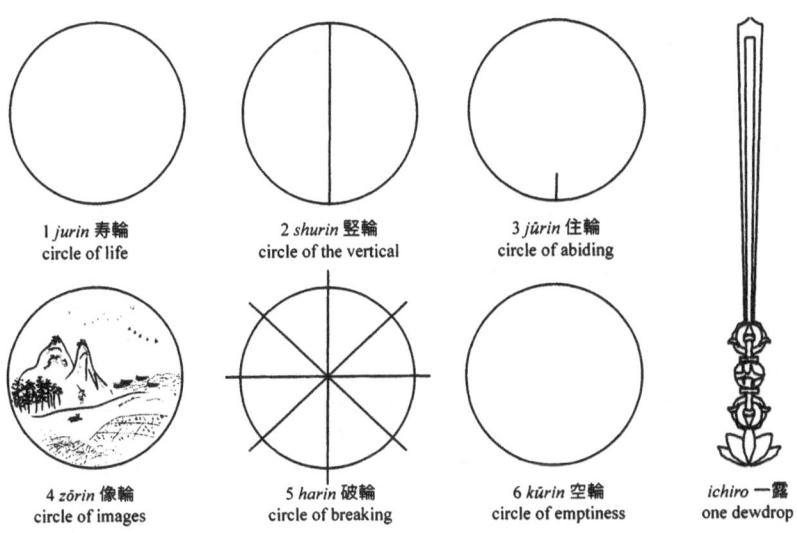

1 *jurin* 寿輪
circle of life

2 *shurin* 竪輪
circle of the vertical

3 *jūrin* 住輪
circle of abiding

4 *zōrin* 像輪
circle of images

5 *harin* 破輪
circle of breaking

6 *kūrin* 空輪
circle of emptiness

ichiro 一露
one dewdrop

Illustration 1: Zenchiku's six circles and one dewdrop diagrams

Zenchiku is primarily associated with the diagrams he called *rokurin ichiro* (six circles and one dewdrop—see illustration 1). Of these, the six circles themselves describe a circular progress, from an empty circle through four increasingly complex circles, to a sixth again empty circle. The "dewdrop," on the other hand, takes the form of a sword, similar to those found in Buddhist iconography, and refers to a quality that penetrates the six circles. In a series of works, Zenchiku presents these diagrams accompanied by cryptic passages of text. These "commentaries" interpret the diagrams in terms of different areas of knowledge, including *sarugaku*, Shinto accounts of the origins of the universe, Buddhist theories of manifestation and Chinese theories of cosmic forces. They include material deriving from readings of the diagrams contributed by two eminent thinkers, Shigyoku, abbot of the ordination hall at Tōdaiji, and Ichijō Kanera, the leading Fujiwara intellectual of his generation. The overall project, however, is completely Zenchiku's. The mysterious combination of materials and the connection with figures of such elevated social position have drawn the attention of scholars for many years, resulting in some detailed analyses, particularly of the external contributions. A sense remains, however, that the project that gave rise to these works has not been adequately described or explained. The main purpose of this chapter will be to fill this gap. We will start by delineating contexts for the *rokurin ichiro* project and proceed to certain fundamental questions: where did the diagrams come from, to what use did Zenchiku put them, why did he believe them appropriate for that use, how successful was the project, and what does the project tell us about how Zenchiku visualized his *michi*?

Medieval discourse characteristically employs a number of universalizing rhetorical modes that assume commonality across traditions. Both Zeami and Zenchiku participated in such modes, but in different ways, drawing on different pretexts. Zeami borrowed ideas from other *michi* to articulate, enrich and define his own. Zenchiku, particularly in the *rokurin ichiro* works, also adopted universalizing textual techniques to build relations with other traditions, techniques that were basically legitimatory and hermeneutic in character. Related to these separate intellectual modes, we should note a further difference between the writings of the two men. Whereas Zeami generally had a settled idea of what it is he wanted to say, and sought the means to express it, Zenchiku was typically in search of new as yet unclear meanings—that is, his writings are marked by an exploratory spirit. We can see this in the repeated combinations and restatements of the typological works we considered in chapter four and it is plainly evident in the researches recorded in *Meishukushū*, as we shall see in chapter six. It is even more evident in the *rokurin ichiro* works, which are the product of repeated searches for meaning, repeated attempts to uncover the deep truths that Zenchiku felt must lie behind his inherited traditions. Essentially, Zeami wrote to express, Zenchiku wrote to discover. Scholars have not always been clear about this, assuming rather that the *rokurin ichiro* works express settled ideas, and so their inquiries have tended to focus on what precisely those ideas were, which they have then found impossible to answer convincingly.[363] In our investigation I shall both trace the

---

363. Scholars actually start from the standpoint that Zenchiku designed the *rokurin ichiro* series to express essential ideas he received from Zeami. Konishi sees the primary ideas as the contrast between the essential and temporary flower (*shōka* 性花 and *yōka* 用花), and the "return from the heights" (*kyakurai*) (Konishi, 1961): 214–240), Itō sees them to be Zeami's analysis of delight in performance: *myō* (thought transcendence), *hana* (charm) and *omoshiro*

universalizing traditions in which the *rokurin ichiro* works participated, and highlight the shifts in their interpretation and how they were developed.

Rhetorical traditions help us to understand the motives behind the *rokurin ichiro* texts, but we also need to investigate the origin of the diagrams themselves. It has generally been assumed that Zenchiku constructed the diagrams himself to express certain basic ideas in *sarugaku* tradition. I will use a general discussion of authority in medieval ideas as well as Zenchiku's own words to argue my view that he did not devise the diagrams himself, but borrowed them from elsewhere. I shall suggest likely sources for them. An inspection of Zenchiku's earliest interpretations shows that he always understood them to be interpretable in cosmic as well as *sarugaku* terms. I shall argue that their initial significance in Zenchiku's mind, wherever they came from, was in fact as an expression of cosmogonic stages. That Zenchiku should have felt it appropriate to apply cosmological structures to his own tradition shall be seen to make sense when we consider the ways in which he characterized *sarugaku* and consider similar uses of cosmological theories in Shinto writings.

If the diagrams expressed stages in cosmic manifestation, then the hitherto unexplained fact that Shigyoku and Ichijō Kanera interpreted them in terms of cosmological processes described in Buddhist and Neo-Confucian works, becomes comprehensible, especially against the background of the theory of the "unity of the three creeds." The cosmological interpretations are merely parallel descriptions of the same processes in different fields. The other side of the interpretation of the diagrams is Zenchiku's application of them to *sarugaku*. What particular area of *sarugaku* did he expect the diagrams to describe? The answer can be seen in Zenchiku's very earliest readings. By a terminological analysis I shall demonstrate that Zenchiku from the start read the diagrams in terms of the received prescription of the life path of the *sarugaku* actor (*shūdō* 習道). The *rokurin ichiro* system then amounts in its early applications to the

---

(conscious awareness of delight), represented in the first three circles (KZK, 162–9), Thornhill refers to three subjective principles and three concrete styles (Thornhill, 1993, 55–6). The fact that the disagreement is so wide indicates the weakness of the primary assumption. In any case, the fundamental problem with these theories is that Zenchiku hardly mentioned any of these elements in the primary work, *Rokurin ichiro no ki!* Further problems are the fact that Itō's terms do not appear in any of the *rokurin ichiro* works at all, and Thornhill's do not seem to correspond to anything in Zeami's works. Both Konishi and Thornhill read back material found in later *rokurin ichiro* works into the primary conception, ignoring the renegotiation seen in the works. If Zenchiku designed the diagrams to express Zeami's ideas, first, why did he not say what those ideas were plainly, up front; second, why did he interpret them in terms of cosmic theories of manifestation; and third, why did he repeatedly change his mind about what the diagrams meant in relation to *sarugaku*?

search for a parallel between the unfolding of the universe and the unfolding of a performer's individual life.

I believe the perception of this parallel to have been Zenchiku's primary intuition when he embarked on the *rokurin ichiro* project. It is the major theme of the first and second works of the series (*Rokurin ichiro no ki* and *Rokurin ichiro no kichū* 六輪一露之記注 (referred to hereafter as *Kichū*)), both of which present material collected and refined over more than a decade. It is clear, however, that Zenchiku, in the later section of this second work, had begun to look for new ways to conceive of and apply the diagrams. It is difficult to determine whether this reflects a loss of interest in the primary approach or a fundamental shift in his thought. The new direction (or lack of direction) characterizes subsequent *rokurin ichiro* works. A full account of these later readings is beyond the scope of this chapter, but one reappearance in them of the primary theme deserves our notice. Zenchiku attempted in the later readings to integrate into his system various ideas associated with Zeami, particularly through his own rereading of them in the typological works. Among these was the theory of nine levels, in which Zeami himself had combined the ranking of qualities in performance with the tradition of stages in training and performance. Zenchiku's absorption of this theory into the *rokurin ichiro* diagrams conflicted with his first reading of them. This incompatibility between the two models of the path points to a deeper incompatibility between Zenchiku's Shinto-based values and Zeami's vision of *sarugaku*, which conformed to Buddhist ideas of the path. We shall close with a consideration of the inherent values expressed within the *rokurin ichiro* diagrams.

In general, then, the aim of this chapter will be to ask about the purposes and origins of Zenchiku's *rokurin ichiro* writings and at the same time to explore the intellectual processes at work in them. Of these the most striking is the borrowing of ideas from quite different traditions, traditions that on the surface appear to have little in common. Why did Zenchiku think that this borrowing could generate or uncover new truths concerning his own field? We shall approach this question by looking more generally at medieval intellectual and textual traditions. These will both make Zenchiku's borrowing more comprehensible in this particular case, and also highlight an important dimension of medieval thought. We shall start, then, by considering what promises to be a useful theoretical approach to such interdisciplinary cross-fertilization, that is Konishi's theory of universality in *michi*.

UNIVERSALITY AND *MICHI*

Zeami's reinterpretations of formulae from other traditions are widely admired. Zenchiku's borrowings are more difficult, for they sometimes combine material that seems quite unrelated. To what extent are these borrowings from other fields to be explained by the belief in the "universality" of *michi*?

Konishi's account of universality (*fuhensei* 普遍性) in *michi* is complex:

> *Michi* are extremely faithful to traditional forms, and yet they give no impression of being bound by those forms. In other words, though the fields of activity may be different, masters who in their own spheres achieve a high level, despite the fact that they might know absolutely nothing about other disciplines, share the state of mind at which they have arrived. That is, the specialization or particularization of *michi*, which makes it appear closed off, surely possesses at the highest level a universal or general character which is shared by all *michi*.[364]

This passage has an impenetrable character; the second and third sentences introduce themselves ("in other words," "that is") as clarifications, but in each case there is a shift of meaning. The first sentence seems to contrast two aspects of *michi*—their discrete spheres of action and their common ability to lead the practitioner from restricted forms to freedom in practice. In the context of the discussion of rigid training that precedes this passage, it seems that what connects the particular methods and the resulting freedom in *michi* must be repetitious training, for constraints become naturalized through repetition. Konishi goes on, however, to redefine the freedom from constraint as a "state of mind." This shifts the significance of "universality" away from practice to a general "*michi*" awareness or knowledge. Again we have to guess at the nature of this state of mind/knowledge. Is Konishi thinking of something along the lines of Nose Asaji's view, that "penetration to the highest level in a single (traditional Japanese) art fosters the power to grasp at a glance the inner significance of all other arts?"[365] When Nose said this, he was talking of Japanese *michi* pursued in his own day. His belief seems a rather modern conceit, not likely to be acceptable to medieval practitioners in general; one cannot imagine a Muromachi master horseman, for example, claiming to be able to grasp the

---

364. Konishi, 1986, 156. (I have tried in my English to match the rather loose structure of the Japanese. For a different translation, see Konishi, 1991, 148).
365. See "Nōgaku to gadō," in *Nose Asaji chosakushū 5* (Kyoto, Shibunkaku Shuppan, 1984): 475.

significance of *waka* "at a glance." Konishi, however, seems to visualize a universality that goes beyond the sphere of "arts." In the last sentence, he suggests that something in *michi* makes the awareness arrived at universally relevant. But it is not clear where this something is to be found.

In another passage Konishi says that the same "state of mind" achieved by masters of *michi* was understood by medieval thinkers as penetration to *ōgi*, profound hidden knowledge.[366] Konishi believes this *ōgi* was of importance to everyone, even those not practicing any *michi*, as the following passages make clear:

> A master practitioner, even in an art as humble as tree climbing, achieved the same state realized by masters in other *michi*. His words therefore contained lessons that could become standards for the world at large.[367]

> This universality is extremely important in *michi*, for unless the specialization in the particular leads to a penetration to universal truth it is not a genuine *michi*.[368]

The idea that *michi* leads to universal truth is perhaps familiar to us from modern descriptions of Japanese arts—one is reminded of Eugen Herrigel's *Zen in the Art of Archery*, where progress was marked by mystical breakthroughs.[369] But such descriptions are very much the product of their time and are no guide to the medieval period.[370] Konishi neither cites evidence for his perception of universality from medieval practitioners themselves nor does he define it clearly, which is a pity, as it is a central feature of his theory. He does, however, describe the intellectual roots in which he believes it to be founded, that is, the idea that each individual phenomenon contains within it all phenomena, and the related proposition that the complete mastery of a single practice is equivalent to the mastery of all. Konishi calls this the "logic of 'one is many and many is one,'" and sees it flowing from Tendai Buddhism and Zen, at work in Dōgen's instructions

---

366. Konishi reports a medieval expectation that "penetration to the root of one's own *michi* would lead to the attainment of the common profound hidden knowledge (*ōgi*) of other *michi*." Konishi, 1986, 165.

367. Konishi, *Chūsei no bungei: "michi" to iu rinen* (Kōdansha, 1997), 18. Konishi here alludes to the celebrated passage in *Tsurezuregusa* (section 109) in which a tree climber's advice on training "accords with the precepts of the sages." We will give an alternative interpretation of this and similar passages below.

368. Konishi, 1986, 156.

369. Eugen Herrigel, *Zen in the Art of Archery*, trans., R. F. C. Hull (London: Routledge and Kegan Paul, 1953).

370. As demonstrated in Yamada Shōji, "The Myth of Zen in the Art of Archery," *Japanese Journal of Religious Studies*, 28/1–2, 2001, 1–30.

to monks to concentrate their efforts on a single practice.[371] "Seeing a world in a grain of sand," however, is the essential characteristic of mystical experience and likely to be a part of any spiritual training, but the suggestion that medieval *michi* were felt to lead to a universal goal needs to be balanced against the overwhelming authority in the period of Buddhism and *waka*. As we shall see, poetry did argue an equivalence to Buddhism; but while we see repeated use of terminology and ideas drawn from these two paths in Zeami and Zenchiku's writings, there is little sign that these two actors considered their achievements as masters to endow them with a universal wisdom of any kind, especially not equivalent to that of a Buddhist saint or *waka* poet.[372]

Konishi's concept of universality does have explanatory force in relation to certain aspects of Zeami's thought: his formulaic borrowings and his use of Buddhist terms for stages in the actor's career. However, it seems that Zeami simply borrowed the structure of the Buddhist path, and not that he believed in any hidden identity.[373] In general, Zeami's borrowings do not need beliefs to explain them. We have seen a typical example (in chapter four) in Zeami's use of the elements of human anatomy to characterize types of performance:

> In this art there are skin, flesh and bone [*hi*, *niku* and *kotsu*]. These qualities are never all present together. In calligraphy, too, there is a tradition that, apart from the work of the great master [Kūkai], these three cannot be present together. Now if we were to indicate the location of skin, flesh and bone in this art, we would have to name the evidence of inherent skill . . . bone, . . . and call the evidence of complete training in performance flesh, . . . the development of this quality to an extreme of elegant beauty . . . we must term skin.[374]

This draws on passages from works on *waka*, which in turn borrow from discussions of calligraphy.[375] The basic idea in each of these applications of the formula, however, is that the qualities of artistic products reflect the characteristics of the artists who produced them—their talent, their

---

371. Konishi, 1986, 164–5.
372. Both expressed considerable deference towards *waka*, clearly feeling unqualified to understand it (see discussion in Minemura, 94–5). As we have seen, Zeami felt his involvement in *sarugaku* to be an obstacle to his spiritual progress.
373. We have seen examples in chapter three. Zeami adopted the vocabulary of the Buddhist path for its structures (specific stages, a moment of primary completion, the need for continuous practice, the appropriate relation between the novice and the master, the adoption of vulgar methods after rising to the heights, etc.) not its Buddhist implications. For example the term *tokuhō* ("gaining the Dharma") simply signified the mastery of basic techniques.
374. ZZ, *Shikadō*, 116.
375. Minemura, 94–100.

technical training, their years of practice and refinement. If such a relationship existed in calligraphy, it seems reasonable to look for it in poetry or performance art. We do not need to call on a mysterious theory of universality to explain it.

On the other hand, Konishi's "universality" is not extreme enough to account for Zenchiku's method in the *rokurin ichiro* works, for there the parallels are between human and non-human processes. In my view both these sets of borrowings and cross-fertilizations across disciplines were not so much driven by ideals and beliefs, as Konishi supposes, but rather resulted from their authors' participations in widespread rhetorical practices. These "universalizing" styles of reasoning may have implied certain beliefs, but those beliefs remained unstated and were, in my view, secondary.

What were these rhetorical traditions? For Zeami I would like to highlight two patterns: the first a series of clichéd parallels between *waka* and Buddhism, and the second a cross-*michi* fertilization developed when court and plebian traditions appeared to have much in common, as the remains of an older culture. For Zenchiku's writings, I would add two more pretexts—one being discussions of the unity of the three creeds brought by Zen masters from China, and the other related textual practices developed by Shinto families and others trying to construct a Japanese worldview in the face of Buddhist hegemony.

THE GENEALOGY OF UNIVERSALITY

Waka was not one of the Heian *shodō* (諸道), as it was not imported from mainland culture,[376] but by the Kamakura period it had become established as the most prestigious of pursuits.[377] Of particular importance in the prestige accorded to *waka* were arguments that characterized it as a Japanese equivalent to Buddhism. These arguments first appeared in connection with the Tang poet Bai Juyi's characterization of poetry as *kyōgen kigo* 狂言綺語—wild words and specious phrases.[378] As Bai Juyi devoted himself to Buddhist practice in later life, he felt the pursuit of poetry to be a perturbation that he should eschew. Referring to the fourth and fifth abstinences enjoined on all Buddhists (*gokai* 五戒), he claimed to have given up drunkenness (the fifth) but not "false words" (the fourth, i.e. *musāvādā*).[379] To his dedications of the Loyang anthology to the Hsiangshan temple in Soochow in 839, he appended the following wish:

376. Ishiguro, 1993, 25.
377. Pandey, 39.
378. Ishiguro Kichijirō, *Chūsei engeki no shosō* (Ōfūsha, 1983), 118.
379. Arthur Waley, *The Life and Times of Po Chü-i, 772–846* (London: Allen and Unwin, 1949), 207. Few Japanese seem to have worried about the fifth abstinence.

that the worldly writings of this life, the error of 'wild words and specious phrases,' should be transformed into a karmic cause in future lives for praising the Buddha vehicle, a karmic circumstance for turning the wheel of the law.[380]

The evident meaning of Bai Juyi's passage was that he hoped that the evil karma of writing sinful words in this life should turn into karmic conditions that would cause him in future lives to use words appropriately, that is, for praising the Buddha vehicle and preaching the Law.[381] This prayer was known to the Japanese through its presence in *Hakushi monjū* and a slightly different version anthologized and translated in *Wakan rōeishū*. It seems that for some time poetry, Japanese or Chinese, that was not specifically Buddhist, along with fictional and other writings, was felt to be an obstacle on the Buddhist path.[382] But the idea of transformation, which Bai Juyi in his prayer applied to his own karma, was eventually taken to apply to the poet or even the art of poetry itself. By the thirteenth century

380. Using the version found in *Hakushi monjū* 白氏文集, cited in Morohashi's *Dai kanwa jiten*, entry for *kyōgen kigo*. "Wild words and specious phrases" is Etsuko Terasaki's translation for *kyōgen kigo* taken from "'Wild Words and Specious Phrases': *Kyogen kigo* in the Noh Play *Jinen Koji*," *HJAS* 49.2 (December 1989): 519–552. The phrase *kyōgen kigo* was a combination of a Taoist term for trivial talk (*kyōgen*) and a Buddhist term for decorative speech that avoids the truth (*kigo*) (Pandey, 10–11).
381. Based on the parallelism in the passage (contrasting "this life" and "future ages") and the Buddhist significance of two characters (*yuán* 縁 and *yin* 因, indicating indirect and direct karmic causes) as well as the general plausibility of this reading. Note that the Japanese equivalent of the passage in *Wakan rōeishū* 和漢朗詠集: (*negawaku wa konjō sezoku no monji no gō kyōgen kigyo no ayamari o mote kaeshite tōrai seze sanbutsujō no in tenbōrin no en to semu*, Ōsone Shōsuke and Horiuchi Hideaki, eds., *Wakan rōeishū (Shinchō Nihon koten shūsei 61)* (Shinchōsha, 1983): 222), fits my reading well, for the subject "*gō*" means action creating karmic consequences, and it is this that is to be transformed into "*in*" and "*en*" karmic manifestations in future lives. This could only make sense if it were the same reincarnating person who carried out the karma and experienced its effects. Other scholarly translations of the passage generally seem to me misleading. Arthur Waley has the poems themselves being transformed into praises in future ages: "May the worldly writings of my present incarnation, all the wanton talk and fine phrases, be changed into a hymn of praise that shall glorify the doctrines of the Buddha in age on age to come, and cause the Wheel of Law forever to turn" (1949, 194). This omits *yin* altogether. A compromise position is found (twice) in *Principles of Classical Japanese Literature*: "I have long cherished one desire, that my deeds on this earth and the faults occasioned by my wild words and fancy language will be transformed, for worlds to come, into a factor extolling the Law and a link to the preaching of the Buddha's Word." (Earl Miner, 1985, 156 and 192.) This matches other translations, for example, Herbert Plutschow's: "May the worldly writings of my present life, with all their excessive words and ornate phrases, serve in future ages as the inspiration of hymns of praise extolling the Buddha's teachings, and turn the Wheel of the Law forever" (in "Is Poetry a Sin?— *Honjisuijaku* and Buddhism versus Poetry," *Oriens Extremus* 25.2 (1978): 208), which converts the explicit Buddhist terms *yuán* and *yin*, direct and indirect karmic causes, into "inspiration." The role of *kyōgen kigo* in Japanese thought is of course well-tramped ground; prominent in English are Plutschow 1978, mentioned above, William R. Lafleur, *Karma of Words: Buddhism and the Literary Arts in Medieval Japan* (Berkeley: University of California Press, 1983), chapter one, and Pandey, 9–55.
382. Ōsone and Horiuchi, 222.

the phrase *kyōgen kigo* was regularly used as a signal that the speaker was about to argue that (secular) poetry could have spiritual benefits. One way to such a conclusion was to see poetry as a kind of expedient means.[383] Another argument appealed to the principle of non-dualism.[384]

In these ways the term *kyōgen kigo* came to signify both the sinfulness of poetry and its transformative potential. The arguments tended early on to operate more as justifications of, or apologetics for, poetry. There were assertions that *waka* could act as a Japanese equivalent to *dhāraṇī*, for spiritual truths could be as well expressed in Japanese as Sanskrit. Fujiwara Shunzei famously described a parallel between Buddhism (its transmission, scripture and meditation) and poetry (the tradition, the imperial collections and its training). This is another case where no strong claims were made.[385] By Zenchiku's time, however, some poets had read back into these earlier arguments a more fundamental identity. Shinkei, for example, claimed that "the way of poetry has always been the *dhāraṇī* of" Japan[386] and attributed a fantastic description of Shunzei's quasi-spiritual absorption in poetry, what Brower and Miner commenting on the passage term a "mystic fusion of the poet and his materials," to Fujiwara Teika.[387] By this time, of course, Teika himself had been converted into a deity. The term *kyōgen kigo*, however, continued to be used primarily as an argument against poetry's

---

383. As in *Shasekishū* (1279–1283): "*Waka* is included among 'wild words and specious phrases.' . . . But if it reports the principle of the Buddha's teachings, is accompanied with the awareness of impermanence, weakens worldly connections and vulgar thoughts, forgets name, fame, passion and clinging, seeing the leaves in the wind, understanding the emptiness of the worldly, singing of snow and moon, awakening us to the pure principle in the heart, then it can act as a means to introduce us to the Buddhist path and to awaken us to the Dharma-gate." Watanabe Tsunaya, *Shasekishū (Nihon koten bungaku taikei 85)* (Iwanami Shoten, 1966), 220.
384. As in the preface to *Jikkinshō* (1252): "'all things are forms of ultimate reality' (*shobō jissō* 諸法実相), so the so-called "entertainment of crazy words and specious phrases" is, contrary to normal expectation, a "karmic connection to the praise of the Buddha vehicle." Cited in Ishiguro, 1983, 119.
385. In *Koraifūteishō* 古来風躰抄, in Hayashiya Tatsusaburō ed., *Kodai chūsei geijutsuron (Nihon shisō taikei 23)* (Iwanami Shoten, 1973), 262–3. For a detailed discussion of the passage in question, see chapter four of Lafleur, 1983.
386. *Sasamegoto*, in Kidō and Imoto, 183.
387. "Very late at night he would sit by his bed in front of an oil lamp so dim that it was difficult to tell whether it was burning or not, and with a tattered court robe thrown over his shoulders and an old court cap pulled down to his ears, he would lean on an arm-rest, hugging a wooden brazier for warmth, while he recited verse to himself in an undertone. Deep into the night when everyone else was asleep he would sit there bent over, weeping softly." (*Sasamegoto*, in Kidō and Imoto, 147, using the translation in Brower and Miner, 257). Brower and Miner participate in these reinterpretations of late Heian attitudes to poetry ("the art of poetry was regarded as a way of life and just as surely a means to ultimate truth as the sermons of the Buddha," 1961, 257), perhaps putting too much trust in later traditions. Similarly, Pandey takes the difficult to date *Togano-o myōe shōnin denki* 栂尾明恵上人伝記 as evidence for Saigyō's supposed claim that "through poetry I have mastered the Law" (47–8).

supposed sinfulness, as a general anxiety that too keen a pursuit of poetry or other arts was an obstacle to spiritual progress persisted for centuries.[388] While poetry turned to Buddhism for justification, the various court *michi*, in the changed atmosphere of the post-Heian era, began to draw from each others' traditions (and *waka* traditions) to create a common vocabulary of ideas. In the late Heian and early Kamakura period, *michi* became closely associated with lineages. The role of the court and its cultural practices became subject to radical self-doubt. As practitioners began to look to other *michi* for ideas through which to define themselves, Ishiguro Kichijirō finds that court musicians led the way. They took ideas particularly from poetics—*toki no koe* (the sounds suited to times), sinfulness of the arts (usually discussed in terms of the above described *kyōgen kigo*) and prescribed stages in training—and located their own practices in relation to them.[389] Their adoption of the idea of *kyōgen kigo* spread to other performance arts. In musical treatises, references to *gagaku* as *kyōgen kigo* signal a subsequent assertion of its spiritual uses, just as it did in poetic works.[390] In the *Tale of the Heike* there is a case of reference to the spiritual power of the flute.[391] Similar uses of *kyōgen kigo*, as a rhetorical signal marking the approach of a counter-intuitive argument for an art's spiritual potential, later appeared in reference to *ennen* and *sarugaku*, both in Noh plays and *sarugaku hidensho*.[392]

The gradual broadening of the category of *michi* stimulated further inter-*michi* borrowing, so that a palette of types and features of *michi* developed, enabling individual specializations to situate themselves within a broad range of possibilities. As we saw in chapter two, commoner *shokunin* traditions began to appear in élite writings and picture scrolls in the late Heian and early Kamakura period. The boundaries between these and more courtly traditions, all perhaps part of an older order under threat, seem to have been felt less deeply than formerly. Yoshida Kenkō's writings illustrate this by repeatedly comparing *michi* across the class divide and across the boundary between secular and spiritual. Kenkō's main interest in

388. A well-known performance of this anxiety being Bashō's deathbed scene, as described by Shikō (Ueda, Makoto, *Basho and His Interpreters: Selected Hokku with Commentary* (Stanford: Stanford University Press, 1991), 413–4.
389. Ishiguro, 1993, 7–14.
390. See Ishiguro, 1983, 120 for two examples.
391. The passage is found in the story of the warrior Kumagai Naozane, who, on seeing the flute "Saeda" in the robes of the boy Atsumori that he has just killed, decides to become a Buddhist monk: "It's name was Saeda. How moving that, according to the principle of *kyōgen kigo*, it should in the end become a cause for the praise of the Buddha vehicle." Takagi Ichinosuke et al., *Heike monogatari 2 (Nihon koten bungaku taikei 33)* (Iwanami Shoten, 1960), 221–2.
392. See examples, Ishiguro, 1983, 120–124, and Terasaki, 1989, 519–552.

this regard seems to have been to generalize training processes—that is, stages on the path. Konishi invokes Kenkō's discussions in support of his idea that masters of *michi* possessed universally applicable knowledge, but that seems to me to miss Kenkō's point.[393] Kenkō never implies in *Tsurezuregusa* that the different paths were bound to have principles in common; but he delighted in finding cases where they did.

Ishiguro notes the important role of fourteenth-century *renga* theory in the cross-fertilization of ideas between plebian and élite *michi*.[394] In the fourteenth century, *renga* was practiced very widely and had two forms—popular and aristocratic. Nijō Yoshimoto, who in his writings on *renga* is thought to have gathered and organized ideas commonly held in his day,[395] presents *renga* in the context of the history of *waka* and makes it subject to the restrictions of *waka*'s diction and aesthetics; he explains the performative and spontaneous values of *renga*, however, in terms of popular performance arts. Yoshimoto's *renga* theories were an important influence on Zeami's *nōgakuron* and probably encouraged his "gentrification" of *sarugaku*.[396]

In my view, then, Kenkō, Yoshimoto and Zeami regarded the theorizing of various *michi* as a kind of storehouse of intellectual structures from which they could pick out elements useful for their needs. They never lost sight, however, of the individual character of particular paths.[397] Their eclecticism was more likely the result of their need to find ways of saying new things than any belief in fundamental identity.[398] In many of Zeami's

---

393. Thus, in section 92 of *Tsurezuregusa*, the caution that the novice archer who takes two arrows rather than one might learn carelessness, Kenkō proposes is applicable to all branches of learning, while in section 109, the tree-climber's warning that the student should be careful when things seem easy he finds to accord with the precepts of sages. The point here is not that the master of tree-climbing possesses universal knowledge, but that rules regarding the training processes in *michi* can be generalized. Kenkō's punch line to the passage notes the similarity of the tree-climber's advice to that given in the art of court football, thus crossing the class divide. In section 150, Kenkō observes that the advice to mix with experts from the beginning, a piece of guidance probably deriving from *renga*, "holds true for every art." Kenkō also finds common ideas in the practice of *michi*, as well as in its training: for example he notes that backgammon shares principles with ruling the state (section 110) and he discovers as a common principle in *michi* that correct external form will lead to correct inner attitude (section 157). He does not, however, convert these commonalities into any kind of quasi-mystical principle (for above examples, see Nishio Minoru, ed., *Hōjōki, Tsurezuregusa (Nihon koten bungaku taikei 30)* (Iwanami Shoten, 1957).
394. Ishiguro, 1993, 46–7.
395. Ueda Makoto, 1967, 38.
396. Ueda Makoto, 1967, 52–3. See also useful discussion in Goff, 35–8.
397. See Pinnington, 2006, 33–37. Kenkō both finds similarities and differences between *michi*. Yoshimoto uses different *michi* to characterize different aspects of *renga* and so does Zeami to characterize *sarugaku*.
398. I know of just one fourteenth-century general assertion of the identity of *michi*: "in the myriad *michi*, the principle is one" (*yorozu no michi sono ri ichi narubeshi*) from *Jinnō shōtōki*. This refers however to *michi*'s social function: "dispelling delusion and fostering

borrowings—whether from the élite or vulgar arts or from religion—it is clear that he has found something in another sphere that he applies differently to his own.[399] In particular, he took ideas from poetics (such as the image of the flower, *hana*) and from Zen (such as the need to continue practicing after the experience of enlightenment), but only applied them insofar as they were useful in the context of his knowledge of performance. There is no sign in these cases that Zeami expected concepts or theoretical models developed in other paths to be *necessarily* applicable to his own.

Zeami marks a high point in the strategy of drawing on images in an ever-widening range of *michi* to define and refine new developments in a traditional art. Where this strategy had legitimating motives they were secondary, and we see few assertions of mysterious or counter-intuitive equivalences. A contrast to this kind of reasoning is found in the Chinese tradition of arguments for the unity of the three creeds. Here, legitimation was from the beginning a primary motive, and obvious differences between the creeds in question were ignored. As we shall see, however, in Japan this rhetorical tradition eventually came to be put to another kind of use, the interpretation of difficult traditions.

The "unity of the three creeds" was a rhetorical ploy developed by Buddhists in China, in the face of Confucian criticism. Instead of answering the charges (of being unfilial, antisocial and foreign) directly, they argued that the Confucian, Taoist and Buddhist traditions were traces (迹 Ch. *ji* Jp. *shaku*) in the world that were equivalent, because they had the same basis (本 Ch. *ben* Jp. *hon*).[400] The *hon/shaku* polarity was used widely in Chinese philosophy, Buddhist exegesis, and syncretic theories in China and Japan.[401] In early discussions of the three creeds, *hon* refers to a "mind" or intention associated with a sage, the resulting tradition of which is called a *shaku*. Thus Ming Qisong 明契嵩 (1007–1072) wrote, "Of old there were the sages Buddha, Laozi, Confucius. Their intentions were one but their manifestations (*shaku*) different. They were one in that they wished all men

---

understanding," not its basic processes (cited in Ishiguro, 1993, 44–5; see also H. Paul Varley, trans., *A Chronicle of Gods and Sovereigns: Jinnō Shōtōki of Kitabatake Chikafusa* (New York: Columbia University Press, 1980), 163.)
399. For example, he adopted the language of secrecy used in the courtly arts (*hiden* secret transmissions), to discuss a quite different kind of secrecy (of tactics when trying to overcome competitors in competition) (Pinnington, 2006, 38–9).
400. I shall use the Japanese pronunciation. My account here follows Haga Kōshirō's study "*Sankyō itchi ron no tenkai*" in *Chūsei zenrin no gakumon oyobi bungaku ni kansuru kenkyū (Haga Kōshirō rekishi ronshū 3)* (Kyoto: Shibunkaku Shuppan, 1981) 221–244. Haga traces the theory to early expressions in terms of the *hon/shaku* polarity starting with: "Buddhist teachings and Confucian and Taoist teachings had the same basis (*hon*) but different traces (*shaku*)", 224.
401. Just like the *tai/yū/sō* triplet, however, it is important to notice that this polarity is used differently in different places.

to be good. They were different in the schools into which their teachings became divided."[402] In general, Sung proponents of the unity of the three creeds looked for similarities in the different teachings to support their assertion of a common source. Thus the five abstentions of Buddhism (killing, stealing, sexual misconduct, lying and drinking alcohol) were matched against the five constants of Confucianism (benevolence, righteousness, propriety, wisdom and sincerity). Such reasoning drew on correlative systems associated with the five courses (that is, wood, fire, earth, metal and water), but was applied with some ingenuity, being fleshed out with equivalences in content.[403] We should note here that we are not so much confronted with a clear belief, that for example the world of manifestation is the product of an essential mind, but rather we have a style of argument which implies some such structure, but the implied structure is not clearly defined.

Zen teachers coming to Japan in the Kamakura period also advanced arguments for the unity of the three creeds, but there was no need in Japan for Zen to defend itself against Chinese native traditions. A subsequent generation of Japanese Zen teachers actually rejected the theory, stressing the distinct superiority of Zen.[404] In the fifteenth century, however, Zen priests, wishing to justify their interests in Chinese thought and literature against Buddhist strictures, began to use the arguments of the unity of the three creeds to that end.[405] The popularity of the theory in this period is reflected in the many paintings of the three "founders," Buddha, Lao-zi, Confucius.[406] At the same time, perhaps as a form of domestication of imported ideology, a new wave of attempts to identify concepts in the different traditions arose. The tradition thus developed from a mode of justification into a bewildering method of elucidating fundamental truths.

---

402. Haga, 1981, 224–5.
403. An example is a parallelism constructed between five categories of Mahayana Sutras and the five Confucian classics that discovered in them shared characteristics, so that the Nirvana scriptures, which "clarify the Buddha nature and its mysterious virtuous actions," were made equivalent to the *Doctrine of the Mean*, which "is wide and great, and exhausts the fine and subtle." Haga, 1981, 225–6.
404. Many examples could be given, but Dōgen's rejection of the theory is particularly intense ("They say that the three paths are indeed compatible; like the legs of a three-legged sacrificial vessel, if one is missing it will fall over, they say. This extremely stupid simile signifies nothing. .... The unity of the three creeds is of less worth than the babble of children," *Shōbōgenzō*, 50, cited in Haga, 1981, 229–230). By the way, this passage casts strong doubt on Konishi's suggestion (discussed in chapter two), that Dōgen considered secular *michi* equivalent to the Zen path.
405. See examples cited in Haga, 1981, 233–237.
406. See John M Rosenfield, "The Unity of the Three Creeds: A theme in Japanese Ink Painting of the Fifteenth Century," ch. 13 of John W. Hall and Toyoda Takeshi, eds., *Japan in the Muromachi Age* (Berkeley: University of California Press, 1977), 205–226.

An extreme is found in the writings of the Confucian expert Kiyō Hōshū 岐陽方秀, who related terms across disciplines in the search for the common truth he believed them to express. Thus, he explained "bright virtue" (*meitoku* 明德 from *Da xue* 大学) in terms of the "one mind" (*isshin* 一心, in its Buddhist sense as the Buddha nature), through the metaphysics of the *Awakening of Faith* (that is: essence *tai* 体, functioning *yō* 用 and appearance *sō* 相): "Bright virtue is the functioning of one mind. One mind is the essence of bright virtue 明德一心之用 / 一心明德之体." This construction of equivalences across disciplines may have been intended to clarify obscure concepts, but it has been said that it resulted in new ideas that were neither Buddhist nor Confucian.[407]

Thus to summarize, the theory of the unity of the three creeds was not originally a hermeneutical method, but was a rhetorical style used to legitimate Buddhist tradition by associating it with others already culturally sanctioned. The association was argued through such polarities as *hon* and *shaku*, ground and manifestation, and was supported by numeric or structural coincidences. In Japan, it was used to justify monks practicing Chinese cultural activities, but it also developed into a hermeneutic technique that operated by looking for similarities of structure and terminology in separate traditions.

A similar search for coincidences between separate traditions was adopted in the last universalizing intellectual tradition I wish to highlight, found in the works of Shinto. These developed from attempts made by aristocrats and shrines associated with the imperial institution to redefine themselves in the thirteenth and fourteenth centuries. A common element of such works was the reinterpretation of the age of the gods as presented in *Kojiki* 古事記, *Nihonshoki* and other texts. These earlier works traced Japanese imperial history in a linear fashion, from an age of gods (*kamiyo* 神代) through legendary emperors, and then to historical emperors. From the early Kamakura period, however, court scholars began to re-read the earliest stage as a paradigm for the present polity.[408] The events described, the splitting apart of heaven and earth (*tenchi kaibyaku* 天地開闢), the generation of gods and birth of the Japanese islands, and the establishment of the imperial and aristocratic lines, were seen to prescribe a sacred political structure. A key text produced by this reinterpretation was

---

407. Haga, 1981, 235–6.
408. Thus we see the appearance both of histories like *Mizu kagami* 水鏡, beginning with Jimmu Tennō, the first human king, and of works treating the age of the gods as sacred. For this and a discussion of paradigmatic and prognosticatory uses of the age of the gods, see Miyai Yoshio, *Nihon no chūsei shisō*, (Seikō Shobō 1981), 77–80.

Kitabatake Chikafusa's *Jinnō shōtōki* 神皇正統記, which took history to justify political power.

Primal events were also seen as models of spiritual experience. Shinto thinkers, lacking the analysis of spiritual states found in Buddhism, read events from the age of the gods as descriptions of the path to spiritual union. One particular event they lighted on was the splitting apart of heaven and earth (*tenchi kaibyaku*).[409] It was thought that if one could return to the state of primal chaos, one would be integrated with divine forces.[410] This interpretation lies behind the intense focus on *tenchi kaibyaku* that one finds in medieval Shinto texts, for example, Watarai Ieyuki's *Ruijū shingi hongen* 類聚神祇本源.

While political and spiritual thinkers inspected Japanese accounts of the ancient past, they also began to compare them with similar accounts from Indian (i.e. Buddhist) and Chinese works. This resulted in a characteristic arrangement of accounts, similar in style to works on the three creeds. If we look at *Jinnō shōtōki*, we see it starts with a juxtaposition of three versions of cosmic events, Shinto, Chinese and Japanese. Similarly, in *Ruijū shingi hongen*, Chinese (Confucian or Taoist), Buddhist and Japanese accounts cosmogonies are collected and listed side by side. In both these examples it is interesting that there is no discussion or explanation of similarities or differences between the accounts, rather it seems that the reader is expected simply to observe and dwell upon the striking resonances between the different versions.

How do fifteenth-century *sarugaku* writings participate in these intellectual practices? Zeami, as we have seen, inherits the tradition of borrowing models and reinterpreting them in his own context. He is particularly concerned with the path itself, as was Kenkō, through the stages of training, performance, and decline in late life, and borrows from formulations of the training process developed both in poetics and Buddhism, especially Sōtō Zen. Zeami's parallel between the Buddhist path and that of *sarugaku* is structural; he does not make any claims that, for example, *sarugaku* leads to spiritual enlightenment. What Zenchiku's aims were, we cannot assume here, but at least we can say that he was interested in the discovery of deep identities. His methods reflect the traditions of the unity of the three creeds. Firstly he does not choose just Buddhism (let alone Zen) as his primary religious model; rather he treats Buddhism itself as one of several sources of knowledge that can be taken up freely and in

---

409. Ōsumi Kazuo, ed., *Chūsei shintōron (Nihon shisō taikei 19)* (Iwanami Shoten, 1977), 352.
410. See Teeuwen's account of this core practice in Watarai thought: 99–126.

parallel to talk about the same realities. Secondly he organizes his material in terms of a polarity prominent in that tradition, distinguishing shared quasi-mathematical structures and contingent content. Related to this is another polarity, between textual and ideological material felt to derive from ancient and sacred sources, and ordinary human interpretations of it, which were provisional and less significant. As we have seen, the discovery of similarities between the three creeds had two purposes, justificatory and hermeneutic, and both these motives can be seen in Zenchiku's *rokurin ichiro* works. These works also participate in the traditions developed by Shinto specialists, with whom Zenchiku clearly identified.[411] On the one hand we see him employing the textual practice of juxtaposing material drawn from different traditions, while on the other, he uses processes of cosmic manifestation as a model for the practice of his own tradition.

ORIGINS OF THE *ROKURIN ICHIRO* DIAGRAMS

The most puzzling element of the *rokurin ichiro* works is the diagrams. They precede the interpretations and take priority over them. Where did they come from? We cannot know for sure, but if we look at what evidence there is and consider the way they are used we can suggest a likely answer. Some have concluded that Zenchiku saw the diagrams in a spiritual vision, others that he devised them himself to express Zeami's theories, and still others have looked for the sources out of which Zenchiku might have developed them. I shall explain first why I think that Zenchiku did not devise them himself and then argue that they most likely originated in a Shinto-style representation of cosmogony.

The focus of most of the discussion in this chapter will be the first two works Zenchiku wrote on the diagrams, *Rokurin ichiro no ki* and *Kichū*. The first, *Rokurin ichiro no ki*, is a composite made up of Zenchiku's own readings and others received from external contributors, to which he applied slight modifications. It consists of seven diagrams (six circles and a sword), Zenchiku's own preliminary reading of them with an introduction, this group called *watakushi kotoba* 私詞 (personal or private notes), an equivalent Buddhist reading of them received from the prelate Shigyoku, a similar Neo-Confucian reading from Ichijō Kanera, and a postscript by the Zen priest Nankō Sōgen 南江宗沅 (1387–1463). The organization of the material is a little complex, and I refer the reader to table 5.[412]

411. As will be discussed in chapter six in connection with Zenchiku's *Meishukushū*.
412. Zenchiku's preliminary reading of the diagrams, the *watakushi kotoba*, includes an introduction and brief readings of each of the diagrams. Interspersed with each of these readings are equivalents by the prelate Shigyoku in Buddhist terms, preceded by an

Rokurin ichiro no ki was completed in 1455. Zenchiku's reading, the *watakushi kotoba* sections, were completed at least eleven years earlier and thus represent his earliest thoughts of the system's significance.[413] It is in them that a brief phrase appears that indicates that Zenchiku did not devise the diagrams himself:

> That is why I have provisionally acquired the forms of the six circles and the dewdrop. . . .[414]

The phrase is "provisionally acquired," by which I translate "*kari ni ete* 假 得*.*" The element: "provisionally," *kari ni*, suggests that the diagrams are a kind of expedient means (*hōben* 方便)—to be applied for the moment to enable the attainment of a higher knowledge, after which they will no longer be required.[415] "Acquired" *(ete)* implies that the diagrams were not invented by Zenchiku, but adopted from elsewhere.

This is important evidence, but it may be thought that it is contradicted by the later passage which concludes the second work, *Kichū*:

> Above, this "six circles and one dewdrop," overall, is not just a record of what I understood from the instructions of my teacher, it is the purport that I realized in spiritual retreat at the Hase Kanzeon Bodhisattva, an interpretation of Kannon's expedient means of benefiting living beings, a path of precepts for all living creatures. That is why I also call this the Six Circles of Kannon.[416]

But it is clear that Zenchiku is in this case talking not about the diagrams, but the particular interpretations of them he records in the work.[417] The

introduction and followed by closing remarks. Ichijō Kanera's Neo-Confucian interpretation is placed after them. Finally there is a postscript by the Zen priest Nankō Sōgen
413. The *watakushi kotoba* are found in a separate commentary on the diagrams written by the prelate Shigyoku much earlier, in 1444. This commentary only exists in a copy, but it is thought to faithfully reflect the original work (KKS, 73). It is clearly the source for Shigyoku's interpretations in *Rokurin ichiro no ki*. It seems that Zenchiku gave the *watakushi kotoba* to Shigyoku, with the diagrams, when asking for his interpretations, and that Shigyoku included them in the material he returned.
414. KKS, 197.
415. This implication of "*kari ni*" was impressed upon me by Professor Hendrick Van de Veere, at a series of seminars on *Rokurin ichiro no ki* at Leiden University in 1992.
416. KKS, 220.
417. The way that the subject "six circles and dewdrop" (*rokurin ichiro*) is modified by the words "above" (右), this (此) and "overall" (凡そ), the use of the term "record" (記する) in the following phrase, and the reference in the predicate to meanings and readings (purport 旨 and interpretation 説—which Lewis Cook informs me in medieval poetics usually describes a traditionally approved interpretation), makes it clear that Zenchiku is referring to the collection of interpretations presented in *Kichū* and not to the diagrams themselves. We shall later conjecture what might have constituted Zenchiku's realization (*kakugo* 覚悟) in retreat if it was not the vision of the diagrams themselves. (Note that Mark Nearman reads this passage to

Table 5
Arrangement of *Rokurin ichiro no ki*

1 Combining Zenchiku's *watakushi kotoba* (*WK*) and Shigyoku's commentary (SG)		
WK Introduction	1st circle (diagram)	WK interpretation 1st circle
SG introduction	SG interpretation 1st circle	
2nd circle	WK interpretation	SG interpretation
3rd circle	WK interpretation	SG interpretation
4th circle	WK interpretation	SG interpretation
5th circle	WK interpretation	SG interpretation
6th circle	WK interpretation	SG interpretation
sword	WK interpretation	SG interpretation
SG conclusion		
2 Ichijō Kanera's *I Ching*-based commentary		
Introduction		
Interpretation of 1st circle		
Interpretation of 2nd circle		
Interpretation of 3rd circle		
Interpretation of 4th circle		
Interpretation of 5th circle		
Interpretation of 6th circle		
Interpretation of sword		
Kanera's conclusion		
3 Nankō Sōgen's commentary/postscript		

passage is a problematic one, typical of Zenchiku, an elucidation which simultaneously obfuscates, but is not enough to override his earlier "*kari ni ete*" which, after all, was passed to Shigyoku, who must have been privy to the origins of the diagrams.

The way Zenchiku and the other interpreters treat the diagrams also implies that he did not invent them himself but adopted them from somewhere else, probably a highly regarded traditional source. Referring to a late reinterpretation, which he justifies on the basis of its roots in his master's instructions, Zenchiku claims that it "is not a personal thing" using the term *watakushi naki*[418] The idea that what is a "personal thing" lacks

refer to the diagrams, concluding that Zenchiku had a direct vision of the circles and dewdrop in meditation—Mark J. Nearman, "The Visions of a Creative Artist. Zenchiku's *Rokurin ichiro* Treatises," *Monumenta Nipponica* 50.2 (summer 1995): 235.)

418. "In particular, this account (*shidai* 次第) of the six circles (*rokurin*) is my own creation, but it is the result of profound deliberation (*kufū* 工夫) over the aesthetic qualities (*kyokumi*) of my teacher, and is not a personal thing." (KKS, 250.) This passage again might be thought to be a claim to have invented the diagrams, but in context it is clear that here too it is the particular reading Zenchiku is justifying. The term *shidai* in medieval works signifies "matters concerning," "an account of" (as, for example, in the title of another of Zenchiku's works: *Go on no shidai*—"An Account of the Five Moods") and Zenchiku only mentions the six circles, not the dewdrop. As we shall see later, this statement comes after a new interpretation of just the six circles in terms of Zeami's nine levels (*Kyūi*), one which contradicts Zenchiku's earlier readings. That Zenchiku is specifically referring to this reinterpretation is further supported by the fact that, as we have seen, Zenchiku understood the nine levels in terms of *kyokumi*. It is

authority pervades medieval thought. Konishi touches on this matter in his discussion of transmission and conformity, where he argues that elements of tradition perceived to derive from a single individual lacked authority. *Michi* could only preserve things handed down over several generations; any practitioner had to renounce his personal ideas in their favor.[419] Similar concepts are found in Shinto traditions.[420] Zenchiku more than once attempted to strengthen the authority of ideas he recorded by arguing that they were *watakushi naki*, that is authoritative, not personal.[421] It is in these terms that we should understand his calling his first readings *watakushi kotoba*. Rather than expressing a contrast to Shigyoku's interpretation (that is "my readings" as opposed to his) as some readers have assumed, the intended contrast is, I believe, with the diagrams themselves: they are authoritative and unalterable—hence *watakushi naki*—but the *watakushi kotoba*, Zenchiku's provisional interpretations of the diagrams, are personal, conjectural.[422] It is only when he can refer to the views of external authorities that Zenchiku can claim that a reading is not "personal," that it has impersonal authority.

The *watakushi naki/watakushi* polarity, then, has implications for a related polarity, that is, intellectual formulae and the interpretations of them when applied to specific practices. It is an important characteristic of the *rokurin ichiro* works that the diagrams themselves (as well as their names) are never modified nor treated as modifiable, whereas the interpretations are exploratory and constantly open to renegotiation. The diagrams hold the same kind of relationship to their readings that we have seen in the borrowed structures found throughout *sarugaku* writings.[423] These received formulae were not to be modified, but could be re-read to fit circumstances—rather as transmitted formula are commonly observed to be in oral cultures. In the many combinations of formulae and interpretations,

---

not the *rokurin ichiro* diagrams that Zenchiku is claiming here to have created, but this new re-reading of six of them.
419. Konishi, 1986, 154–5.
420. Mark Teeuwen notes the contrast between what is authorized (*kō* 公) and private (*shi* 私, or *watakushi*) made by disputants in the Inner and Outer Shrines over the priority of the Inner Shrine. Those favoring the Inner Shrine argued that the Secret Books of the Outer Shrine were private i.e. unofficial, and could not be evidence in a "public" procedure. Teeuwen, 68–7.
421. See for example KKS, *Kabuzuinōki*, 140 and KKS, *Bunshōbon*, 249.
422. That is, the *watakushi kotoba* are not simply "personal remarks" as Thornhill has them (1993, 20–1).
423. For example, the triad of *jo* 序, *ha* 破 and *kyū* 急 (taken from *gagaku*), the ten forms *jittei* (from *waka*), *hi*, *niku* and *kotsu* (from calligraphy), the nine levels (ultimately from Chinese rankings of officials), as well as in its own transmitted formulae, like the two arts *nikyoku* and three forms *santai*.

the formulae themselves are not generally presented as inventions of ordinary individuals. The persistence of such models and their power to yield profound interpretations depended on their provenance. Medieval thinkers seem to have expected a wide range of phenomena to be amenable to profound interpretations, for example, Chinese characters, texts, statues, natural formations and so on. However, it was not every object that could be so interpreted, but only culturally sanctified objects—the *Kokinwakashū*, Mt. Hiei, or well-known Buddhist phrases. For objects to be deeply significant they not only could not be *watakushi*, they also had to have a particular provenance, for example origins associated with the divine, the imperial or the ancient past. Such persistent bases for interpretation were of a different order of authority from temporary and personal ideas.

In the case of the *rokurin ichiro* theory, Shigyoku and Kanera seem to have accepted that the diagrams were not personal, not open to revision. Although strains are evident in their attempts to align their readings with the diagrams, there is no sign that they went back to Zenchiku with suggestions to modify them to better fit their own systems, which were themselves derived from works of the highest prestige. As all the participants in the *rokurin ichiro* works acted as if the diagrams were fixed elements, it seems likely that they all believed them to have originated somewhere other than Zenchiku's own devisings.

If we can accept that Zenchiku "acquired" the diagrams from somewhere else, then we should now turn to the question of from where. In this connection, the fact that both Shigyoku and Kanera were prepared to read them in terms of cosmic processes makes it seem likely that that was their application in their original context. Indeed, this would explain why Zenchiku himself from the start read them in cosmogonic as well as *sarugaku* terms. But where might such a diagrammatic representation of cosmic processes come from? Japanese scholars have considered the origins of the diagrams somewhat indirectly, asking about their "sources" (*yoridokoro*). In an early study, Konishi suggested that Zenchiku's system had its roots in esoteric Buddhist theories met with in works on music.[424] Itō Masayoshi responded by showing that the terms Konishi traced to esoteric Buddhism actually came to Zenchiku from Watarai-related Shinto writings.

---

424. He conjectured that Zenchiku might have noticed the image of water, symbolized in esoteric Buddhism by the circle, and visualized this image, associated with the "wisdom of the great mirror," as having the potential to reflect performance art through a series of circles containing various designs. Konishi, 1961, 249–253.

It is in such Shinto works that Itō suggests that we look for the origins of Zenchiku's ideas.[425]

Are there diagrammatic representations of cosmic processes in Shinto theory? There certainly are; indeed the stages of cosmic manifestation were an obsession of Shinto theorists in the medieval period. Scholars have shown that Zenchiku must have had access to a version of the widely copied Watarai Shinto work, *Ruijū shingi hongen*.[426] The first section of this work is a collection of accounts of cosmic beginnings taken from Neo-Confucian and Classical Chinese works, as well as Japanese courtly, shrine and Buddhist traditions. It includes a number of diagrammatic representations of cosmic manifestation, including a version of Zhou Dun-i 周敦頤's *Diagram of the Supreme Ultimate* (*taikyokuzu* 太極図) (see illustration 2).[427]

How likely is it that a Shinto version of the *Diagram of the Supreme Ultimate* would look like the six circles and the dewdrop? As Zenchiku himself reads them in that way, it is not an unreasonable supposition. Shinto theorizing about first things was still open to a variety of versions.[428] A later set of diagrams in the Yoshida Shinto tradition, however, is strikingly similar to the *rokurin ichiro* diagrams. This later set is found in a collection of Shinto traditions gathered by Hayashi Razan 林羅山 (1583–1657) in the 1640's text *Shintō denju* 神道伝授 (see illustration 3).[429] Razan's source for them is not known.[430] It is possible that they derived from the same set of diagrams from which Zenchiku borrowed his system. In any case, Razan's set shows that a diagrammatic representation of the manifestation of the universe in Shinto tradition, deriving from Ieyuki's writings, could look

425. KZK, 171–190.
426. A "digest of Watarai Shinto thought from 1320" (Teeuwen, 98). For Zenchiku's use of this or similar works see KZK, 179–186, and Thornhill, 1993, particularly, 151–2. We do not know how Zenchiku came to have access to such works. My guess is that it was through a form of Miwa Shinto propagated in the Hasedera complex. We discuss other indications of this connection in chapter six.
427. Ōsumi Kazuo, 83.
428. Watarai Ieyuki collected many cosmogonic accounts in *Ruijū shingi hongen*, but seems not to have been able to synthesize them into a single version. See Ōsumi' discussion, 353–356.
429. Taira Shigemichi, Abe Akio, eds., *Kinsei shintōron, zenki kokugaku (Nihon Shisō Taikei 39)* (Iwanami Shoten, 1972), 43. Nearman says of these diagrams that they are "almost identical" (1995, 238, fn. 8) to Zenchiku's. They are not, but they do have striking similarities (for differences, see footnote below).
430. Scholars have conjectured that he (or someone else) constructed them by combining a simple four-part diagram known as the *Diagram of the Three Beginnings* (*sanshizu* 三始図) found in Watarai Ieyuki's *Shintō kanyō* 神道簡要 and a version of the *Diagram of the Supreme Ultimate*. See Hayakawa Junsaburō, *Shintō sōsetsu* (Kokusho Kankōkai, 1911), 4.

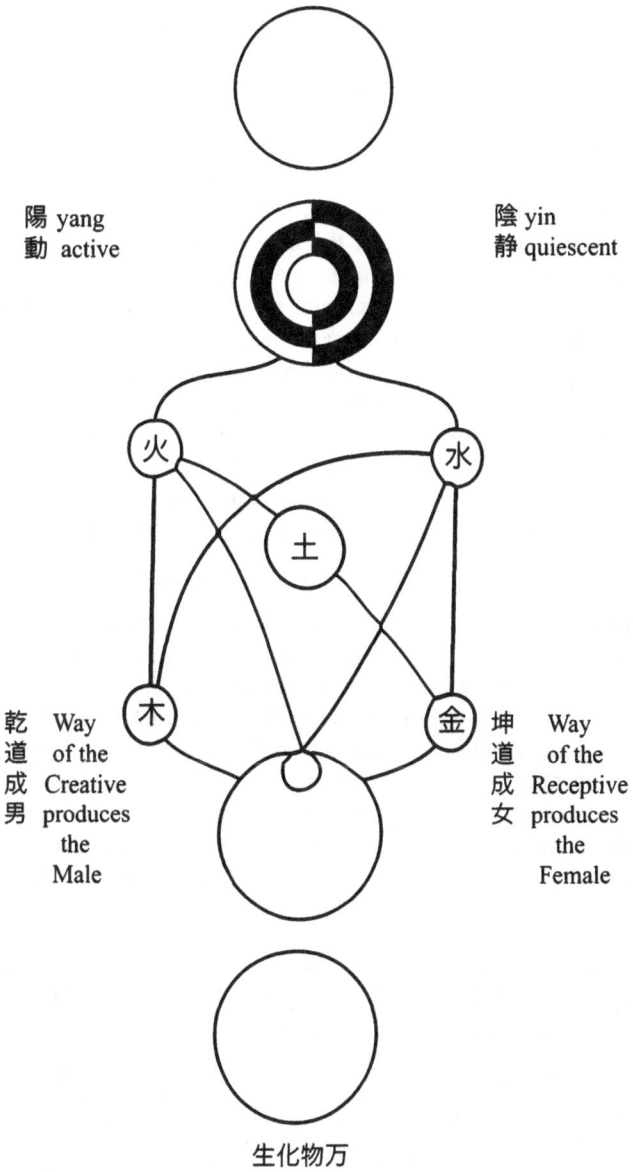

陽 yang　　　　　　　　　　　　陰 yin
動 active　　　　　　　　　　　　静 quiescent

火　　　　　　水

土

木　　　　　　金

乾　Way　　　　　　　　　坤　Way
道　of the　　　　　　　　道　of the
成　Creative　　　　　　　成　Receptive
男　produces　　　　　　　女　produces
　　the　　　　　　　　　　　the
　　Male　　　　　　　　　　Female

生化物万

The myriad things are born

Illustration 2: Diagram of the Supreme Ultimate

very like Zenchiku's *rokurin ichiro* diagrams.[431] My guess is that such a set of diagrams was a part of Shinto lore, now lost to us, that came to Zenchiku along with the other Shinto writings he acquired in his early maturity.

Zenchiku repeatedly combined *sarugaku* and cosmological readings of the *rokurin ichiro* diagrams. Scholars have generally thought that he must have designed them primarily to represent *sarugaku* traditions. My argument, however, is that the diagrams were borrowed from Shinto theorists' representations of stages in cosmic unfolding. That they were borrowed explains their persistence and the intellectual authority that all contributors were prepared to afford them. That they primarily described cosmic manifestation from a Shinto standpoint explains why Shigyoku and Kanera expected them to yield Buddhist and Neo-Confucian equivalents (according to the logic of the unity of the three creeds). If such a set of diagrams existed in Shinto traditions in Zenchiku's day, then they provide a source for the similar diagrams that reappear in Razan's work several generations later. A final fundamental question now arises: why would Zenchiku himself have thought it worthwhile to reinterpret diagrams representing cosmogonic processes in terms of the arts of *sarugaku?*

A SHINTO COSMOLOGICAL MODEL FOR *SARUGAKU* TRADITIONS

In the interpretative passages of the *watakushi kotoba*, Zenchiku combines two specific types of vocabulary: the first, present mainly in discussions of the first three circles, from *sarugaku*, and the second, mainly in the later circles, from accounts of cosmogonic processes. This dual conception of the *rokurin ichiro* system (combining *sarugaku* and cosmogony) is present from its earliest reading. Although the formulations that Shigyoku and Kanera applied to the system are squarely in the realm of cosmic forces, they also possess some degree of application to the human life cycle.[432] Such dual readings are furthermore explicit in the conclusion of Zenchiku's

---

431. I feel that this is not the place for a detailed comparison of Razan's diagrams with Zenchiku's, which I leave to the interested reader. I would just point out one important difference and a less obvious similarity. The first is the presence of the five elements in Razan's system. As I discuss below there were two basic versions ot the early stages of cosmic unfolding in Chinese thought, represented by the numbers: 1, 2, 5, many, and 1, 2, 3, many. The first set of course corresponds to the *Diagram of the Supreme Ultimate* as well as Razan's system, but the second, found in Lao-tzu for example, and also represented in *Ruijū shingi hongen*, matches Zenchiku's system. As for the similarity, there is no *ichiro* in Razan's system, but he does state at the end, "the significance of the above six circles: all are equipped with one mind," which corresponds to the *ichiro*'s role as a non-dual unity pervading the *rokurin* cycle.
432. I read the primary application to *sarugaku* to be to the actor's life path. The formulations that Shigyoku and Kanera applied to the diagrams can be taken to describe general processes of manifestation but they also had a history of applications to the human life cycle (discussed further below).

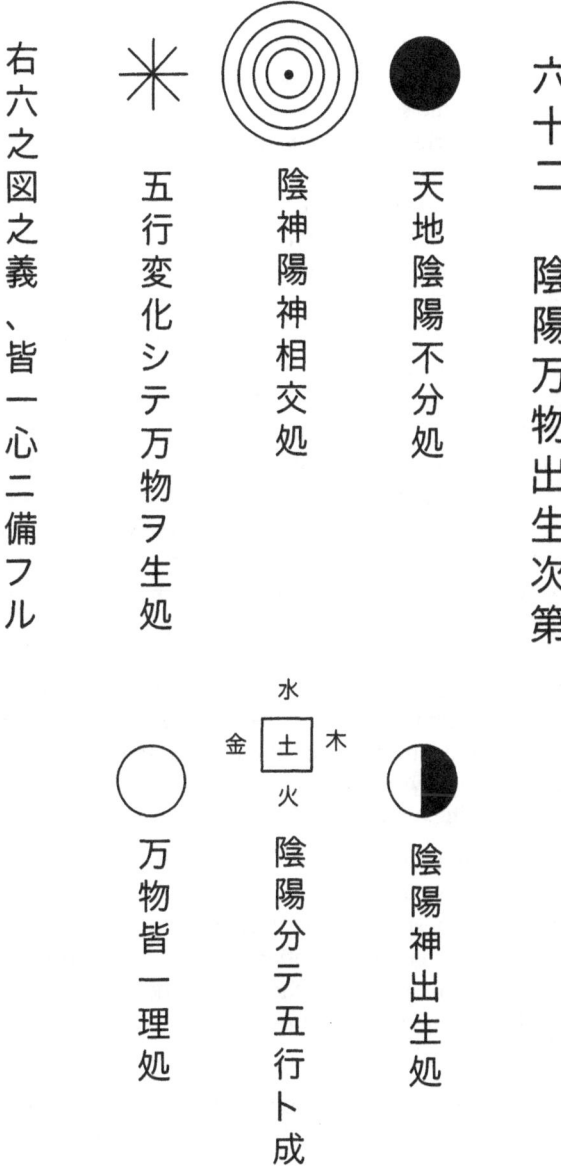

右六之図之義、皆一心ニ備フル

五行変化シテ万物ヲ生処

陰神陽神相交処

天地陰陽不分処

六十二　陰陽万物出生次第

万物皆一理処

水
金　土　木
火

陰陽分テ五行ト成也

陰陽神出生処

Illustration 3: Diagram from Hayashi Razan's *Shintō denju*

first stage of interpretation, the *Kichū*, where we find the two aspects separated out into a Shinto cosmogonic interpretation and a *sarugaku* one. Why should Zenchiku have thought that cosmogony and *sarugaku* might at a profound level share the same structure?

Let us begin by considering other terms in which Zenchiku described *sarugaku*. These used models drawn from various fields representing a single basic idea: *sarugaku* was the end result of a process by which essential, superb or absolute forces took form in the phenomenal world. In the typological works, as we have seen, Zenchiku used the model of instinctive reactions flowing forth from the depths of human nature through poetry, chanting, gesticulating and treading, borrowed from Chinese poetics. [433] He also converted Zeami's use of the *hi, niku, kotsu* triad into a description of steps from the "single thought of the Sanskrit character 'A,'" symbol of the primal manifestation of reality, through organs, bone, flesh and skin.[434] This built a bridge between ultimate spiritual reality and Noh performances. Another parallel was the adoption of form by the ancient Buddha—softening his light and taking up a human body.[435] As we shall see in the sixth chapter of this study, a similar vision was expressed in *Meishukushū*, in which all aspects of the *Okina* performance were seen to be manifestations of an ultimate spiritual being—identified with absolute reality. Actors are of course interested in the mechanics of manifestation, but in Zenchiku's case it was not that he wished to create an illusion of phenomenal reality, but rather that he believed *sarugaku*, properly performed, to be the direct manifestation of ultimate reality itself.

A description of *sarugaku* as the manifestation of primary spiritual forces is expressed in opening phrases of the *watakushi kotoba*:

> Now, the way of the household task of *sarugaku* is to exhaust beauty with the body and to "create pattern with the voice." Hereby "unwittingly the hands gesture and the feet tread." Consequently, this must surely be the mysterious operation (*myōyū* 妙用) of what is fundamentally without master and without phenomena. That is why I have provisionally acquired the forms of the six circles and the dewdrop. . . . [436]

Zenchiku is saying that *sarugaku* is the mysterious operation through the actor of the hidden, the absolute. Thus we can understand why Zenchiku

433. See pages 125–6, above.
434. See pages 132–3, above.
435. See page 141, above.
436. KKS, 197.

should have been predisposed to believe that a structural representation of essential stages in manifestation at all levels should describe the processes by which *sarugaku* is brought to performance. We still need to see why Zenchiku might have in the first place identified such processes operating in the individual life with those active on a cosmic scale. This, however, was very close to the way in which Shinto theorists were using their own investigations of the first cosmic events. For example, the diagram of the Great Ultimate was interpreted in terms of stages of cosmic manifestation, but it had Taoist precursors which were read in reverse as a plan for the achievement of spiritual union by dissolving mental elaboration and returning to an undivided mental state.[437] This was also the way in which Watarai priests were interpreting accounts of cosmic processes in the age of the gods. Teeuwen describes this as the new form of worship developed by the Watarai hereditary priests. Priests converted the stages of cosmic development into a paradigm of mental processes of ritualists seeking spiritual union. It was through this ability to achieve union with the deity that they could justify their social position.[438]

We might expect that the example set by Shinto theorists would have inspired Zenchiku to apply the diagrams to the processes of performance itself. As it happens there are signs in the third section of *Kichū* that he did try to map moments in a Noh play on to the diagrams, but they are not fully developed. As we shall see, the primary application was not to the Noh play but to the actor's lifeplan. I think the reason Zenchiku read the diagrams in this way in the first phase of interpretation is that there is in fact a fairly good parallel to be drawn between his cosmogonic reading and the prescribed stages in the training and performance of a *sarugaku* actor. I believe that it was in fact the observation of this coincidence that was the substance of "the purport" that Zenchiku "realized in spiritual retreat at the Hase Kanzeon Bodhisattva," described at the end of *Kichū*.[439]

ROKURIN ICHIRO DIAGRAMS AS STAGES IN THE WAY OF PERFORMANCE

I have attempted to unravel my first question, the origins of the diagrams, and the related matter of what inspired Zenchiku's peculiar use of them. Let us now look at how that inspiration worked out in his early interpretations of the system. We shall start by analyzing the reading of the diagrams

437. See Fung Yu-lan, *History of Chinese Philosophy: Vol. II The Period of Classical Learning*, trans. by Derk Bodde (Princeton: Princeton University Press, 1983), 434–42.
438. Discussed by Teeuwen, 85–126.
439. See citation on pages 162–3, above.

expressed at the very start of the *rokurin ichiro* project in the *watakushi kotoba*. As I say, it is my view that Zenchiku noticed certain similarities between the prescriptions of training and performance handed down among *sarugaku* actors and certain well-known accounts of cosmic manifestation; and this became the basis of the *rokurin ichiro* project. The terms used in the *watakushi kotoba* in the main relate either to cosmogony or to *sarugaku* (although sometimes they can be applied to both). The major problem for scholars reading the *watakushi kotoba* has been the obscurity of the *sarugaku*-related vocabulary. My view, that these terms describe stages in the actor's lifeplan (*shūdōron*), will need to be demonstrated, then, which I will do through a close analysis of terminology. The less problematic cosmological elements will be handled separately, when we look at their fuller description in *Kichū*.

Before we look at the *watakushi kotoba* terminology, however, we should note that in fact Zenchiku himself said certain things that imply that he understood his primary *sarugaku* interpretation of the *rokurin ichiro* diagrams to be in terms of the actor's path. In *Go on sangyoku shū*, he wrote: "Now I composed a volume on training in the way (*shūdōron*) called *Rokurin ichiro*."[440] This is probably *Rokurin ichiro no ki*. In the later work *Nika ichirin*, he referred to a document in which the practice of training in the way (*shūdō no keiko*) was explained through the *rokurin ichiro* diagrams.[441] The document referred to in this case was almost certainly *Kichū*.[442] The structure of *Kichū* itself supports this theory, for it is primarily a summary of the interpretations of *Rokurin ichiro no ki*, and in it the readings of *watakushi kotoba* are clearly separated out into two more developed ones. The first relates to Shinto theories of cosmogony, and the second presents an explicit reading of the *rokurin ichiro* as stages in the actor's life. From his own remarks, then, it seems that Zenchiku understood the primary *sarugaku* reading of the diagrams informing the first two *rokurin ichiro* works to be in terms of the actor's path.

An analysis of the problematic vocabulary of the *watakushi kotoba* leads us to the same conclusion.[443] We shall start by overviewing the stages in the actor's career as reported by Zeami, and paying particular attention to the terminology that he employs. His most complete account is found in

440. KKS, 182.
441. KKS, 222.
442. KZK, 116–7.
443. I labor the point because other scholars have not read the *watakushi kotoba* in this way, as noted above.

Shikadō.[444] It operates by distinguishing between those *sarugaku* arts which were representational (*monomane* 物まね, usually translated mimicry) and those which were artificial, or artistic (primarily *kabu* 歌舞, song and dance). Thus an actor in the role of an old man would mimic an old man's posture (as illustrated in Zeami's *Nikyoku santai ningyō zu*, for example) and appearance (using costume, wig and mask), but he would sing rather than speak his lines and express his emotions through dance—activities that few old men do. The first stage in training was to learn the artificial elements, song and dance. Later stages concentrated on representation. Children started by practicing passages of singing and particular dance routines, and could even perform roles, but they were not to introduce into their performances any of the elements of mimicry (they could not, for example, use masks). In this way, the innate grace (*yūgen*) of the child would be preserved and persist in his performances throughout his life. Once pure song and dance were mastered, in order ultimately to attain what was called the full fruition (*jōka* 上果) of artistic performance, the actor studied three basic role types in turn—old man, woman and warrior—concentrating on adjusting the two arts of singing and dancing to suit each of them. At this stage masks were still not used and complex roles not attempted. When the three roles were completely mastered, however, it was believed that particular qualities required for the next stage—complex roles including the vigorous demonic roles *seikyoku* or *ikitaru kyoku* 生曲—would emerge of their own accord.[445]

Zeami noted that the order of these stages was crucial.[446] In an important passage of *Shikadō*, he regretted that certain recent performers skipped the separate study of the two arts and three roles and went directly to complex and even heterodox (*isō* 異相) styles. Zeami calls techniques attempted in this fashion *mushu* 無主, originally a legal term for a found object, the true owner of which was unknown.[447] In a later passage, Zeami clarified the term.[448] *Mushu* techniques were those which, while they might resemble those displayed by a properly trained actor, were not "fully mastered" (*nushi* or *shu nari* 主也). The process of training was to observe and copy what one was taught. Even when learning the basic two arts, if

444. My account here, except where stated otherwise, is based on this work, particularly those sections found in ZZ, *Shikadō*, 112–4.
445. This term, *seikyoku*, is glossed in a headnote of ZZ as the vigorous performance style of *monogurui* (that is people driven mad by unhappiness) and demon roles (ZZ, *Shikadō*, 113).
446. He further stresses this point in ZZ, *Kakyō*, 94.
447. See for example the entries for *mushu* in Morohashi's *Dai kanwa jiten*, and in Shōgakkan's *Kokugo daijiten*. This summary is still following Zeami's description in ZZ, *Shikadō*, 113.
448. ZZ, *Shikadō*, 114.

one could not reproduce them just as taught, they were still *mushu*, not one's own possession. If one practiced the examples given by the master teacher, however, and made them one's own, one eventually became established in the "settled stage" (*yasuki kurai*) where one achieved "living performance" (*ikitaru nō* 生きたる能). One had to develop the power of basic skills to become a performer whose "techniques were all owned" (*ushufū* 有主風).[449]

After the basic program of training was complete, the actor still had further stages to pass through, this time defined in terms of types of performance. In the beginning he had to restrict himself to the orthodox techniques he had studied. When his practice had reached a point of full maturity (*taketaru kurai* 蘭位, also read as *ran'i*), however, he could occasionally employ "irregular styles" (*ifū* 異風 or *isō*) to great effect. Zeami warned that one who had not attained mastery of orthodox techniques should not attempt such admixtures.

The above stages are all described in *Shikadō*, but Zeami also reports a further stage in the later works *Kyūi* and *Kyakuraika*. After the age of forty, an actor was permitted to employ a technique known as *kyakurai* 却来 (the style of returning). The precise nature of this technique is not clear, unfortunately, but it seems to have involved the master actor's use of elements considered vulgar when performed by a less qualified actor. It is associated with the Buddhist pairing, *kōkokyakurai*, which Zeami used to describe singing as one pleased (as we saw in chapter four).[450]

Let us now read Zenchiku's *watakushi kotoba* within the framework of the above program. Table 6 summarizes the reasoning behind my reading, matching terms and phrases used by Zeami to describe the stages in the actor's life against the *watakushi kotoba*. The reader may also wish to consult the diagrams themselves as reproduced in illustration 1 (at the start of this chapter).

The *watakushi kotoba* reading of the first circle is as follows:

> The first, the circle of life (*jurin* 寿輪), is the source of *yūgen* (grace) in song and dance, the vessel that generates emotion when dance is seen and chanting heard. Because it makes the lifespan complete and long, it is called the circle of life.

---

449. ZZ, *Shikadō*, 112–114.
450. The use of the term seems to be somewhat different in two works. See ZZ, *Kyūi*, 176–177, and ZZ, *Kyakuraika*, 246–7, and Konishi, 1961, 231–7. See also the reference to *kōkokyakurai* in ZZ, *Go ongyoku jōjō*, 199, and our discussion above, 149–50.

Table 6
Zeami's description of the path and *watakushi kotoba*

Training	Zeami's descriptions	Diagram	*Watakushi kotoba*
Stage 1: Adolescence	Study two arts: 二曲 (=歌舞) apply to various roles, without any of the elements of mimicry. This is the root of those stylistic elements that will cause *yūgen* to manifest in performances long after 是則、 後々までの芸態に幽玄を残すべ き風根なり.	Circle 1	In song and dance 歌 舞 The source of *yūgen* 幽 玄の根源 When dance is seen and chanting heard 見 風聞曲
Stage 2: Adulthood	Study of three role-types without any further techniques 三体のみ 別の曲道習ふべからず. Only path to highest fruition 上果. Skipping to other techniques is not to own them 主也.	Circle 2	vertical, horizontal appear give rise to pure performance roles 横 竪顕レ清曲生ず feeling of the highest fruition 上果の感 fully possessed 主たり
Stage 3: Mastery	Mimicry of other roles (including 生曲) arises naturally. Achieve the settled stage of mastery 安き位.	Circle 3	many roles, vigorous roles 諸体生曲 settled locus 安所
Mature performer	The mature level 闌けたる位 Heterodox appearances 異相 (also called 異風、非風).	Circle 5	heterodox forms 異相
Post-mature performer	*Kyūi*: returning 却来して *Kyakuraika*: the style of returning, only for those over forty years old 却来風とて四十以後	Circle 6	facing, leaving and coming back 向去却来

I understand this first circle to represent the first stage in training, when the young performer studied song and dance. According to Zeami, if he mastered these technical skills fully and separately in the first stage, then his later performances, no matter how complex and forceful, would always possess the quality of *yūgen*. Zenchiku links this idea here to another theory, that song and dance were the basic artistic elements that produced an emotional impact on the audience.[451] He further connects this to the matter

451. Zenchiku's words: "the source of *yūgen* (grace) in song and dance" 歌舞幽玄の根源 correspond to Zeami's description of the effect of early training in the two arts, song and dance, free of mimicry, "the root elements that will cause *yūgen* to persist in performances long after." 後々までの芸態に 幽玄を残すべき風根 (ZZ, *Shikadō*, 112). In the phrase "the vessel that generates emotion when dance is seen and chanting heard" 見風聞曲而成感之器也, we see a telescoping of a complex of ideas related to Zeami's term "root element" 風根. In *Goi* 五位 (*Five Levels*), Zeami analyzed the sources of the impact of performance on audiences (*kan* 感) in terms of five different elements, termed *fū* 風. Zenchiku's *kenpū* 見風, what is seen,

of the "lifespan" (*jumyō* 寿命). (This was the widely-held belief that properly done, performance art lengthened the life of both those attending, and the performers).[452] The commentary of the first circle thus asserts that the extension of *yūgen* into performances "long after" (後々までの) extends the "life" of the actor, his troupe and of his audiences too.[453] The lengthening of the lifespan is doubtless intended to resonate with the name of the circle, the *circle of life*.

The *watakushi kotoba* associated with the second circle reads:

> In the second, the circle of the vertical (*shurin* 竪輪), the rising stroke having become spirit, the vertical and horizontal appear and give rise to pure roles (*seikyoku* 精曲). Here, then, the feeling of the highest fruition (*jōka no kan* 上果の感) is fully possessed (*nushi / shu tari* 主たり).

The "rising stroke" in the passage refers to the vertical line in the diagram that divides the circle into two halves. A problematic compound in this passage is *seikyoku*, a term not found in Zeami's works.[454] The graph *kyoku* 曲 in *sarugaku* has a number of significations, including "performance role."[455] *Sei* 精 (purity, essence) is probably connected to Shinto readings of the diagram that we consider in a later section. If we consider the relationship to the second stage of training in the table given above, however, we can interpret *seikyoku* as meaning the "pure" roles of old man, woman and warrior, that Zeami refers to as *santai*.[456] If we read the term in this way, the rest of the passage makes immediate sense. In Zeami's

and *kyokumon* 曲聞, what is heard, are the terms used in *Goi* for two of them, visual and aural elements. (The visual element is termed *kenpū* and the vocal *shōfū* 声風. This last is further described as *kyokumon no zuifū* 曲聞の瑞風, the element of beauty in what is heard (*ZZ, Goi,* 171). These are the two most basic of the five, the others being the element of mind, of feeling and of the spirit.) In the form of the arts of dance and song, these are the basic artistic elements, the non-representational, beauty-creating elements of performance.

452. This idea is expressed in the term *ennen* (life-extending), both a genre of performance and also used by Zeami to refer to *sarugaku* plays (which he called *sarugaku ennen*). Zeami discusses this quality in ZZ, *Fūshikaden*, 45. See also additional note 23, ZZ, 438–9, and additional note 1, ZZ, 427–428.

453. This reading of the first circle will perhaps seem too concrete and small in focus for those who have interpreted Zenchiku's words in a more abstract way, as indicating a realm of higher reality from which grace and vitality flow. But that is to create a boundary between the contingent and essential that I think inappropriate. In my view the identification of patterns in both the contingencies of *sarugaku* tradition and the larger realms of cosmic processes is the essence of the *rokurin ichiro* project.

454. Note that this *seikyoku* 精曲 is not the same as the *seikyoku* 生曲, found in the reading of the next circle.

455. Other meanings are: sung passages, technical arts (as in song and dance: *nikyoku* 二曲), types of main roles (as in vigorous roles: *seikyoku* 生曲 see below) and the distinctions of *hi*, *niku* and *kotsu* (*sangyoku* 三曲)

456. The reading of *kyoku* 曲 here as role is supported in *Shikadō* where Zeami contrasts the *santai*, the three roles in their pure form, with *betsu no kyokudō* 別の曲道, other role types.

account, it is only when the basic three role types are fully mastered, without "skipping," that the young performer can develop the level of performance that is "fully mastered" (*shutari*), and can have an impact on the audience's feelings (*kan*) that is the "highest fruition" (*jōka*).

In the third, the circle of abiding (*jūrin* 住輪), the position of the short stroke is a settled locus (*ansho* 安所) that forms the many roles (*shotei* 諸躰) including such vigorous performance roles as mad women and demons (*seikyoku* 生曲).

My reading of this stage depends in particular on the compound *shotei seikyoku* 諸躰生曲. The first element *shotei* signifies the many types of role. This *seikyoku* (distinct from the one in circle two, which has different orthography) is usually found in Zeami's works in some version of the form *sokutō seikyoku* 足踏生曲, vigorous foot-stamping roles, the most complex roles that need to be mastered in training.[457] Thus we can read the third circle as indicating the stage in which these complex roles, too, as well as the three plain roles, are mastered. Zeami refers to just such a stage as the "settled stage," *an'i* or *yasuki kurai* 安位. Zenchiku's term, the "settled locus" *ansho* or *yasuki tokoro* 安所, can be seen as a modification of Zeami's so that it at the same time refers to the position of the point settled at the base of the third circle.

The remaining diagrams in the *watakushi kotoba* contain fewer references to *sarugaku* vocabulary.

The fourth is the circle of images (*zōrin* 像輪). Heavenly objects and earthly phenomena—all things are in order within this circle.

This seems a straightforward depiction of a cosmic state. Nevertheless a potential application to stages in training can be discerned without difficulty. Zeami prescribed three performance styles permissible after the completion of technical training. The first style, in which only orthodox techniques are used, corresponds with the idea of "all things" being "in order." The reading of the fifth circle is open to a similar interpretation:

The fifth is the circle of breaking (*harin* 破輪). The generation of inexhaustible different forms (*isō*) in the ten directions of heaven and earth originally emerges from within this circle. Because the circular form is temporarily broken, however, it is called the circle of breaking.

---

457. In *Nikyoku santai ningyō zu*, for example, we see the phrase: 二曲より、三体、足踏生曲に至まで "from the two arts, the three roles, to the vigorous foot-stamping roles." ZZ, 123.

Here the term *isō* is a kind of "*kakekotoba*," allowing two readings. The first, as translated here, corresponds to a stage in cosmic manifestation. This reading of the term was to reappear in Shigyoku's commentary. But as we have seen, Zeami used the same term to describe the heterodox techniques employed in the second period of performance, at the stage of maturity, *ran'i*.[458] This *sarugaku* reading of the term in relation to the fifth circle is made explicit in the later *Kichū*.[459]

Finally, a similar hint at a *sarugaku* interpretation appears in the sixth circle:

> The sixth, the circle of emptiness (*kūrin* 空 輪) is the level of masterlessness and formlessness; facing, leaving and coming back (*kōkokyakurai*), one again takes refuge in the (first) circle of life.

As we have seen, Zeami used the term *kōkokyakurai* for either a return to vulgar styles or complete freedom in performance. This reading, then, fits the *sarugaku* lifeplan, but we should note that it does not match the sixth diagram itself very well (an empty circle). In *Kichū*, Zenchiku found another interpretation of the sixth circle, which was more effective.

Finally there is the *watakushi kotoba* reading of the single dewdrop:

> The one dewdrop (*ichiro* 一 露), not falling into the duality of emptiness and form, is free and unobstructed, not hindered by a speck of dust. It therefore takes the form of the essential sword.

This passage is different in kind from the other sections of the *watakushi kotoba*, for it seems to no obvious connection with either cosmic manifestation or performance.

As we have seen, the *watakushi kotoba* for the first three circles is dominated by the terminology of *sarugaku* training, while for the remaining three circles the vocabulary of cosmogony is dominant, yet there are clear hints of further *sarugaku* connections. There is a convincing match between these *sarugaku* readings of the *watakushi kotoba* and the description of the stages in *sarugaku* training and performance found in Zeami's writings. My view, then, is that Zenchiku understood the circles to have as their primary interpretation a cycle of cosmic emergence and degeneration derived from Shinto writings, but that he observed in them a structural coincidence with his received tradition of stages in *sarugaku* training and practice. (The *watakushi kotoba* were probably notes Zenchiku made for Shigyoku to

458. "*Hifū isō no kyoku*," ZZ, 115, l. 16.
459. KKS, *Kichū*, 219.

remind him of technical matters which he had described more fully in discussion.)

In justifying this interpretation of the *watakushi kotoba*, I have drawn closely on Zeami's account of the program of training and performance, but I should stress that I consider it inappropriate to treat this program as purely Zeami's personal invention. It is difficult to know just what in Zeami's writings derives from his received tradition, what from his generation's shared discourse and what from his own private cogitations. Scholars tend to treat everything after the early part of *Fūshikaden* as Zeami's private creation. Moreover, they are sometimes simplistic about what sort of innovation Zeami himself, let alone his colleagues in the family and troupe, would have regarded acceptable. Concerning stages in training and practice, Zeami himself wrote as if they were organized in an established and agreed pattern, which he regretted that younger actors of his time sometimes ignored.[460] In my view, it is particularly the program of training that would be unlikely to change radically from generation to generation.[461] A study of

460. See, for example, the section starting "When you look at how *sarugaku* actors train in the present generation, however, . . ." (*koko ni, tōsei no sarugaku no keiko o miru ni*), in *Shikadō* (ZZ, 113), or else the description of the continuity of *michi* in the Kanze lineage that opens *Go on*, cited in chapter four, above.

461. Quinn takes a different approach, seeming to view Zeami's stress on mastering *nikyoku* (dance and song) before proceeding to the *santai* (mimicry), described in mature works, like *Shikadō*, as his personal invention, reflecting his reorientation of the relation between mimicry and song and dance. In fact, this order in training, at least, is made explicit in the very first section of *Fūshikaden* (song, movement and dance, before any teaching of mimicry—ZZ, *Fūshikaden*, 15) and must therefore derive from the tradition Zeami received from his father and his associates. It is true that Zeami does not happen to use the formula: *nikyoku santai* in *Fūshikaden*, so it is possible that Zeami developed these terms later himself (although not certain). Even if we read it in this way, what we have here is at most selection and emphasis. It is interesting to note how in *Shikadō*, Zeami introduces the formula in a language that is close to the terms listed in *Fūshikaden*; (*nikyoku to mōsu wa buga nari. Santai to mōsu wa monomane no jintai nari*). Quinn's argument for the innovatory nature of *santai* itself is more convincing than for the order: *nikyoku/santai*, but even that is open to doubt. First we should note that *santai* is a term that already existed in calligraphy (the three styles). So we have yet another case of a formula from outside *sarugaku* being taken up to aid the transfer of oral to written expression (see Pinnington, 2006, esp. 34–5). Scholars have noted that when Zeami first used *santai*, its precise application (like that of *nikyoku*) was more open than its later uses. *Santai* seems at first to have referred to the role types of woman, old person and man (ZZ, *Kakyō*, 88). As these three correspond to the first three role types described in the order of training listed in the early part of *Fūshikaden*, the idea that these are the core roles from which the others naturally emerge was probably already there in the tradition. That is presumably why in *Sandō*, Zeami's assertion that Kannami and Inuō had achieved appropriate levels of skill in all of the *santai* or three basic role types is not the anachronism that Omote and others take it to be, except (perhaps) in terms of terminology (ZZ, *Sandō*, 134, and ZZ, extra note 49, 455). Zeami's innovation (at least as far as the order of training—the matter of writing plays is a separate issue, also problematic) would then consist of finding a traditionally approved formula in élite tradition to represent a received idea in his own oral tradition. At some point, Zeami determined that the essential male role was best represented as *guntai*, the warrior, rather than *nantai* 男体, the man. Overall this is the kind of process that we see throughout Zeami's writings. Zeami appropriates, reinterprets and reapplies various formulations, but (like Zenchiku) he is always operating within received and shared tradition, always conscious of its

what was and was not innovative in Zeami needs another forum, but let us recall that Zenchiku's only reference to Zeami as the originator of new ideas was as the one who "cured" the nine levels.

In any case, there is no sign that Zenchiku interpreted the six circles at this first stage in terms of the path in order to represent "Zeami's" personal inventions (in which, as I have argued, he had little interest). I would suggest a grander and less personal vision behind the *rokurin ichiro* project. Zenchiku perceived that diagrams describing cosmic events could be read as well in terms of what he took to be the traditionally received life path of *sarugaku*, and he saw this as evidence of an essential and profound relation between *sarugaku* and the world, one that he was determined to uncover.

COSMIC READINGS—BUDDHIST, NEO-CONFUCIAN

As well as interpreting the diagrams in terms of the *sarugaku michi*, Zenchiku collected three primary commentaries on, or interpretations of, them in terms of cosmic processes, derived from Buddhist, Neo-Confucian and Shinto sources. The commentaries of Shigyoku and Kanera that are included in *Rokurin ichiro no ki* are two of them; and his own Shinto reading, hinted at in the *watakushi kotoba* and more fully described in *Kichū*, is the third. There are two aims that might explain the presence of these readings: first, they might be intended simply to legitimate Zenchiku's received tradition of training—by exposing striking similarities to universal processes—and second, they might be intended to provide a basis for a deepening or correction of that tradition. The readings Zenchiku obtained from Shigyoku and Kanera operated by constructing a network of cultural authority that absorbed Zenchiku's own interpretations, and thus may be thought of as being primarily concerned to satisfy the first aim (which may be how the two men understood their contributions). On the other hand, we can see amendments to the *sarugaku* reading in *Kichū* that derive from the cosmic readings, indicating some presence, in Zenchiku at least, of the second motive. It is something of an irony that Shigyoku's commentary, which has dominated scholarly investigations of the *rokurin ichiro* works (and even of Zenchiku's writings in general), has no impact on the subsequent *sarugaku* reading at all.[462] Even Kanera's interpretation has only

legitimacy, for he lived in a medieval community of actors whose social position depended on inheritance, in which personal invention, like "genius," carried little weight (see Quinn, 73–4, and ZZ, *Shikadō*, 112). In any case, a major problem reading Zeami is that we do not know what his father and other people around him thought, and even considering the body of his own work, the writing can only be a small part of his thought. The situation with Zenchiku is more firmly based, as we have both Zeami's and Zenchiku's writings.

462. As we shall see. The external commentaries became increasingly insignificant in Zenchiku's second period of writing about the *rokurin ichiro* diagrams.

a slight impact, and that corresponds to nothing central, but rather is the result of an accident of phrasing. In light of the limited relevance of these readings to Zenchiku's, I shall restrict myself here to a brief summary of them. I shall however make some observations about the hermeneutical methods that the two men employ, which are of general importance. I shall then proceed to an exploration of the Shinto reading as it appears in *Kichū*, which, as I have made clear, I believe to be the root interpretation of the diagrams.

Both Shigyoku and Kanera found standard formulations of the cycle of manifestation in their own areas of expertise that they mapped onto the *rokurin ichiro* diagrams. While both sets of qualities described a progression of general states of being, they also were associated in their own contexts with stages in the human life cycle and thus possessed a similar duality to the readings of the *watakushi kotoba*. Shigyoku's formulation derived from Kegon Buddhist traditions. The quality of "true emptiness," *shinkū* 真空, he assigned to the first and sixth circles, and he mapped the "four appearances" *shisō* 四相 of phenomenal manifestation: arising (*shō* 生), abiding (*jū* 住), changing (*i* 異) and vanishing (*metsu* 滅) onto the second to the fifth circles. Kanera, with his interests in Neo-Confucianism, took a set of terms originating in the *Classic of Change (I Ching* 易経)—that is *qian* 乾, the creative, name of the first hexagram, and four qualities (*side* 四徳): "originating growth" *yuan* 元, "prosperous development" *heng* 亨, "advantageous gain" *li* 利 and "correct firmness" *zhen* 貞, used to discuss the first hexagram—and applied them to the first five circles. He took a polarity from the *Diagram of the Supreme Ultimate* ("Supreme Ultimate" *tai ji* 太極 and the "Ultimateless" *wu ji* 無極) for the sixth circle and the dewdrop.[463]

The resulting commentaries operate by citing or alluding to passages in authoritative works. These citations are chosen to establish connections between the author's chosen qualities and the elements of the system as received from Zenchiku: the diagrams, the names and terms of the *watakushi kotoba*, and in Kanera's case, elements of Shigyoku's interpretation, too. There is an interesting story to be told of how the commentaries both take advantage of felicitous coincidences—for example the identity of the Shigyoku's second "appearance" *jūsō* (abiding appearance, assigned to the third circle) and Zenchiku's name for the third circle, *jūrin* (circle of abiding)—and negotiate problematic ones—for example, Shigyoku's third "appearance" *isō* (changing appearance,

---

463. For a full discussion of these formulations, see Thornhill, 1993, 25–42, 88–149.

assigned to the fourth circle), which appears in Zenchiku's *watakushi kotoba* for the fifth circle, where it signified heterodox forms, and not the fourth, as we have seen. We should note, however, that the commentaries depend far more than has been recognized on textual factors (matters of arrangement, orthography, visual coincidences and so on) than on any kind of rational argument. We can see in the array of citations and allusions, and the formulaic correspondences that they support, not so much expressions of complex ideas as networks constructed to demonstrate that relations *of some kind* exist between the diagrams, Zenchiku's readings of them and authoritative textual traditions. [464] These commentaries thus textually embody their social function, which was to establish Zenchiku's (and his art's) relations with high culture and its representatives. That is not to say that the commentaries were insincere, for connections observed in

---

464. My assertions as to the methodology of the commentaries need a different forum for demonstration, but let me provide one example here of the kind of interpretative technique that traditional "scholarly" readings have missed. Shigyoku faces a problem in that the fourth of his "appearances," "vanishing" (*metsu*), does not correspond well with the quality of breaking (*ha*) that constitutes Zenchiku reading of the fifth circle, to which it has to be applied. Zenchiku wrote:
The fifth is the circle of breaking (*harin*). The generation of inexhaustible different forms in the ten directions of heaven and earth originally emerges from within this circle. Because the circular form is temporarily broken, however, it is called the circle of breaking. (第五破輪者、天地十方無尽異相之形を成も、本来此輪中生ず。然共、仮以破円相之儀故、破輪と名付也。).
Shigyoku's commentary was:
The fifth is the stage of extinction, the revelation of defilement as enlightenment, the return of saṃsāra to nirvāṇa. The passage of the Avataṃsaka Sūtra: "The three worlds are just one mind; apart from mind there are no separate dharmas; mind, Buddha and living beings; there is no distinction between these three," the commentary of the great Tendai master that "the conditions of hell are totally situated in the body of the great sage, the realm of Vairocana does not surpass a single thought of an ordinary man" correspond with this stage. The quatrain from the *Awakening of Faith*: "he breaks through the form of compound consciousness, destroys the form of mutually succeeding mind, manifests the *dharma-kāya*, for his wisdom becomes clear and pure" has the same meaning.
(第五は滅の位、煩悩も即菩提と顕れ、生死も即涅槃に帰。「三界唯一心、心外無別法、心仏及衆生、是三無差別」の華厳経の文、「阿鼻依正全処極聖之自身、毘廬身土不超凡下之一念」と云天台大師の解釈、当此の位。「破和合識相、滅相続心、顕現法身、智純浄故」の起信論之文、又此の心なり。)
Why does Shigyoku add the quatrain from the *Awakening of Faith*, which he says merely "has the same meaning"? Its value only becomes apparent when we look at its Chinese orthography. The first two lines are *tsuiku* 対句—parallel phrases—in which the first line starts with the character to break (*ha* 破) and the second with the character to vanish (*metsu* 滅) (i.e. 破和合識相、滅相続心). I suggest that an important motive for the choice of this passage was its apparent bridging of the semantic gap between Zenchiku's "breaking," and Shigyoku's "vanishing." Rather than trying to argue for a semantic equivalence between "breaking" and "vanishing," which would be difficult, Shigyoku provided a quotation in which the relative positions of the two graphs, according to Chinese conventions of parallelism, were a spatial demonstration of their close relationship. The force of Shigyoku's quotation lies not so much in its meaning, but its combination in parallel of Shigyoku's *metsu* and Zenchiku's *ha* in a single prestigious citation (for cited passages see KKS 202–3).

Table 7

Arrangement of *Rokurin ichiro no kichū*

1 Combined readings of the diagrams ("Shinto" (ST), Buddhist (B), Neo-Confucian (NC), and *sarugaku* (S))			
1st circle (ST)	1st circle (B)	1st circle (NC)	1st circle (S)
2nd circle (ST)	2nd circle (B)	2nd circle (NC)	2nd circle (S)
3rd circle (ST)	3rd circle (B)	3rd circle (NC)	3rd circle (S)
4th circle (ST)	4th circle (B)	4th circle (NC)	4th circle (S)
5th circle (ST)	5th circle (B)	5th circle (NC)	5th circle (S)
6th circle (ST)	6th circle (B)	6th circle (NC)	6th circle (S)
Sword (ST)	Sword (B)	Sword (NC)	Sword (S)

2 Summary of *sarugaku* readings
1st circle read in relation to *sarugaku*
2nd circle read in relation to *sarugaku*
3rd circle read in relation to *sarugaku*
4th circle read in relation to *sarugaku*
5th circle read in relation to *sarugaku*
6th circle read in relation to *sarugaku*
Sword read in relation to *sarugaku*

3 Further *sarugaku* based readings
1st circle read in relation to *sarugaku*
2nd circle read in relation to *sarugaku*
3rd circle read in relation to *sarugaku*
4th circle read in relation to *sarugaku*
5th circle read in relation to *sarugaku*
6th circle read in relation to *sarugaku*
Sword read in relation to *sarugaku*

prestigious texts were thought to point directly to connections in the real world.[465]

COSMIC READINGS—SHINTO

For Zenchiku's Shinto interpretation of the circles we have no equivalent document to the full statements of Shigyoku and Kanera. We can, however, extract a summary of that interpretation from *Kichū* where it is combined with other readings into a typically complex Zenchiku structure. At this point let us overview the organization of this work. As will be seen from table 7, the work is made up of three sections. The first constructs a series of spatial clusters similar to those seen in the typological works. Associated

---

465. See the discussions of the social functions of Kanera's prefaces and other contributions to artistic works in Steven D. Carter, "Ichijō Kaneyoshi and the Literary Arts," in *Literary Patronage in Late Medieval Japan*, edited by Steven D. Carter (Michigan Papers in Japanese Studies, 1993), 19–44, esp. 22–37.

with each diagram in turn are four layers of commentary. The first layer, consisting of a few phrases, is cast in terms of Shinto cosmogony, the second layer is Buddhist, being extracted from Shigyoku's commentary, the third is Neo-Confucian, selected from Kanera's commentary, and the last is an elaborated reading in terms of the *sarugaku* path. The second section of *Kichū* distills the material of the fourth layer in each case to make a complete reading of the diagrams in *sarugaku* terms. The third section is also a *sarugaku* interpretation, a new one, tentative and not fully worked out.

The first section combines interpretations in four fields, and we can extract from it material related to the first that is Shinto cosmogony. The term "Shinto" is commonly applied to this interpretation, but what makes it Shinto? As I have mentioned, "first things," the early stages in the manifestation of the universe, were of particular interest to both hereditary shrine families and supporters of the imperial family for their potential as political and spiritual models. These Shinto thinkers collected non-native accounts of cosmogony and aligned them with the descriptions found in the early Japanese histories. As these histories originally drew on Chinese accounts for some of their imagery and terminology, and as some Buddhist thinkers also borrowed terms from the *Classic of Change* and related sources, the various traditions were overlapping and mutually reinforcing. This is particularly apparent in the collection of such accounts in the section of the Watarai Shinto digest *Ruijū shingi hongen* related to cosmic origins.[466] Zenchiku's cosmogonic reading of the first five circles is drawn from these or similar texts, and so in that sense this layer of his interpretation can be called "Shinto." The placing of this reading at the head of the other readings, before even the commentaries of Shigyoku and Kanera and before the *sarugaku* readings, is further support for the view that this was the system's primary significance.

The Shinto interpretation of the *rokurin ichiro* diagrams follows a well-attested series of stages: a single reality (chaos), dual reality (heaven and earth, or rising purity and sinking impurity), a triad (heaven, man and earth), and multiplicity (all phenomena). This pattern can be found in various

---

466. Called the *Tenchi kaibyaku hen* 天地開闢編 (*Section on the Separation of Heaven and Earth*) and included in Ōsumi, 82–106. This section is divided into citations from Chinese Works and Japanese Works. The second group is arranged into works from court families, Shinto families and Buddhist traditions. The last includes specifically Indian traditions, such as the account of the universe's origins in Brahma the creator, who emerges from a lotus linked to the navel of Vishnu floating on universal waters. It also includes accounts that draw directly from Chinese traditions, including the four qualities of the creative, the basis of Kanera's interpretation.

places in Chinese tradition, including Taoist accounts and the *Classic of Change*.[467] Zenchiku adds to it a further stage: multiplicity (heterodox phenomena), diagrammatically similar to Razan's fifth stage: all phenomena.[468] For the last and sixth stage, he draws on a Buddhist conception of universal destruction. There is no significant incompatibility between these stages and the cosmogonic elements of *watakushi kotoba*, so this reading was probably present in Zenchiku's mind from his first thoughts about the system.[469]

The readings of the first two circles are as "Shinto" as they could be. The first, the circle of life, is "the form of undivided heaven and earth, round like a bird's egg. It is the source of the gods of heaven and earth." The second, the vertical circle, is "the form in which heaven and earth are already separated, the pure rises, impure sinks, and one energy arises; this is the source of the gods of heaven and earth." These two passages allude to the first few lines of *Nihonshoki*, the primary canonical Shinto text.[470]

The commentary for the third circle reads: "The form in which heaven is heaven, and earth, earth. All things are settled in their dwelling places." This describes three elements: heaven, earth and "all things." The commentary on the fourth circle, however, says that it has arisen out of the

---

467. It has its roots in such works as *Laozi*, the *Classic of Change*, and *Liezi*, and is quoted in *Ruijū shingi hongen*, from the Sung work *Xinduan fenmen zuantu bowenlu*, Osumi, 1977, 84. Note, however, that the *Diagram of the Supreme Ultimate* and Razan's diagrams in *Shintō denju* follow the alternative pattern: single reality (chaos), dual reality (heaven and earth, or yin and yang), a mixed duality (mixtures of yin and yang), a set of five elements (courses), multiplicity (all phenomena), also well attested in Chinese tradition. Both these schema appear in *Ruijū shingi hongen*, see Ōsumi, 104–5.
468. This might be thought to correspond to the "altered appearances" in the commentary on the *Diagram of the Supreme Ultimate*: "The way of the creative makes the male, the way of the receptive makes the female. The two energies work on each other and give rise to the many things. The many things give birth repeatedly, and the altered appearances have no end," Ōsumi, 83.
469. Further support for this position is the presence of the ideas of rising and the birth of the pure in the *watakushi kotoba* for the second circle, which allude to the same Shinto ideas that appear here.
470. Sakamoto Tarō et al., eds., *Nihonshoki 1 (Nihon koten bungaku taikei 67)* (Iwanami Shoten, 1965), 76. The passage is translated by Aston: "Of old, Heaven and Earth were not yet separated, and the In and Yō not yet divided. They formed a chaotic mass like an egg which was of obscurely defined limits and contained germs. The purer and clear part was thinly drawn out, and formed Heaven, while the heavier and grosser element settled down and became Earth" (Aston, W. G. trans., *Nihongi : Chronicles of Japan from the Earliest Times to A.D. 697* (London: George Allen & Unwin Ltd, 1956), 1–2). One term, from the Shinto reading of the second circle in *Kichū*, that is, *ikki*, "one energy," does not appear in *Nihonshoki*, but it is found in a parallel Chinese description of first things collected in *Ruijū shingi hongen* (Ōsumi, 84). Thornhill, discussing the term in the context of its appearance in Kanera's introduction to his commentary, which as it happens cites another passage found in *Ruijū shingi hongen* (Notes on the Perfect Enlightenment Sutra, ibid, 105), translates it following sinological traditions as the "primal pneuma."

"three powers" (*sansai* 三才), that is, heaven, earth and man.[471] This reading is made explicit in the later *Kanshōbon*.[472]

The fourth and fifth circles are read much as they were in the *watakushi kotoba*, the fourth representing the multiplicity of things in proper order, and the fifth the production of heterodox forms.[473] The sixth circle is interesting in the Shinto context. Zenchiku finds a Buddhist correspondence: "The circle of emptiness is the total disappearance of the universe when the three great disasters strike." The "three great disasters" derive from the Indian doctrine of the great temporal cycles called kalpas. Great kalpas come to an end after a series of fires, floods and typhoons, known as the three great disasters.[474] Why did Zenchiku suddenly need to introduce this exclusively Buddhist reading? Razan's *Shintō denju* diagrams also end with a sixth empty circle. Razan's accompanying comment is "the stage where all things are one principle."[475] Thus, for Razan, the circle does not represent a further temporal stage, but rather refers to a unifying common element present in all things—that is, it plays a role similar to that played by the dewdrop, or *ichiro,* in Zenchiku's system. Zenchiku, however, reads his sixth circle as one more temporal event, a return to the beginning. Cyclic time, fundamental in Indian cosmology, and present in some Neo-Confucian thought, has no place in Shinto conceptions of history. The age of the gods proceeded to the age of human kings, which then had to continue forever.[476] What about the Neo-Confuction interpretations of the sixth circle? Kanera sidestepped the issue in his reading by separating the sixth diagram from the first five and uniting it to the dewdrop through the

---

471. "Man" in Chinese tradition had the wider meaning of the human world; perhaps this is what Zenchiku meant in his reference in the third circle to "all things." His lack of clarity over the connection between all "things" here and the third of the "three powers" mentioned later might have been the result of his particular interest in the idea of things being "settled" (*rakkyo* 落居—important for his *sarugaku* reading) in their "dwelling places" (important in connecting to the other layers of interpretation).

472. I.e. *Rokurin ichiro hichū (kanshōbon),* KKS, *Kanshōbon,* 235.

473. These two stages may be connected to states described in the *tenchi kaibyaku* section of *Ruijū shingi hongen.* In the first, all things accord with the Great Way and they do not harm the spirit, and in the second, they do not accord with the Way, and the spirit is scattered. Ōsumi, 104–5.

474. The myth is well described in the first section of *Jinnō shōtōki* (translated in Varley, 58–9).

475. See accompanying illustration of Razan's diagrams.

476. There were political reasons to deny cyclic schemes, for courtly conservatives could not accept Chinese ideas of dynastic change. This matter was particular sensitive in the Muromachi period. In his preface to *Kojiki,* Ō no Yasumaro 太安万侶 had referred to one hundred human kings. The theory then developed that the hundredth king (i.e. emperor descended from Amaterasu) would be the last. This was calculated to be Go-Komatsu who reigned from 1392 to 1412. The shogun Yoshimitsu showed particular interest in this theory, for it seems that he wished to install his son as the first of a new dynasty of Japanese rulers—Imatani and Kōzō, 1992, 73–4 and 76.

pair of Supreme Ultimate and Ultimateless. Thus, for Zenchiku, there was no ready alternative to a Buddhist reading. In terms of performance art, too, the sixth circle posed difficulties. In the *watakushi kotoba*, Zenchiku interpreted the return to emptiness through the term *kōkyokyakurai*, the return to inferior or vulgar styles of performance. Equating emptiness and vulgarity does not seem very satisfactory; as we shall see Zenchiku found a more convincing alternative in the *sarugaku* section of *Kichū*.

THE *SARUGAKU* INTERPRETATION

Zenchiku had gathered together Shinto, Buddhist and Neo-Confucian commentaries; how did they contribute to his model of the *sarugaku* actor's lifeplan? His discussions in the first sections of *Kichū* show evidence of considerable elaboration of the *watakushi kotoba* elements. Nevertheless, apart from the readings of the first and sixth circles, which are revised, the interpretations follow the same basic plan. The second section of *Kichū* summarizes them as follows:

> First, the circle of life. The breath in singing, the form of a circle from beginning to end. The circle at the start of dance, joining the beginning to the end. This circle has front and back. Oral transmission.
>
> Second, the circle of the vertical. The form of singing rising supreme, pure and cold. The emotional impact of the ultimate *yūgen* in the appearance of dance is manifest from here.
>
> Third, the circle of abiding. In dance and song each note, syllable and movement is without disarray. Each is settled in its level, ordered in this absolute place.
>
> Fourth, the circle of images. Singing, dance and technique become like each thing portrayed, the stage where things are ordered and differentiated, without forgetting the upper three circles of higher levels.
>
> Fifth, the circle of breaking. Singing is fully mature and dance has heterodox appearances (*isō*) and reverse styles, but the actor naturally keeps within the constraints of the upper three fruitions.
>
> Sixth, the circle of emptiness. Penetrating deeper and deeper, song and dance dry up and are exhausted, the style of blossoms remaining on an old tree. The roles are few and unadorned, he returns to the original circle of life.

The one dewdrop is the spirit that connects these six circles.[477]

All the circles pointedly refer to singing and dancing in parallel. We shall discuss the first circle separately below. The stages of training have been redistributed over the second and third circles and are completed in the fourth circle. The fifth circle makes explicit the reading that we saw hinted at by the term *isō* in *watakushi kotoba*. The sixth circle is made to correspond to the last stages of an actor's career using an image famously employed by Zeami.

In the second circle, we have "the form of singing rising supreme, pure and cold. The emotional impact of the ultimate *yūgen* in the appearance of dance is manifest from here." Mastery of the two arts, *nikyoku*, song and dance, is now the central idea. The image of pure rising resonates with the Shinto reading of the circle in which "the pure rises" (creating the world of the gods). In the third circle, "each note, syllable and movement is without disarray. Each is settled in its level, ordered in this absolute place." This is where the non-representational arts of dance and song have been fully mastered and applied to the various role types without the introduction of mimicry. In the fourth circle, these arts are now modified to fit the performance of actual roles. "Singing, dance and technique become like each thing portrayed, the stage where things are ordered and differentiated, without forgetting the upper three circles of higher levels."[478] Following my interpretation, which roots these readings in the traditions Zeami described in *Shikadō*, the "upper three circles" can be understood to correspond to the mastery of basic techniques in early training. The fifth circle is *ran'i*, the stage where the polished actor admits heterodox techniques, as indeed we saw foreshadowed in the *watakushi kotoba*. "Singing is fully mature and dance has heterodox appearances (*isō*) and reverse styles, but the actor naturally keeps within the constraints of the upper three fruitions." To these four stages, instead of reading the sixth as *kōkokyakurai*—a return to the vulgar world—which as we noted seemed a problematic image for a return to the pure emptiness of the first stage, Zenchiku adds a new interpretation. "Penetrating deeper and deeper, song and dance dry up and are exhausted, the style of blossoms remaining on a old tree. The roles are few and unstylish, he returns to the original circle of life." This metaphor of the old tree was famously used by Zeami to describe his father Kannami, performing two weeks before his death. In the same passage Zeami stated

---

477. KKS, 219.
478. In my translation: "become like each thing portrayed" corresponds to *sono mono sono mono ni narite*, which conveniently fits my analysis. I felt justified in this reading by Thornhill's: "become like the objects portrayed" for the same passage. (Thornhill, 1993, 50).

that in ordinary circumstances actors over the age of fifty should stop performing, but mentioned his father as the exception, someone whose achievements were so great that even at the end of his life he still had the power to charm.[479]

This interpretation of the second to sixth circles, then, spans the life of an actor, closing with the loss of abilities developed earlier. But what about the first circle? In the *watakushi kotoba*, the first circle was the vessel from which *yūgen* arose. If it corresponded to a stage in training at all, it was the inherent vitality brought by a youth to the first steps on the path. The first and last circles could be understood as placing the limits at either end of the actor's career. Here in *Kichū*, however, the reading of the first circle is quite new. As it is summarized in the second section it opens with the words: "The breath in singing, the form of a circle from beginning to end. The circle at the start of dance, joining the beginning to the end." It is still possible to read this as a stage in the actor's life cycle—breath-control and phrasing might have been an important part of the first training in singing. But it is a different kind of reading from earlier ones, for the circle is being interpreted in terms of a general performance principle. Where does this new reading come from?

Inspection shows that it derives ultimately from Kanera's commentary on the first circle. How it does so exemplifies the concrete and visual ways in which texts could be interpreted. Zenchiku's replacing of the *watakushi kotoba* readings of the first and sixth circles with the new ones here is moreover the first in a series of renegotiations that appear increasingly in subsequent works, exemplifying the provisional and exploratory nature Zenchiku's interpretations.

To understand how Zenchiku came to the new reading of the first circle, we must consider the more detailed version he gives in the first section of *Kichū*. The central image is still the breath:

> Interpreted in terms of song and dance, the breath of vocal art joins the circle of chanting from beginning to end. The outgoing breath should directly join its sound to the stage of the ingoing breath. Without breath the voice makes no sound, but breath and sound are separate and so, in the first place, one should make this breath a string to join the sound of the syllables. In this world, if there is a gap of a single breath, then one cannot live. If one does not forget this circular form, then the life of one's singing will be long. Singing and dancing are essentially one, and so this circular form is also the breath of dance. Even if one abandons

technique, if one joins the dance in a continuous circular form, this will give life to the dance. This is the vessel that gives birth to all things. This is the source of *yūgen*.[480]

The last two sentences refer back to the original interpretation in *watakushi kotoba*, but the dominant idea now is a fluid continuity joining together moments in performance. The "circle of the breath" refers to a constant flow stringing together the consecutive syllables in singing. Zenchiku links this image to the idea of "life" (the name of the first circle), both literally, through the dependence of life on breathing, and figuratively, through the idea of "the life of singing," which needs a continuous flow. The idea of continuity is straightforward, the image of the circle seems well designed to express it and it seems sensible to extend its application from song to dance. But why is it expressed primarily through the image of the breath, and why is it suddenly introduced here? The answer becomes evident when we look at the preceding sentence in *Kichū*, which paraphrases Kanera's interpretation:

> The meaning in the way of the *Classic of Change*: this is the stage of the creative (*qian*); the wheel of heaven revolves day and night, without the break of a single breath, the form of the circle in the circle of life signifies perpetual revolving without the slightest rest. [481]

We can immediately see that this image, of the ceaseless revolution of heaven "without the break of even one breath," inspired Zenchiku's new interpretation. For surely there were traditions in the training of *sarugaku* relating to control of the breath, including advice about not breaking the continuity of sound mid-phrase.[482] It is interesting to consider, however, what lay behind Kanera's adoption of his image. It will be recalled that Kanera's commentary involved the assignation of the quality of the creative (*qian*), name of the first hexagram of the *Classic of Change*, to the first circle. This was achieved by creating a series of allusive links:

> The circle of life is what is called the circle of the creative. Now the circle of heaven revolves day and night, and, without the break of even one breath, "the four seasons pursue their course and all things are

---

480. KKS, 215–216.
481. KKS, 215.
482. See, for example, the sensible advice in ZZ, *Fushizuke Shidai*, 151, section headed: *ongyoku ni iki no koto*. Technical matters to do with singing generally involve a particularly difficult vocabulary, which does not seem consistently applied (see extra notes 29–32, ZZ, 440–444). The discussion of phrasing here, however, which begins by describing the breath as " the basic source which links the elements of a song together," is clear and practical, and corresponds closely with Zenchiku's interpretation of the circle of life here.

produced." Surely this is the power of the creative. "Thus complete sincerity is without break;" it is called the creative. "The creative is also health/action." Ceaseless health is thus the meaning of the circle of life. [483]

As I have said, Kanera's aim was to establish, by associative links and allusion to authoritative texts, connections between his chosen correspondences and prominent aspects of the other interpretations of the diagrams, including their names and interpretations in the *watakushi kotoba*. This reading of the first circle is a good example, bringing together Kanera's principle, *qian* the creative; Zenchiku's *jurin*, the circle of life; and the idea of a long or complete lifespan mentioned in the *watakushi kotoba*. How these are linked is as follows: the circle 輪 from *jurin* 寿輪 is appended to *qian* 乾, the creative, to make the compound *qian lun* 乾輪, the circle of the creative. The traditional identification of *qian* and *tian* 天 then leads to *tian lun* 天輪, the circle of heaven. Kanera alludes to a commentary from the appendices to the *Classic of Change*: "*Qian* is represented by Heaven and revolves without ceasing," and then cites a well-known passage in *The Analects* that describes heaven silently producing all things. [484] He uses the idea of this wheel's continuity to link to two images of ceaselessness—that of complete sincerity (from the *Doctrine of the Mean*) [485] and that from the "commentary on the image" on the first hexagram *qian*: "Heaven's movements are healthy. Thus the superior man makes himself strong without break." This idea of endless health conveniently resonates with the final element of Zenchiku's interpretation: "complete and endless lifespan" 円満長久之寿命.

The interesting thing is that none of this reading has any essential connection with the breath, but the Chinese citations used an idiom to express the idea of "ceaselessness" that is literally 無息 "no breath," which Kanera expanded in one phrase to the more explanatory Japanese 一息の間断無し "without the break of one breath." What appears to have happened, then, is that Zenchiku, seeing in Kanera's interpretation of the first circle the fortuitous use of an idiom signifying "unceasing," expressed as "no break in the breath," associated this with *sarugaku* traditions on phrasing. From this he developed his new *sarugaku* interpretation of the first circle, extended to both singing and dancing. He later applied the imagery

---

483. KKS, *Rokurin ichiro no ki*, 210.
484. "The four seasons pursue their course and all things are produced," *Analects*, ch. 17, 19 (in Legge, 1893, 326)). The commentators of KKS miss this allusion, picking up the less close connection to a phrase in the *Diagram of the Great Ultimate*, KKS, 210, headnote 2.
485. *Doctrine of the Mean*, ch. 26, 1 (Legge, 1893, 419).

developed here, separated from its *rokurin ichiro* context, in *Go on sangyoku shū*.[486] In this whole process, we again see the associative nature of the interpretative principles employed.

We have seen above that Zenchiku conceived of an analog between a diagrammatic representation of cosmogony and the stages prescribed for the *sarugaku michi*. I have argued that he was inspired in this by the similar analog set up by Shinto thinkers between accounts of the first cosmic events and prescriptions for the state of spiritual union. He then combined this analog with his vision of *sarugaku* as a manifestation of fundamental forces through the channel of the mind and body of the actor. Zenchiku believed this analog to have been authorized by the circumstances in which he noticed the similarity, a retreat at the Hase temple. I have argued that for Zenchiku this analog, at least for the first decade of the *rokurin ichiro* project, centered on an attempt to simultaneously map the traditional plan of stages in the *sarugaku* path and a Shinto-style account of cosmic processes onto the diagrams. His concatenation of Buddhist and Neo-Confucian readings mimicked the textual juxtapositions found in works of Shinto spiritual and imperial political theorizing.

The hermeneutic techniques employed in the production of these readings are associative and do not distinguish between intellectual, orthographic or textual connections. As such they are similar to other medieval Japanese texts, poetic and spiritual, and have much in common with Zenchiku's own intellectual procedures in the last of his works, which we shall explore in the next chapter. Zenchiku constructs from all these readings complex arrays of phrases similar to those we have seen in his categorical works. In both sets of works, these textual combinations describe networks of authority. The citations of Buddhist and Chinese texts and commentaries in the *rokurin ichiro* works play a similar role to the references to poetical and other external material in the typologies: they hint at deep significance through apparent connections to works of undisputed authority. Zenchiku sought to authorize and universalize his views—views which might be suspected otherwise of being *watakushi*, private and provisional—by demonstrating their similarity to what was *watakushi naki*, established and permanent.

---

486. KKS, *Go on sangyoku shū*, 177.

Table 8

Six circles and nine levels in *Kanshōbon*

Order in *Rokurin*	Names of the six circles	Zeami's names for the Nine Levels	Order in Nine Levels
1	circle of life	*myōkafū*, absolute flower	1
2	circle of the vertical	*chōshinkafū*, charming profound flower	2
3	circle of abiding	*kankafū*, still flower	3
4	circle of images	*shōkafū*, correct flower	4
5	circle of breaking	*kōshōfū*, broad and pure	5
		senmonfū, shallow and patterned	6
		kasanfū, remaining lower styles	7, 8, 9

Table 9

Six circles and nine levels in *Yūgen sanrin*

Order in *Rokurin*			Order in Nine Levels
1			1
2	upper three circles	upper three flowers	2
3			3
			4
4	circle of images	middle three styles	5
			6
			7
5	circle of breaking	remaining lower styles	8
			9
6	circle of emptiness	the level of the highest fruition	

INHERENT VALUES IN THE *ROKURIN ICHIRO* SYSTEM
AND CONTRASTS WITH ZEAMI

Before we conclude this study of the *rokurin ichiro* writings, let us take up one case where Zenchiku tries to integrate into his theory a conceptualization closely associated with Zeami. The problematic nature of that integration reflects differences in values inherent in Zeami and Zenchiku's theories, values which, as we shall consider in the next chapter, led Zenchiku to identify *sarugaku* as (what we might consider) a spiritual rather than an artistic activity.

The division of performances (or plays) into nine grades was, as noted in chapter four, probably a common tradition. Zeami, in his work *Kyūi*, used this division in two ways, first as an analysis of aesthetic qualities—the first being the finest and the ninth being the poorest—and second as a framework for a prescription of the actor's progress. This secondary development he summed up in his formulae: middle first, upper middle, lower after, which meant that the aspiring actor should start his training at the bottom of the middle group (the sixth grade) and work himself up step by step to the highest (the first grade) after which the now mature actor was free, if he wished, to descend to the lower three (the seventh, eighth and ninth grades). Zenchiku, in *Kabuzuinōki*, took the same nine levels as an aesthetic typology of plays (rather than performances), calling them by the same poetic names used by Zeami. He also linked them to his six circles in a number of works of the *rokurin ichiro* series. The first is *Kanshōbon,* written in 1459, four years after *Kabuzuinōki*. *Kanshōbon* gathers together material from earlier works related to each diagram. It also adds the names of the nine levels to the first five circles, as shown in table 8.

Zenchiku does explain his reasons for this arrangement, but it seems relatively straightforward: the circles are simply being aligned with the aesthetic styles in order from the finest to the crudest.[487] As we noted above, while writing *Kichū*, Zenchiku began to consider the first three of his six circles to be inherently superior to the others. The correspondence described here between the circles and the nine levels allows these three "upper circles" to be aligned with the three higher levels of performance.

A similar set of correspondences is described in the undated work *Yūgen sanrin*, as illustrated in table 9. This time Zenchiku gives his rationale, matching superior, middling and inferior qualities in each system:

> Now the training path of the "six circles, one dewdrop" makes the upper three circles the source of *yūgen*. Extending to the many orthodox roles (*jittei*), and even performing heterodox form and

---

487. The nine levels are distinguished into three groups. The idea that the better performance pieces belong in the first three circles, and the more ordinary ones in the fourth and fifth is interestingly expressed in the introduction to *Kanshōbon*: "The upper three circles are the three ritual pieces (*Shikisanban*), the divine technique (*kamiwaza*). From the circle of images, the sixty-six *kagura*, up to the forms of other styles, these must all be arts that praise the Buddha and turn the wheel of the law." (KKS, 231.) "Other styles" is probably referring to the "*isō*" of the breaking circle, so the sixty-six *kagura* are being apportioned to the fourth circle and the heterodox styles to the fifth. This reflects Zenchiku's neo-conservative evaluation of *okina sarugaku*, discussed in chapter six.

demonic creatures, as long as one is accompanied by the *yūgen* of the upper three circles, . . . these shall be the bright path guiding creatures to nirvana and benefiting living beings. In this regard, piling up the classes of grades, Zea[mi] cured the ninefold essential levels. Now if we consider this carefully, the upper three qualities are the upper three of the six circles. The middle qualities are various, the circle of images. The lower three qualities are the circle of breaking.[488]

As we have seen, however, Zeami himself in *Kyūi* apportioned the nine levels to the stages of the actor's life in his own specific order.[489] This means that in creating the correspondences between the six circles and nine levels, Zenchiku is also willy-nilly generating a new correspondence with the path of training. This becomes explicit in *Bunshōbon*. A new starting point for the path is found in the six circles corresponding to Zeami's entry point at the lower middle stage of the nine levels:

> The entry point of training, however, is at the circle of images, from the orthodox style of the three roles. The beginner having attained the complete training must rise in level up to the upper three circles. First, the study of the beginner from childhood must be based on the two arts of song and dance. From there, following the different stages in order, achieving success and winning fame, he should not attempt the two circles of breaking and emptiness. Essential are the highest grades; these three circles are techniques of the mind, the others techniques in the handling of the body.[490]

The fourth circle, the circle of images, which corresponds to three of Zeami's middle levels, has to bear the burden of representing "the complete training," the two arts, and the "different stages in order." This contradicts

---

488. KKS, 264–5. The reference to the "various, circle of images" (雑、像輪) seems to indicate an alternative orthography for the circle: *zōrin*.

489. It is possible to map out the order of training Zeami describes in *Fūshikaden, Shikadō* and elsewhere onto his path through the nine levels in *Kyūi* by inspecting Zeami's descriptions in the second half of that work. It does not operate through one to one correspondences. (I number the nine levels from 1 at the bottom to 9 at the top.) Studying the two arts, song and dance, brings the actor in at level 4 ("shallow and patterned"). Pursuing the training more broadly and bringing everything to complete fruition (*zenka* 全課) brings him to level 5 ("broad and pure"). Applying these arts to the three roles brings him to level 6 ("the correct flower"). The achievement of the settled level (*an'i* or *yasuki kurai*) brings him to level 7 ("the still flower"). After rising through the two higher levels (8, "charming profound flower," and 9, the "absolute (or language-transcending) flower"), the actor may descend from the heights (*kyakurai*) on occasion and play freely in the lower levels (1 to 3). Note here that the distinctions of the three highest levels (7 to 9) do not correspond to any distinct stages in the earlier descriptions of *Shikadō* and other works, and also that it is doubtful whether *kyakurai* can be identified with the employment of heterodox techniques (*ran'i*) of the earlier system. (See ZZ, *Kyūi*, 176–7).

490. KKS, 249–250.

the readings that we saw culminating in the second section of *Kichū*, where the actor simply proceeded through his life from the first circle to the sixth. It is this final reading that Zenchiku justifies with his statement that:

> In particular, this account (*shidai*) of the *rokurin* is my own creation, but it is the result of profound deliberation over the aesthetic qualities (*kyokumi*) of my teacher, and is not a personal thing.

What we see, then, from this survey of the relationships set up between the *rokurin ichiro* system and the nine levels, is that Zenchiku, in attempting to establish such a correspondence, is forced to alter his own earliest readings of the *rokurin ichiro* system in a fundamental way. Why is this important? Partly because this is one very clear occasion where Zenchiku takes a prominent theory that he himself closely associated with Zeami and tries to represent it in his own system. This is evidence that the *rokurin ichiro* system was not simply a device for reproducing Zeami's theories. But more importantly it leads us to ask what it was about the Zenchiku's vision of the path that rendered his major theoretical structure incompatible with Zeami's systematization of the way.

THE STRUCTURE OF THE WAY

Zenchiku's repeated negotiations of the *rokurin ichiro* system (only a small part of which we have been able to consider here) hardly reaches a satisfying conclusion, partly because of the increasing difficulty he finds in achieving a good fit between his diagrams and his ideas, and partly because of the widely different types of issues that he tries to have it represent. In the cases of the two commentaries of Shigyoku and Kanera, we see the beginning of such problems. There was the evident amenability of the structure: emptiness followed by progressive elaboration and a final decay back into emptiness, to cyclic patterns of the rise and disappearance of phenomena. Yet when it came to the details, matching the particular sets of stages which they had chosen from their traditions to the diagrams—let alone to the *watakushi kotoba* and to each other—was impossible without some fudging.

When it comes to the representation of the *sarugaku* path, the situation again appears promising. Let us step outside the cultural context for a moment, and recall the cliché of western musical and artistic biographies: the artist goes from simplicity in childhood through increasing complexity to perhaps over-complexity, followed by a return to simplicity in old age. This would seem to be a natural pattern, one likely to be well represented by the *rokurin* diagrams. The empty circles at the beginning and the end, indicating the *tabula rasa* at birth and the final exhaustion at death, fit well.

The pervading and unchanging dewdrop could represent the unchanging talent or spirit of the artist throughout. In *sarugaku* traditions as we find them in Zeami's writings, particularly those in which Zenchiku shows an interest, the dominant image is the path of the performer from childhood to old age, inherent in the word *michi*. We might expect that the *rokurin* system would be well able to represent such a *michi*. Still, we must not ignore the system of values inherent in the diagrams themselves. The empty circle, within Taoism and also in Zen, because of its emptiness, was always likely to stand for a desirable and superior state in contrast to elaborated circles. Alicia Matsunaga discusses this in the context of the intellectual history of China. While for Buddhism, the realm of the formless and the world of form were considered to be at root identical and equivalent, in Taoist writings the return to the formless was the great goal, so that the Ultimateless was superior to the Supreme Ultimate, *wu* 無 superior to *yu* 有.[491] Watarai Shinto thought had spiritual union couched in similar terms: it was a return to the beginning, to what was undifferentiated. Throughout Zenchiku's readings of the six circles, we find the weight of value to lie on the empty circles. For him, it is to the origin in particular, the *mushu mubutsu*, that we must look for the significance of literary art—whether in its first and purest manifestation as poetry, or in its extended and hence slightly less prestigious manifestation as song and dance.

Elsewhere Zenchiku distributed the polarity of *shō* 性 (essence) and *yū* 用 (function) onto the circles, making the simpler first three circles *shō*, hence primary, and the complex fourth and fifth *yū*, hence secondary. Konishi took this polarity to be the primary idea that Zenchiku derived from Zeami to construct his *rokurin ichiro* system; but if this does come from Zeami, it is a considerable misreading of Zeami's theory.[492] Zenchiku treats the sixth circle as a return to the first, i.e. again a valuation of emptiness. If one now considers the appropriateness of this structure to acting tradition, it is indeed problematic. The acting tradition, as described, for example, in

491. Matsunaga, Alicia, *The Buddhist Philosophy of Assimilation: The Historical Development of the Honji-Suijaku Theory* (Tokyo: Sophia University in cooperation with Charles E. Tuttle Company, 1969), 105–7.
492. Zenchiku's interpretation is found in *Nika ichirin*, in the final passage: "The profound storehouse of this *michi* is not only for one full lifetime. That "essential flower" that vertically spreads through the three worlds and horizontally extends through the ten directions is the three upper circles. The "apparent flower" is the two circles of images and breaking. The two levels of empty and dew are the spirits of sun and moon, the level of complete realization, the fruit of faith in the Buddha, beyond which one cannot go." (KKS, 223). This is far from Zeami's essential flower (the charm that lasts, being rooted in thorough training) and apparent flower (the charm of a young actor that passes with his youth) (ZZ, *Shūgyokutokka*, 187). Zenchiku has read this through a *Lotus Sutra* inspired duality of absolute and provisional reality, with a ying-yang polarity tacked on the end, presumably to generate a correspondence with the desired seven elements of his system.

Zeami's early work *Fūshikaden*, proceeds from unskilled, through increasing training to highly skilled, and then eventually to decline and failure. The value here would likely be placed on the fourth and fifth stages. This image of the path has much in common with many formulations of the Buddhist path, as indeed is evident in Zeami's adoption of Buddhist terminology in his later theories. The aspirant starts in a state of ignorance, and by repeated discipline and practice purifies the mind of illusion, resulting eventually in enlightenment. Some schools of Zen may have attempted to undercut the idea of steady progress to a goal. Nevertheless, the pattern of development adopted by Zeami from Tendai thought and Sōtō Zen revolved around a basic conception of training: developing physical techniques, acquiring knowledge, and finally breaking through to emptiness (*mu*).[493] It is no accident that this conception of ability that increases with time (and thus seniority) coincides with the power structure of the household—the older you are, the higher your degree of training, the more capable you probably are (before retirement, at least). Though the Buddhist aspirant was not conceived of as sinking back into ignorance in old age, the actor could expect to lose his abilities and looks, a fact which posed repeated problems in Zeami's thought.[494] The idea of the attainment of the permanent or essential flower, and its superiority (as recognized by the refined aficionado in the audience) over the callow charm of youth, should perhaps be seen as an expression of denial in Zeami's theories—denial of the preferences of shoguns, elderly aristocrats and clerics, for the young and charming over the sophisticated but unfortunately old.

What I am saying, then, is that there is a fundamental conflict of values between the *rokurin ichiro* diagrams, embedded as they are in traditions that place a high value on origins and emptiness, and the image of *michi* in Zeami's works, which stresses progressive training and the acquisition of skills that must be carefully maintained. These contrasts can in fact be found in the ideological roots from which the two men drew their models— Buddhism in general stressed seniority and a forward progress along the path, achieved by rigorous practice, but Shinto families saw their legitimacy to lie in their ancient origins, their descent from divine ancestors in a perfect past. Zenchiku's adherence to Shinto (and Taoist) paradigms reflected his sense that in performance it was the actor's purity of mind that was most important, for that drew the regard of the gods, even if the audience was not entertained. This purity of mind he began to think was

493. This basic pattern is analyzed by Nose Asaji in "Zeami ni okeru kokoro no shomondai," in *Nose Asaji Chosakushū 5* (Kyoto: Shibunkaku Shuppan, 1984), 93–185.
494. See Pinnington, 2006, 36–7.

something to be earned not by training, but rather by the adoption of appropriate attitudes, for example of freedom from the thought of gain when making offerings. If this power of mind were to be achieved, it would be not so much by strict training and a highly developed sensitivity to audience mood, but rather by a general spiritual attitude, supported by heredity, particularly descent from the semi-divine figures he was willing to believe established the art in the first place. Such a view characterizes Zenchiku's attempts to present *sarugaku* as a quasi-Shinto ritual, as we shall see in the next chapter.

6 Authority
Meishukushū and the Ideology of Okina

How does a tradition claim authority? If its importance is self-evident it does not need to; otherwise it turns to ideological means. Konishi sees authority in *michi* as something that was granted by medieval society to traditions possessing the four elements of specialization, transmission, conformity and universality. Such a statement is difficult to evaluate; it is not clear to what degree medieval society did grant *michi* authority, and, where it did, on what basis. Rather than speculate on the attitudes society had towards traditions, it seems more profitable to ask about the claims for authority made by specialists themselves. Such claims were primarily based on ancient founding occasions and secret interpretations. With these types of material, traditions of all kinds sought to establish the importance of their practices and the legitimacy of their practitioners.

Such stories already existed in medieval *sarugaku* traditions. They included theories of three founding occasions and of hidden identities for certain performance roles. Zeami described some of this lore in a disengaged fashion in his early work, but in his later writings he used it to discuss certain questions that concerned him: the nature of audience response, the correct balance between artistic and mimetic elements in performance, and the relationship between duty and financial reward in troupe performances. Zeami thus used the material for its normative potential but did not dwell on its authorizing force. This is not surprising. First, his line had its own authority through its ties to the Muromachi shogunate. Second, *sarugaku* lore was conservative, and Zeami and his father were innovators. Third, the founding occasions were linked by transmission to the Komparu line, so that any use of them to legitimate the Kanze could only put it in a secondary position.

Zenchiku took a greater interest in this material. He was happy to use it to authorize his family line, and indeed he developed it further, intensifying *sarugaku*'s importance and strengthening his family claims. But he also pored over it along with legends and interpretations from other traditions in search of the knowledge that he felt sure lay behind it. The results of his investigations are collected in the fragmentary text, *Meishukushū*. This work constructs a vision of *sarugaku* to challenge Kanze ideals and current trends, a vision that we can see in retrospect to have been present in Zenchiku's imagination from the beginning: *sarugaku* performers are religious functionaries, and performance is a means by which the actor experiences the divine and the world is blessed.

Before we look more closely at Zeami and Zenchiku's use of traditional lore, we must consider certain contexts. How does this material relate to Konishi's formula for authority, and were there broader contexts for the Komparu and Kanze styles of legitimation? What was the historical background to Zenchiku's resuscitation of *sarugaku* mythology?

ESTABLISHING THE AUTHORITY OF *MICHI*

Konishi states:

> The elements of *michi*, that is, specialization, transmission, conformity and universality, arose one by one in turn, starting with specialization. At each stage *michi*'s authority increased. Authority was born not from one particular element but closely connected with all of them.[495]

This is the kind of satisfying conclusion to Konishi's theory that is unlikely to be supportable by evidence; in any case he does not provide any. Konishi makes it plain that he means by authority a respect felt by society towards *michi* and their practitioners. Whether society actually felt such a respect, though, is difficult to demonstrate. For example, in *sarugaku*, eminent figures allowed Zeami and Zenchiku a surprising intellectual intimacy, but authorities treated other actors of similar station badly.[496] The relationship between practitioners of the arts and society in the fifteenth century is sometimes characterized in the following terms: warrior leaders sought prestige by patronizing courtly and metropolitan arts, so artists tried to sell themselves as bearers of metropolitan culture.[497] This is intrinsically interesting (bearing comparison with what was happening in Italy at the same time: in both cases artists turned themselves into intellectuals), and shows that society must have valued traditions which could demonstrate their connections with the old court. But it does not otherwise connect directly with Konishi's theory.[498]

---

495. Konishi, 1986, 158.
496. For example, the Enami, discussed in chapter two.
497. We see this pattern described in relation to painters in Imatani Akira, Miyajima Shin'ichi, *Gadan tōitsu ni kakeru yume—Sesshū kara Eitoku e* (Bun'eidō, 2001), 24–7.
498. Clearly it conflicts with specialization as Konishi describes it.

Konishi sees his elements as progressively establishing the authority of *michi*, but an unsystematic survey suggests that *michi* themselves did not in fact routinely claim all his elements; rather different traditions favored some and rejected others. *Renga*, for example, in the hands of Nijō Yoshimoto, claimed ancient origins and a form of universality but rejected the need for specialization and conformity to the past.[499] *Sarugaku*, through Zeami, on the other hand, showed little interest in ancient transmission or universality, but did require specialization and conformity. Counter-examples can be given in both these fields.[500] These self-characterizations are perhaps best understood not merely in terms of claims to authority, but rather as position-taking, the adoption of distinct points of view within a field of practitioners. This is evident in the negotiation of the same elements in the writings of teachers of sword-fighting a century later. In *Gorin no sho* 五輪書, Miyamoto Musashi states that he mastered many arts and had no teacher.[501] His authority as a swordsman came from the fact that he always won his fights.[502] He claims universal wisdom: by "thinking of things in a wide sense" and "taking the void as the way," he found the Way of Heaven, a way applicable to all arts.[503] Musashi adopts a position that contrasts with his competitors, such as Yagyū Munenori 柳生宗矩 (1571–1646), who stress descent and conformity to standard models. Konishi's elements thus figure repeatedly in characterizations of *michi*, not as parts of a fixed set, but as a number of issues in relation to which different practitioners can situate themselves.

It is hard to say what relation this position-taking has to the establishment of cultural authority. Yoshimoto's definition of *renga* was perhaps designed to deepen its connections to courtly traditions without alienating or stifling the popular styles of his time. His tracing of its ancient history may have been designed to increase its prestige, but he himself of course had cultural capital to spare. In the other cases, the positions adopted seem rather the means by which practitioners distinguished themselves from each other. If Bourdieu's suggestions are correct, the positions must have paralleled sources of patronage, but in any case resulted from jostling within *michi* themselves, rather than attempts to dignify given *michi* per se.

499. Nijō Yoshimoto describes the ancient history of *renga* and compares it in practice to Buddhism, but he does not demand the renunciation of other pursuits and denies the need to study with a teacher or copy former works. See Ueda, 1967, 37–54.
500. In *sarugaku*, I mean Zenchiku, obviously, and in *renga* I am thinking of Shinkei.
501. Kamiko, 13–14, (for translation see Victor Harris, trans., *A Book of Five Rings* (London: Allison and Busby, 1974), 35).
502. Kamiko, 13; Harris, 35.
503. Kamiko, 221–2; Harris, 95.

Let us approach the question of authority in *michi* afresh. Arguments for the authority or social necessity of traditional practices must be distinguished from arguments for the legitimacy of particular practitioners. In the cases of Musashi and Zeami, the importance of the skills they had mastered seemed self-evident. In Musashi's life, skill in sword-fighting was "a matter of life or death" (only later would it need spiritual or other justifications), and in Zeami's time powerful audiences clamored for Noh plays. Neither of them sought ideological ways to lend their arts prestige. When it comes to the way they justified their personal legitimacy, Musashi won his fights and lived to a ripe age, and Zeami's father, Kannami, gained the support of the *bakufu* through winning competitions. They thus proved the superiority of their skill over competitors. How about traditions whose value was open to doubt, or practitioners who could not prove themselves against competitors? A standard technique had developed for demonstrating the significance of medieval traditions: describing ancient founding occasions (what Klein calls "etiologies") from which the traditions developed. Both prestige and necessity could be asserted by situating these occasions in ancient time and by including in them the participation of spiritual and imperial beings. Such occasions could also be seen as a pure source, and so the practice described at that point could be interpreted as its true or essential form. Thus historical accounts disguised arguments for particular styles and purposes. For those practitioners who could not compete directly, these accounts could be used to shift the ground; if for example the aim of the primordial *sarugaku* was to attract the gods, then the importance of winning competitions might be negated.

Originating occasions, then, did the work of characterizing and justifying the practice or tradition. Another kind of typical telling, the transmission account, was used to legitimate particular practitioners. Such accounts could be mere genealogies, but they could also modify or emphasize elements of the original founding. Thus we see new precedent-setting occasions described to justify changes of practice. Accounts of transmission needed supporting evidence—links to official histories, transmission documents, inherited sacred treasures, regular rituals and the possession of secret knowledge. Inherited treasures are especially interesting objects, for like documents they have concrete and symbolic force and like formulaic teachings they can be productive of and justify new interpretations.

Secret knowledge was particularly associated in *sarugaku* with the performance piece *Shikisanban*. It is interesting to see how in the

Muromachi period, secret interpretations of *Shikisanban* repeatedly uncovered hidden identities for the old man roles.[504] This is similar to the secret knowledge found in other traditions, for example the ubiquitous identification of spiritual beings, usually in terms of *honji/suijaku* 垂迹 pairings, declared in Shinto works. In poetic traditions, identifying objects in poems and uncovering secret identities of authors of poems were considered highly significant. Zenchiku managed to combine these various types of identifications to a bewildering degree in the secret knowledge he manufactured for *Shikisanban*.

There is then a contrast between a theory of authority that arises out of demonstrable and undeniable power and another that appeals to origins, transmission, and evidence of transmission. These two styles are of course fundamental to medieval theories of political authority: when the Kamakura *bakufu* discussed Go-Daigo's plotting, they referred to Chinese theories of rule, including the mandate of Heaven.[505] The belief that success in battle was a mark of Heaven's approval was part of a military society's worldview, just as the competitive display of skill was part of warrior culture. In *Fūshikaden*, probably reflecting Kannami's close involvement in the competitive warrior ethos of Kyoto, we see the ideal of *hana* explained in terms of military metaphors, and success or defeat in *sarugaku* competitions in terms of the determinations of the gods of battle.[506] On the other hand, the same period saw the completion of the theory of imperial authority (at a time when its power was least demonstrable) in the works of Kitabatake Chikafusa (1293–1354) and Jihen (late Kamakura). That theory was based on its founding in the age of the gods, its precise transmission, its rituals, and its possession of the three regalia taken to possess both symbolic and magical force. Zenchiku's construction of his family's authority gives it equivalents to all of these.

Transmission-based ideologies similar to the imperial one are found throughout medieval traditions. *Waka* developed its version, as did the Watarai shrine at Ise and the Miwa shrine. Zenchiku, however, took the relatively simple stories of *sarugaku* lore and turned them into something more impressive, enriching them and his conception of his family line, by borrowing from all three traditions: imperial, poetic and Shinto. For the ideology he inherited was not, as it stood, appropriate to his needs. It was rooted in an earlier period when conditions were different. For example, the

---

504. See Pinnington, 1998.
505. See Ochi Reiko, *Buddhism and Poetic Theory: An Analysis of Zeami's "Higaki" and "Takasago"* (Ann Arbor: U.M.I. Dissertation Information Service, 1984): 308–319.
506. ZZ, *Fūshikaden*, 62–3. For analysis, see Pinnington, 2006, 38–9.

three sacred treasures of the Komparu family were not as originally interpreted quite right for Zenchiku's image of his family's current role. There was one anachronistic element of his lore, however, that Zenchiku was prepared to embrace, albeit in a neo-conservative fashion. The traditional ideology did not discuss Noh plays, but rather traced *sarugaku* to the tradition of *okina sarugaku*, through the centerpiece of the Nara ritual calendar, *Shikisanban*. In *Meishukushu*, *Shikisanban* is returned to the center of *sarugaku* duties. To understand the significance of this, let us look at how *Shikisanban* differed from other Noh plays and how the roles of the two types of performance in the life of the *sarugaku* troupes changed in the late fourteenth century.

OKINA SARUGAKU AND THE *SARUGAKU* TROUPES

Shikisanban was not the same genre as the plays we now call Noh,[507] and was, moreover, problematic and incoherent, lending itself to theories of mysterious origins. It was emblematic of the older *sarugaku* of Kōfukuji in Nara before Noh became fashionable among members of the military government in Kyoto. It was thus bound to be more appealing to those Yamato troupes like the Komparu who had been unable to attract the new sources of patronage.

Let us contrast the two genres. Noh plays characteristically have specific authors and draw on clearly defined sources. They virtually always focus on a single main role (*shite* シテ), often masked, mediated to the audience by a secondary character (*waki* ワキ). They are set in a particular location and season, and the identities of the roles are explicitly defined. In general Noh plays are constructed of two scenes, through which a fundamental emotional fact or memory is progressively exposed, through narrative, song and dance in turn. Between the two scenes there may appear a third role-type (*ai-kyōgen* 間狂言), who explains the action in more colloquial language.

Shikisanban does not share any of these characteristics. The name *Shikisanban* literally means ritual three pieces, or rounds, and we know that early performances featured three old men (*okina*) roles (*Okina*—the old man, *Sanbasō* 三番叟—the third old man and *Chichi no Jō* 父尉—the old father),[508] corresponding to which were three masks of old men. These

---

507. As they say, nowadays, regarding its current form, "*nō ni shite nō ni arazu*;" it is "Noh which is not Noh."

508. The fact that the name of the second old man role contains the number three (*sanban*=third round) (rather than two) has exercised minds, but the problem is a relatively old one, as we find that Zenchiku himself is pleased to discover a solution, KKS, *Meishukushū*, 301 (that past, present and future all meet in the middle).

masks are varieties of a single type, but that type is fundamentally different in construction from the masks used in Noh plays. Associated with each old man role was a set of elements—a dance, a dialog between the old man and a younger role, and a song. The older libretti were preserved in three separate scenes: one involving *Okina* and a younger man called *Senzai* 千歳, one involving *Sanbasō* and another younger role and one involving *Chichi no jō* (the old father) and a third younger role, *Enmei kaja* 延命冠者 (life-extending prince). *Shikisanban* was in fact a collection of three distinct performance pieces, each constructed to a similar pattern, with two roles, a masked older man and a younger man.[509] It is thought that there were other performances of similar structure; the genre to which all such pieces belonged is referred to as *okina sarugaku*.

Shikisanban is the ancestor of the present-day *Okina*, performed in a number of traditional theaters as a program opener at the New Year. The *Okina* section of *Shikisanban* has changed little since the fourteenth century, but the *Sanbasō* element, the responsibility of *kyōgen* actors, has been more fluid.[510] The scene featuring *Chichi no jō* has now been dropped and is preserved only as an alternative dialog. Medieval interpretations are mainly concerned with the first scene, in which *Okina* appears, and we can get a good idea of what that must have been like from the present day *Okina*.

The performers are *Okina*, *Senzai*, *Sanbasō* and *Menbakomochi* 面箱持ち. *Menbakomochi* enters the stage first, carrying a box containing two old man masks, white and black. *Okina*, *Senzai*, *Sanbasō*, musicians and chorus follow. *Okina* goes to center stage, bows to the front and sits to the side. *Menbakomochi* takes out the white mask and places it before *Okina*, who starts to sing, in dialog with the chorus, a rhythmic set of syllables: "*dō dō tarari tararira tarari agari rari dō. . . .*"[511] Out of these incantations emerges a celebratory *imayō* 今様 (a late Heian popular song): "May our lord live for a thousand ages and we serve a thousand years. . . ." *Senzai* then sings some lines of another *imayō*: "We hear the sound of the waterfall although the sun shines . . . " and dances a cheerful, rhythmical dance. Meanwhile *Okina* dons the white mask. *Okina* then rises and addresses a garbled version of an older Heian erotic song (*saibara* 催馬楽): "The two

509. This description might seem unnecessarily labored, but care is necessary because the version of *okina sarugaku* performed today, deriving from Kanze traditions, was treated as the traditional form by earlier scholars. That form only involves two old men, so that the element of three in the title *Shikisanban* was mistakenly interpreted in terms of the two old men and one young man role, *Senzai*. See Nogami Toyoichirō, *Nō: kenkyū to hakken* (Iwanami Shoten, 1930), 181–222, and Omote Akira, *Nōgakushi shinkō 1* (Wan'ya Shoten, 1979), 350–5.
510. See Amano Fumio, "Okina sarugaku no hensen," *Geinōshi kenkyū* 109 (1990): 14–28 and Oda Sachiko, "Sanbasō no mondō no hensen," *Geinō* 32.1 (1990): 12–18.
511. The Kanze troupe pronounces this as *tō tō tarari* etc.

youngsters sat out of each other's reach . . . " to *Sanbasō*, who turns away. *Okina* intones a *waka* and some lines of a Chinese verse, praying for peace in the realm and divine protection. He then wonders out loud who *Sanbasō* might be before starting his dance, the stately *Okina no mai* 翁の舞, after which he bows again to the front and quits the stage with *Senzai*. In the second section, *Sanbasō*, having donned a large black hat, runs out chanting benedictions and dancing a wild and vigorous piece called the *momi no dan* 揉みの段. He then returns to his seat and puts on the black old man mask. Now in the character of an old man, he banters with *Menbakomochi*: ("Sit down and I'll dance!" "No, you dance first, then I'll sit down!"), who eventually hands him a bell tree (*suzu* 鈴) and takes his seat. *Sanbasō* performs a final calm dance, the *suzu no dan* 鈴の段, after which both actors withdraw from the stage.

As this modern version exemplifies, the characters in *Shikisanban* do not explain their identities, their geographical location, or the time and season in which the action is situated. Thus these plays demand explanation. Even before Zenchiku's time, there was associated with *Shikisanban* a tradition of secret interpretations intended to find the meaning beneath its surface. [512] Whatever the reason for its incoherence, or apparent meaninglessness, those qualities made it suitable as a focus for Zenchiku's assertion of his tradition's identity precisely because it was rich in triggers for esoteric interpretation.[513] Such interpretations were just the kind of thing that a group whose main claim was unbroken transmission from the art's earliest days was likely to possess.[514]

Shikisanban was also emblematic of a conservative stance taken in relation to *sarugaku* patronage in the fourteenth and fifteenth centuries. The four Yamato troupes were organized by the Kōfukuji temple to carry out a calendar of performances. The most important of these was the performance of *Shikisanban* at particular sites—before the Kasuga Shrine, at the Tōnomine complex, and at the Wakamiya Shrine, an extension of the Kasuga complex. As we mentioned in the second chapter, *sarugaku* troupes had a number of performance genres in which they specialized, of which

512. See Pinnington, 1998. The interpretation in *Hokegobukukanjo*, a Tendai study of the *Lotus Sutra*, converts the apparent meaninglessness of *Shikisanban* itself into its hidden message, for it claims that the pieces were deliberately designed by monks to demonstrate the fact that both "pure and vulgar truths are illusory . . . and to show that the ten worlds . . . have no actual substance" (1998, 501–2).

513. Borrowing Klein's term for apparent inconsistencies, lacunae and inexplicabilities that attract esoteric interpretations in poetry and elsewhere (22–24).

514. In fact, the lore which included the claims of the Komparu line was already closely associated with *okina sarugaku*, but not as closely as it became in Zenchiku's development of it.

the Noh play was just one that assumed great importance from the late fourteenth century onwards. *Shikisanban* in Nara was reserved to troupe elders and its main role, *Okina*, was the responsibility of the leader of the troupe, the *osa*, whose duties included liaison between the Kōfukuji authorities and other actors, and who received the larger share of the troupe's income. It was younger actors, generally possessors of the title *tayū* who became the specialists in performing Noh plays. The two sets of performers were distinct: a *tayū* could not play an *okina* role until he retired, nor could an *osa* play *shite* roles in Noh plays.[515]

When *sarugaku* was taken up by élite warrior society in Kyoto, however, it seems that *Shikisanban* was not popular. Zeami describes how before noble audiences it was gradually dropped. The steady curtailment of this piece began when Kannami first performed before Yoshimitsu at Imagumano in 1374. The modern *Okina* seems more or less the same as the reduced form of *Shikisanban* that was performed at that time, in that they both omit the *Chichi no jō* section. The reduced importance of *Shikisanban* on such occasions was for actors not just an aesthetic decision; it was also a rejection of the authority of the *osa*, and hence of the traditional seniority system in the troupe. In fact, at the Imagumano performance, Kannami performed the *Okina* role at the suggestion of the member of Yoshimitsu's entourage who seems to have organized the occasion, Ebina Nan'amidabutsu 海老名南阿弥陀仏. Nan'amidabutsu's motive was simply to put the spotlight on Kannami from the start, and he may not have realized that Kannami was thereby usurping the *osa*'s prerogative. It appears that afterwards, however, the *osa* was no longer required as a member of the troupe except when it was performing its traditional calendar in Nara. In Zeami's *Shūdōsho*, instructions to members of his troupe, neither the *osa* nor other senior officers described in the troupe rules are mentioned. In his place the leader of the troupe is described by a new name: the master actor, *tōryō* 棟梁 *no shite*, identifiable as the leading *tayū*.[516]

---

515. For documentary evidence for these assertions, see Omote 1976, 1977 and 1978.
516. We do not know whether similar changes affected the organization of the *shimogakari* troupes, Kongō and Komparu, which hardly appeared in the capital region. Zenchiku records the traditional Enman'i troupe rules in which a series of titles indicating a hierarchy based on seniority, headed by the *osa*, and divided into three groups: older *okina sarugaku* actors, adult Noh play actors, and child actors (*KKS, Enman'iza kabegaki*, 312–4). A similar troupe structure was recorded in the Kanze troupe rules, too (*ZZ, Sarugaku dangi*, 308–310). The anxiety about age, which pervades Zeami's writings, is not present in Zenchiku's. It seems from *Meishukushū* that the transition from *tayū* to *osa* was marked by the adoption at about the age of sixty of the style: *koji* (居士) ("*Ōsa* is the status of *koji*" (長者居士身), KKS, *Meishukushū*, 279). As we have seen Zenchiku himself used *koji* in his self-namings after that age (chapter two). We might conclude that Zenchiku himself was happy to accept that older style of promotion in his troupe.

As it stood, the claims of the Kanze troupe were associated with the rise of the Noh play, the priority of the *tayū* in the troupe and the gaining of the Ashikaga shogun's patronage. By constructing an alternative legitimation of *sarugaku* squarely based on *okina sarugaku* and hence the *osa*, its primary performer, the Komparu could negate those claims and instead propose themselves as the true heirs to *sarugaku* tradition, possessors of its most mysterious secrets. The significance of these secrets, morever, bore no relationship to appraisal of performance by any human audience, however exalted.

TRADITIONAL LORE CONCERNING *SARUGAKU*

The body of the *sarugaku* lore transmitted to Zeami and Zenchiku naturalized the priority of *Shikisanban*, associating it with courtly and religious traditions. It included three accounts of ancient origins—one set in the age of the gods, another during the life of the Buddha and a third situated in the Japanese age of human kings. This last was the starting point for an account of transmission through the centuries to the Komparu house. Associated with this story was an interpretation of elements of *Shikisanban*, of which only fragments remain. Zeami related some of this traditional lore in *Fūshikaden* and subsequently used elements of it to discuss the purpose of *sarugaku* performance and to analyze audience experience, but he showed little interest in it otherwise. Zenchiku, for his part, was particularly interested in the origins of *sarugaku*, but the two mythical occasions did not fit his own vision of the art very well. The transmission account was central to his inheritance, and he was particularly concerned to clarify and deepen his knowledge of it. In his earlier works we see his interest in origins, and in *Meishukushū* we see him incorporating techniques developed in Shinto and poetic works to enrich his accounts of them further.

This *sarugaku* lore of origins, secrets and transmission accounts was probably developed in the Kamakura period. It predated Zeami and Zenchiku, for they both refer to older works, no longer extant. The focus on *okina sarugaku* and the failure to mention Noh plays implies it was developed before Kannami's rise to fame. The first account of it we have is in Zeami's works, in the fourth section of *Fūshikaden*. This account seems not to have been Zeami's own, but rather one received from a non-performer, probably a Kōfukuji priest.[517] We can therefore take it as to

---

517. The general priestly stance is reflected in the references to *seinō* 細男 and the interpretation of the motives for *ennen* (see below). For further discussion, see Omote Akira, "Zeami no 'sarugaku ikōru sarugaku' setsu o megutte—'Fūshikaden daishi shingi' no seiritsunendai, sono ta," *Nōgaku kenkyū* 18 (1993): 41–48.

some degree independent of differences in standpoint between Zeami and Zenchiku, a version which, although inevitably with its own biases, can be compared to later interpretations of the material in both men's works.

The first of the mythical origins described in this text is the performance of Uzume no Mikoto before the cave of heaven during the age of the gods, an event described in *Kojiki*, *Nihonshoki* and other canonical works. It is part of a typical myth in which the sunlight is going to be lost from the world and ritual action is required to bring it back. Zeami records it as follows:

> The origin of *sarugaku* in the age of the gods is as follows: the Sun Goddess, Amateru Oongami, had secluded herself in the cave of heaven and the world had entered everlasting darkness, so the eighty myriads of gods gathered at the heavenly Mount Kagu and tried to divert the mind of the great deity, performing *kagura*, starting with comic pieces (*seinō*). As this was going on, the heavenly Uzume no Mikoto came forward with *sakaki* branches hung with *shide* 紙垂 (white ritual hangings), raised her voice, lit the fire, thunderously stamped her feet, and became divinely possessed, singing and dancing. The great deity faintly heard voices and opened the door slightly. The realm became light again. Behold the faces of the gods were white. The entertainments of that time are said to be the start of *sarugaku*.[518]

As told in canonical works this story describes the origin of *kagura* and Shinto worship. It was linked to a clan of female performers of *kagura* who worked for the Jingikan ("Department of Shinto") under the name Sarume. Sarume no Kimi was a later name for Uzume no Mikoto. *Kagura* and *sarugaku* are separate traditions, but a kind of identity could be asserted through the presence of "*saru*" in the name Sarume.[519]

The aim of *kagura* according to this story is to attract the attention of a powerful deity, resulting both in general happiness and blessings. In Zeami's telling, the performance is partly ritual in character, as revealed in the phrase *kamugakari su* 神懸りす (became divinely possessed) which derives from traditional accounts of the story; but it also aims to entertain, as we can see among other things from the reference to *seinō* 細男, a comic performance genre.[520]

518. ZZ, 38.
519. As Ichijō Kanera does in his reading of the *rokurin ichiro* theory, KKS, *Rokurin ichiro no ki*, 209. See also Thornhill's discussion in 1993, 37, f.63.
520. *Seinō* was a genre of male performer that appeared in the Kasuga Wakamiya festival. The idea of divine possession is found in both *Nihonshoki* and *Kojiki* accounts of the heavenly cave incident.

The other mythical founding of *sarugaku* is set in the time of the historical Buddha (the story has no known scriptural pretext):

> When the Buddha dwelt on earth, the wealthy Sudatta built the Jetavana monastery, and the Tathāgata Sākyamuni was to preach at its dedication ceremony, but Devadatta, accompanied by ten thousand non-Buddhists, hung branches and bamboo grass with *shide*, and when they started dancing and shouting, it became difficult to carry out the dedication service. The Buddha glanced at Sariputra, who, receiving the power of the Buddha, arranged drums and flutes at the back door. Sixty-six pieces of mimicry were performed through the talent of Ānanda, the spiritual knowledge of Sariputra and the eloquence of Purna. The unbelievers, hearing the sound of flute and drums, gathered at the back door to watch and became quiet. The Tathāgata used the interval to preach the dedication service. This was the occasion when this art started in India.[521]

The story contrasts strikingly with the other. There, Uzume no mikoto was described "singing and dancing," but here the disciples perform *monomane* (mimicry). As we have seen, this was a fundamental polarity organizing the way in which actors thought about their technical arts—what might be called artificial and figurative. Again there is a contrast in the way the audience is viewed. Before the cave of heaven, the performance was intended to attract the benevolent gaze of a goddess, but here it is to divert noisy unbelievers. These unbelievers appear to be worshippers of *kami*, carrying out some form of *kagura*, dancing with branches hung with *shide*. The stance of the passage overall is clearly that of Buddhists looking down on Shinto religious activity. If it represents the views of Kōfukuji priests in relation to the *sarugaku* performance and the Kasuga shrine, it is important in our understanding of the origins of the Kōfukuji patronage of the troupes. Such a conjecture is supported by Zeami's subsequent remark:

> In the present age, at the Vimalakirti festival at Kōfukuji, when Dharma-tasting is being carried out in the assembly hall, *ennen* dances are held in the dining hall. It pacifies non-Buddhists and settles obstructive influences. In front of the dining hall the scriptures are intoned. This is based directly on the ancient precedent set at Jetavana.[522]

---

521. ZZ, *Fūshikaden*, 38.
522. ZZ, *Fūshikaden*, 40–1.

This explanation of the monks' performances of *ennen* at the end of the Yuima-e is interesting in itself. How similar in motive were the ritual performances required of the *sarugaku* troupes affiliated to Kōfukuji?[523] In any case, according to this story the purpose of *sarugaku* was to pacify and divert disruptive forces, especially those of non-Buddhist religious practitioners. Another aspect of this story is its characterization of performance. It seems to be suggesting that the actors should be talented (like Ānanda), that plays should express Buddhist spiritual knowledge (like that possessed by Sariputra) and that the language of the performance should be eloquent (like Purna). Although there is no specific mention of Noh plays here, this might be thought an appropriate ideal for performances in Zeami's day.

Explicitly connected to and based on this origin of *sarugaku* in the age of the Buddha were two more founding occasions, each set in Japan in the age of human kings, and each taken as a precedent for subsequent *sarugaku* tradition. The first drew on stories developed in the popular medieval cult of Prince Shōtoku and associated beliefs developed in Hada no Kōkatsu's temple, Kōryūji in Yamashiro province. In the following paragraph I paraphrase salient elements shared by both Zeami and Zenchiku's accounts:

The River Hase overflowed and a jar [524] was washed ashore. It contained a child who claimed to be the first emperor of China;[525] he was brought to court where he showed great talent and grew up to be named Hada no Kōkatsu.[526] When there were "disturbances in the land," Prince Shōtoku made sixty-six masks and ordered Kōkatsu to perform the sixty-six

523. As I have said, these all involved the troupes being sent off to other locations, twice to the Kasuga shrines and once to the Tōnomine temple-shrine complex. Are we to understand the sending of *sarugaku* performers from Kōfukuji to the Kasuga deities to be to apotropaic, intended to avert their negative attentions? Was some similar motive behind the sending of troupes to Tōnomine? This sending of troupes has been a puzzle in light of the intense hostilities between the two institutions in the fourteenth and fifteenth centuries (see Pinnington, 1998, 500–501).

524. A related elaboration of the brief mentions of Hada no Kōkatsu in *Nihonshoki* is found in *Seiyoshō* 聖誉鈔, a work on Prince Shōtoku. Sake no Kimi (Lord Ricewine), a great grandson of the first Chinese emperor, got his name because he grew up in a jar. He fled China and came to Japan via Naniwa bay in Settsu where he was awarded the name Hada by Empress Suiko. He had two sons, Toshiyuki, who was ennobled, and the younger, Kōkatsu, who became a servant (see KZK, 284). Elements of this story are transposed in the Yamato *sarugaku* account (location, ancestry, jar, name). In *Kogoshūi*, Emperor Yūryaku put Sake no Kimi in charge of the Hada clan (see Katō Genchi and Hoshino Hikoshiro. trans., *Kogoshūi—Gleanings from Ancient Stories* (Tokyo: Meiji Seitoku Kinen Gakkai, 1925), 41).

525. The Emperor Shih-huang (259–210 B.C.) known for his oppression of intellectuals and burning of books.

526. Hada (Hata) is a Japanese reading of the character Qin 秦, the name of the dynasty of the first emperor of China.

piece performance at the *Shishinden* of the Tachibana palace. "The country soon became peaceful."[527] This story gives *sarugaku* a substantial legitimacy. Prince Shōtoku brought the prestige of both the historical Buddha (in the contemporary cult he was viewed as Japan's *nirmāna-kāya*) and the imperial family.[528] Hada no Kōkatsu, too, is a useful figure. In *Nihonshoki* he was merely a figure at court who founded a temple and did various other tasks, but according to Kōryūji traditions he was a semi-divine reincarnation of the first Chinese emperor.[529] As such he was a founder of Chinese traditions in Japan. Zenchiku, for example, notes his establishment of three *michi* lineages: *sarugaku*, court music at Tennōji, and the martial arts transmitted at Hasedera.[530] Looking at the motives ascribed to Prince Shōtoku in this account, we notice the familiar politicization of "pacification" in Japan: the disturbances here are social in nature, not just the interruptions to preaching that prompted the Buddha's disciples to perform. Hence the performance now possesses a politico-magical force, pacifying the realm.

The second originating occasion set in Japan involved one of Kōkatsu's descendants. According to the account in *Fūshikaden*, in the tenth century, Emperor Murakami read Prince Shōtoku's writings on *sarugaku*, which noted its origins and stated that according to the principle of "wild words and specious phrases" it would "protect the praise of the Buddha and the teaching of the Dharma, repel evil karma, and invite plenty." When the *sarugaku* dance was performed, the realm would become quiet, the people peaceful, and life would be lengthened." Murakami then decided to make *sarugaku* a "rite for the benefit of the nation" and had it performed by a descendant of Kōkatsu, Hada no Ujiyasu.[531] Ujiyasu did so helped by his brother-in-law, Ki no Gonnokami. Later they reduced the sixty-six pieces to

---

527. The Tachibana palace of Prince Shōtoku did not have a *Shishinden*, the ceremonial court where formal business was conducted at the imperial palace. See Hattori Yukio, 1974, "Shukushin ron—geinōshin shinkō no kongen ni aru mono jō," *Bungaku* (October 1974): 56, for an ingenious origin for this location in the story.
528. *Sarugaku* actors could and did perform in the presence of the retired emperor (see additional note 86, ZZ, 469–470), but it seems that there was no sufficient precedent to justify performance before a current emperor. Zenchiku alludes to this in KKS, *Meishukushū*, 284.
529. Kōryūji claims to be the temple founded by Hada no Kōkatsu to house the famous image of Maitreya given to him for safe keeping by Prince Shōtoku. The image can still be seen there today.
530. These were actual lineages in the fifteenth century that claimed descent from Hada no Kōkatsu. KKS, *Meishukushū*, 288.
531. The name Hada no Ujiyasu appears in *Honchō monzui* 本朝文粋, as that of the author of a reply to a question from Emperor Murakami about the origins of *sangaku* (Ōsone Shōsuke, Kinpara Tadashi, Gotō Akio, eds. *Honchō monzui (Shin koten bungaku taikei 27)* (Iwanami Shoten, 1992), 29–33). It is not thought to correspond to a real person, but nevertheless the existence of this text very likely played some part in the invention of the legend under discussion.

three, creating the *Shikisanban*. Yamato *sarugaku* descended from Ujiyasu and the troupes based at the Hie shrine in Ōmi descended from Ki. The leaders of the Komparu (i.e. Enman'i) troupe were Ujiyasu's descendants. They held in their possession three rare treasures handed down from Ujiyasu, who had inherited them from Kōkatsu.[532]

This story, too, characterizes the purposes of *sarugaku*. It is a Buddhist rite, operating on the principle of *kyōgen kigo,* with exorcistic, political and life-lengthening powers.[533] As an originating occasion, this tenth-century performance legitimates the *Shikisanban* performed by *sarugaku* actors, and also legitimates Yamato and Ōmi traditions, while making plain the priority of the first. This last issue was of some importance, for Ōmi and Yamato performers were competing representatives of different styles. This account, with its elevation of Yamato *sarugaku,* was likely to have been embraced by the Kōfukuji priests as well as performers; but it must also have originated in part in the family traditions of Zenchiku and his forebears, the stories they told about their origins and the origin of their family treasures.

The lore also included secret interpretations of *Shikisanban,* primarily expressed through the identity of the old man roles. Zeami mentions them in passing in the fourth section of *Fūshikaden,* when discussing Ujiyasu's performance:

> Afterwards it proved difficult to perform the whole sixty-six pieces in one day, so they selected *Inatsumi no okina* (*Okina omote*), *Yonatsumi no okina* (*Sanbasarugaku*) and *Chichi no jō,* and decided to do these three. This is the present day's *Shikisanban.* These roles are modeled directly on the three bodies of the *Tathāgata: dharma, sambhōga* and *nirmāna.*[534]

It is not clear whether Inatsumi and Yonatsumi, whom scholars have failed to identify, refer to hidden identities or simply to alternative names.[535] The Buddhist identification of the roles (*dharma, sambhōga* and *nirmāna*) refers to the doctrine of the *trikāya,* the three-fold body of the

---

532. This summarises material found in *Fūshikaden,* and *Sarugaku dangi* (ZZ, 38–40, 302) and in *Meishukushū, Sarugaku engi,* and *Enman'iza keizu* (KKS, 283–4, 287–9, 291–2, 308–9, 311).

533. In the parts of *Fūshikaden* that refer to this legendary lore, *sarugaku* and *ennen* are treated as one tradition. *Ennen* literally means "long life," but its relation to beliefs in the life-extending effects of performance is unknown, see ZZ, additional note 1, 427–8.

534. ZZ, *Fūshikaden,* 40.

535. It might be that the first is linked to *Ina no mi no kimi* who, according to *Engishiki,* appeared in the *Daijōsai,* but the second, of whom the reading is anyway in doubt, is unknown (see NGK, 215–221, Omote, 1979, 344–50, and ZZ, headnotes, 40).

Buddha and appears to be a "deep interpretation,"[536] although it is not described in those terms, and could have been derived from hints in the libretto itself.[537]

ZEAMI'S USE OF TRADITIONAL LORE

In the preface to *Fūshikaden*, apparently a late addition to the work, Zeami refers to *sarugaku*'s originating occasions. His stance towards the first two is skeptical and unengaged:

> Now, when one enquires into the origin of the profession of *sarugaku ennen* one is told that it arose in the time of the Buddha, or that it has been handed down from the age of the gods, but times have passed and those ages are remote, so the power required to master those styles is hard to attain.[538]

The placing of the information: "when one enquires . . . one is told" distances Zeami from the two mythical accounts, their concatenation weakens their credibility, and the authorizing force of their temporal distance is converted into a reason why they can be ignored—they are already out of reach. Zeami goes on to mention the origin in the age of human kings:

> That [*sarugaku ennen*] has become in recent times everybody's entertainment. But in Empress Suiko's reign, Prince Shōtoku commanded Hada no Kōkatsu to perform it, on the one hand for the safety of the realm, and on the other, for everyone's enjoyment. The sixty-six-piece carnival was put on, and called *sarugaku*. Since that time, generation by generation, men have borrowed the scenes of wind and moon and made them the medium for this diversion.[539]

---

536. That is, it does not have any ordinary explanatory power. The doctrine of the *trikaya* arose from the problem of the status of the Buddha's body: how did it compare with the body of an ordinary man? This was at first solved by the idea of a dual manifestation—a delusory or birth-body (生身) and a perfect body (*dharma-kaya* 法身)—and was later extended to three bodies. The *dharma-kaya* then came to represent absolute reality, the *sambhōga-kaya* (報身) the form of the Buddha in a Pure Land experiencing the bliss of his good karma, and the *nirmāna-kaya* (応身), equivalent to the birth-body, the form of the Buddha appearing to people according to their capacity (Taya Raishun, *Bukkyogaku jiten* (Kyoto: Hōzōkan, 1955), 383–6). There is a possible connection between the identification of the three old men with the *trikaya* and the Tendai interpretation recorded in the *Hokegobukukanjō* that I mentioned above. If Zeami's informant was a Buddhist priest, it is possible that he had access to, or had heard of, this interpretative work.
537. The *Chichi no Jō* section of extant libretti mentions the historical Buddha, the prime example of a *nirmāna* body. That, and the fact that there were three old men roles, would be sufficient to imply a connection with the *trikāya*.
538. ZZ, *Fūshikaden*, 14.
539. (I also discuss this passage in chapter three, above) ZZ, *Fūshikaden*, 14.

While this mentions the politico-magical motive, it highlights the pleasurable aspects of performance. It also justifies the composition of new plays and their sources in the court poetic literary tradition. This naturally had no relevance to the *Shikisanban*, which resisted innovation. The story of Uzume's performance in the "age of the gods" was generally taken to be a precedent for *kagura*, offerings of songs and dances to the gods, rather than for *sarugaku*. In *Shūgyokutokka*, however, Zeami used the story as a basis for the analysis of the mental events of an audience during the superb moments in the performance of Noh plays.[540] His discussion revolves around three particular terms: *myō* (ultimate reality),[541] *hana* (flower), and *omoshiro* (fascination).

There are these three: *myō*, *hana* and *omoshiroki*, but they are one phenomenon, distinguished into first, second and third. The experience of ultimate reality occurs when words cease and the activity of the mind is extinguished. When this is seen to be *myō*, there is *hana*. When a point is added it is *omoshiroki*. Now, as for the name *omoshiroki*, when the great goddess was attracted by the playful performance of *kagura* on Mount Kagu in heaven, she pushed open the cave door, and the faces of all the gods became clearly visible. This was when the term *omoshiroki* was first applied. . . . When the goddess has shut the cave door, and in utter darkness language has ceased, this is *myō*. When it has already brightened it is *hana*. When it has been noted as such, it is *omoshiro*.[542]

This interpretation depends on the folk etymology of the term *omoshiroki* 面白き, which was added to some tellings of the *kagura* myth[543] (*omo* 面 = face, *shiroki* 白き = whiteness—hence sight of the gods' white faces when the goddess emerged was felt to be *omoshiroki* = fascinating). Zeami has

---

540. Strictly speaking, Zeami's discussion does not distinguish the experiences of actor and audience. This reflects the structure of the myth itself: Uzume no Mikoto is certainly a performer, but the many gods are both participants and observers, and the sun-goddess does not see the performance (she only hears the inexplicable laughter of the gods outside). When she opens the cave door, it is herself that she sees (in mirrors) and the other gods who experience the pleasure.
541. *Myō* in the Buddhist contexts translates the sanskrit "sat," which has two connotations: that which is real or true, and also that which is wonderful or awe-inspiring (a well-known use is *myōhō* = *saddharma* (the true or wonderful law) in the title of the *Lotus Sutra* (*Myōhōrengekyō* = *Saddharmapundarikasutra*)). In aesthetic contexts *myō* is often understood to signify splendour or perfection. In Noh plays and in *nōgakuron* the term *myō* is invariably accompanied by an explanation that bridges its aesthetic and ontological connotations: declaring that *myō* is a mental state in which language ceases and the mind merges with absolute reality.
542. ZZ, *Shūgyokutokka*,188.
543. Notably in *Kogoshūi*.

taken the mythical event and projected its structure onto a moment of rapturous appreciation during performance.

Zeami made no equivalent use of the derivation of *sarugaku* from the performance at the Jetavana monastery, nor of its transmission through Hada no Kōkatsu and Ujiyasu. These were to be understood by Zenchiku as conservative arguments for the primacy of *okina sarugaku*. Zeami, growing up, fully identified with the avant-garde, and justified the reduced importance of *okina sarugaku* and the usurpation of the *osa*'s performance rights by recounting a new "founding event," the performance at Imagumano. The presence at that performance of the supreme political figure of the time, Yoshimitsu, and the participation of his favorite actor, Kannami, and the fact that it was a first event—Yoshimitsu had never seen *sarugaku* before—qualified it to be a precedent-setting occasion. Still, much later in Zeami's career, when, like many a former path-breaker, he was marooned by current fashion, and when the troupe was in his nephew's hands and Motoyoshi was about to retire to a monastery, he appears to have taken a conservative stance to troupe duties, regretting the tendency to abandon the ritual performances in Nara, including *Shikisanban*:

> Item. To be careless about sacred performances, or to be late in going up to, or else not appearing at, the Kasuga Shrine festival, on the excuse that one is traveling to and from the capital. Such things as these will cause your life on earth to get worse and worse. You may escape for a while, but you will be punished in the end. One should make sacred performances the basis, and commute to the capital in the intervals to add to one's income.[544]

Zeami also found himself resisting the fashion among the next generation for more dramatic and representational plays, and here he found the derivations of *sarugaku* from *kagura*, on the one hand, and from *okina sarugaku*, on the other, useful to argue for the song and dance style he preferred:

> The path of musical entertainment is said to be all mimicry, but *sarugaku* is *kagura*, so its essential style must be the two arts of dance and song. Then what shall we take as the dance of *sarugaku*? Surely it should be the *Okina* dance, for this is the basis of this artistic tradition.

---

544. ZZ, *Sarugaku dangi*, 307.

Again if we are to say what is the basis of chanted song, surely we should say the *kagura uta* of *Okina.*[545]

The story of the *kagura* origin represented the non-representational elements of performance, the importance of which Zeami consistently emphasized. The model for such elements, however, he took not from *kagura* but *okina sarugaku.*

Zeami drew on these stories of origin to describe the psychology of aesthetic appreciation and to argue for a particular form for the Noh play. Otherwise, however, he showed little interest in them, having no need to accept their assumptions of Komparu priority, traditional troupe structure and Kōfukuji patronage.

ZENCHIKU'S DEVELOPMENT OF
TRADITIONAL LORE AND *MEISHUKUSHŪ*

Zenchiku, on the other hand, had every reason to embrace a vision of *sarugaku* which granted his troupe an inherent prestige, against which his family's failure to win Kyoto patronage in the previous two generations would seem unimportant. The normative element of the lore, which concentrated on *okina sarugaku,* was ideal from his point of view, for *Shikisanban* was no part of Kanze success in the capital.[546] Again Zenchiku naturally welcomed the lore's legitimation of the Yamato transmission, in which his own lineage claimed precedence, which it could prove through its inheritance of treasures. But, as we have seen, Zenchiku was a man in search of a knowledge that he felt sure lay behind the surface, and so he went further, exploring this material in search of hidden meanings and significance. His explorations included the collection of new material, appeals to deities, and new interpretations, mimicking the styles of the other traditions he revered, poetic and Shinto. By such means, he greatly elevated the cultural significance of *sarugaku* and shifted its purposes in the direction of ritual. He developed an exaggerated view of the prestige of his line, but could do no more than bewail the contrast between that view and the reality of his troupe's circumstances.

In our presentation of Zenchiku's use of this material we shall first look at his handling of three elements: the stories of origins, the transmission accounts, and his family heirlooms. We shall then move to the results of his investigations—the hidden meaning of *Shikisanban* performance and the

---

545. ZZ, *Sarugaku dangi,* 260. The *kagura uta* was the chant which opened the *Okina* performance, sung by the *Okina Men* role, starting with the nonsense (?) syllables "*tō tō tarari tararira tarari agari rari to. . . .*"
546. See Pinnington, 1998, especially 494.

hidden identities of the divine power it manifested. The main source of our account is Zenchiku's work *Meishukushū*, although we shall consider other works too. Before moving on to Zenchiku's use of the stories of origin, we should introduce this work, the condition of which will impact on our own investigation.

Meishukushū is an incomplete draft (with erasures, amendments and interlinear notes), a working document written for Zenchiku's own use and addressed in several places to himself (to add material later, for example) and also sometimes to a reader, probably his son. It is often obscure, because it makes no attempt to express its ideas explicitly, but on the other hand, we sometimes see Zenchiku's thought unusually clearly, for it is relatively free of the clotted concatenations of formulaic phrases and allusions that constitute his other works.

Meishukushū lacks an introduction or consistent organizational plan,[547] but the purpose and character of the work is usefully indicated by two titles, one of which was replaced by the other. The former title is *Meiōshū* 明翁集, which can be translated: *A Collection Illuminating Okina*.[548] The term "Collection" is appropriate, for the work is made of twenty-two sections,

---

547. There is a reference to an introduction, but it is missing. *Meishukushū* was discovered in 1964 among Komparu family documents. Two members of the Komparu family read it in the eighteenth century and a copy was made, but otherwise it seems to have been a closely guarded secret that was eventually forgotten. There are signs of its contents in Yoshida initiations in the Tokugawa period (see Pinnington, 1998, 515). The attribution to Zenchiku is based on handwriting and internal references to many of Zenchiku's favorite topics. The work is a late one, but there has been a good deal of speculation about just when it was written. *Meishukushū* refers to a vow made to Sumiyoshi on the 13th day of the 9th month, when poems were offered (KKS, *Meishukushū*, 282, 299–300). At the end of the work *Kabuzuinōki* are several *waka*, and after the first three is the remark that " . . . in this path one especially relies on the fulfillment of prayers to Sumiyoshi Myōjin. Thus I relate my wishes in offerings of *waka*" (KKS, *Kabuzuinōki*, 142). If these were the offerings in question, the date of authorship would be about 1456. Other textual characteristics, however, lead the editors of KKS to take a later date, nearer 1465, (KKS, 81). Itō elsewhere adopts a different approach. Considering the extremely bitter and pessimistic reflections on other *sarugaku* performers found in *Meishukushū*, he characterizes them as "craving for the world," "extremes of immorality," (KKS, *Meishukushū*, 296). Even in reference to the original Yamato troupes, he compares their despoliation of the Kasuga environs during ritual performances to a "raid on an army camp" (KKS, *Meishukushū*, 296–7). Itō sees these as of a piece with Zenchiku's tone of depression in certain *waka* written in 1466, when he handed over the troupe to his son Motouji. (For example, Zenchiku writes: "I no longer seem to know the way, the aged horse whose travels are not yet done," and "What stage have I reached? With such thoughts I console myself of the misfortunes of life, in the evening of old age.") Itō wonders whether some unknown unhappy event connected all these writings, setting *Meishukushū* in Zenchiku's old age, after retirement (KZK, 141–4). If we consider that *Shikisanban*, the performance piece at the center of *Meishukushū* was reserved, in Nara at least, to actors in retirement from the performance of Noh plays, this last proposed date seems to me the most likely.

548. It is also possible to read *Meiōshū* as "Collection concerning the Bright Okina." The character *mei* 明 in the title can be read as a verb: to make clear, or as a modifier: bright. As it is used in both titles and as I think it unlikely that Zenchiku was both thinking of a "Bright Okina" and a "Bright Shuku," I read it as a verb.

each containing material loosely related to given topics. It is evident that Zenchiku herein attempted to gather material from a number of sources. The purpose of the work is clearly to "illuminate Okina," but this Okina is not the old man role of *Shikisanban* but rather an ancient spiritual entity, one manifestation of which is *Shikisanban*. The second title, which replaced the first, is *Meishukushū: Collection Illuminating the Indwelling Deity*. For the moment let us note simply that this indicates Zenchiku's belief that the spiritual being, Okina, was identical with a deity he called Shukushin 宿神. Scholars have theorized that Zenchiku took this deity from a widespread cult among medieval performers, but I will argue a different derivation. Shukushin, as Zenchiku understood it, was a continuous presence "residing" (*shuku*) in the hearts of human beings. It should be noted that *Meishukushū* asserts several other identities for Okina, too, including Buddhist and Shinto deities, but the stance taken throughout is that of Shinto ideology; in particular there is a close connection of ideas to Watarai and Miwa Shinto.

ZENCHIKU'S INVESTIGATIONS OF ORIGINS

Zenchiku's interest in the origins of *sarugaku* is evident in a number of works. In *Meishukushū*, however, both the *kagura* and Buddhist story proved problematic and he constructed a new originating story. Not only did the two mythical origins contradict each other, but they were also problematic in other ways. The origin in *kagura* was suitably related to Shinto traditions, but its highlighting of the comic, entertaining and female meant that, while at a stretch it could be associated with Noh plays, it was hardly appropriate to *okina sarugaku*. Even in *Kabuzuinōki*, where the focus was Noh plays, Zenchiku had shifted the focus by using a Watarai Shinto version of the story [549] and adding an eclectic series of citations [550] to emphasize *sarugaku*'s ritual potential:

> This, then, is the start of *kagura*, the source of song and dance, of the poetic arts. Amateru Oongami commanded, and from among the many, Amanokoyane spoke. The mind transcended words and Amateru, considering the speech to be properly worded, had Tajikara O no Mikoto open the rock door, and Amateru emerged. One yin, one yang, one sound—the origin of the myriad things. When we observe that mind long ago, and consider it well, that superb mind in which the

---

549. The "one yin, one yang, one sound the origin of all beings " is close to a passage in *Ruijū shingi hongen* (see KKS, additional note 6, 580, and KZK, 272).
550. Most of which will be recognized by now (for references see headnotes to the passage in KKS, *Kabuzuinōki*, 121–2).

realm had been eternally dark and started to brighten slightly, the realm of white faces, this is the occasion of that state of emotion where the ways of language cease, unthinkable, where the activities of mind become extinguished. If you steep your mind in that state, and create the mood of profound emotion in your song and dance, as "there is scenery in mind, and mind in scenery," if you offer performance to the gods and buddhas, then in truth "crazy words and fancy phrases, too, become the causes for praising the Buddha and turning the wheel of the law" and there is no doubt that it will "benefit living beings from the binding of fate through the softening of the light and mixing with the dust, to the attaining of enlightenment by the Buddha."[551]

The purpose of performance clearly emerges as spiritual benefit. The "extinguished" mind does not represent the transports of the audience as it did in Zeami's reading, but rather the desired mental state aimed at by the performer (achieved by "steeping"). This is faithful to the shamanistic aspect of ancient tellings of the story, in which Uzume no Mikoto entered a "divine trance" (*kamugakari*). The combination of this state and the offering of the performance to the gods transforms human artistic acts into ritual, resulting in magical benefits.

Zenchiku mentions this Shinto origin of *sarugaku* in *Meishukushū*, too. The Shinto connection was no doubt welcome, but here it was the stately old man dance (*Okina no mai*) of *Shikisanban* that Zenchiku sought to elevate, so Uzume's erotic performance needed to be played down.[552] Perhaps that is why his reference is very brief and the performers are not mentioned:

That deity performed *kagura* outside the cave of heaven and Amateru Oongami deigned to open the door. That *kagura* is *sarugaku*.[553]

The other story of the origin of *sarugaku*, set in the time of the Buddha, refers explicitly to *okina sarugaku*, for it mentions the sixty-six piece *monomane* from which the tripartite *Shikisanban* was selected. But this story, too, was problematic. First, it had no connection with the Buddhist origins of performance that Shigyoku had managed to uncover[554] and was

551. KKS, *Kabuzuinōki*, 121–2.
552. In the *Kojiki* version of Uzume's performance, she deliberately exposes her breasts and genitals, setting off a shout of laughter from the assembled gods. Uzume has been compared to the mythical Greek crone, Baubo.
553. The last sentence refers to a theory (also mentioned by Zeami) about how *kagura* 神楽 came to be named *sarugaku*, through manipulation of the Chinese character 神 into the form 申, which can be read "*saru*." See KKS, 284.
554. Zenchiku had Shigyoku and Kanera both outline what they knew of the origins of performance art when he asked for their commentaries on the *rokurin ichiro* diagrams.

thus suspect, and second, it characterized the audience as Shinto-style disturbers of the peace, which contradicted Zenchiku's pro-Shinto stance. In *Meishukushū*, Zenchiku again only briefly describes the event, but he alters it to solve the second of these problems:

> When the Buddha carried out the dedication ceremony at the Jetavana retreat, Ānanda and Sariputra and others danced this *kagura* at the rear entrance to pacify the disturbance of Tenma. This is that same *sarugaku* that is performed today.[555]

We see that he has replaced the implicitly Shinto *shide* hangers of Zeami's version with the more neutral *Tenma* (a generic disturber of the Buddhist way) and that he calls the performance itself *kagura*, transferring the Shinto connotations from the unruly audience to the performance itself.

Neither of these origins is really satisfactory. Zenchiku appropriated another origin, however, through the fundamental idea that *Shikisanban* was a manifestation of a god. This was the origin of the universe, the moment when heaven and earth separated, which had figured in the interpretations of the *rokurin ichiro* diagrams. *Meishukushū* opens:

> Now when we inquire into the origin of the mysterious reality of Okina, it becomes clear that it came into being when heaven and earth started to split apart. Throughout the age of human kings up to the present day it has unceasingly protected the imperial throne, benefited the realm, and aided the people.[556]

The tracing of a deity to the state of chaos before heaven and earth had separated was a technique used by Kamakura shrine theorists to elevate a given deity to an unchallengeable status.[557] *Sarugaku*, by similarly tracing itself to the beginning of the universe, could now be presented as a cultural tradition of the highest prestige. Having identified *Shikisanban* with a deity in this way, it was necessary to create for him some history of appearances

---

Shigyoku mentioned the origin in the age of the gods and also gave a Buddhist genealogy refering to Prince Shōtoku and to the Kasuga deity, but not the origin in India (see Thornhill, 1993, 31–33 for translation and useful footnotes). Kanera, for his part, discussed various Confucian theories of music as well as providing further material from *Nihonshoki* linking the first *kagura* to *sarugaku* (see Thornhill, 1993, 35–7).) Zenchiku seems to have found Kanera's reading interesting for he wrote a short work, *Sarugaku engi*, which added it to his own version of his genealogy. This mechanical juxtaposition cannot hide the fact that there is no connection between the story and his family origins.

555. KKS, *Meishukushū*, 284–5.
556. KKS, *Meishukushū*, 279.
557. As Ōsumi Kazuo describes, 350–356. Teeuwen describes the Watarai case in detail in 29–48. This passage is also strikingly similar to one describing the Miwa deity in the Kamakura document *Miwa daimyōjin engi*, found in Tanikawa Ken'ichi ed., *Jinja engi (Nihon shomin seikatsu shiryō shūsei 26)* (San'ichi Shobō, 1983) 555–558, particularly 555.

that would demonstrate his persistent significance. Ideally such a history would be linked to the Komparu house, turning it into a transmission narrative.

ZENCHIKU'S TRANSMISSION NARRATIVES

At its simplest a "transmission narrative" is an account of a lineage connecting an originating occasion to a current practitioner. It is thus a kind of genealogy. Such a line only needs a few prominent figures; unnamed progenitors are imagined to fill the generations between. The narrative's primary aim is to legitimate the present member of the lineage, but it can do other work, too. The activities of the various figures can be taken as normative, reinforcing and refining the messages found in the originating occasions about the true purposes of the tradition. These activities can be understood in a slightly different way, too, that is as instances of the action in the world of the original impulse informing the tradition. If that is primarily spiritual, then we can interpret the transmission narrative as a catalog of that spiritual force's interventions in human history. Both these kinds of readings appear in the transmission narratives that Zenchiku constructed in *Meishukushū*.

Zenchiku's interest in his genealogy is seen in other works as well as *Meishukushū*, particularly in his diagrammatic family tree, *Enman'iza keizu* 円満井系図, and its narrative version, *Sarugaku engi*. It is generally thought that the family tree was written late in Zenchiku's life, probably for his son, to mark his succession to the Enman'i troupe. If so, then, like a Zen transmission document, its primary function would have been to authorize its possessor.[558]

In *Meishukushū*, Zenchiku gathers together similar material, but his interest here is rather to search out its deeper significance. He is particularly concerned with events involving Prince Shōtoku and Hada no Kōkatsu. He brings into his account material that otherwise we only know through the play *Moriya* and tells of a research visit he made to the temple Kōryūji, where the cult of Hada no Kōkatsu was active.[559] This new version of the

---

558. The family tree is interesting for its layout; the importance of each person is reflected by the size of the writing. (The largest characters are used to write Prince Shōtoku, then progressively smaller characters represent Hada no Kōkatsu, Hada no Ujiyasu and Bishaō Gonnokami. These are followed with middle-sized characters for the five leaders of the Enman'i: Mitsutarō, Bishaōjirō, Komparu Yasaburō, Komparu Ujinobu (i.e. Zenchiku himself) and Komparu Shichirō Tayū Motouji (Zenchiku's son, Sōin). Surrounding these main figures are discussions of their involvement in *sarugaku*, written in the smallest writing).

559. Kōryūji (also known as Uzumasadera) was believed to be the temple built by Kōkatsu to house a statue given to him by Prince Shōtoku. The statue that Zenchiku saw on his visit can still be seen today, along with a number of other splendid and ancient representations of buddhas and bodhisattvas.

Kōkatsu's activities exposes behind them a counter-intuitive spiritual purpose:

> Now concerning this Kōkatsu. . . . When the prince destroyed the rebel minister Moriya, shooting him with a magic arrow, as he fell from the scaffold Moriya intoned a passage from the *Lotus Sutra*:
>
> "Thus my many wishes of long ago are now fully satisfied."
>
> Kōkatsu intoned the next phrase:
>
> "Transforming all living beings, all are brought into the Buddhist way."
>
> At the time the *Lotus Sutra* had not yet been brought from China. It is thus clear that both were the expedient means of incarnations benefiting living beings. It is this same Kōkatsu who was commanded to perform *sarugaku* and first danced *Okina* at the *Shishinden* of the Tachibana court. So it is recorded. [560]

Thus, what appeared to be a bloody war between the Mononobe (of which Moriya was the leader) and the Soga (who supported Shōtoku) was in fact the acting out of a secret agreement by Moriya and Kōkatsu to bring enlightenment to all creatures. This was evidenced by their mysterious knowledge of the *Lotus Sutra* and the verse they intoned. By placing this interpretation of Kōkatsu's military activities next to his establishment of *sarugaku*, the reader is led to interpret *sarugaku*, too, as having a hidden spiritual purpose. [561]

Zenchiku later discusses Kōkatsu's descendent Ujiyasu's performance in the time of Emperor Murakami. On that occasion, Ujiyasu had his brother-in-law, Ki no Gonnokami, help him perform the *Shikisanban*, three pieces selected from the sixty-six piece *sarugaku*. Ki no Gonnokami became the ancestor of the Hie and Yamashina troupes in Ōmi, while Ujiyasu was the ancestor of the Enman'i troupe in Yamato. This is clearly a story to both legitimate and distinguish the relative importance of the Yamato and Ōmi streams of *sarugaku*. Zenchiku finds a striking way to

---

560. KKS, 287. Zenchiku cites the *"Prince's summary"* (*Taishi no onmokuroku*). Elsewhere in *Meishukushū* he similarly refers to *Jōgū Taishi no jihitsu no mokuroku* (*Prince Shōtoku's summary in his own hand*, 285). This work may correspond to Zeami's *"Jōgū Taishi no mifude no sarugaku ennen no ki"* (Prince Shōtoku's handwritten account of *sarugaku ennen*, ZZ, *Fūshikaden*, 40). While some details of Zenchiku's version accord closely with Zeami's, others contradict it (for example the reign in which Hada no Kōkatsu appears is different, and his claim to be the reincarnation of the first Chinese emperor is reported in an oracle rather than in an imperial dream). The two *Lotus Sutra* citations come from the *Hōben* (Upāya) chapter.
561. The Kōkatsu who appears in *Nihonshoki* has no military character at all (see Aston, 127 and 141).

give this connection a spiritual basis. There was a connection between the Miwa deity in Yamato and the Sannō Shrine on Hieizan, which Zenchiku probably knew of through Miwa Shinto.[562] It seems that when Saichō founded the Tendai institution, he invoked the Miwa deity from Mt. Mimuro in Yamato to act as the protective deity of Mt. Hiei, where it was known as Sannō Gongen.[563] Miwa and Sannō were thus the same deity active in two places. Zenchiku had developed the idea that *sarugaku* was closely associated with the Miwa deity.[564] He could therefore explain the existence of two *sarugaku* traditions in Yamato and Ōmi as a reflection of the Miwa deity's two manifestations in the two provinces. This theory gave the Yamato troupes priority over the Ōmi troupes, but Zenchiku went on to extend the hierarchy downwards to all the *sarugaku* groups in the provinces of Japan:

> As Sannō and Miwa are one essence, *sarugaku* also starts in Yamato and divides to Ōmi, performing the divine ritual. It is the binding of fate (*kechien* 結縁) that causes it to be thus. After that [*sarugaku* traditions] divided, spreading far and wide throughout Japan, performing the divine ritual *sarugaku* in place after place in the sixty-six provinces. If there were none in a province they crossed over from a different province to perform the divine ritual. This troupe—the source—as the master and basis, of old received yearly tribute from every troupe in every province. Old men say that it was like this up until recent times. Nevertheless, now is a time when the latter days are strong and full, this is unused, rather the headship ritual is mocked, the head is shaken, the tradition is stopped. Therefore, now it has reached a point where one hesitates to tell of it, and one just thinks of it in the bottom of one's heart. I am anxious about talking like this, but as outsiders will not read these two volumes of secret teaching, I am able to speak without restraint.[565]

562. The story is told in *Miwa daimyōjin engi* (see Tanikawa, 557).
563. On the model of the Shanwang (=Sannō) shrine on Mt. Tiantai (=Tendai) in China. See further discussion of Sannō and Miwa below, in relation to the interpretation of the mask.
564. The deity worshipped at Ōmiwa Jinja (大神神社), which claims to be the oldest shrine in Japan, is referred to by Zenchiku as Miwa no Myōjin 三輪の明神 (KKS, 282). The Miwa cult played a role in the development of Shingon Shintō, that is Ryōbu Shintō. The mountain was identified with the regions of mandalas, and also believed to be a "pure land." Amaterasu was identified with Dainichi Nyorai, which manifested once in the sky as the sun, and twice on earth as the shrine deities of Miwa and Ise. See Murayama Shūichi, *Honji suijaku (Nihon rekishi sōsho 33)* (Yoshikawa Kōbunkan, 1974), 322–327.
565. KKS, *Meishukushū*, 289–90.

There is no evidence that any of this was ever true, but it seems that Zenchiku believed that the Enman'i lineage had formerly occupied this leading position. The final link in the chain of transmission was between the Enman'i line and the Komparu branch. Zenchiku managed to find a tradition to justify that, too. Certain geographical locations figure prominently in Zenchiku's discussions. One of them is Hase—both the river, which is important in the story of Hada no Kōkatsu, and the temple, which is related to the origin of the *rokurin ichiro* theory. Zenchiku builds a number of relationships between Hase and *sarugaku*, one of which is the following:

> Long ago the priest of the Hase Yogi Shrine, Aimasu Tayū, a man of divine favor and spiritual powers, composed a poem:
>
> *hatsuse yama / tani no mumoregi / kuchizu shite / kon haru ni koso / hana wa sakitsuge*
>
> Mount Hase! The buried tree in the valley has not decayed; in the coming spring it will blossom again and again.
>
> That he wrote thus makes me feel that he had profound knowledge.[566]

Aimasu Tayū was one of a line of shrine priests of the Yogi subtemple in the Hase complex that had close *sarugaku* links.[567] Zenchiku interpreted Aimasu's poem as a prophecy concerning himself and his grandfather: the term "coming spring" could be read: "komparu," so the poem could be understood to say that the buried tradition would bloom again and again in the Komparu line.[568]

Zenchiku adds a quite new transmission narrative, which he constructed from poetic traditions. This time the starting point is the deity Okina, who emerged at the beginning of the universe. As we shall discuss below, one of the primary identities Zenchiku proposed for Okina was the Sumiyoshi Daimyōjin, which was treated as the tutelary deity for *waka* in the esoteric commentary tradition deriving from Fujiwara Tameaki. Certain poetic figures had been identified with Sumiyoshi by the simple fact that

---

566. KKS, *Meishukushū*, 290.
567. Little is known of these people. There was a *sarugaku za* at Hase, connected in some way to the Jūni performers. The thirteenth-century actor Miroku Tayū was based at Hase and the fifteenth-century playwright Jūni Rokurō Shigehisa was the head priest of the Hase Yogi Hachimangū shrine. See NGK, 868–9 for details.
568. The poem itself is otherwise unknown, but it is reminiscent of a poem dedicated to the Kasuga shrine by Fujiwara Ietaka, numbered 1793 in *Shinkokinwakashū*. Zenchiku composed his own poem in reply: *Kare ni ide shimizu no nagare ya hatsuse kawa sono mama fukaki e ni komoruran*, "Emerging for a moment, the flow (lineage) of pure water, River Hase, hidden deep in the bay" (KKS, *Meishukushū*, 291).

they had been represented or named as old men. Sumiyoshi Daimyōjin manifested himself as an old man in some versions of episode 117 of the *Ise monogatari*. Hitomaro was represented as an old man in a tradition of portraits used in poetic ceremonies. Ariwara no Narihira was referred to as *katai okina*—"humble old man" in *Ise monogatari*. The word *okina* thus, in certain poetic texts, had come to be treated as a marker of a manifestation of the Sumiyoshi deity.[569] In the *Kokinwakashū* there is a reference to three poems being composed by *mitari no okina*, three old men. This, too, was a trigger for secret interpretations in Kamakura commentaries.[570] Zenchiku converted all of these into manifestations of his "Okina":

> In the age of human kings, Okina, as Zaigo Chūjō Narihira, author of the *Ise monogatari*, was born into a family practicing the art of poetry. Called *katai okina*, humble old man, he guided fickle-hearted women, teaching them the way of yin and yang. Among the poetic sages of the *Kokinwakashū*, the single substance separated into different forms as *mitari no okina* (the three old men), and composed poems on birth, old age, sickness and death. These are all temporary forms taken up as expedient means. Things conform to the names by which they are called, so how can these not be this ultimate essence?[571]

This last remark is a reference to the Hossō theory *myōsenjishō* 名詮自性 that Kanera alluded to in his commentary on the *rokurin ichiro* diagrams.[572] The theory asserts that names reflect the true nature of their referents, in other words it denies the arbitrariness of signs. Zenchiku claimed that the presence of the word "*okina*" in the names he lists must indicate a hidden connection to Okina.

INTEGRATING THE THREE TREASURES

The three treasures had a dual function: as possessions passed down in the Komparu family they were evidence of the transmission of the art, and as "texts" they could be interpreted to give information about both the possessors and their practices. In this duality they were similar to *hidensho*, which both marked authority and embodied profound knowledge. They also resonated (through the number three) with the regalia of the imperial family: mirror, jewels and sword. Fourteenth-century courtiers had explored

569. See Klein, 87–8 and 204.
570. See extra note 28, KKS, 588.
571. KKS, *Meishukushū*, 280.
572. The entry in Morohashi's *Dai kanwa jiten* cites a passage from *Yuishikiron*. Kanera simply uses the term 名詮, KKS, *Rokurin ichiro no ki*, 209. Zenchiku uses the full term in KKS, *Meishukushū*, 295.

the meanings of the regalia, finding them to be both symbolic and magical. Zenchiku sought appropriate interpretations of his treasures, too, and also treated them as sacred.

The treasures were a picture, a reliquary and a mask, and had been put together in an earlier period when the self-image of the Enman'i troupe was significantly different from the one developed by Zenchiku. Their original implications were no longer helpful and Zenchiku needed to reinterpret them. What for us is his "creative misreading," was for him more in the nature of the solution of a puzzle, one for which he sought spiritual guidance. The gods gave Zenchiku an obscure message, out of which developed what many have taken to be the primary idea of *Meishukushū*: the identity of Okina and the deity Shukushin.[573]

The need for a new slant on the treasures led Zenchiku to reconfigure them, adding others and making new combinations, but still highlighting the number three. As we shall see, his process of alteration was continued by future generations, so that in the eighteenth century the troupe reported a different set. The number three, however, persisted.

Zenchiku's firm belief in the centrality of *Shikisanban* complicated his interpretion of his inherited treasures. Zeami had described the objects in *Fūshikaden*:

---

573. The identity between Okina and Shukushin are generally taken to be the central ideas of *Meishukushū*, see, for example, KKS, 80: "*okina sunawachi shukushin no tachiba kara sarugaku gei no shimpisa o toita mono de aru.*" This idea is central to the scholarly theory of a Shukushin cult among medieval performers. That theory, however, is built on weak circumstantial evidence; once one sees the interpretative process I outline here, the need to conjecture a common cult disappears. Hattori developed the theory of a Shukushin cult among medieval performers based on studies by Kita Sadayoshi of outcast performer beliefs, Yanagita Kunio's discovery of widespread worship of deities with names like Shukushin in modern Shikoku, and *Meishukushū* (see Hattori 1974, and "Shukushin ron—geinōshin shinkō no kongen ni aru mono, ge," *Bungaku* (February 1975)). Kita's studies (esp. Kita Sadayoshi, "Shukushin kō," *Minzoku to rekishi* 4/5 (1920): 253–266) were based on Tokugawa period records and the Shukushin (宿神) in question was clearly related to the *shuku* (宿), dormitories in which such performers were organized. Yanagita's deities were called a variety of names including *shukushin no kami* (肅慎の神) and *shugoshin* (守護神). These may well have been separate varieties of protective deity (*shugoshin* 守護神), but the links to medieval *sarugaku* are too thin. There is no evidence that I know of for a cult to Shukushin among *sarugaku* performers in the fifteenth century. Zeami never mentioned Shukushin, and outside *Meishukushū* (which the text itself explains as an astrological god, one of several tens of deities identified with Okina) Zenchiku never mentioned Shukushin. One needs to be careful about treating deities as if they were like physical objects that either are or are not the same. With a deity, identity depends on the believer's conception. The coincidence between Kita's Tokugawa period "dormitory deity," Yanagita's twentieth century "protective deity" and Zenchiku's fifteenth century "god of the constellations," is too weak to propose a widespread performer's cult. (It is for similar reasons that I pay little attention here to Hattori's related arguments about Matarashin, which he sees as a kind of hidden identity of Shukushin informing *Meishukushū*. Zenchiku never mentions Matarashin.)

Three things from Ujiyasu are transmitted in (the Enman'i) house: an *oni* mask made by Prince Shōtoku, a sacred image of Kasuga, and a Buddhist reliquary.[574]

In the context of the Enman'i troupe's role in previous generations, these objects were obviously appropriate. Zenchiku's forebears were famous for *oni* (=demon) performances—hence the *oni* mask. Of the two founding occasions, it was the Buddhist one that was directly linked to the Enman'i—thus Buddha relics. Finally, the prime duty of the Yamato troupes was the offering of performances at the Kasuga shrine—thus the Kasuga portrait. To Zenchiku, however, developing his theory of Okina as spiritual essence, the same objects now needed a different explanation, for why was the mask not an *okina* mask and why the picture not a picture of Okina? Zenchiku dealt with the fact that the mask was a demon by conjecturing that Okina had two manifestations, the cheerful old man of the *Okina* mask and the terrifying demon of the *oni* mask:

Concerning the fact that, in contrast to *Okina*, an *oni* mask is enshrined in this troupe. Prince Shōtoku made it. He gave it to Kōkatsu when he ordered him to perform *sarugaku*. This is therefore a mask with the same essence as *Okina*. The various heavenly and protective deities, the Buddhas and bodhisattvas, and human beings too, all have two forms, mild and fierce. . . . Thus, when angered, the demon-quelling form is manifest in the wrathful deities, but when expressing the mild, forbearing and compassionate form, the countenance is serene; it is the wonderful being of the original Tathāgata.[575]

Zenchiku did not record any interpretation of the second treasure, the Buddhist reliquary, explaining instead that it came from Prince Shōtoku, as a reward to Kōkatsu "for cutting off Moriya's head."[576]

Of the three objects, the picture was the most difficult. In the first place, unlike the other two, which Zenchiku traced to Prince Shōtoku, the picture's origin seems to have been unknown, for Zenchiku fails to report it. Zeami mentioned it as one of a group passed down from Ujiyasu, but

---

574. *ZZ, Fūshikaden*, 40.
575. *KKS*, 291. The phrase "in contrast to" (*okina ni taishitatematsutte*) can be read "paired with." This is how Hattori reads it, concluding that such masks came in pairs (1974, 71–4).
576. An idea with unfortunate resonances. Hattori theorizes that *Okina* traditions derive from propitiatory performances made to the Chinese obstructive deity, Matarashin, worshipped at the *ushirodo* (or back door) of temples, and sees this as being behind the violent element projected on to the stories of Hada no Kōkatsu (Hattori, 1974, 75).

Zenchiku talks about it as if it had closer and more recent origins.[577] Still, it is clear that Zenchiku and Zeami are talking about the same picture.[578] Zenchiku writes:

> Item. What is represented in the picture, it is a bit sudden, but as I say in the introduction, I had a deep wish and prayed to Sumiyoshi, and it is represented according to the oracle.[579]

Unfortunately the "introduction" is not extant. It seems, however, that the "deep wish" Zenchiku had was for an explanation of this painting.[580] First he describes an inscription that was already on the picture and then he breaks off and tells us what the "oracle" (*o-tsuge* 御告げ) he received was:

> The inscription to the picture says, "The hundred felicitous sublimities of the unchanging *dharma*-body, etc." The meaning of this is, and so on and so forth. *[The writing breaks off here and starts on a new line]* It matches what was indicated in the Sumiyoshi oracle: "Verily sun, moon, and constellations, house the image."[581]

The old inscription, not surprisingly, is Buddhist in character. The term "hundred felicitous sublimities" (*hyakufukushōgon* 百 福 荘 厳) is a formulaic reference to the blessings that a Buddha is born with as a result of good deeds in previous lives. Zenchiku's new oracle, however, *hi tsuki hoshiyado kage o yadosu zo,*[582] has no obvious connection to the inscription. What does Zenchiku mean then when he says "it matches?" It seems it matches the picture itself, as Zenchiku says in another passage:

---

577. He uses "humble" language for the picture, "What [we] represent in the picture" (御エイ ニアラハシ申すコ ト). A headnote (19), however, weakens the reliability of the transcription of the passage (KKS, 282).

578. Zeami's term for the inherited picture was *Kasuga no goshin'ei* 春日御神影, a sacred picture of Kasuga. Zenchiku, in *Enman'iza keizu,* also refers to one of his inherited treasures as a *miei* 御影. In *Meishukushū,* when referring to the ritual worship to be offered to the three treasures he again mentions a *miei.* It seems that these must all be the same picture. (That is how Itō reads it: see KZK, 296).

579. KKS, *Meishukushū,* 282.

580. He must have been aware of Zeami's belief that it represented the Kasuga deity, but he does not seem to have placed much faith in it, because he does not mention the picture when he discusses the connections between the Kasuga deity and *sarugaku* (KKS, *Meishukushū,* 294).

581. KKS, *Meishukushū,* 282-3. The phrase "and so on and so forth" translates Zenchiku's *shikashika.*

582. Note that the phrase takes the form of the lower *ku* (7/7) of a *waka;* only natural for a message from the patron deity of poetry.

My wish seemed to penetrate to the divine will and I immediately received a spiritual dream, and opening the picture the evidence was clear.[583]

It is interesting here to note that the oracle came to him through a *reimu* 靈夢, a sacred dream—in other words, it was not mediated by a third party. This sacred dream came to Zenchiku as a result of a standard procedure, going and praying at the Sumiyoshi shrine on the thirteenth day of the ninth month.[584] He could therefore think of it as being *watakushi naki*. It had, moreover, the appropriate form for a message from Sumiyoshi—the last two phrases of a *waka* (two sets of seven syllables). Zenchiku's subsequent interpretation of the person portrayed in the picture is based on the oracle:

The formal cap manifests the two lights, sun and moon, the prayer beads string in a line the constellations, the cypress fan makes manifest the twelve months, the form which binds itself to living beings day and night without rejection.[585]

Zenchiku reads into the images in the picture the presence of astronomical phenomena mentioned in the oracle. As we shall see in Zenchiku's interpretations of the *Okina* dance, he also believed that the picture represented the *Okina* dance in its "original" form. Thus the oracle, for Zenchiku, identified the original *Okina* performance with the sun, moon and constellations. The next section of *Meishukushū* shows that Zenchiku took these heavenly phenomena to be closely related to the deity Shukushin. The section opens:

Item. The fact that I call Okina Shukushin. This perfectly matches that mysterious manifestation of Sumiyoshi. The light of the sun, moon and constellations descends, dividing day and night, giving birth to things and residing in man. These three lights are thus the *Shikisanban* and so, on the basis of the formula of "sun, moon and constellations," it is named Shukushin.

The connection is through the word *shuku* or *yado*, meaning dwelling, but also in astrological terms, constellation. Zenchiku here understands Shukushin to be the god of the constellations. We shall see how he interpreted this later, when we consider the identities of Okina. It seems here that the seed of this fundamental identification between Okina and

583. KKS, *Meishukushū*, 300.
584. Klein notes that this was the appropriate time to approach the Sumiyoshi deity for an oracle concerning one's artistic practice (196).
585. KKS, *Meishukushū*, 283.

Shukushin, expressed in the painting, and elaborated in *Meishukushū* in several directions, was in fact the dream message received from Sumiyoshi. Zenchiku thus re-interpreted the demon mask and the Kasuga picture. These along with the reliquary not only bore meaning, but sacred power. As such he made them the obects of monthly rituals, but in these rituals he added other articles to further emphasize the connection to Okina:

> Therefore collect your prayers and make offerings to the three treasures month by month. On the pre-ordained day, the first of the month, you must worship the *Okina* mask and likewise hang up the picture, and show your respects and make offerings. It is a deity of infinite compassion, and does not spurn the expedient means of taking life, so you should offer flesh as a sacred offering. Sake has always been used by the various gods. Moreover, if you offer sake porridge, with a scoop of water, to show your gratitude, your prayers will be heard to your benefit, it is clear as pointing to the back of your hand. On the fifteenth day, make offerings to the relics, do the relic ritual, and read from the *Lotus Sutra*. On the twenty-eighth day make offerings to the *oni* mask. This day has connections with Kōjin (the wild deity) so there is an accord between principle and manifestation.[586]

Zenchiku appears to be addressing his successors in the troupe, probably his son, Komparu Motouji. The threefold grouping now adds the *Okina* mask to the picture, emphasizing its new reading as Okina and not Kasuga, adds *Lotus Sutra* to the relics, and worships the old *oni* mask on a day symmetrically opposite that of the *Okina* mask, implying that they are the two poles of a single principle. The number three is still emphasized. Leading into this passage Zenchiku wrote:

> This tradition of transmitting these significant treasures cannot be copied by other troupes. But you should consider simply the degree to which one has faith or not. The sacred traditions say that the mysterious body of the Tathāgata is his relics, the mysterious speech of the Tathāgata is the sutras, and the mysterious mind of the Tathāgata is the gods. If there are relics and sutras, and if you praise them and the gods in the two masks of *okina* and *oni*, yours will be a troupe that protects the three treasures (*sanbō shugo*), karmically bound to the three mysteries. . . .

586. KKS, *Meishukushū*, 291–2.

This deliberately conflates various groupings of three here as if they are equivalent: the three mysteries (*sanmitsu*), the three treasures, and the three rituals. The phrase three treasures (*sanbō*) usually refers to the three refuges: Buddha, Sangha and Dharma, [587] and "protecting the three treasures" (*sanbō shugo* 三宝守護) is a term normally indicating the function of protecting Buddhism. Here, however, it also means protecting the three inherited treasures, the *oni* mask, picture and Buddhist reliquary. Zenchiku is implying that his troupe in possessing these three objects can claim to be a "protector of Buddhism."

It seems that Zenchiku by including an *Okina* mask into the schedule of offerings caused it eventually to be considered one of his family's sacred objects. In 1721 the Komparu troupe reported its treasures to the *bakufu* as follows:

1: a frightening mask not used in Noh performance,

2: an *okina* mask, believed to have magical powers, made by Prince Shōtoku and passed down from Kōkatsu, and

3: a *Sanbasō* mask similarly made by Prince Shōtoku.[588]

There are still three treasures but the details have changed. The first mask may well be the *oni* mask mentioned by Zeami, but it is now the other two masks (which can be used in the *Shikisanban*) that are ascribed to Prince Shōtoku. We can understand the Komparu treasures to play a similar role to ideological formulae in oral cultures, affording both formal conservatism and practical flexibility through new interpretation. The number must be three, but the objects themselves can change.

Zenchiku's research into his family's origins focused on the three treasures that were evidence of its transmission. As such they could not be random objects left over by the passage of the generations; they were bound to be significant. If there was a spiritual entity, Okina, expressing itself in both the poetic and performance traditions, then the *oni* mask was not just a mark of the Komparu troupe's excellence in demonic performances, it was also a representation of Okina. Similarly the picture must represent Okina, but nothing about it seemed connected to the *Okina* role and it lacked a useful story of its origin. Appeal to spiritual forces resulted in an astrological message, and the picture appeared to be interpretable in those terms. Such astrological ideas were the province of the "constellation" deity Shukushin. While Zenchiku pursued this route in the development of his

---

587. That is the Buddha himself, the community of monks and nuns, and the Buddhist teachings.
588. Cited in Hattori, 1974, 74.

theories of Okina, he also added an *Okina* mask to his treasures, which eventually was to supplant the picture.

INTERPRETING ASPECTS OF *SHIKISANBAN* PERFORMANCE

A secret knowledge of an art based on Okina needs an interpretation of elements of *Shikisanban* performance. Zenchiku's reading centered on two particular elements: the *Okina* mask and the *Okina* dance. There was a tradition of magical *Okina* masks at the Tōnomine temple of which Zenchiku was aware, but he focused on spiritual rather than magical connotations. He raised the perhaps inevitable question of whether *Okina* masks were conscious or not. To common sense they are inanimate, but in use they appear to be alive. Zenchiku came to the conclusion that at a high level of consciousness they could be seen to be alive. In this way he related mask lore to the transformation of the actor's awareness. A similar idea informs his reading of the *Okina* dance. There seems to have been a traditional interpretation of it as the manifestation of the Buddha Amida. Zenchiku reports this but also argues that if the dance is the manifestation of a divine being, the actor who plays the main role must experience the identity of his consciousness with absolute reality. In Zenchiku's reading this experience is the primary legitimation of the actor, whose role thereby is to bless audiences. The idea that the state of mind of the actor is the key to true performance is a consistent element of Zenchiku's thought, but here the achievement of that state of mind is the mysterious product of religious faith and the power of ritual.

Actors believed that *Shikisanban* was a shortened form of a series of sixty-six performance pieces established by Kōkatsu. A Kanze text shows that a full sixty-six pieces were still performed at Tōnomine in the sixteenth century. [589] Associated with those performances were magical masks that exhibited signs of life—going red when drunk or growing whiskers:

> The sixty-six pieces are even now performed at Tōnomine. It is the Dharma ritual at the start of each year. The focus of worship (*honzon*) is an *okina* mask. After the ritual there is a great drinking session. . . . They force down sake in incalculable quantities. . . . As the temple followers get drunk, one after the other, the color of the mask, which is

589. Early scholars of *sarugaku* history thought the tradition of sixty-six pieces was a mere legend, partly because the founding occasions were not in themselves believable and also because the number sixty-six looked symbolic—either related to the number of provinces or a doubling of the thirty-three faces of Kannon (Zenchiku himself develops these connections: KKS, *Meishukushū*, 289–280). It is now accepted that such a group of performances did exist (see Omote Akira, "Tōnomine no sarugaku," *Nōgaku kenkyū* 1 (1974): 88–120).

hung up, gets redder. This miracle still works even in these latter days of the law. . . . The sixty-six pieces were condensed into the *Shikisanban*, but the effect in each case is the same. The [present] mask was made with short facial hairs but with each year they have grown longer, now reaching a foot in length. These evidences of spiritual presence are quite awesome.[590]

This New Year's performance put on by the Tōnomine priests was not the same as the Yamato *sarugaku* performances at Tōnomine during the Yuima-e, but there was clearly a connection between the beliefs involved. We saw that Zenchiku added an *okina* mask to his monthly rituals. It seems likely that it was the one mentioned in a collection of poems (*Tsukigusa*) by his *waka* teacher, Shōtetsu:

I composed this poem on the occasion when Komparu Tayū requested an inscription for a religious image (*honzon*). The image was in the form of an *okina* mask.

Chihayaburu / kami wa hotoke no / kage nareba / okina sugata / ei no koromo zo

千ハやふる神は仏の影なれハ 翁すかたえひのころもそ

Since the fierce deities are projections of the Buddha, the guise of *Okina* is a purple/drunken robe[591]

Shōtetsu's use of the term *honzon* 本尊 indicates the ritual purpose of the mask, and the pun on drunkenness indicates the similarity to the Tōnomine tradition.[592]

Zenchiku of course knew of the performance of the sixty-six piece *sarugaku* in his time:

The ancient ritual at that temple [Tōnomine] is not reformed, and the sixty-six piece *sarugaku* is performed every new year. Similarly there is a magical and excellent mask of *Okina*. It is said that it is when they have had much experience of this ritual, after having put on this mask, that they make the grade of first elder (*ichirō* 一﨟).[593]

This highlights the authorizing aspect of the *Okina* performance—it is a rite of passage by which the wearer becomes an elder.

590. Quoted in additional note 36, KKS, 589–590.
591. See KZK, 27–30, KKS, 81, and Hattori 1975, 95. I preserve the orthography in order to enable recognition of the pun (next footnote).
592. The pun is えひ (酔ひ) drunk, and えび (葡萄), a purple weave. Hattori notices this in 1975, 95, fn 18.
593. KKS, *Meishukushū*, 295.

Zenchiku seems less interested in the gross manifestations of magic associated with the *okina* mask and more in understanding its special nature in terms of traditional discussions of religious images. How can images or masks represent what is beyond the realm of form?

Now what can be used to represent the superb form of "thusness"? It is said:

"When you play with a flower, scent fills your robe,
when you scoop up water, the moon is in your hand,"[594]

or again:

"When the moon has hidden itself in the serried mountains
I hold up my fan and liken the two."[595]

The image of the flower in the first poem suggests that association with it leads to the absorption of its invisible qualities; so, too, the physical connection through the mask brings an invisible connection with what it cannot express. The moon in the scooped water likewise brings the unreachable into one's grasp.[596] The second poem uses a Buddhist metaphor: the moon is the true teaching, the fan is expedient means and the serried ranges are earthly passions.[597] The representation is necessary to point to otherwise hidden reality. Zenchiku goes on to discuss the mask in the terms used regarding statues. Once the Buddha had died, the three-fold refuge needed concrete representations: statues of the Buddha, texts of his teachings, monastic institutions. But seen rightly, the statues of the Buddha and his embodiment as Sākyamuni were equivalent, for both were the descents into form (*suijaku*) of thusness (*tathatā*).

In the rule of the three treasures,[598] wooden and clay images are treated as the Buddha, yellow volumes and red scrolls as the Dharma, and shaven heads and dyed robes as the Sangha. The enlightenment form of the living body of Sākya has entered the cloud of *nirvāna*, and so in the present evil world of the five impurities, wooden carvings, molded mud and drawings are treated as Buddha. The same kind of thing is true of the Dharma and the Sangha. Therefore as long as one has sincere conviction, there is no distinction between living bodies and simulacra.

594. From a poem by Yu Liang-shih.
595. From a poem by Chih-I, appearing in *Wakan rōeishū* (Ōsone and Horiuchi, 221).
596. Zenchiku also referred to these images in KKS, *Bunshōbon*, 258.
597. See the note in Ōsone and Horiuchi, 221.
598. Here, of course, it is the three refuges, Buddha, Dharma and Sangha, which are referred to, not the family heirlooms.

Descending into form as an expedient means of benefiting living creatures is unchanged up to the present age. Use this to know this. It is only in conviction and doubt that there are differences. There should be no distinction between the living body and the wooden body.[599]

That is, the *Okina* mask is a descent into form equal to a living manifestation of Okina in its power to bless.

This sets up a theoretical basis for treating the mask as if it were a living being. Zenchiku identifies that aliveness with the presence of the senses:

To start with, the mask is equipped with the six senses: eyes, ears, nose, tongue, body, and mind. The first four: eyes, ears, nose and tongue, are clearly present as the world understands them. As for the remaining two senses they too pose no difficulty. The body refers to the fleshly form, and as I have said above this cannot be different from the wooden form. Now, what indeed should be understood to be the sense of mind? Regarding this one must contemplate and cogitate so that one might understand that within this mask the sense of mind is present. If that can be understood, then you have reached the stage wherein you will achieve Buddhahood in this very body.[600]

Seeing the life in the mask indicates a transformation in one's own consciousness.

In the interpretations of the performance of *Shikisanban* itself as well, ideas of the border between contradictory states and the transformation of consciousness drive Zenchiku's interpretations. The central element is the role of *Okina*, especially his dance, known as *Okina no mai*. Zenchiku claims that this manifests Amida and his two Bodhisattvas coming to meet the souls of believers at death.

As for the *Okina* dance, one sounds out the drums, and shakes the tinkling bells. These are the actions of Amida coming to welcome souls [at the moment of death]. *Kuriku-sa-saku, kuriku-sa-saku*, these sounds of the bells are the seed syllables of Amida and his accompanying two Bodhisattvas. They must not be performed carelessly. When the mask is put on and the 'Agemaki' sung, it is directly perceived that the ordinary mind is, as it is, the absolute reality. This should be in a separately recorded secret teaching. This being the case, there must be a gathering of the living creatures of every place into this divine

599. KKS, *Meishukushū*, 281.
600. KKS, *Meishukushū*, 281.

binding of fate. Whether in regular shrine ritual or special performances, there is this Amida coming to meet, so it is a form that makes the karmic connection to all the living creatures that make up the great gathering of noble and base.[601]

The specific character of these assertions gives the impression that they reflect an inherited tradition.[602] The idea that the sound of the bell-trees is the seed syllables (*bija-mantra*) is clever. The seed syllables of Amida, Kannon and the Bodhisattva Mahāsthāmaprāpta are indeed pronounced in Japanese *kuriku*, *sa* and *saku*; and placed in succession they are perhaps similar to the sound of a bell-tree shaken in a dance.[603] Seed mantras cause spiritual forces to manifest themselves. The dance is thus transformed into an invocation of Amida and his companions. The appearance of this group is generally thought to occur at the moment of death, when Amida "comes to meet"[604] those who have made the all-important karmic connection (*kechien*) to him, to escort them to the Pure Land from which there is no return to suffering. The *Shikisanban* performance represents this moment, and at the same time, it becomes the means of making the connection by which the audience will actually see Amida coming to help them when they die. While *Shikisanban* has this external effect, it also transforms the mind of the actor. "Agemaki" refers to an old Heian erotic *saibara* ("The two youngsters sat out of each other's reach . . . ") that the actor in the *Okina* role sings early in his performance. At this moment the actor perceives directly *tōisokumyō* 当意即妙, the identity of ordinary mind and absolute reality. This is the Buddhist interpretation of this term, but in performance contexts, *tōisokumyō* is generally read to mean spontaneous improvisation.[605] For Zenchiku it has both readings, which are of course connected:

> Item. *Okina no mai*—this is of profound importance. It is the original dance of *sarugaku* and so one must especially contemplate and consider before proceeding to dance. . . . There must be only the form of dance of *tōisokumyō*. . . . The state of mind to be attained in the dance is: not considering material things, not thinking about the gaze of men, having achieved the attitude and appearance that is within no-

601. KKS, *Meishukushū*,283.
602. I am informed (by Nakano Chieko in a private communication), however, that it was common for pictures of Amida to be used to establish the "binding of fate" with followers in the Pure Land sects. This might be the inspiration behind a reading of the *Okina no mai* fulfilling the same function, especially if that dance is being read through a religious picture.
603. See headnote 33, KKS, 283.
604. *Raigō* 来迎.
605. See entry in Taya, with the orthography 当位即妙, 335, and entry in *Kōjien* for 当意即妙.

mind and no-form, making dance and song, body and mind into one thought, to dance as impelled by the music.[606]

This is not merely an abandonment of restraint and a surrender to the spirit of the music, it is also the destruction of illusion:

Make its level like the sun and moon, its essence like the auspicious sword, and perform the dance without the least speck of an obstacle. This auspicious sword essence in itself generates the techniques of entertaining music and dance. When this is kept within the mind to the very end without clouding over, truly it becomes a strong Noh form, achieving the level at which one is not overcome by material things. This sword actually must be the auspicious sword of Acala (Fudō), the sword of wisdom of Manjusri. Truly it is the sword of 'not one (illusory) thought arises.'[607]

The moment of *tōisokumyō* is also a transcendence of the worldly—an absorption in which no thoughts arise. It is interesting to see here how Zenchiku employs the imagery of the sword taken from the *rokurin ichiro* system to express this idea, for it shows that it is not in his mind restricted to *Shikisanban* alone, but has a more general presence in Noh performances, too.

The identity of the transient world of appearances and unchanging reality is a constant theme of medieval Buddhism, and along with a number of other identifications of opposites, repeatedly appears in Noh plays. Magic rites convert such theories into practice, where contrary realms overlap and their identity is inwardly felt. In Zenchiku's reading, the *Okina* dance is a rite of transformation: through it the audience is bound to Amida, and the actor's mind penetrates the absolute. But this transformation also operates on a worldly level: after many years of acting in Noh plays, the troupe elder wins the right to don the *okina* mask and perform the *Shikisanban*. Not only does he experience higher consciousness, he also thereby exhibits his leadership of the troupe and his right to the major share of its rewards.

DEFINING AND IDENTIFYING OKINA

The opening passage of *Meishukushū* defines Okina as a spiritual force arising at the start of the universe. It continues with a list of identities: first there are three so-called *honji,* here signifying Buddhist identities:

---

606. KKS, *Meishukushū*, 286.
607. KKS, *Meishukushū*, 286. Note that the swords of Acala and Manjusri, were mentioned in Shigyoku's commentary on the *ichiro* sword, KKS, 204.

When one enquires into the *honji*, it is Dainichi transcending the two
realms, it is also the Tathāgata Amida, of the supramundane
compassionate vow, and it is also the Buddha Sākyamuni, the
responding form—the three embodiments: *dharma, sambhōga* and
nirmāna, fully complete in the one function. When [Okina] divides that
single function into three forms, he directly appears as the *Okina
Shikisanban.*[608]

This is simply an elaboration of Zeami's statement that the old men roles of
Shikisanban represented the three bodies of the Buddha: *dharma-kāya,
sambhōga-kāya* and *nirmāna-kāya*. The most commonly identified
examples of those bodies were Dainichi, Amida and Sākyamuni. Zenchiku
goes on to provide a matching trio of Shinto deities:

> When we enquire into the *suijaku*, they are distinct and clear. The first
> is the Daimyōjin of Sumiyoshi. He also appears as the Myōjin of Suwa,
> and also as the deity of Shiogama.[609]

The origin of these identifications is less clear. The number of them is three
perhaps for symmetry. The identity with Sumiyoshi is based on Zenchiku's
perception of identity between poetry and *sarugaku*, but the connection to
the other two deities is less clear. Both Sumiyoshi and Suwa were sites of
ritual *sarugaku* in the Muromachi period.[610] The local deity at Shiogama is
the old man of the tides that was linked to poetic *okina*.[611] Zenchiku goes on
to refer to other Shinto manifestations of Okina at Mount Sōtō and Mount
Tsukuba about which little is now known.[612] After this he states that there
have been *suijaku* in many places, but cloudy eyes and foolish minds cannot
perceive or understand them.[613]

Zenchiku next enumerates the appearances of Okina in history based
on the use of the referent "*okina.*" These statements of equivalence are
joined later in *Meishukushū* by identifications of Okina with one after the
other sage or divinity, including the Kasuga deity, Tenman Tenjin, Hindu
heavenly beings, the god of war, and the founders of Buddhist sects. These

---

608. KKS, *Meishukushū*, 279. The "one function" (一得) is unknown, but may have Shinto
roots, related to the *suitoku* 水得 of Watarai Shinto theory.
609. KKS, *Meishukushū*, 279.
610. See NGK, 1516–7 and 345.
611. There he is called *Shio-tsuchi-no-oji-no-kami* (Tyler, 163, fn. 12). This old man was also
considered a manifestation of Sumiyoshi Daimyōjin. There are a number of such linkages
across deities and shrines, but it is hard to see what an exhaustive investigation of them might
yield.
612. The editors of KKS reproduce in a note a legend of a miraculous spirit at Mt. Sōtō in the
third century, which has similarities with the story of Hada no Kōkatsu's origins.
613. KKS, *Meishukushū*, 279.

assertions of identity seem steadily more pointless and the flimsy "logic" with which they are supported seems even more misguided. In a number of cases, however, it is clear that Zenchiku perceived these identities as carrying with them moral and other messages. As *Meishukushū* itself is incomplete, one cannot tell what he intended to do with all these identifications, but he does fill out the significance of some of them. We will consider three exemplary cases, Shukushin, Miwa and Sumiyoshi.

The identity with Shukushin, which we saw arose from Sumiyoshi's astrological message, was used by Zenchiku to discuss inner divinity, the mind in performance, and the moral duties of actors. As we have seen, the original purpose of the message was to interpret the picture. The oracle referred to heavenly bodies and constellations (*shuku*). Zenchiku, who took the picture to represent the "original" appearance of the *Okina* dance, used the astrological connections to develop *sarugaku* into a purely religious practice and to draw conclusions related to the moral behavior of contemporary performers.

The picture is primarily read in terms of the message from the Sumiyoshi deity. The term *yado* appeared in that message in two cognates ("Verily sun, moon, and constellations (*yado*) house (*yadosu*) the image"). The character used to write *yado*, 宿, usually interpreted "dwelling" or "house," also signified astrological constellation (as indeed does "house") and could be read "*shuku*," yielding the name Shukushin 宿神 "dwelling deity." This character had associated with it one of those interpretations based on the elements out of which it was constructed: a roof (宀), a man (人), and the number one hundred (百="myriad"). These are the basis of Zenchiku's reading of the picture:

> The light of the sun, moon, and stellar houses descends, dividing day and night, making things arise, and residing in man. As the three luminaries[614] are the *Shikisanban*, it is this principle of sun, moon and stellar houses that is named Shukushin (宿神). The character for *shuku* (宿) signifies a star descending and facing a man, practicing myriad techniques. In any house the blessings of the stellar houses must be invoked, but especially the awesome power of that Okina that is called Shukushin, cannot be revered enough.[615]

Shukushin is a divine transmitter of knowledge to man. Shukushin also resides ("*yadosu*") within the human being, as a kind of inner voice. Therefore he is an inner moral regulator, or conscience:

---

614. 三光—sun, moon and stars.
615. KKS, *Meishukushū*, 285.

The sight of Heaven is clear. There is nothing hidden from the gaze of the gods of earth. You may think that you think alone, but in your head are the stellar houses. How should they cloud over?[616]

Shukushin is always watching!

If all people contain the divine within, how should one distinguish between them? The difference is in the level of awareness they achieve of the inner voice:

> Item. As said above, Okina, that is sun, moon, and stellar houses, resides in the minds of men. Each person is fully equipped, but there are those who know and those who do not know. . . . When one does not know, one must fear the possibility of becoming distant. One must concentrate one's mind in contemplation and thought.[617]

Zenchiku sees this knowledge or awareness as coming to one as a kind of enlightenment. Unusually, he draws on Zen terminology:

> In general, when one contemplates the satori essence of Okina, one realises that it is the absolute form of emptiness, the ancient one of the distant past that is called Okina. As it is the original face before father and mother were born, it is called Okina. When you do not see samsara (life and death) it is called Okina. As it is unlimited it is called Okina. As it is ever-present it is called Okina. The compassionate mind is called Okina. Looking deeper and further, does it exist or not, facing the ruler of the mind, behold this Okina. If you meet this Okina, he must be that person who directly answers to the field that is your original portion.[618]

Sarugaku thus has mystical roots, and performers as representatives of the divine bear responsibility accordingly: they must not mislead people, must be honest, of good character, and dedicated to their duties:

> There is a passage about people who, preaching as envoys of the Tathāgata, indiscriminately explain the law to the sullied world, and confuse the minds of others; they are like rice, hemp, bamboo and reeds (the correct passage should be quoted).[619] When we understand this, truly *sarugaku* troupes in the present latter age are like "rice, hemp,

616. KKS, *Meishukushū*, 297.
617. KKS, *Meishukushū*, 306.
618. KKS, *Meishukushū*, 285–6. This passage is rare for Zenchiku in that it uses Zen terms for the Buddha nature: the face before birth, the field that is your original portion.
619. The note enclosed in parentheses was written by Zenchiku to himself. There is a mention of rice, hemp, bamboo and reeds in the *Lotus Sutra*, in the second book, *Hōben*, but it bears quite a different significance from the one intended by Zenchiku here.

bamboo and reeds," for they have become separated from the roots into branches and from those ends again, several varieties of troupes have appeared. If one pursues one's art by behaving honestly in the correct path, and becoming a master of one's calling, one revives one's art, then indeed must one truly be that rare "envoy of Okina." If craving after the world, one is just engaged in earning a living, confusing the minds of others under the mere title of a shrine servant, an extreme of immorality, then one is an evil obstacle in the path. It is not enough just to talk about it. If one has the power to establish a troupe, and makes plans, even supposing that one has not the karmic inheritance, one should perform the divine ritual (i.e. *Shikisanban*) and consider well how to be in accord with the deity's hidden wishes. This is the essential point.[620]

Zenchiku naturally rated birth into a family of traditional performers as important, but he also considered sincerity and faith combined with the practice of *Shikisanban* to be essential. He criticized the recent behavior of the Yamato troupes:

Moreover, even in the unchanging *sarugaku* of the original troupes, one must understand that there is that which is an evil obstacle in the path. Lately under the pretext of performing *Shikisanban*, they go to that place and make unreasonable demands, coveting sacred objects and the rewards for performance, which are limited. There is an ancient saying: "He neither dilutes nor thickens, comparing it with the traditional way."[621] Thus if you dilute what is thick, you go against the wishes of the deity. If you thicken what is thin, the *sarugaku* must differ from divine intent. However, they go in to place after place, and not only take sacred objects, but, making pretexts to the *gakutō*,[622] take wood from the mountain, taking it to their households and transporting it to other places. Despoiling the village, they go too far. The taking of wood at the time of the divine ritual is for use while one is in that place. To take more is not as it should be. . . . Nevertheless in recent years the going up to the place of ritual is like a raid on an army camp. With things thus, when the tide of events eventually turns, the family task

---

620. KKS, *Meishukushū*, 296.
621. Origin unknown. I read "*gi to tomo ni hisu*" differently from the editors of KKS, who suggest 秘す for the last word. I prefer 比す.
622. 楽頭, the temple official responsible for performances on ritual occasions.

will naturally be cast aside. What thing could be more of an obstacle in the path than this![623]

The Kasuga mountain and its produce were sacred, off-limits even for shrine officials. [624] It seems that the *sarugaku* troupes had a special dispensation to use the wood on ritual occasions. Zenchiku regrets the exploitation of these rights. The performer's character should be correct and straight:

> But if one is born into this family task of Okina, then, if one should whole-heartedly master this art, performing one's task without duplicity, making the essence of the mind[625] correct and straight,[626] and believing in Okina, then one would need no other religious practice. One must see that this very thing is the wonderful *Lotus Sutra*; this very thing is that straight road on which Amida comes to greet [souls at death]. Thus indeed was established the idea of the non-dual absolute. Things that face different ways are not the same and those that face the same way are not different. All I ask is that you should know the consciousness of Okina. Once that is understood one is directly in the land of the Tathāgata. . . . As I said above, the mysterious mind of the Tathāgata is the conscious self, so it must be contemplated as that mysterious mind. This is what is called in the Buddha-mind (Zen) sect 'the field that is our original portion' and 'the original face.'[627]

---

623. KKS, *Meishukushū*. 296–7.
624. Killing animals and cutting wood on the mountain were strictly forbidden by the Fujiwara in 841 (Nagashima, 1987, 47). It seems that there were occasions when *sarugaku* could use those resources, probably at the meetings of the troupes on the mountain to decide the troupe offices that took place before the start of the year's performance calendar on the fifth day of the second month.
625. 心性, the unchanging aspect of mind.
626. 正直.
627. KKS, *Meishukushū*, 298. Zenchiku is alluding to his discussion of the esoteric doctrine of the three mysteries (*sanmitsu* 三密, the three arenas of the Buddha's activity: body, speech and mind) in which, referring to an unknown source, he identifies the Buddha's body with relics, his speech with scripture, and his mind with *shinmei* 神明 (which I render here as "conscious self"). This last term operates as a kind of swivel-word to identify Buddhism and Shintō. The graph 神 in Buddhist contexts refers to the part of the living being that reincarnates in successive lives—what is called in Sanskrit the *purusha*. As *shinmei* it can mean the gods of heaven and earth (not necessarily Shinto gods) or the conscious subject in living beings. In *Laozi*, the compound *shinmei* means pure consciousness, and it seems likely from the next part of this passage that Zenchiku is aware of that kind of reading. The compound was also commonly used in this period to indicate the gods worshipped at shrines. In the passage Zenchiku refers back to, he identified *shinmei* with the two masks, *okina* and *oni*, which he treats as two aspects of the deity Okina. It is not clear, therefore, whether he is recommending the contemplation of the empty mind (as the subsequent sentence seems to imply) or the images of Okina (as in his earlier passage). See Taya, 285 (entry for *shinmei*) and 177 (entry for *sanmitsu*) and also KKS, *Meishukushū*, 291.

This "consciousness of Okina" seems to be the spiritual union that we saw elsewhere described in performance, the primary legitimation of the actor. *Okina* performance is now a religious path:

> It is my humble heartfelt wish that *sarugaku* should have a religious tradition to be known as *shinshinshū* 神真宗, the true sect of the deity.[628] Even supposing one does not achieve that direct mind that leads to enlightenment, if one whole-heartedly relies on the wonderful power of Okina, it is utterly without doubt that it will establish the connection to rebirth in the pure land. Do not think that this is just a worldly and irreligious way to make a living and thereby enter into evil ways. . . . We must revere, we must revere. Once you have known completely the profound depth of this source, the spirit of Okina, then there should be no obstacle at all if you should wish to practice other religious activity.[629]

Consciousness of Okina, a direct spiritual awareness akin to Zen-enlightenment, is the primary aim of the actor, but failing that, a whole-hearted faith will be effective. What *sarugaku* requires is faith.

Zenchiku developed this spiritual and religious dimension through the idea of Okina as Shukushin, which signified for him the indwelling cosmic spirit. Another identity of Okina was the Miwa deity. The invocation of the Miwa deity at the Sannō shrine was used to justify *sarugaku* history and the relative authority of the Yamato and Ōmi troupes, as outlined above. Zenchiku extended the interpretation of this relationship to derive a theory of the appropriate attitude when offering performances at shrines. His argument follows his interpretation of the *Okina* mask:

> Moreover, the *Shingi* says that the mask has the seven holes of eyes, ears, nose and tongue. These then are the seven stars. As these stars are called the seven upper shrines of Sannō, they must also be revered as Sannō Gongen.[630]

The seven stars refer to Ursa Major, a set of stars that in Sannō beliefs were a heavenly manifestation of a group of seven religious structures on Mount

---

628. An interlinear note states that this *shinshinshū* is "in *Shinpūwaki*." The term does not however appear there (in Jihen's *Toyoashiwara shinpūwaki*). It is unclear whether the second and third graph 真宗 are linked to 浄土真宗 the term for the True Pure Land Sect.
629. KKS, *Meishukushū*, 298–9.
630. KKS, *Meishukushū*, 281–282.

Hiei.[631] Zenchiku establishes the connection with Okina simply through the number seven.

As Sannō is the famed deity of Miwa, one must directly revere the Mimuro mountain of Miwa as a form of *Okina shikisanban*.[632]

Shrine deities were usually believed to be particularly present in some sacred object. In the case of the Miwa deity, this object was the mountain on which the shrine is sited. This mountain's name Miwa was written with characters meaning three circles 三輪. This orthography had already been used in Miwa Shinto writings to absorb the Buddhist doctrine of Dāna Pāramitā: purity of offering, told in the form of a dialog between the Nara period priest Genpin and the Miwa deity. Zenchiku relates a version of the story to claim the same doctrine for *sarugaku* (this version also appears in the Noh play *Miwa* as well as in later Miwa Shinto documents):

> Long ago in the time of the prelate Genpin, the deity of Miwa received the Dharma and the robe, and composed a divine poem:
>
> *miwa gawa no / kiyoku mo kiyoki / karagoromo / kururu to omou na / toru to omowaji*
>
> Even as the River Miwa is pure, this pure Chinese robe, do not think that it is given; I do not wish to think that I take it.
>
> The expression of the state of mind that there is nothing to be gained, with the attitude of the most profound compassion of the three circles of purity (*sanrin shōjō* 三輪清浄), without any distinction of self and other, in donating and being donated to, being without ideas of gain, is utterly free from blame.

The term *sanrin shōjō* derives from Buddhist scriptures, where it indicates the ideal of detachment found in the act of religious donation.[633] Miwa Shinto writings make the following commentary on the poem:

---

631. There were twenty-one structures controled by the Hiei Jinja on the mountain, divided into three groups of seven. The upper group was the most important, and was believed to manifest in the heavens as Ursa Major (the Big Dipper). The Tendai institution in Japan became dominated by the Sannō cult in the Kamakura period. The primary statement of Sannō belief was *Yōtenki* (c. 1221). It replaced the idea of *honji suijaku* with that of *inbon suijaku* (隠本垂迹), which claimed that the Buddha deliberately hid the basis and only manifested the traces in different countries according to their national characteristics. In Japan the Buddha manifested as Sannō. See Murayama, 313–8 and Ishida Ichirō, ed., *Shintō shisōshū* (Chikuma Shobō, 1970), 12–15.

632. KKS, 282.

633. Found for example in the *Hannya kyō*—see Taya, entry for *sanrin*, 178.

This concerns the Dāna Pāramitā (the ideal of giving). If he who gives is pure of heart and he who receives is pure of heart, then what is given will also be pure. . . . This is a poem about the practice of charity, one of the six virtues of Bodhisattvas, about *sanrin shōjō*.[634]

Zenchiku applies *sanrin shōjō* to *sarugaku* performance:

> As this deity is of the same essence as Okina, performers of this art must bear in mind the meaning of this divine poem when performing at regular shrine ritual or special events. When it comes to receiving payment, they should attain that freedom from ideas of gain expressed as: "do not think that it is given, I do not wish to think that I take it." Simply perform in order to create a karmic connection with the Buddha mind.[635]

Identification of Okina, Sannō and Miwa thus fulfils two functions—explaining the existence of two *sarugaku* traditions in Yamato and Ōmi and determining the appropriate spirit of performance. At the same time the link of *sarugaku* to *sanrin shōjō* could be made by a different route; in the *rokurin ichiro* works, Zenchiku equated the first three of the six circular diagrams to it.[636] This is typical of Zenchiku's thought, a densely interwoven fabric of ideas, all reaching in several directions at once.

The situation is similar with the identification of Okina and Sumiyoshi. It provided Zenchiku with a source for hidden knowledge through the oracle, but it also allowed him to bring in the beliefs about *sarugaku* he had developed from his study of poetry. The following citation is long, but I leave it as it is so that the reader can see the way all the different ideas derived from the identification of poetry and *sarugaku* have become one grand idea, symbolized by the identification of Sumiyoshi and Okina:

> Item. The vow to Sumiyoshi.
>
> There is a particular reason why I prayed to Sumiyoshi rather than Ise or Kasuga concerning the sacred picture. This deity is not only essentially the same as Okina; it is also the protective deity of *waka*. Now *sarugaku*'s artistic style started from Okina and makes dance and song its essence. I am afraid that performers today hear the terms dance and song, but they do not understand their true significance. The salutary verses of India, the poems and airs of China, and our own

---

634. From *Miwaryū shintō shimpi shō*, quoted in additional note 21, KKS, 586. The version of the poem given is slightly different from Zenchiku's.
635. KKS, *Meishukushū*, 282.
636. The first reference is in KKS, *Kichū*, 217.

country's songs are the same. The *Great Preface* says: "Poetry is the movement of the mind. What is in the heart is the movement of the mind, what comes out in words is poetry. When this is insufficient to tell it, one shouts and cries. When it is not enough to shout and cry, the hands gesture, the feet tread." The character preface to the *Kokinwakashū* says: "Japanese songs have their root in the ground of the mind and open their flowers in the forests of words." The syllabic introduction says: "The songs of Yamato make people's hearts their seeds, and become the leaves of a thousand words." Considering the drift of these basic Chinese and Japanese texts, one notes that there are ten styles in *waka*. They distinguish varieties of mood, but *yūgen* is the first. It penetrates from here to the most profound realm. Write out and sing the old poems of the masters of ancient times, who with pure hearts composed like flowing water, understanding distant and near verses, experienced in the five sounds of the phrases of five, seven, five, seven and seven syllables. Containing that aesthetic quality, understanding its emotional significance, if one unites it with the singing voice and moves the body, the elegance of the poetic syllables will be expressed of their own accord. When sound, meaning and dance, the three actions of body, voice and mind, have a single intent, the style of dance will be of the ultimate *yūgen*, not externally obvious but subtle and superb. Thus this play of "crazy words and fancy phrases" has become "the circumstances for praising the Buddha and turning the wheel of the Law." That is why Shinto deities accept *sarugaku* performances as offerings. If you extend this essential root to the physical movements and steps of those vital roles of warriors and demons with human hearts, then you can be a performer who all his life performs in the *yūgen* style, without any vulgarity. Thus *waka* must be revered as the life of *sarugaku*.[637]

The identity of Sumiyoshi and Okina is more than a symbol of the relationship between *waka* and *sarugaku*, it is a spiritual reality that brings together, explains and manifests the essential elements of Zenchiku's view of performance, spiritual, artistic and practical.

THE SEARCH FOR AUTHORITY AND THE SEARCH FOR TRUTH

This chapter opened with a consideration of Konishi's theory that authority accrued to specialties that were perceived to possess a set of qualities. It is true that they were claimed repeatedly in certain generic passages in works

---

637. KKS, *Meishukushū*, 299–300.

on *michi*, but it is difficult to see a direct relationship between them and cultural authority. Certain particular types of passages, however, in *michi* works, seemed designed to assert authority, both of the *michi* and of practitioners. These included accounts of originating occasions and of historical instances leading from those beginnings to the present, and also claims of secret transmitted knowledge. In *sarugaku* such material existed in lore transmitted to both Zeami and Zenchiku. Perhaps because this lore was inherently conservative, Zeami did not at first find much use for it, but he recognized its normative potential, and later he also found that one particular part of it, borrowed from *kagura* traditions, provided a useful paradigm for the discussion of aesthetic response. Zenchiku was in search of secret knowledge, but he also had a fairly settled sense of what he thought *sarugaku* really ought to be. He therefore approached the traditional lore as a series of hints or starting points from which he could discover what he needed to know by imaginative investigation.

In *Meishukushū*, Zenchiku constructs a story about *sarugaku* that borrows a great deal from *waka* and Shinto ideologies. He makes *sarugaku*—in its supposed "original" form as *Shikisanban*—the manifestation of a god, as well as a magic offering to the gods, a manifestation that transforms the world, the audience and the actor. This new deity is expanded into an ultimate spiritual principle, and its origins are shifted to the beginning of the cosmos. In medieval Shinto works, tracing practices to the beginning of the cosmos was a way to give them priority over Buddhist and other traditions. It was the way that the Watarai radically elevated their object of worship at the outer shrine at Ise. The Watarai also reinterpreted ritual worship as the achievement through purity of mind of union with the deity. Zenchiku makes the actor's state of mind the central issue in performance and characterizes it in terms of the experience of Okina. Again, Zenchiku borrows ideological techniques from poetic traditions, not only taking over their history of a line of *"okinas"* and their special connection with Sumiyoshi Myōjin, but also constructing house rituals focused on offerings to inherited objects of mysterious provenance (including an old man picture). There are even signs that he was considering instituting initiation ceremonies for the transmission of secrets.[638] This coincides with much found in poetic traditions, particularly as described by Klein in relation to the development of the Rokujō as a poetic family.[639] It might be said that Zenchiku merely used these

---

638. See the first lines of *Rokurin kanjō hiki*, KKS, 229 and the reference to *himitsu kanjō*. KKS, *Meishukushū*, 258.
639. Klein, chs 5, 8.

techniques to construct an obvious and excessive authorizing rationale for his own line and its special activities. But that is not the whole story. The way Teeuwen and Klein describe it, the authorizing constructions of poets and shrine priests must, to some extent at least, be seen as cynical manipulations designed to benefit their houses. The situation with Zenchiku appears somewhat different. While one might reject his intellectual means, and pity his gullibility, one recognizes his sincerity. He really does want to understand his destiny, and searches in every way he can to discover the significance of his house and its task. Zenchiku is an indefatigable searcher for truth. The means he uses are simply the common means of his culture. That the result of his investigations turns out to be the kind of theory that completely satisfies his hopes is perhaps human nature.

7 Conclusion
Practitioners, the Way, and Secret Writings

We opened this book with a discussion of three interrelated matters: the practitioner, the way and writings about the way. Let us now take these as three perspectives to look back over the ground we have covered.

ZENCHIKU—*SARUGAKU* PRACTITIONER

First, Zenchiku's works can be read as an expression of the views he developed as an individual practitioner, views which can be analyzed in terms of his situation, of their relation to the thought of Zeami and contemporary discourses. Zenchiku himself recommends the position advanced in Confucius's adage: "cherishing the old and knowing the new" (albeit replacing "cherishing" 温 with "investigating" 尋). Confucius's advice concerns the present use of received knowledge and must have felt particularly relevant to *michi* traditions in the fifteenth century. When Zenchiku's father-in-law Zeami used the term "*michi*," he was claiming the authority of a tradition that traced itself back across generations of public service. To openly deviate from such received tradition was to risk forfeiting its authority. But in the age of *gekokujō* (the victory of ability over social position) practitioners had to respond to fashion, or "omit the tide that leads on to fortune."

Confucius's approach to the role of received knowledge is very similar to a key idea informing Zeami's early work. Some have interpreted 温 "cherishing" to signify repeated practice and maintenance of something learned earlier, and the general aim of Confucius's advice to be the production thereby of the new.[640] This is similar to Zeami's well-known phrase: "never forget the beginner's mind" (初心忘るべからず) which refers to the maintenance through repeated practice of inherited skills

---

640. See Legge's comments in 1893, 149, footnote 11.

249

received in early training.[641] Zeami and Kannami saw this "old"—the techniques acquired in early training—as a means to create the new, using them at appropriate times to produce novelty (*mezurashiki*).

But Zenchiku's investigation of the old was another kind of "cherishing"—not just a maintenance of traditional techniques, but an intense belief that there was a knowledge rooted in the past which he had to rediscover. His method of uncovering that truth can appear as a deliberate "creative misreading," a cynical attempt at self-legitimation. He himself, however, surely thought of his interpretations as genuine inquiry into "the old." Even his production of the new (for example, his readings of the *rokurin ichiro* diagrams) was a search for what he believed was the truly old. Of course, Zenchiku's conservatism was itself fashionable—a participation in the intellectual currents of his time, the widespread invention of tradition. The choices he made, moreover, siding with neo-conservative trends, can be seen as an appropriate response to his circumstances.

We can speculate on the personal reasons for Zenchiku's mystical neo-conservativism. The choice of an inner justification of performance art over the concrete demonstration of skill may have reflected the insecurities he felt succeeding to the Enman'i line in his youth. The troupe had failed in the struggle for new cosmopolitan patronage, yet it had a history that proclaimed its superiority. How could this be explained except by arguing that performance was not to be judged by its perceived effects alone. Zenchiku's mystical interests, and his beliefs in the importance of the actor's state of mind, make it likely that he was one of those people who find altered states accessible. He was one of those people to whom transformations of consciousness are significant ends in themselves, more important than mere aesthetic sensations.

But Zenchiku's commitment to externally unverifiable higher states of mind was also an alignment with the intellectual authority of his day and of a piece with the justifications of Shinto institutions and the new Buddhist groups. His identification of lineage and authority was common to institutions that derived from the court period. The positions that he adopted in the field of *michi* thought were appropriate to his social circumstances. Zenchiku adopted a position that was in essence away from the support of the warrior establishment in the capital and back to the barer institutional position in Fujiwara's Kōfukuji in Nara. In Yoshinori's time, *bakufu*

---

641. 初心, "first mind" is used in various ways by Zeami, but a primary meaning is the knowledge and skill acquired at the completion of one's youthful training (see Konishi, 1961, 190–196, and ZZ, *Fūshikaden*, 17).

patronage appeared fraught with danger, in a way inconceivable in Yoshimitsu's age. As life in the capital became more and more unstable through the middle years of the fifteenth century, Kōfukuji—and positions there that derived from precedent—promised security.

Zenchiku's reconstruction of *sarugaku* tradition drew extensively on Zeami's writings, but in so doing, it undid much that Kanze tradition had achieved. The theory of *hana* and the ideal of maintaining multiple techniques to win the appreciation of any audience were put aside. The cultural flowering of Kitayama society, with its rejection of the crude and demonic and its elevation of the elegant and feminine (*yūgen*), which informed Zeami's received tradition, was left behind. By omissions and reinterpretations, Zenchiku reintegrated performance traditions that had been marginalized. His belief that *yūgen* derived from the actor's state of mind, not from the role being performed, enabled him to recover the demon Noh, his family specialty. The virtual erasure of *Okina* in Kanze performances was reversed; *Shikisanban* was returned to its place as the performer's primary duty.

Zenchiku repeatedly juxtaposed the aesthetics of *kanshi* 漢詩 (poetry in Chinese), *waka* and *sarugaku* to elevate *sarugaku*, implying identity by proximity. But the treatment of *sarugaku* as an extended manifestation of *waka*, while it could have been a first step to a performative aesthetics, in fact obscured *sarugaku*'s performative potential, which lay in its mimetic power, its narrative potential, the emotional impact of its music and the magic of spectacle. Though these are all important in Zeami's writings, his insider perspective and concern with the processes through which art is produced rather than with the artifact itself meant that Zeami never developed an analysis of a play of the kind that we find in Aristotle's *Poetics*, for example. Zenchiku's interest, though, is quite clearly to justify *sarugaku* through its relation to something else, rather than the performance situation, and so the defining characteristics of performance art that Zeami never loses sight of came to be ignored.

Some schools of poetics had recast poetry as a spiritual path. Zenchiku's borrowings from these schools enabled him to emphasize *sarugaku*'s ritual power, lifting it out of the arena of aesthetic criticism into a world where time stood still and absolute reality was made present through the actor in trance. If we look over Schechner's criteria—efficacy versus enjoyment, the Other versus the present audience, highlighting time or abolishing it, trance versus intentional action, inviting or resisting critical appreciation, attitudes to individual creativity—it is clear that while Zeami's thought moves from a thoroughly theatrical perspective to one open to some ritual aspects, Zenchiku consistently gives priority to ritual.

Zenchiku repeatedly tried to construct parallels between *sarugaku* and the new Shinto ideology. Eventually he redefined *sarugaku* through *Okina* as a Shinto rite. This justified *sarugaku* tradition by the possibility of spiritual union in performance, both in the actor and as a *kechien*, binding of fate, embracing the audience. Zeami may have perceived parallels between certain kinds of knowledge developed through the performer's training and experience and the enlightenment achieved on the Zen path, but Zenchiku stretched these parallels to the point of identity—*sarugaku* was not like a spiritual path, it was a spiritual path. This collapse of the distinction between figure and essence is a consequence of the conception Zenchiku had of manifestation: similar appearances in traditions are demonstrations of identical roots in reality. From this point of view, the actor, too, is rooted through lineage to archetypal performances in legendary time. This may have been convenient for Zenchiku with his family claims, but he did not feel that lineage alone was sufficient. God judged from within. Zenchiku saw traditional troupes despoiling the precincts of the gods. The essential qualification was not training and skill but selflessness, morality and dedication. *Sarugaku* was a religion and actors needed to be good men.

The general assumption that Zenchiku was a devoted systematizer of Zeami's teachings is based on a belief in Zeami's greatness, his decision to pass his tradition to Zenchiku, and the reappearance of Zeami's terminology and theories in Zenchiku's writings. It reflects an ideological image of the relation between medieval master and pupil, characterized by wise judgment on the part of the first, and loyalty and self-denial on the part of the second. It has, however, meant that Zenchiku's works have appeared virtually incomprehensible. Why is he so uninterested in the ideas for which Zeami is so admired today—refinement and sensitivity to the audience? And why does he seem to misunderstand Zeami's thought—using for example the nine levels as a means of categorizing main roles? Yet, in fact, the changes in the social circumstances facing the two generations, the very different positions of the Kanze and Komparu lines, and the altered intellectual climate of the courtier intellectuals in which the two men associated are well known. I have attempted in this book to give Zenchiku his own place as a thinker about *sarugaku*, one quite distinct from Zeami, one equally a creative response to the life of a tradition in interesting times.

SARUGAKU QUA *MICHI*

Zenchiku's writings, and their relation to Zeami's writings, constitute a case study of the worldview of *michi*. Of course, this is merely one case, but it is one about which we know a good deal, and it is useful for a number of reasons. *Sarugaku* performers occupied a social position of crucial importance to *michi*; that is, lower class groups who redefined themselves through the language of courtly arts. The period in question is moreover one that was central to the creation of later Japanese culture, one to which many later *michi* traced themselves.[642] Konishi's theory of *michi*, which I take as the framework for the study, is admirable as a serious attempt to analyze something that many refer to but few define. It is moreover a satisfying characterization, which highlights the importance of *michi* for Japanese cultural history. But it carries assumptions about intellectual history which I do not share, assumptions reflected in the title of one of its expositions: "a medieval ideal." Konishi sees intellectual and cultural history in terms of ideas, derived from beliefs and intellectual fashions. We only have to look at current artistic, political and other discussions today to be reminded forcefully that ideas and ideals draw their force from outside mere intellectual realms. Another problematic aspect of an intellectual history thought of in terms of ideals is the attitudes to words that it implies—that is, as representing definite and clear ideas. I see words as the foci of multiple meanings, subject to change, negotiation and new interpretations; and find it difficult to believe in the existence of fixed ideas behind their uses. It is perhaps inevitable, then, that while I see Konishi's elements as being more or less central to *michi*, I also see them as approximations of families of ideas, sites of conflict and reinterpretation, arising out of creative responses to particular conditions, rather than as essential shared concepts. Let us review then the way we have discussed the elements.

Specialization as Konishi discusses it embraces two ideas: exclusive practice and wholehearted dedication. There were expressions of a belief that practitioners of one tradition should not practice others, but it was not widely emphasized. The origin is not clear, but I think it unlikely that it arose, as Konishi has it, simply from Buddhist beliefs in the power of single practices. Dōgen's reference to the duties of household occupations clearly envisages plebian occupations. Employing institutions most likely thought that *shokunin* households, being freed from taxes, should keep to their given duties and not diversify. I know of no equivalent restriction in the aristocratic arts and scholarly traditions—which would in any case have contradicted the courtly ideal of *suki*. It may be that some restrictive convention applied to the "dusty professors" of the Heian universities.

---

642. The characteristic traditional arts of Japan, tea ceremony, *shoinzukuri* 書院造り architecture, flower-arranging, incense ceremony, Zen gardens, can all be traced to the late fourteenth and fifteenth centuries.

When Zeami mentions exclusivity of practice, it is only to immediately nominate an exception. Shinkei, too, having raised the subject, modifies the restrictions with multiple exceptions. Both men, however, took for granted an attitude of total dedication. This attitude had a very strong presence in aristocratic culture, having become a topos in numerous stories in the twelfth century, when courtly privileges were proving vulnerable to military force. If you could not prove your aristocracy by real power, perhaps you could prove it by commitment to the marks of aristocracy, its arts and culture. As courtly arts and *shokunin* traditions began to appear comparable, both being remains of a disappearing world, the two types of dedication, that enjoined by employers determined to get their money's worth, and that idealized by courtiers, coincided. Nevertheless, a broad general education, including Chinese and esoteric Buddhism at least, was expected of aristocratic specialists, and the refashioning in the period we are considering—of less élite traditionalists as intellectuals—led to another convergence. If narrow, restrictive specialization ever was enjoined in the arts, it disappeared and was replaced by the idealization of the polymath, abreast of cultural developments in all the arts. An early example of such a master is Zenchiku's grandson, Komparu Zenpō.

Essentially we can see the issue of specialization as one side of a dual image of culture. In the *Tale of Genji*, Genji is presented as one type of artistic ideal: he masters the various court *michi* by breeding and blood, with little sustained practice, and his productions are the effortless expression of his innate ability. The effects of the dusty professors and the painting masters are the product of effort, and are therefore contrived and inferior. Genji is an amateur of his whole culture. In contrast, the master carpenter, *ki no michi no takumi*, knows one thing only, but he knows it very well. These two images converged in the rise of the medieval professional, a polymathic intellectual whose knowledge was rooted in intense training in one primary traditional art.

The next element of *michi*, transmission, is obviously essential to tradition. Popular writings about *michi* sometimes draw on images of transmission that are purely benevolent. The dedicated master looks for an appropriate vessel able to withstand the rigors of training and embody the tradition for another generation, and the idealistic pupil looks for a master to whom he can submit his life in quest of higher truths. This, however, masks the conflicts inherent in transmission. Such conflicts seem particularly characteristic of Japanese life in general, for primogeniture has never been deep-rooted, and Japanese history can be read as a series of succession disputes. In specialist traditions, knowledge was typically passed from one teacher to several students. Only one of them, however, could receive the social position through which that knowledge could be fully enacted. Medieval norms gave office-bearers great power over potential successors through their right to choose and change their minds. But ultimately the patron had higher authority and could override the master's choice.

Zeami's transmission can be read as a classic case, bringing out all the conflicting elements. Despite the still unsolved problems of Zeami's banishment, Motomasa's death and Motoyoshi's retirement to a monastery, which may have political aspects,[643] we can still see elements of inherent transmission problems in these events. Zeami at first favored succession through his brother, Shirō, as marked by the transmission of the "secret" *Besshi kuden*. Zeami changed his mind, but Shirō's son, Onnami, armed with his father's *Besshi kuden*, won the support of the prime patron, the shogun Yoshinori. Zeami's later choice, his son Motomasa, received the full transmission and all the major works, but died at the peak of his powers. The younger son, Motoyoshi, was not talented enough to receive the full transmission. The son-in-law, Zenchiku, was talented, but he had his own household name and, inextricably associated with it, a different story of *sarugaku*'s significance. Zeami was by now in his seventies and spent most of his remaining years in exile. Under these circumstances, the works Zenchiku received were not symbols and records of transmission already received, but substitutes for the transmission. What was passed from one generation to the next thus became vulnerable to specifically textual reinterpretation. From Zenchiku's side, the authorizing power of the works within the Kanze line was insignificant in relation to his own lineage, but the texts of the works themselves could be useful in his search for an original truth behind the tradition. Zenchiku has been thought of as Zeami's artistic successor, but the separation of knowledge, training and household naturally weakened Zenchiku's commitment to the Kanze worldview.

Konishi notes that the importance of transmission in *michi* results in the privileging of inherited knowledge over that developed by individuals. Transmission takes place in an ethos of conformity. The individual sacrifices his own ideas to conform to his tradition. In this regard, *michi* is like any oral tradition, but in oral tradition, what is preserved is adjusted over the generations by the reinterpretation of formulae and "structural amnesia." As Zenchiku's reception had a considerable textual element, his use of Zeami's texts in his own writing provides us with an unusual opportunity to see similar adjustments enacted textually. Selection and

---

643. See Imatani Akira's arguments, in "Zeami Sado hairyū no haikei ni tsuite," *Geinōshi kenkyū* 141 (1998.4): 105–113.

reinterpretation are primary strategies, particularly in the series of works developing out of Zeami's *go on* system. Zenchiku selected poetic aspects and omitted the technical, shifting the emphasis from Zeami's effective training, designed to enhance the impact of singing on audiences, to Zenchiku's conflation of *sarugaku* and *waka*, intended to unearth a fundamental similarity in their relation to deep mental (or unconscious) forces. Zenchiku achieved this shift partly through techniques not possible in oral transmission, which depended on the concrete character of writings. To Zeami, writing was attractive as a way to resist the loss and change inherent in oral transmission, but in the event writing itself proved liable to its own specific types of manipulation and reinterpretation.

Konishi's next element, universality, is different in kind from those that precede it, for it is an expression not just of what he concludes medieval people to have believed, but of what he himself experienced in his own connections with *michi* arts, that is, that they lead to a universal truth of general applicability.[644] It is perhaps for this reason that this element is less clearly described. Still, we are more interested here in how the idea of *michi* was conceived in the medieval period than how it is experienced now or at some time in between. In medieval writings, we see people adopting certain images of the Buddhist path to express their knowledge about their own arts. It would be ironic for us to conclude thereby that those arts were felt to be types of Buddhism—paths to universal truth. We have mentioned above the problem of distinguishing identity and analogy, and the related question of worldviews, encouraged by textual techniques, that see analogy as implying at some profound level identity. But still, it is clear that there is a distinction, in poetry for example, between those earlier thinkers who found analogies between it and Buddhism and others who wanted to treat the two activities as equivalent.

In the case of Zeami, it seems clear that he observed an analogy between various expressions of the Zen path and *sarugaku* without ever believing they were substantially the same. Training proceeded under discipline to a preliminary moment of mastery. Subsequently, performance could be accompanied by increasing freedom from the restrictions of orthodoxy. Similarly in the Zen path, practice led to a preliminary breakthrough, and subsequent enlightenment justified the release of

---

644. " . . . at the highest level possesses a universality shared with all other fields. This reality is not just what I happen to have experienced myself, indeed it has been widely acknowledged for a long time, and my own experience is simply one case of many that have confirmed it." Konishi, 1986, 156.

constraints, the "return to the marketplace."[645] Zeami used the terms of one to describe the other, but the underlying model can as much be read as reflecting the realities of human institutions based on seniority, as the spiritual powers of *michi*. After a successful novitiate, time brings increasing autonomy. Who is going to tell the abbot or senior performer what he can or cannot do?

On the other hand, medieval authors themselves seemed happy not to distinguish analogies and identities, and indeed for Zenchiku, certain analogies implied identity. The promiscuous borrowing of intellectual structures across fields seems to be the central characteristic of *michi* thought, and it lies behind many expressions that can be read as beliefs in the universality of *michi*. It has been traced from *waka*, *gagaku*, *renga* to *sarugaku* and beyond. The related interest in shared structures of the path is found repeatedly in *Tsurezuregusa* and again can be thought of as self-redefinition by court traditions, religious and artistic, at a time when minor aristocrats like Yoshida Kenkō lost the self-evident justification of court wealth and power. A number of universalizing intellectual traditions, including textual ones, developed in the medieval period, with legitimating and hermeneutic purposes. Such techniques encouraged the mapping of particular traditions onto universal structures.

But the boundaries between traditions or discourses were also deeply felt. It is striking that Zenchiku's repeated concatenations in the *rokurin ichiro* works consistently preserve their distinctions. While an idea in one field could stimulate a reading in another (as in the case of the cycle of breath), it was always clear to which field a particular piece of text belonged. This technique of combining while preserving distinctions was characteristic of the textual techniques of Shinto that we looked at, and it is also characteristic of Japanese culture as a whole, reappearing in many contexts. A modern example is linguistic vocabulary. Japanese constantly imports words, but the origins of lexical items are to a great degree distinguished and preserved in the writing system: *kanji*, *hiragana* and *katakana*.

Zenchiku found his structure for the path in Shinto rather than Buddhist tradition. The *rokurin ichiro* structure, by describing increasing complexity leading to a return to simplicity, at first seems quite appropriate to the actor's path. Yet it also reflects certain inherent values that Zenchiku's situation might have him favor: the valuation of origins over training, of simplicity or emptiness over complexity, of the unmanifest over the

---

645. That is, *kōkokyakurai*.

manifest. These values, shared with Shinto shrine specialists, who sought a return to the inchoate, conflicted with the forward-looking ideal of increasing skill, wisdom and autonomy inherent in Zeami's Buddhist terminology. Perhaps it is for this reason that the *rokurin ichiro* system failed to come to a satisfactory conclusion.

Konishi's idea that society spontaneously granted authority to those traditions which possessed his first four elements ignores the widespread loss of *michi* traditions in the fourteenth and fifteenth centuries. Authorized (*michi*) and unauthorized (*te*) groups competed for patronage, and the majority of the first did not survive. *Michi* groups that wished to survive surely had to reinvent themselves. By developing the Noh play, constructed out of *dengaku*, *sarugaku*, *kusemai* and *ennen* (and, of course, works like the *Tale of Genji* and *Tale of the Heike*), and by preserving a rationale for the spiritual function of *okina*, *sarugaku* actors won the support of local warrior leaders and of new-style religious institutions, and survived the sixteenth century. *Michi* writings of all types routinely record authorizing rationales, particularly important for those groups who could not demonstrate their utility or entertainment value directly. There is a variety of justifying methods, but most are similar to those used by the imperial family, aristocrats and shrines (these also being groups whose utility was difficult to demonstrate), centering on ancient origins with divine and imperial participants. Accounts of origins authorized descendents and set precedents for their traditions. *Sarugaku* had manufactured its stories; Zeami exploited their normative potential and Zenchiku looked for ways to expand and adjust them, through borrowings from poetics and Shinto writings, to authorize his particular characterization of his tradition.

Konishi's elements provide us with the basis for an analysis of *michi* writings, but that analysis needs to recognize that those elements were not fixed, at least not in the fourteenth and fifteenth centuries. In the various *michi* writings we have looked at, the elements are all unstable, objects of negotiation, interpretation and manipulation. In each case, the construction of *michi* is deeply embedded in social contexts, and not the mere product of intellectual worlds.

WRITING—THE NATURE OF *NŌGAKURON*

In a world of mass printing and digital data, writings are routinely imagined as texts, separate from their embodiments, but in the medieval world, where access to writings was limited, their concrete aspect was inseparable from their expressive power. Possession of or access to texts was always significant. Noh *hidensho* have been thought of as treatises on aesthetics, but in the world of *michi* the emblematic force of such works cannot be ignored. Their distribution reflected the oral transmission of the knowledge they inscribed, and they certified the transfer of corresponding authority: position in the household, access to patronage or office.

In this way, the line between texts and other artifacts was less firmly drawn. We can see this by contrasting Zenchiku's inherited treasures—picture, mask and reliquary—with the texts he cited. His picture was a representation demanding interpretation, but it also bore an inscription and was associated with an oracle. One of the frustrations of the body of scholarship on orality and literacy is the assumption that writing should be limited to the representation of language. This distinction is quite inappropriate for Far Eastern traditions, at least. Written characters were frequently read figuratively or diagrammatically; the spatial characteristics of written material (for example position, size and color of marks) were significant, and the distinction between writing, drawing and painting was not linguistically highlighted, for all three were produced by the same media and similar skills.[646] Zenchiku's interpretation of his inherited picture was achieved through words (the oracle), orthography (the character *shuku*), and other associations both verbal and visible. Considering the mask, it too, like writing, was a bearer of meaning through its plastic form, and also it could be used in performance, as the knowledge in a text might. Finally, the reliquary, by physical association with the ancient past, possessed spiritual force. Whether Zeami's and other texts to which Zenchiku gained access had for him numinous force (like a Buddhist text) is not clear, but reliquary and texts were both valued, and access to them was restricted. In any case the possession of his inherited objects conferred authority on Zenchiku and his house, and so did the possession of Zeami's writings as well as the copies of poetic and religious *hidensho* he acquired.

It seems that Zeami first wrote his works simply to record oral tradition, but he increasingly saw their other possibilities. At first he was concerned to preserve knowledge, appropriate in a time when knowledge and traditions were disappearing. This can be seen in two ways, as a benevolent freezing of tradition so that it could be recovered by future generations, or an imposition of a dead hand over later generations, not trusting them to find their own way. In either case, it was an attempt to manage the future. As Zeami wrote the books of *Fūshikaden,* his consciousness of their certificatory potential became prominent, as is clear in *Besshi kuden* in

---

646. The discussion of *Eawase* in the chapter so named in *Genji monogatari* is interesting in this regard. As Seidensticker notes, no distinction can be discerned therein between painting pictures and calligraphy (Edward G. Seidensticker, *Genji Days* (Tokyo: Kodansha International Ltd, 1977), 169).

particular, which appeared to mark the successor. The distribution of works later followed patterns typical of the distribution of property by landed officials—a major portion for the heir, minor portions for siblings leaving the house, and a marriage portion for a daughter marrying out. Zeami increasingly exploited the non-oral possibilities of writing, constructing tables, aligning formulae of different origins and interpreting Chinese characters.

To Zenchiku these works demanded interpretation, but he appears not to have submitted to the particular constraint that the more traditional of us might take for granted in reading—faithfulness to authorial intent. I have suggested that rather than interpret this as disloyalty or mendacity, we must recognize that it was appropriate to a worldview in which personal readings were considered provisional. As we mentioned above, Zenchiku's interpretative techniques included ones that would have been used in oral tradition: omission and selection. The reinterpretation of traditional formulae was exemplified by Zenchiku's over-reading of skin, flesh and bones, reinforced by borrowing from Shinto uses of the same formula.

Zenchiku used ways to extract meaning from Zeami's writings that were not only textual, but depended on their concrete character. He took the construction of tables (broadly defined) to a new extreme in the spatial collections and arrangements of the typologies. It seems that just as the insertion of other *michi* traditions into the Noh play was felt to be legitimate (not "change"), the combination and rearrangement of elements of Noh writings with material from other traditions was felt to be a valid form of reading. The oral explanatory element in Zenchiku's typologies is notably weak. Zeami's writing is marked by its comprehensibility, for he saw it as a substitute for oral transmission; but Zenchiku makes no concessions to the reader, in many cases abandoning discursive modes altogether.

In the *rokurin ichiro* works, Zenchiku brought to bear other possibilities, the investigative and authorizing potential of associations exposed across traditions. The gathering of contributions from authoritative sources, themselves inscribing material from sacred and normally inaccessible texts, endowed the commentaries with significant cultural legitimacy, but it is clear that Zenchiku took the investigative aspect most seriously, repeatedly trying new readings in the hope of discovering a grand synthesis. The power of writing as simply a way to collect material and to organize one's thoughts is evidenced in *Meishukushū*. At the same time, this work demonstrates a full range of interpretative and rhetorical techniques applied to other cultural material: legends, orthography, objects, performance traditions, and natural formations.

When we see Zenchiku's extraordinary textual constructions, it is tempting to think that his freedom from the constraints that we have naturalized, distinguishing form from meaning, valid from invalid inference, the significant from the accidental, made his reading indiscriminate and injudicious. But we should recognize the other constraints operative in his work, evident in his concern to preserve textual origins, his awareness of hierarchies of authority, and the priority of the received over the personal. Writings, in a world of handwritten texts in private libraries, must have appeared to medieval artists breaking into élite circles as exciting gateways to hidden truths and also promises of new possibilities of thought. In Zenchiku's writings we see his creative excitement at the moment when his tradition became textual. Zenchiku was in fact as much a writer as he was a performer, and like us, he used writing to interrogate his world.

Bibliography

Amano Fumio. "Okina sarugaku no hensen." *Geinōshi kenkyū* 109 (1990): 14–28.
_____. *Okina sarugaku kenkyū.* Osaka: Izumi Shoin, 1995.
Amino Yoshihiko, Nihon chūsei no minshūzō (Iwanami shinsho 136). Iwanami Shoten, 1980.
Aston, W. G. trans. *Nihongi : Chronicles of Japan from the Earliest Times to A.D. 697.* London: George Allen & Unwin Ltd, 1956.
Atkins, Paul. *The Noh Plays of Komparu Zenchiku.* Ph D dissertation: Stanford University, 1999.
_____. *Revealed Identity: The Noh Plays of Komparu Zenchiku.* Ann Arbor: Center for Japanese Studies, University of Michigan, 2006.
Bloom, Harold. *The Anxiety of Influence: A Theory of Poetry.* New York: Oxford University Press, 1973.
Bourdieu, Pierre. *Pascalian Meditations.* Translated and edited by Richard Nice. Stanford: Stanford University Press, 2000.
_____. *The Field of Cultural Production: Essays on Art and Literature.* Translated and edited by Randall Johnson. New York: Columbia University Press, 1993.
Bowring, Richard. "The Ise Monogatari: a Short Cultural History." *Harvard Journal of Asiatic Studies* 52.2 (December 1992): 401–480.
Brower, Robert H. and Earl Miner. *Japanese Court Poetry.* Stanford: Stanford University Press, 1961.
Brown, Steven T. *Theatricalities of Power: The Cultural Politics of Noh.* Stanford: Stanford University Press, 2001.
Bussho Kankōkai, ed. *Honchō kōsōden 1.* Bussho Kankōkai, 1913.
Carter, Steven D. *Regent Redux: A Life of the Statesman-Scholar Ichijō Kaneyoshi.* Ann Arbor: Center for Japanese Studies, University of Michigan, 1996.
_____. "Ichijō Kaneyoshi and the Literary Arts." In *Literary Patronage in Late Medieval Japan,* edited by Steven D. Carter, 19–44. Ann Arbor: Center for Japanese Studies, University of Michigan, 1993.
_____, ed. *Literary Patronage in Late Medieval Japan.* Ann Arbor: Center for Japanese Studies, University of Michigan, 1993.
_____, ed. *Conversations with Shōtetsu (Shōtetsu Monogatari).* Translated by Robert H. Brower. Ann Arbor: Center for Japanese Studies, University of Michigan, 1992.
De Poorter, Erika. *Zeami's Talks on Sarugaku: An Annotated Translation of the Sarugaku Dangi with an Introduction on Zeami Motokiyo.* Amsterdam: J. C. Gieben, 1986.
Dōmoto Masaki. *Zeami.* Geki Shobō, 1986.

Ebersole, Gary. *Ritual Poetry and the Politics of Death in Early Japan*. Princeton: Princeton University Press, 1989.

Emmert, Richard. "Okina—the Ritual Piece of Ritual Theatre." *In the Noh* 1.2 (March 2004): 2.

Feng, Gia-Fu and Jane English, trans. *Chuang Tsu Inner Chapters: A New Translation by Gia-Fu Feng and Jane English*. London: Wildwood House, 1974.

Fukui Kyūzō. *Ichijō Kanera*. Koseikaku, 1943.

Fung Yu-lan. *History of Chinese Philosophy: Vol. II The Period of Classical Learning*. Translated by Derk Bodde. Princeton: Princeton University Press, 1983. Originally published in 1953.

Geinōshi Kenkyūkai eds. *Nihon geinōshi*. Hōsei Daigaku Shuppan Kyoku, 1981–1990.

Goff, Janet. *Noh Drama and the Tale of Genji: the Art of Allusion in Fifteen Classical Plays*. Princeton: Princeton University Press, 1991.

Goody, Jack. *Literacy in Traditional Societies*. Cambridge, UK: Cambridge University Press, 1968.

_____. *The Interface Between the Written and the Oral*. Cambridge, UK, Cambridge University Press, 1987.

Grapard, Allan G. "The Shintō of Yoshida Kanetomo." *Monumenta Nipponica* 47:1 (1992): 27–58.

_____. *Protocol of the Gods: a Study of the Kasuga Cult in Japanese History*. Berkeley: University of California Press, 1992.

Haga Kōshirō. "Higashiyama bunka no seikaku to sono seiritsu." In *Higashiyama bunka no kenkyū*. Kawade Shobō, 1945.

_____. *Chūsei zenrin no gakumon oyobi bungaku ni kansuru kenkyū (Haga Kōshirō rekishi ronshū 3)*. Kyoto: Shibunkaku Shuppan, 1981.

_____. *Higashiyama bunka no kenkyū*. Kawade Shobō, 1945.

_____. *Higashiyama bunka*. Hanawa Shobō, 1962.

Hall, John W. and Toyoda Takeshi, eds. *Japan in the Muromachi Age*. Berkeley: University of California Press, 1977.

Hare, Thomas B. *Zeami's Style: the Noh Plays of Zeami Motokiyo*. Stanford: Stanford University Press, 1986.

Harris, Victor trans. *A Book of Five Rings*. London: Allison and Busby, 1974.

Hattori Yukio. "Shukushin ron—geinōshin shinkō no kongen ni aru mono, jō," *Bungaku* (October 1974): 64–79.

_____. "Shukushin ron—geinōshin shinkō no kongen ni aru mono, ge." *Bungaku* (February 1975): 76–97.

Hayakawa Junsaburō. *Shintō sōsetsu*. Kokusho Kankōkai, 1911.

Hayashiya Tatsusaburō. *Chūsei geinōshi no kenkyū*. Iwanami Shoten, 1960.

_____, ed. *Kodai chūsei geijutsuron (Nihon shisō taikei 23)*. Iwanami Shoten, 1973.

Hayashiya Tatsusaburō (with George Elison). "Kyoto in the Muromachi Age." In *Japan in the Muromachi Age*. Edited by John W. Hall and Toyoda Takeshi, 15–36. Berkeley: University of California Press, 1977.

Hendry, Joy. *Understanding Japanese Society*. London: Croom Helm, 1987.

Herrigel, Eugen. *Zen in the Art of Archery*. Translated by R. F. C. Hull. London: Routledge and K. Paul, 1953.

Hiraoka Jōkai. *Tōdaiji*. Kyōikusha, 1977.

Hirose Mizuhiro. *Nō to Komparu*. Shoon Shobō, 1969.

Hisamatsu Sen'ichi and Nishio Minoru, eds. *Karonshū (Nihon koten bungaku taikei 65)*. Iwanami Shoten, 1961.

Hisamatsu Sen'ichi. *The Vocabulary of Japanese Literary Aesthetics*. Tōyō Bunko, 1963.

Ienaga Saburō et al., eds., *Iwanami kōza: Nihon rekishi (7 chūsei 3)*. Iwanami Shoten, 1967.

Ijichi Tetsuo, Omote Akira and Kuriyama Riichi, eds., *Rengaronshū, nōgakuronshū, haironshū (Nihon koten bungaku zenshū 51)* Shōgakkan, 1973.

Imatani Akira and Miyajima Shin'ichi. *Gadan tōitsu ni kakeru yume—Sesshū kara Eitoku e*. Bun'eidō, 2001.

Imatani Akira and Yamamura Kōzō. "Not for Lack of Will or Wile: Yoshimitsu's Failure to Supplant the Imperial Lineage." *Journal of Japanese Studies* 18.1 (winter, 1992): 45–78.

Imatani Akira. *Kujibiki shōgun Ashikaga Yoshinori*. Kōdansha. 2003.

_____. *Muromachi no ōken*. Chuōkōronsha, 1990.

_____. "Zeami Sado hairyū no haikei ni tsuite." *Geinōshi kenkyū* 141 (1998.4): 105–113.

Innes, Matthew. "Memory, Orality and Literacy in an Early Medieval Society." *Past and Present* 158 (1998): 3–36.

Ishida Ichirō, ed. *Shintō shisōshū*. Chikuma Shobō, 1970.

Ishiguro Kichijirō. *Chūsei engeki no shosō*. Ōfūsha, 1983.

_____. *Chūsei geidōron no shisō: Kenkō, Zeami, Shinkei*. Kokusho Kankōkai, 1993.

Itō Masayoshi and Omote Akira, eds. *Komparu kodensho shūsei*. Wan'ya Shoten, 1969 [KKS].

Itō Masayoshi. *Komparu Zenchiku no kenkyū*. Kyoto: Akao Shōbundō, 1970 [KZK].

Kamiko Tadashi, ed. *Gorin no sho*. Tokuma shoten, 1963.

Katō Genchi, Hoshino Hikoshiro trans. *Kogoshūi—Gleanings from Ancient Stories*. Meiji Seitoku Kinen Gakkai, 1925.

Kawamoto, Kōji. *The Poetics of Japanese Verse: Imagery, Structure, Meter*. Tokyo: University of Tokyo Press, 2000.

Keene, Donald, trans. *Essays in Idleness: The Tsurezuregusa of Kenkō*. New York: Columbia University Press, 1967.

_____. *Some Japanese Portraits*. New York: Kodansha International, 1978.

Kidō Saizō and Imoto Nōichi, eds. *Rengaronshū haironshū (Nihon koten bungaku taikei 66)*. Iwanami Shoten, 1961.

Kita Sadayoshi. "Shukushin kō." *Minzoku to rekishi* 4/5 (1920): 253–266.

Kitagawa Tadahiko. *Zeami*. Chuōkōronsha, 1972.

Klein, Susan Blakeley. *Allegories of Desire: Esoteric Literary Commentaries of Medieval Japan*. Cambridge (Massachusetts): Harvard University Press, 2002.

Kobayashi Shizuo. *Zeami*. Hinoki Shoten, 1958.

Kodera, Takashi J. *Dōgen's Formative Years in China: An Historical Study and Annotated Translation of the Hōkyō-ki*. London: Routledge and Kegan Paul, 1980.

Koga Hidehiko, ed. *Zengo jiten*. Kyoto: Shibunkaku Shuppan, 1991.

Konishi Jin'ichi. "*Michi*" *chūsei no rinen*. Kōdansha, 1975.

_____. *Chūsei no bungei: "michi" to iu rinen*. Kōdansha, 1997.

_____. *Nihon bungei shi 3*. Kōdansha, 1986.

_____. *Nōgakuron kenkyū*. Haniwa Shobō, 1961.

_____. "*Michi* and Medieval Writing." In *Principles of Classical Japanese Literature*. Edited by Earl Miner, 181–208. Princeton: Princeton University Press, 1985.

_____. *A History of Japanese Literature Volume Three: the High Middle Ages*. Translated by Aileen Gatten and Mark Harbison. Edited by Earl Miner. Princeton: Princeton University Press, 1991.

Kōsai Tsutomu. *Zeami shinkō*. Wan'ya Shoten, 1962.

_____. *Zoku Zeami shinkō*. Wan'ya Shoten. 1970.

Kuroda Toshio. "Historical Consciousness and Honjaku Philosophy in the Medieval Period on Mount Hiei." In *The Lotus Sutra in Japanese Culture*. Edited by George J. Tanabe Jr. and Willa J. Tanabe, 143–158. Honolulu: University of Hawaii Press, 1989.

Lafleur, William R., *The Karma of Words: Buddhism and the Literary Arts in Medieval Japan*. Berkeley: University of California Press, 1983.

Lama Anagarika Govinda. *Foundations of Tibetan Mysticism*. London: Rider and Company, 1960.

Legge, James, trans. *The Texts of Confucianism part II: The I Ching*. Volume XVI of *Sacred Books of the East*. Oxford: Clarendon Press, 1899.

_____, trans., and ed. *Confucian Analects, The Great Learning, and The Doctrine of the Mean* (Volume 1 of *The Chinese Classics*, 2nd edition). Oxford: Oxford U.P., 1893.

Mass, Jeffrey P. *Lordship and Inheritance in Early Medieval Japan: a Study of the Kamakura Sōryō System*. Stanford: Stanford University Press, 1989.

_____, ed. *The Origins of Japan's Medieval World: Courtiers, Clerics, Warriors, and Peasants in the Fourteenth Century*. Stanford: Stanford University Press, 1997.

Matsunaga, Alicia. *The Buddhist Philosophy of Assimilation: The Historical Development of the Honji-Suijaku Theory*. Sophia University in cooperation with Charles E. Tuttle Company, 1969.

McCullough, Helen Craig, trans. *The Tale of the Heike*. Stanford: Stanford University Press, 1988.

Mills, Douglas E. trans. *Collection of Tales from Uji: a study and translation of Uji Shūi Monogatari*. Cambridge, UK: Cambridge University Press, 1970.

Minemura Fumito. "Nōgakuron to chūseikaron." In *Yōkyoku kyōgen*. Edited by Nihon Bungaku Kenkyū Shiryō Kankōkai, 94–100. Yūseidō, 1981.

Miner, Earl, ed. *Principles of Classical Japanese Literature*. Princeton: Princeton University Press, 1985.

Miyai Yoshio, *Nihon no chūsei shisō*. Seikō Shobō, 1981.

Morris, Ivan. *The Nobility of Failure: Tragic Heroes in the History of Japan*. New York and Toronto: Holt, Rinehart and Winston, 1975.

Murai Yasuhiko. *Kyōyōjin no Nihonshi (2) (Gendai kyōyō bunko 582)*. Shakai Shisō Sha, 1966.

Murayama Shūichi. *Honji suijaku (Nihon rekishi sōsho, 33)*. Yoshikawa Kōbunkan, 1974.

Nagashima Fukutarō. "Kasuga taisha no rekishi." In *Kasuga Myōjin: ujigami no tenkai*. Edited by Ueda Masaaki, 41–67. Chikuma Shobō, 1987.

_____. "Kōfukuji no rekishi." *Bukkyō geijutsu* 40 (1959): 1–22.

_____. *Ichijō Kanera*. Yoshikawa Kōbunkan, 1959.

_____. *Nara bungaku no denryū*. Chuōkōronsha, 1944.

Nakanishi Susumu. "The Spatial Structure of Japanese Myth: the Contact Point between Life and Death." In *The Principles of Classical Japanese Literature*. Edited by Earl Miner, 106–129. Princeton: Princeton University Press, 1985.

Nearman, Mark J. "Kyakuraika: Zeami's Final Legacy for the Master Actor." *Monumenta Nipponica* 35.2 (Summer 1980): 153–97.

_____. "The Visions of a Creative Artist, Zenchiku's Rokurin Ichiro Treatises." *Monumenta Nipponica* 50.2 (Summer, 1995): 235–261.

Nishino Haruō. "Zeami bannen no nō: nōhon sanjūgoban mokuroku o megutte." *Bungaku* 39:5 (1971): 37–48.

Nishio Minoru, ed. *Hōjōki, Tsurezuregusa (Nihon koten bungaku taikei 30)*. Iwanami Shoten, 1957.

Nogami Toyoichirō. *Nō: kenkyū to hakken*. Iwanami Shoten, 1930.

Nose Asaji Chosaku Shū Henshūiinkai, eds. *Nose Asaji chosakushū 5*. Kyoto: Shibunkaku Shuppan, 1984.

Nose Asaji. "Nōgaku to gadō." In *Nose Asaji chosakushū 5*, 475–482. Kyoto: Shibunkaku Shuppan, 1984.

_____. "Zeami ni okeru kokoro no shomondai." In *Nose Asaji Chosakushū 5*, 93–185. Kyoto: Shibunkaku Shuppan, 1984.

_____. "Zeami no geijutsuron ni okeru 'kurai.'" In *Nose Asaji chosakushū 5*, 143–166. Edited by Nose Asaji Chosaku Shū Henshūiinkai. Kyoto: Shibunkaku Shuppan, 1984.

_____. *Kodai geki bungaku (Nihon bungaku taikei 21)*. Kawade Shobō, 1939.

_____. *Nōgaku genryu kō*. Iwanami Shoten, 1938 [NGK].

_____. *Zeami jūrokubushū hyōshaku 2*. Iwanami Shoten, 1944.

O'Neill, P. G. "The Letters of Zeami: One Received from Jūni Gonnokami and Two Sent to Zenchiku." *Nōgaku kenkyū* 5 (1979): 134–150.

Oda Sachiko. "Sanbasō no mondō no hensen." *Geinō* 32/1 (1990): 12–18.

Olson, David R. "Literacy as Metalinguistic Activity." In *Literacy and Orality*. Edited by David R. Olson and Nancy Torrance, 251–270. Cambridge, UK: Cambridge University Press, 1991.

Omote Akira and Amano Fumio. *Nōgaku no rekishi (Iwanami kōza nō kyōgen 1)*. Iwanami Shoten, 1987.

Omote Akira and Katō Shūichi, eds. *Zeami Zenchiku (Nihon shisō taikei 24)*. Iwanami Shoten, 1974 [ZZ].

Omote Akira. "Yamato sarugaku no osa no seikaku no hensen (chū)." *Nōgaku kenkyū* 3 (1977): 1–72.

_____. "Yamato sarugaku no osa no seikaku no hensen (ge)." *Nōgaku kenkyū* 4 (1978): 1–92.

_____. "Yamato sarugaku no osa no seikaku no hensen (jō)." *Nōgaku kenkyū* 2 (1976): 1–40.

_____. "Tōnomine no sarugaku." *Nōgaku kenkyū* 1 (1974): 88–120.

_____. "Zeami no 'sarugaku ikōru sarugaku' setsu o megutte—'Fūshikaden daishi shingi' no seiritsunendai, sono ta." *Nōgaku kenkyū* 18 (1993): 1–48.

_____. *Nōgakushi shinkō 1*. Wan'ya Shoten, 1979.

Ong, Walter J. *Orality and Literacy*. London: Routledge, 1982.

Ōsone Shōsuke and Horiuchi Hideaki, eds. *Wakan rōeishū (Shinchō Nihon koten shūsei 61)*. Shinchōsha, 1983.

Ōsone Shōsuke, Kinpara Tadashi and Gotō Akio, eds. *Honchō monzui (Shin koten bungaku taikei 27)*. Iwanami Shoten, 1992.

Ōsumi Kazuo, ed. *Chūsei shintōron (Nihon shisō taikei 19)*. Iwanami Shoten, 1977.

Ōyama, Kyōhei. "The Fourteenth Century in Twentieth Century Perspective." In *The Origins of Japan's Medieval World: Courtiers, Clerics, Warriors, and Peasants in the Fourteenth Century*. Edited by Jeffrey P. Mass, 345–365. Stanford: Stanford University Press, 1997.

Pandey, Rajyashree. *Writing and Renunciation in Medieval Japan: the Works of the Poet-Priest Kamo no Chōmei*. Ann Arbor: Center for Japanese Studies, University of Michigan, 1998.

Pinnington, Noel J. "Invented Origins: Muromachi Interpretations of *Okina Sarugaku*." *Bulletin of the School of Oriental and African Studies* 61.3 (1998): 492–518.

_____. "Crossed Paths: Zeami's Transmission to Zenchiku." *Monumenta Nipponica* 52:2 (Summer 1997): 201–234.

_____. *Strategies of Legitimation: an Approach to the Expository Writings of Komparu Zenchiku* (Cambridge, UK: University of Cambridge (Ph. D. dissertation), 1994).

_____. "Models of the Way in the Theory of Noh." *Japan Review* 18 (2006): 29–55.

Plutschow, Herbert. "Is Poetry a Sin?—*Honjisuijaku* and Buddhism versus Poetry." *Oriens Extremus* 25.2 (1978): 206–18.

Quinn, Shelley Fenno. *Developing Zeami: the Noh Actor's Attunement in Practice*. Honolulu: University of Hawaii Press, 2005.

Raz, Jacob. "The Actor and his Audience, Zeami's Views on the Audience of the Noh." *Monumenta Nipponica* 31:3 (1976): 251–274.

Rosenfield, John M. "The Unity of the Three Creeds: A Theme in Japanese Ink Painting of the Fifteenth Century." In *Japan in the Muromachi Age*, edited by John W. Hall and Toyoda Takeshi, 205–226. Berkeley: University of California Press, 1977.

Ruch, Barbara. "Medieval Jongleurs and the Making of a National Literature." In *Japan in the Muromachi Age*. Edited by John W. Hall and Toyoda Takeshi, 279–309. Berkeley: University of California Press, 1977.

Rüttermann, Markus. "Anstand durch Abstand. Notizen zum 'Angleichen und Aussparen' (*heishutsu ketsuji*) in der sino-japanischen Briefetikette." *Japonica Humboldtiana* 5 (2000): 144–188.

Sakamoto Tarō et al., eds. *Nihonshoki 1 (Nihon koten bungaku taikei 67)*. Iwanami Shoten, 1965.

Schechner, Richard. "From Ritual to Theatre and Back." In *Ritual, Play and Performance: Readings in the Social Sciences/Theatre*. Edited by Mady Schuman and Richard Schechner. New York: Seabury Press, 1976.

Seidensticker, Edward G., trans. *The Tale of Genji (Volume 1)*. London: Secker and Warburg, 1976.

_____. *Genji Days*. Tokyo: Kodansha International Ltd, 1977.

Tagawa Shun'ei. *Nara Kōfukuji: ayumi, oshie, hotoke*. Shōgakkan, 1990.

Taira Shigemichi and Abe Akio, eds. *Kinsei shintōron, zenki kokugaku (Nihon shisō taikei 39)*. Iwanami Shoten, 1972.

Takagi Ichinosuke et al. eds. *Heike monogatari 2 (Nihon koten bungaku taikei 33)*. Iwanami Shoten, 1960.

Takemoto Mikio. "Nōsakusha Retsuden." In *Nō (Bessatsu taiyō 25)*. Heibonsha, 1978: 62–74.

Tamba, Akira. *La Structure Musicale du Nô: Théâtre Traditionnel Japonais.* Klincksieck, 1974. Translated by Patricia Matoré as *The Musical Structure of No.* Tokyo: Tōkai University Press, 1981.

Tanaka Noboru. "Ōchō josei to Hasedera mōde: Michitsuna no haha to Takasue no musume." In *Nara to bungaku: kodai kara gendai made.* Edited by Tezukayama Tanki Daigaku Nihon Bungei Kenkyūshitsu, 32–40. Ōsaka: Izumi Shoin, 1988.

Tanikawa Ken'ichi ed. *Jinja engi (Nihon shomin seikatsu shiryō shūsei 26).* San'ichi Shobō, 1983.

Taya Raishun. *Bukkyogaku jiten.* Kyoto: Hōzōkan, 1955.

Teeuwen, Mark. *Watarai Shintō: An Intellectual History of the Outer Shrine at Ise.* Leiden: Research School CNWS, 1996.

Terasaki Etsuko. "*Kyogen kigo* in the No Play *Jinen Koji.*" *Harvard Journal of Asiatic Studies* 49.2 (December 1989): 519–552.

Thornhill III, Arthur H. "Yūgen after Zeami." In *Nō and Kyōgen in the Contemporary World.* Edited by James R. Brandon, 36–64. Honolulu: Hawaii University Press, 1997.

_____. *Six Circles, Single Dewdrop: the Religio-Aesthetic World of Komparu Zenchiku.* Princeton: Princeton University Press, 1993.

Tsunoda Ryūsaku, Wm Theodore de Bary and Donald Keene, eds. *Sources of Japanese Tradition 1.* New York: Columbia University Press, 1958.

Tyler, Royall. *The Miracles of the Kasuga Deity.* New York, Columbia University Press, 1990.

Ueda Makoto, trans. *Bashō and His Interpreters: Selected Hokku with Commentary.* Stanford: Stanford University Press, 1992.

_____. *Literary and Art Theories in Japan.* Ann Arbor: Center for Japanese Studies, University of Michigan, 1967.

Ueda Masaaki, ed. *Kasuga Myōjin—ujigami no tenkai.* Chikuma Shobō, 1987.

Ueki Yukinori. "Gakusho no seikō to geiron." *Geinōshi kenkyū* 45 (1974.4): 31–43.

Ury, Marian, trans. *Tales of Times Now Past: Sixty-Two Stories from a Medieval Japanese Collection.* Berkeley: University of California Press, 1979.

Usui Nobuyoshi. *Ashikaga Yoshimitsu (Jinbutsu sōsho 38).* Yoshikawa Kōbunkan, 1960.

Varley, H. Paul, trans. *A Chronicle of Gods and Sovereigns: Jinnō Shōtōki of Kitabatake Chikafusa.* New York: Columbia Press, 1980.

Waley Arthur. *The Life and Times of Po Chü-i, 772–846.* London: Allen and Unwin, 1949.

Watanabe Tsunaya. *Shasekishū (Nihon koten bungaku taikei 85).* Iwanami Shoten, 1966.

Wilson, William Ritchie. "The Way of the Bow and Arrow: the Japanese Warrior in Konjaku Monogatari." *Monumenta Nipponica* 28:2 (1973): 190–233.

Wong, Siu-kit, ed. *Early Chinese Literary Criticism.* Hong Kong: Joint Publishing Company, 1983.

Yamaji Kōzō. *Okina no za: geinōmintachi no chūsei.* Heibonsha, 1990.

Yamazaki Masakazu, ed. *Shōbōgenzō zuimonki.* Kōdansha, 1972.

Yoshida Tōgō, ed. *Zeami jūrokubu shū.* Nōgaku Kai, 1909.

Index

CORNELL EAST ASIA SERIES

Order online: www.einaudi.cornell.edu/eastasia/CEASbooks, or contact Cornell East Asia Series Distribution Center, 95 Brown Road, Box 1004, Ithaca, NY 14850, USA; toll-free: 1-877-865-2432, fax 607-255-7534, ceas@cornell.edu